Mathematics Teaching, Learning, and Liberation in the Lives of Black Children

With issues of equity at the forefront of mathematics education research and policy, *Mathematics Teaching, Learning, and Liberation in the Lives of Black Children* fills the need for authoritative, rigorous scholarship that sheds light on the ways that young Black learners experience mathematics in schools and their communities. This timely collection significantly extends the knowledge base on mathematics teaching, learning, participation, and policy for Black children and it provides new framings of relevant issues that researchers can use in future work. More importantly, this book helps move the field beyond analyses that continue to focus on and normalize failure by giving primacy to the stories that Black learners tell about themselves and to the voices of mathematics educators whose work has demonstrated a commitment to the success of these children.

Danny Bernard Martin is Chair of the Department of Curriculum and Instruction in the College of Education and Associate Professor of Mathematics at the University of Illinois at Chicago.

STUDIES IN MATHEMATICAL THINKING AND LEARNING

Alan H. Schoenfeld, Series Editor

Mathematics Teaching, Learning, and Liberation in the Lives of Black Children

Edited by
Danny Bernard Martin
University of Illinois at Chicago

Routledge
Taylor & Francis Group

NEW YORK AND LONDON

First published 2009
by Routledge
270 Madison Ave, New York, NY 10016

Simultaneously published in the UK
by Routledge
2 Park Square, Milton Park, Abingdon, Oxon OX14 4RN

*Routledge is an imprint of the Taylor & Francis Group,
an informa business*

© 2009 Taylor and Francis

Typeset in Minion by Swales & Willis Ltd, Exeter, Devon
Printed and bound in the United States of America on
acid-free paper by Walsworth Publishing Company,
Marceline, MO

Library of Congress Cataloging in Publication Data
Mathematics teaching, learning, and liberation in the lives of black children/
edited by Danny Bernard Martin.
p. cm.—(Studies in mathematical thinking and learning)
1. Mathematics—Study and teaching (Elementary)—United States.
2. African American children—Education. I. Martin, Danny Bernard.
QA135.6.M3857 2009
372.7089'96073—dc22
2009008559

ISBN 10: (hbk) 0–8058–6463–6
ISBN 10: (pbk) 0–8058–6464–4
ISBN 10: (ebk) 0–203–87770–5

ISBN 13: (hbk) 978–0–8058–6463–2
ISBN 13: (pbk) 978–0–8058–6464–9
ISBN 13: (ebk) 978–0–203–87770–8

Contents

SECTION III
Socialization, Learning, and Identity

SECTION IV
Collaboration and Reform

Preface

Mathematics Teaching, Learning, and Liberation in the Lives of Black Children represents an attempt to change the direction of research on Black children[1] and mathematics. In working toward such an audacious task, we make note of two significant
occurrences within mathematics education over the last 30 years.

First, we cite the fact that the knowledge base of rigorous, explanatory research
for success and failure outcomes has remained relatively thin over most of this 30-
year period. What little progress that has been made is due to the work of a small
number of equity-minded mathematics education scholars who have remained
committed to writing about Black learners over this period. We make note of two
volumes produced with support of the National Council of Teachers of
Mathematics (NCTM). The first, *Challenges in the Mathematics Education of
African American Children: Proceedings of the Benjamin Banneker Association
Leadership Conference,* appeared in 1997 and was edited by Carol Malloy and Laura
Brader-Araje. The other, *Changing the Faces of Mathematics: African American
Perspectives,* appeared in 2001 as part of the NCTM *Changing the Faces of
Mathematics* series and was edited by Marilyn Strutchens, Martin Johnson, and
William Tate.

Second, we note that, during the last 10 years, there has been precipitous
growth in the number of mathematics educators who have built on the work of this
earlier generation and who have continued to focus attention on issues of teaching,
learning, curriculum, assessment, and policy with respect to Black learners. In particular, the growing number of African American scholars, many of whom have
been mentored by recognized leaders in the field, is unprecedented in the history of
mathematics education. This book brings together several of these African
American scholars and their colleagues who are also doing cutting-edge work in
diverse contexts where Black children live and learn. Collectively, these scholars
share a commitment to framing the content, structure, ideology, and purpose
of mathematics education for Black children that will contribute to these
children's ongoing struggle for liberation and human existence (Martin & McGee,
2009).

We focus on the overarching theme of *liberation* for two reasons. First, we realize
that any framing of the mathematical education of Black children that ignores their
experiences *as Black children* is bound to be limited. These experiences include continued and pernicious assaults on their racial and academic identities in societal,

research, policy, and school contexts. Second, unlike many prior analyses of Black children in mathematics, we connect this project to a larger body of research (e.g., Anderson, 1988; DuBois, 1903; Harding, 1981; Woodson, 1990/1933) that frames education for Blacks historically and beyond narrow concerns with labor market participation. The historical record reveals the depth of struggle for education on the part of freedmen and women and landmark legal battles to insure quality education for Black children. These efforts were intertwined with the demand to be recognized as full citizens, free from the devastating effects of racism and discrimination. The chapters in this book illuminate contemporary manifestations of the struggle for meaningful and liberatory education and will help reshape the scholarly discourse on Black children and mathematics.

There are several hallmarks of the scholarship of the scholars highlighted in this book. First, these scholars have engaged in rigorous and insightful critique of extant research, pointing out limitations not only in the theories and methods that have been used to understand the mathematical experiences of Black children, but also in the very framing of these students and their experiences.

Second, many of the authors introduce *new* research questions focused on topics that are rarely addressed or that are underconceptualized in mathematics education in the United States: race, racism, and racialization processes; Black male and female identity; mathematics socialization and mathematics identity; Black mathematics teachers; and liberatory pedagogy. Although they are very familiar with many of the traditional theories of learning and teaching in mathematics education, many of the authors introduce theories not typically used in mathematics education research, including critical postmodernism, Black feminist thought, Black liberation theology, and Critical Race Theory (CRT). In juxtaposing these new perspectives with traditional approaches to mathematics learning, teaching, and assessment, the authors merge psychosocial, cognitive, sociopolitical, and historical concerns in ways that help us better understand how and why Black learners become more or less engaged in various mathematical practices and how combinations of forces influence participation, non-participation, marginalization, and success.

Third, many of these researchers address *success* and within-group diversity among Black learners. While some researchers focus on "students of color" by seeking to apply a singular lens of analysis or develop assumptions about a fixed set of traits across groups, we respect the fact that diversity within and across groups requires a diversity of approaches. We address diversity within Black populations and offer principled analyses that can inform and deepen the understandings of those who are sincerely concerned with making meaningful interventions on behalf of Black learners across various contexts. Given the urgency of the issues confronting the education of Black children, there is often a demand for quick fixes and strategies that can be taken back to classrooms immediately. While we do offer deeper understanding of these issues, we do not offer any quick fixes or prescriptions in this book but rather provide a means to think *differently* about the relationships between Black children and mathematics. We encourage those working in specific contexts to take the ideas presented here and apply to them in ways that make sense for those contexts.

Fourth, the authors address teaching and teacher practice through the lens of *culturally relevant mathematics pedagogy*, affording readers the opportunity to understand teaching with respect to the social realities of Black children.

Fifth, the scholars in this book take the position that, rather than beginning with a fixed set of operating assumptions about Black children, subsequently utilizing a single research methodology, and then generating theory and interventions that can be applied uniformly to all contexts, a more informative and culturally sensitive research strategy is to conduct principled studies of localized contexts as a necessary first step. As stated by Carnine and Gersten (2000), localized and "descriptive research is a very useful tool for analyzing problems and making complex problems more manageable and comprehensible. It can be very useful to build theory, to shape interventions, and help one understand the target or focus of an intervention" (p. 139).

The diversity of topics presented in this book is a major strength. This diversity helps the field move beyond analyses that continue to focus on and normalize failure, essentialize the experiences of Black children and, more insidiously, that reify *race* as a cause of problematic outcomes. We believe that these failure-focused analyses often contribute to a larger societal narrative that has served the purpose of constructing Black children as mathematically illiterate.

This book does two things that will appeal to those who want to move beyond analyses of failure typically found in mainstream research: (1) it gives primacy to the stories that Black learners tell about themselves and (2) it gives primacy to the voices of mathematics educators of African descent and mathematics educators who are committed to meaningful mathematical education for Black children.

This book is an essential resource for researchers in mathematics education, graduate students, and mathematics teacher educators. It will also prove useful to policy-makers and administrators who take seriously the notion of research-informed practice and decision-making.

We also believe this book will appeal to teachers, parents, and community organizers in African American contexts and that our work will be relevant to researchers whose work focuses on the mathematical educations of Latino/a learners, Native Americans, and marginalized white and Asian American students. Because of its diverse theoretical and methodological approaches to the study of learning, teaching, and social context, the book may be useful for researchers and students in sociology of education, multicultural education, and African American studies. Finally, the book will have international appeal, particularly in nations where sociopolitical changes now highlight the needs of indigenous groups, minority Black populations, and majority Black populations who were once denied access to high quality mathematical educations via political and legal exclusion or discrimination. For example, South Africa, New Zealand, Australia, and Canada are four locations that we note.

Danny Bernard Martin

---

1   We use the terms "Black" and "African American" to encompass the diverse ways that group members self-identify and are identified by others. We acknowledge the sociopolitical and power implications in each. We also acknowledge the shared history and experiences of group members despite different labels.

Acknowledgements

We wish to thank our colleagues, especially Alan Schoenfeld, who have offered their support for, and feedback on, this project. We thank our editor, Catherine Bernard, for her valuable feedback and guidance as the project progressed. We extend a special thank you to those colleagues who served as outside reviewers for the chapters and whose comments made the manuscript much stronger: Martha Allexsaht-Snider, Betsy Brenner, Michaele Chappelle, Dan Chazan, Lawrence Clark, Traci English-Clarke, Megan Franke, Rico Gutstein, Victoria Hand, Richard Kitchen, Jacqueline Leonard, Sarah Lubienski, Janine Remillard, and Edd Taylor.

Section I

Mapping a Liberatory Research and Policy Agenda

1 Liberating the Production of Knowledge About African American Children and Mathematics

Danny Bernard Martin

Liberation in its fullest sense requires the securing of full human rights and the remaking of a society without roles of oppressor and oppressed. . . . It involves challenging gross social inequities between social groups and creating new relationships that dispel oppressive social myths, values, and practices. The outcome of this process contributes to the creation of a changed society with ways of being that support the economic, cultural, political, psychological, social, and spiritual needs of individuals and groups. (Watts, Williams, & Jagers, 2003, pp. 187–188)

Liberation is a value worthy of science. That should be the perspective from which the minority scientist seeks to advance knowledge, always in the spirit of respect for logical canons, multiple perspectives, and methodological rigor; not for the purpose of simply predicting, controlling, and understanding, but for the purpose of emancipating (liberating) the bodies, minds, communities, and spirits of oppressed humankind. (Gordon, Miller, & Rollock, 1990, p. 19)

One of the charges given to the authors in this book was to address mathematics education for African American children through the theme of *liberation*. As suggested by the two quotes presented above, this charge acknowledges the continuing struggles against oppression and degradation that must be waged in U.S. society on behalf of African American children. These struggles are particularly necessary in research and policy settings, where ongoing discussions of *racial* achievement gaps and comparisons to white and Asian American students contribute to a pernicious assault on Black identity and humanity (Themstrom & Themstrom, 1997, 2004). This charge also suggests a need to examine mathematics education—and its logical canons—not only as a site where degradation of African American children occurs but also as a site where liberatory resistance against oppressive social myths and practices can, and must, be enacted.

Liberatory resistance can take many forms, including mathematics success by African American children in the face of lowered expectations and conditions that are believed to predict their failure (Berry, 2003, 2005; Jackson, 2007; Martin, 2000, 2006a, 2006b; McGee, 2007; Moody, 2001; Stinson, 2004; Thompson & Lewis, 2005); powerful and culturally relevant teaching that empowers African American children mathematically, epistemologically, and socially (Ernest, 1991, 2002; Gay,

2000; Ladson-Billings, 1994; Leonard, 2008); and culturally appropriate assessments of African American children's mathematical competence. Liberatory resistance can also include generating new knowledge aimed at deconstructing and challenging existing understandings and explanations of African American children's mathematical experiences, development, and outcomes.

Guided by the liberatory theme of this book, my primary goals in this chapter are to critically analyze the nature of the knowledge that is produced about African American children and mathematics and offer a reconceptualization of what that knowledge should be and how it should be generated and acted on. I contend, as African American scholars in other disciplinary areas have done (e.g., Gordon, 1985; Gordon, Miller, & Rollock, 1990; Jones, 1998; Ladson-Billings, 2000; McLoyd, 1991; White, 1991), that mainstream research and policy contexts have served as particularly fertile grounds to aid in socially constructing African American children as learners with particular kinds of deficiencies in relation to other children.

I distinguish *mainstream* mathematics education research and policy as that which has relied on traditional theories and models of teaching and learning (e.g., information processing, constructivism, situated cognition) and research approaches (race-neutral analyses, race-comparative analyses) developed primarily by white researchers and policy-makers to normalize the mathematical behavior of white children. Simultaneous to their use for normalization and generalization, these models have generated and validated conventional wisdoms about African American children and mathematics.

My arguments are not meant to imply that all mainstream mathematics education research and policy is detrimental to African American children. Meaningful and insightful research findings have sometimes led to the creation and implementation of policies that have had beneficial effects for these children.[1] However, research and policy do not always move together in a positive direction. In the case of African American children, I claim that there is often an unsettling convergence of research and policy that results in problematic representations of these children and their competencies and recommendations that are not always in their best interests (e.g., National Research Council, 1988).

Literacy scholar Lisa Delpit, in two highly influential and controversial *Harvard Educational Review* articles (1986, 1988), highlighted this last point in her critical analysis of skills-based and process-based approaches to writing. Delpit argued that these approaches, as conceptualized and implemented primarily by white scholars and practitioners, failed to consider the perspectives of scholars, practitioners, and parents of color or the relevance of these approaches to the needs and social realities of African American children. As a result, Black scholars and practitioners were limited in accessing, and challenging, the culture of power that allowed white scholars and practitioners to determine what is best for Black children. Further, Black children were harmed by approaches to literacy that did not provide them access to the codes, linguistic forms, and communicative strategies necessary for success.

Taking a cue from Delpit's critical analysis in the area of literacy, I find it reasonable to ask whether mainstream mathematics education theories, policies, and interventions have been inappropriately applied to African American children, where the major goal is to simply have the mathematical experiences and outcomes of African American children match those of white children. My analysis suggests that problematic constructions and representations of African American children and their competencies in mathematics are a direct result of this tendency.

Although this chapter is a scholarly critique, my arguments do not represent a dispassionate analysis. I draw on my teaching and research experiences over the last 20 years, where I have worked with African American learners in many different contexts (Martin, 2000, 2006a, 2006b). During this time, I have remained committed to remedying the often oppressive mathematics educations experienced by African American children and adults. These mathematical experiences often reinforce the social devaluation of African American identity and help to reproduce the inequities experienced by African Americans in the larger society. I have also remained committed to better understanding how African American learners remain resilient and succeed in mathematics in spite of the societal, school, and community forces that often work against them (Martin, 2000, 2006a, 2006b; McGee, 2007).

It is important to note that these two broad trajectories of mathematical experience for African American learners—oppression and resilience—have unfolded within the matrix of cutting-edge theories of learning, teaching, curriculum, and assessment that have been developed in mainstream mathematics education over the last 25 years. However, these theoretical perspectives have generated little in the way of better understanding African American children's mathematical experiences and behaviors. Many of the same questions about achievement and persistence asked more than 20 years ago (Johnson, 1984; Matthews, 1983; Stiff, 1990) are still being asked today (Lubienski, 2002; Strutchens & Silver, 2000; Tate, 1997). Unresolved, or unattended to, by most scholars and policy-makers is why advances in mathematics education research and policy have not translated into meaningful and transformative mathematical experiences and outcomes for African American children.

In my view, the inability to translate research and policy into strategies that benefit African American children is also due to the fact that mainstream mathematics education researchers and policy-makers have not taken seriously the differences between (a) research and policies generated for general student populations and that might residually apply to African American children and (b) research and policies that are based on, and apply to, the mathematical experiences of African American children *as African American* children.

In the remaining pages of this chapter, I explore this distinction as well as how research and policies in the first area have given rise to impoverished views of African American children. First, I highlight the dominant ways that mainstream research and policy perspectives *outside* of mathematics education portray African American children. The broader portrayals serve as a backdrop for understanding the ways these children are similarly constructed *inside* mainstream mathematics education research and policy. I also discuss how African American scholars have put forth counternarratives that challenge these dominant perspectives and constructions.

Second, I discuss the dominant research and policy orientations toward African American children and mathematics including the prevailing truths that have emerged about African American children and their development in mathematics.

Third, I offer an analysis of the dominant discursive frames and interpretive lenses on mathematics education that have been used as part of the knowledge construction process about African American children. My critical analysis of mainstream mathematics education research and policy contexts will also facilitate an analysis and understanding of the discursive frames (Bonilla-Silva, 2002, 2003) that are used to help common-sense beliefs about African American children gain status as truth when they reinforced via research and policy. The power of these discursive frames lies in their ability to help to conceal the scholarly racism that is normal to the ways that researchers and policy-makers talk about African American children.

Because a critical analysis of the nature and production of knowledge about African American children and mathematics is insufficient without offering alternatives to problematic approaches, I discuss the principles embedded in what some African American scholars have called a *culturally sensitive research approach* (Gordon, Miller, & Rollock, 1990; Tillman, 2002, 2006) and suggest that future research and policy efforts in mathematics education utilize such an approach.

I close the chapter by posing the question, *What should the study of African American children be the study of?* and offering some suggestions on how to address this question in future mathematics education research and policy efforts.

Some readers may misinterpret my critical analysis of mainstream mathematics education research and policy literatures as an attempt to romanticize African American children by rejecting findings that are typically accepted as fact. Indeed, there are real issues of underperformance and limited persistence in mathematics by some of these children. However, these are often symptoms of how these students experience mathematics instruction in school and classroom settings and, in many cases, reflect students' interpretations of, and rational responses to, their experiences and devaluation (e.g., Jackson, 2007; Martin, 2000, 2006a, 2006b; Spencer, 2006).

A Tale of Two Stories: Young, Gifted, and Black or Mathematically Illiterate?

As I sat in my office writing an early draft of this chapter, I scanned my bookshelves looking for resources that might help me in constructing my thoughts about African American children, liberation, and mathematics. I decided that I did not want to restrict my search to sources from mathematics education and that focused only on mathematics teaching and learning. Instead, I wanted to consider sources that focused on African American children's schooling experiences in relation to broader societal contexts and in relation to societal forces like racism. This would help me bring to light how African American children are constructed as persons in society and how well researchers and policy-makers address African American children's humanity and social realities.

I realized that some sources would take forces like racism as vital considerations and frame their discussions in ways that highlighted the "extra social, emotional, cognitive, and political competencies required of African-American youth, precisely because they are African-American" (Perry, 2003, p. 4). Other sources might be more dismissive of such considerations. I also wanted to consider sources that appeared to take particular stances on characterizing *Blackness*. By this, I mean that I decided to examine texts where the authors, implicitly or explicitly, appeared to define and conceptualize what it means to be Black, either from the point of view of day-to-day experiences or with respect to the societal meanings that have been imposed on this term and that have been used to configure the larger opportunity structure.

While continuing to scan my shelves, I noticed two books in front of me. Neither of these books came from the literature in mathematics education. However, each book, in its own way, had come to be identified as an authoritative source of information on the education of African American children. One book is titled *Young, Gifted, and Black: Promoting High Achievement Among African-American Students* and was written by African American scholars Theresa Perry, Claude Steele, and Asa Hilliard (2003). The other book is titled *America in Black and White: One Nation, Indivisible* and was written by Stephen and Abigail Thernstrom (1997), a white husband and wife author team.

I did not stop at these two books because they were unfamiliar to me or because I wanted to discover the arguments being put forth in each. I knew the arguments well. In fact, there were several other books on my shelf similar to the one by Perry, Steele, and Hilliard (2003). These books have titles like *Going to School: The African-American Experience* (Lomotey, 1990), *Learning While Black: Creating Excellence for African American Children* (Hale, 2001), *Black in School: Afrocentric Reform, Urban Youth and the Promise of Hip-hop Culture* (Ginwright, 2004), *The Mis-Education of the Negro* (Woodson, 1990), and *The Education of African-Americans* (Willie, Garibaldi, & Reed, 1991). I had referenced many of these in my previous research on mathematics socialization and identity among African American adolescents and adults (Martin, 2000, 2006a, 2006b).

There were also books similar in tenor and scope to the one by Thernstrom and Thernstrom (1997). These books have titles like *The End of Racism* (D'Souza, 1991), *Losing the Race: Self-Sabotage in Black America* (McWhorter, 2001), and *The Content of Our Character: A New Vision of Race in America* (Steele, 1990).

I could have chosen any of these books but I selected those by Perry, Steele, and Hilliard (2003) and Thernstrom and Thernstrom (1997) because they encapsulated the perspectives in many of the other texts and because they articulated uncompromising positions on African Americans. Having previously read *Young, Gifted, and Black* and *America in Black and White*, I knew that the authors of these books offered what amounted to a theory of African American achievement and, to some extent, a theory of what it means to be Black in relation to education and society. Yet this is where any similarity ended and where serious questions can be raised about the production of knowledge about African American children.

For example, Chapter 13 of *America in Black and White* is devoted to discussing what the Thernstroms and many other scholars and policy-makers describe as the *racial gap* in cognitive skills. To illustrate and document this racial gap, the Thernstroms examined differences in test scores and orientations to schooling among students identified as African American, white, and Asian American. As one example of their test score analysis, they utilized results from the National Assessment of Educational Progress (NAEP) to conclude that the average African American 12th grader demonstrated math skills and ability at the same level as the average white 9th grader. Years later, that particular framing of the mathematical abilities of African American children continues to be used (Education Trust, 2003; Lubienski, 2002).

In the same chapter, and arguing from what can be characterized as a conservative point of view, the Thernstroms also launched scathing attacks on what they saw as heightened, but debilitating, racial consciousness among African Americans. They suggested that, as a result of this heightened consciousness, African American students come to devalue and reject academic achievement as *acting white*, a term borrowed from educational researchers Signithia Fordham and John Ogbu (1986). Continuing their scholarly assault, they countered critiques of standardized tests as being culturally biased, disparaged Afrocentric curriculum, caricatured the call for more African American teachers, and cited school violence and disorder and negative home and peer socialization as additional factors affecting Black student school performance. They ended their chapter with suggestions for what they characterized as a disciplined, tough education for African American children.

The book by Perry, Steele, and Hilliard (2003) took a very different stance on African American education and began with the premise that:

> African American students face challenges unique to them as students in American schools at all levels by virtue of their social identity as African Americans and of the way that identity can be a source of devaluation in contemporary American society. . . . Before we can theorize African-American school achievement, we need to have an understanding of what the nature of the task of achievement is for African Americans *as African Americans* . . . . The task of academic achievement for African Americans in the context of school in the United States is distinctive . . . . and the ideology of the larger society has always been about questioning the mental capacity of African Americans, about questioning Black intellectual competence . . . . The conversation about African-American achievement is problematic because it fails to begin with a careful examination of all aspects of the school, with an eye toward understanding how the school's day-to-day practices participate in the creation of underachievement. (pp. vii-9, italics in original)

Perry (2003), in particular, articulated a vision and conceptualization of the purposes of education for African American children that resonate with the liberatory theme of this chapter and book. That conceptualization framed the purpose of education as *freedom for literacy and literacy for freedom* and considered not only the historical legacy of African American struggle for education but also the contemporary context of education for African American children. Unlike the Thernstroms, Perry raised several questions that speak to the realities of many African American children:

- Why should African American youth take school seriously if they cannot predict when and under what circumstances their intellect or intellectual work is likely to be taken seriously?
- Why should African American youth commit themselves to doing outstanding intellectual work if—because of the color of their skin—this work is likely to be undervalued, evaluated differently from that of whites, or ignored?
- Why work hard at school, or at anything else for that matter, if these activities are not inextricably linked to and address one's status as a member of a historically oppressed people?

My own interpretation of these questions is that they do not represent either-or propositions with respect to education because African American children can embrace education as a way to exercise their agency to resist oppressive schooling practices. Moreover, many African American children achieve at very high levels even in the face of such practices (e.g., Berry, 2003; Martin, 2000, 2006a, 2006b; McGee, 2007).

As I considered how the perspectives in these two books differed and as I reflected on the liberatory and emancipatory themes of this book, I began to think more deeply not just about educational outcomes among African American children but also about the aims and goals of scholars and policy-makers who purport to explain these children's academic achievement and human development. In the particular instances of these two books, I found myself asking why two very divergent stories about African American children were being told and put forth as truth. Why were the authors telling their scholarly stories in the ways that they did, with one group of scholars focusing on supposed race differences in cognitive skills and using test scores and the performance of white students as the primary measures of academic ability among African American children and the other group of authors focusing on understanding historical and structural *racism* and the societal and institutional assaults on African American identity as precursors to understanding academic outcomes? What scholarly norms and cultural frames of reference were the authors drawing on in telling their stories? What paradigmatic and epistemological traditions guided the work of these scholars in producing their perspectives (Ladson-Billings, 2000)? Whose version of the truth should consumers of knowledge believe? How did the patterns of explanation seen in these two perspectives play out in the areas that I wanted to consider in this chapter: mathematics education research and policy?

One way to answer the question about truth would be to say both sets of authors are correct. Yet such a simple resolution would ignore the fact that knowledge production is a political enterprise. Knowledge construction and production are even more political when African Americans are the focus of study (Gordon, Miller, & Rollock, 1990; McLoyd, 1991; Tillman, 2002, 2006). Moreover, discussing problematic educational outcomes in terms of deficiencies in African American children and their cultures and suggesting solutions that are contingent on the status and well-being of white students is a very different approach than focusing on the social realities and experiences of African Americans *as African Americans* and subsequently devising solutions to pressing educational problems that are responsive to these realities. Therefore, it becomes imperative to understand the nature of these discussions and the orientations toward African American children that they exemplify.

Power and Privilege in the Production of Knowledge: Mathematics Education Research and Policy as White Institutional Space

An important question that must be asked at the onset of developing such a critical understanding is, *How can one characterize the broad research and policy contexts in which African American children and their mathematical development and competences are socially constructed and discussed?* The answer to this question must include specifications of the concepts and ideological frames that are invoked to talk about African American children, an analysis of the research methods and policy orientations used to generate and perpetuate these concepts and frames, and a consideration of who has the power to set the parameters and boundaries of these methods and orientations. In other words, those who wish to develop liberatory mathematics education scholarship for African American children must examine the existing relations of power that influence the construction of knowledge about these children.

In my view, it is especially important to consider the dominance and privilege of white scholars in shaping the broad methodological and ideological contexts of mathematics education research and policy. However, I wish to caution that any interpretation of my arguments which suggests that they are focused on individual white researchers and policy-makers or that white researchers should not conduct research with African American children would make little sense given that: (1) some advances in mainstream knowledge about mathematics teaching, learning, curriculum, and assessment have benefited African American students (e.g., Silver, Smith, & Nelson, 1995; Treisman 1985) and (2) there are also African American, and other, scholars who have appropriated mainstream methods and perspectives in ways that have contributed to negative representations of African American children.

It is true, however, that the vast majority of mathematics education researchers and policy-makers are white, that very little mainstream research and policy has focused on African American children *as African American* children—but rather on how they differ from white children—and that the overwhelming majority of studies in mainstream mathematics education do not explicitly use race, class, and gender-based *theoretical* frameworks in the analyses (Lubienski & Bowen, 2000; Martin, 2009). Theoretical frameworks, research agendas, and policies that do not adequately consider race, class, and gender are then allowed to proliferate based on the assumption that what is good for all children is good for African American children (e.g., NCTM, 1989, 2000; RAND Mathematics Study Panel, 2003; U.S. Department of Education, 2008).

An important, but little-discussed, consequence of the numerical and theoretical dominance of white researchers and policy-makers is that mathematics education as a field continues to be validated and reified as a *white institutional space* (Moore, 2008); that is, as a space where scholarly norms and conceptions of teaching, learning, and assessment are based primarily on the perspectives of white scholars. As indicated by Moore (2008), "many institutional norms, policies, and procedures make ... institutions normatively white including the history of the institutions, the racialized practices and policies ... and the dominant white culture and discourse that often employs racism to signify [people] of color as outsiders in these spaces" (p. 26).

In thinking of mathematics education as a white institutional space, one can visualize a large white projection screen (Martin, 2008). Although up-close inspection of the screen reveals bits and pieces of color, it is the overall whiteness of the screen that serves as its defining characteristic. Moreover, the screen appears neutral yet it has the power to project "meanings and symbols that are associated with the dominant culture, thus reproducing an ideological framework that rationalizes and reproduces structures of inequality" (Moore, 2008, p. 17).

One can also understand mathematics education as white institutional space by considering who dominate positions of power and who regulates the production of knowledge from those positions. Among journal editors, handbook editors, and conveners of major panels and working groups, it is white scholars who occupy the most prominent roles. What this reveals is that mathematics education, as a research enterprise, is not immune to the structural and institutional racism that characterizes many other areas of society. This structural and institutional racism exists above and beyond the good intentions of individual white scholars (Trepagnier, 2006). As indicated by Moore (2008), the "concept of institutional racism captures how racist relations can be reproduced without individuals' intentional racist acts, because racism is deeply entrenched within our institutions" (p. 25). Within the white institutional space of mathematics education, white perspectives often rise to the level of authority, even when issues particular to African American children are the focus.

A case in point is the *National Mathematics Advisory Panel.* The panel was created through an executive order by President George Bush. The charge given to the panel was to use the best available scientific research to advise on improvements in the mathematics education for *all* of the nation's children (U.S. Department of Education, 2008). The *Final Report of the National Mathematics Advisory Panel* (U.S. Department of Education, 2008) contains significant recommendations for future research involving African American children. However, it is noteworthy that the panel included no African American mathematics education researchers and that the final report made no references to research produced by African American scholars in mathematics education (see Martin, 2008 for a race critical analysis of the Math Panel). Moreover, the list of experts cited in the final report and called on to examine materials, offer opinions on specialized topics, and examine drafts of sections of the report included no African American math education scholars (U.S. Department of Education, 2008).

A second example is the *Critical Issues in Education Workshop: Teaching and Learning Algebra* that was held at the Mathematical Sciences Research Institute (MSRI) in Berkeley, California during May of 2008. This two-and-a-half-day workshop was aimed at a national audience and was intended to address important questions related to helping students make the transition from arithmetic to algebra and helping them achieve success in pre-collegiate and collegiate mathematics. The organizing team included some of the most well-known and senior mathematics educators in the country, scholars who could be considered stewards of the field. However, there were no African American mathematics educators on the organizing team, as listed on the conference website, and only one African American panelist across all of the sessions.[2]

In the context of equity-oriented rhetoric and the focus on *Algebra for All* in mainstream mathematics education policy and research (NCTM, 1989, 2000; RAND Mathematics Study Panel, 2003), the limited presence of African American scholars as key discussants of algebra teaching and learning is troubling and serves to preserve the privileged status of white scholars and white perspectives (Gordon, B., 1990; Gordon, Miller, & Rollock, 1990; Gordon, E., 1985; Tillman, 2002, 2006).

A clear and consistent pattern emerges when one also considers the editors, authors, and contents of major mathematics education publications over the last 20 years (e.g., Boaler, 2000; English, 2002; Grouws, 1992; Lesh, Hamilton, & Kaput, 2007; Lester, 2007; Silver, 1985; Steffe, Nescher, Cobb, Goldin, & Greer, 1996). African American authors and chapters devoted to mathematics education for African American children received minimal, if any, representation in these publications.

The result of such practices and marginalization is a knowledge base in mainstream mathematics education that is not informed by African American insights and perspectives and, therefore, is limited in its explanatory power with respect to African American children's mathematical development (Martin, 2008).

As I point out in Martin (2008), some readers might suggest, correctly, that not all African American mathematics education scholars produce research or advocate for policy that is in the best interests of African Americans, while some white scholars do. This is indeed the case. However, based on the small amount of mainstream research focused on African American children, I would argue that these white scholars are a minority within a much larger majority. Moreover, while I agree that the voices of critical white scholars are important, I do believe that, given the high stakes for African American children, the voices of white scholars cannot serve as a direct substitute for the voices of critical African American scholars (Martin, 2008). The numerical dominance of white scholars in meaningful research and policy contexts, whatever their orientation, only insures that white perspectives become the *only* perspectives that matter.

Although individual white researchers and policy-makers may carry out their work seemingly on behalf of African American children, I believe it is more important to take a deeper, more critical look at mathematics education research and policy contexts as white institutional spaces. In doing so, my efforts parallel those of scholars who have studied the sociology of knowledge more broadly (e.g., Berger & Luckman, 1967) and the construction of knowledge about African Americans, in particular (e.g., Banks, 1993; Gordon, B., 1990; Gordon, E., 1985; Gordon, E., Miller, & Rollock, 1990; Tillman, 2002, 2006). Scholars in the latter category have continued to offer challenges to impoverished conceptualizations of race and racism in relation to the experiences of African Americans.

Research and Policy Orientations Toward African American Children

> This conversation [about the achievement gap] will almost surely reinforce the national ideology of Black intellectual inferiority. And, as such, the conversation is likely to be the location of yet another narrative that further undermines how African-American students are seen by others and by themselves. (Perry, 2003, p. 8)

Given my characterization of mathematics education research and policy as white institutional spaces, I claim that the ideologies and norms within these spaces are what shape mainstream orientations to African American children. In choosing to focus on the *nature* and *production* of knowledge within these spaces, I have decided to forego the two main strategies used by many mathematics education researchers and policy-makers in their discussions of African American children: (1) starting with taken-for-granted, *negative* outcomes in mathematics achievement and course-taking patterns—which have remained the preferred areas of investigation—and subsequently working backwards to try and explain these outcomes or (2) deliberately setting out to document patterns of difference in achievement and course completion between African children and children from other ethnic and racial groups but in ways that often mark African American children as less than ideal learners.

Both of these strategies often require that one accept test scores as factual and indisputable measures of ability and accept course-taking and persistence patterns as proxies for student motivation and interest in mathematics. Lacking in these approaches is a critical reflection on whether achievement and persistence are the best, and only, lenses through which to understand African American children's mathematical development. A focus on achievement and persistence without a simultaneous exploration of the ways African American children *experience* mathematics, especially in terms of success and resilience and across a range of school, community, and social contexts, is necessarily incomplete (Martin, 2007).

Another characteristic of these two approaches is that there is often a troubling attribution to African American identity that is legitimized and accepted under the guise of research objectivity and progressive policy. Within both of these approaches, to *be* African American is to be mathematically illiterate, incompetent, and unmotivated. This attribution is an outgrowth of larger societal discussions that render African American children as intellectually and culturally inferior and, as a result, in need of being rescued from their Blackness, on one hand, or worthy of being cast off as expendable from society, on the other (Figueira-McDonough, 1995; Kozol, 1992). Elsewhere (Martin, 2007, 2009), I have highlighted statements such as the one presented below, taken from *Everybody Counts* (National Research Council, 1989), which serve as examples of how these attributions are made in mainstream mathematics education research and policy contexts. This statement, one among many, makes a clear association between mathematical illiteracy and African American identity:

Because mathematics holds the key to leadership in our information-based society, the widening gap between *those who are mathematically literate* and *those who are not* coincides, to a frightening degree, with *racial* and economic categories. We are at-risk of becoming a divided nation in which knowledge of mathematics supports a *productive, technological powerful elite* while a *dependent, semiliterate majority, disproportionately Hispanic and Black*, find economic and political power beyond reach. Unless corrected, *innumeracy* and *illiteracy* will drive America apart. (p. 14, italics added)

Similar statements can be found in the *Final Report of the National Mathematics Advisory Panel* (U.S. Department of Education, 2008) where it is again evident that oblique references are made to African American children as being mathematically illiterate upon entering schools and that this illiteracy is a threat to the nation's well-being:

Moreover, there are large, persistent disparities in mathematics achievement related to race and income—disparities that are not only devastating for individuals and families but also project poorly for the nation's future, given the youthfulness and high growth rates of the largest minority populations . . . . Unfortunately, most children from low-income backgrounds enter school with far less knowledge than peers from middle-income backgrounds, and the achievement gap in mathematical knowledge progressively widens throughout their PreK–12 years. (pp. xii–xviii)

Stereotypical images and constructions of African American children and their competencies are also reinforced through research by invoking conclusions such as the one presented below, taken from the *Second Handbook of Research on Mathematics Teaching and Learning* (Lester, 2007). Such statements are clearly intended to apply to African American children given their disproportionate poverty rates:

We believe the pattern of results suggest that, although low-income children have pre-mathematical knowledge, they do lack important components of mathematical knowledge. They lack the ability—because they have been provided less support to learn—to connect their informal premathematical knowledge to school mathematics. Children must learn to mathematize their informal experiences, abstracting, representing, and elaborating them mathematically, and using mathematical ideas and symbols to create models of their everyday activities. This includes the ability to generalize, connecting mathematical ideas to different situations and using the ideas and processes adaptively. (Clements & Sarama, 2007, p. 534)

Whereas the preceding statements imply that African American children lack mathematical knowledge, other perspectives highlight so-called shortcomings in their effort and efficacy. The following quote from the final report of the National Mathematics Advisory Panel exemplifies this view:

Experimental studies have demonstrated that changing children's beliefs from a focus on ability to a focus on effort increases their engagement in mathematics learning, which in turn improves mathematics outcomes: When children believe that their efforts to learn make them "smarter," they show greater persistence in mathematics learning. Related research demonstrates that the engagement and sense of efficacy of African-American and Hispanic students in mathematical learning contexts not only tends to be lower than that of white and Asian students but also that it can be significantly increased. Teachers and other educational leaders should consistently help students and parents to understand that an increased emphasis on the importance of effort is related to improved mathematics performance. (p. xx)

The following quote, taken from the *Report of the Task Group on Learning Processes* (2008) subgroup of the National Mathematics Advisory Panel cites family characteristics, race and ethnicity as predictors of mathematical knowledge and represents the combined forces of cultural racism and deficit theories:

Differences in mathematical knowledge of U.S. children at the beginning of kindergarten reflect many aspects of the children's background . . . . One predictor is a mother's education . . . . Another group of predictors involves risk factors such as single-parent families . . . and families living in poverty. Children from families with fewer risk factors usually enter kindergarten with greater knowledge of numbers and shapes than children from families with more risk factors. A third predictor is race and ethnicity: White, non-Hispanic children and Asian children usually enter kindergarten with greater mathematical knowledge than Black and Hispanic children. (p. 75)

Viewed collectively, the statements presented above reveal several shortcomings in how African American children and their competencies are socially constructed. Because the tasks, assessments, and standards for competence used to draw these conclusions are typically not normed on African American children's cultural and life experiences, one could also argue that the standards for *less extensive mathematical knowledge* and *less support* as well as the preferred ways of *abstracting, representing,* and *elaboration* called for in these studies and reports are based on the normalized behavior of white, middle-class and upper-class children. In fact, beyond specifications of the preferred ways of engaging in mathematics, it also true that the behavior of white children has been normalized even when research has focused on misconceptions, maladaptive arithmetic counting strategies and errors, and maladaptive measurement strategies and errors (e.g., Cobb, 1986; Erlwanger, 1973).

In my view, the statements presented above highlight the fact that very little consideration is given to exploring patterns in the ways that low-income and African American children *do* engage in abstraction, representation, and elaboration to determine if these ways are mediated by their cultural experiences in out-of-school settings and whether the preferred ways of engaging in these processes serve useful functions relative to those experiences (e.g., Nasir, 2002; Taylor, 2005).

Related to this argument is the fact that these statements carry with them certain assumptions about what counts as mathematics and mathematics knowledge. It is clear that school mathematics knowledge is privileged over children's out-of-school knowledge and that low-income children's out-of-school math knowledge is valued even less. Given such a restrictive view of mathematics knowledge, it is very likely that mathematical competencies linked to the cultural contexts and everyday life experiences of African American children are under-assessed and under-valued because these competencies do not fall within dominant views of what counts as mathematics knowledge.

These conclusions generated in the statements above also reveal the impoverished ways that both race and social class are conceptualized in mainstream mathematics education research. Although *low-income* is often used as a broad signifier for African American children, there is no acknowledgement that being low-income is likely to be experienced differently across socially constructed racial groups because income and wealth are not synonymous. Research has shown that Black and white families with the same low levels of income have significant differences in wealth and that racism accounts for much of this difference (Conley, 1999). To the degree that wealth provides greater access to the kinds of cultural capital that are valued in school contexts, African American children will likely experience greater disadvantage and under-appreciation for the skills and abilities that they do demonstrate. Therefore, class-based analyses of mathematics achievement and development that do not consider forces like racism are incomplete. Failure to highlight this point represents a simplistic view of African American children life circumstances and development.

Also inherent in the conclusions generated in these statements is the belief that race and social class are deterministic in children's mathematical development. However, research on African American students' success in mathematics shows that mathematically successful students come from varied socioeconomic backgrounds (e.g., Berry, 2003; Martin, 2000; Moody, 2001; Stinson, 2004). Moreover, the concept of race, as referenced in these statements, is overly simplistic. Although invoked across several of the statements, none of these reports, as is generally true in mathematics education research, provided a careful definition of the concept of race or attempted to account for structural and institutional racism in their discussions of student learning. As is often the case, the concept of race was used only to disaggregate data so that it could be cited as a causal variable and used to rank students in a racial hierarchy of mathematical ability (Martin, 2009).

Left unchecked, conclusions such as those generated above could easily lead readers to believe that African American students underachieve because they do not try hard enough and they lack mathematical knowledge. Missing from the analyses, however, are observations and questions such as those made by Theresa Perry (2003) and presented earlier in this chapter. As indicated by Perry, it is not simply the case that African American children do not put forth effort in academic settings. One must consider their responses to schooling as a function of their social realities and the ways that their identities are devalued in school, society, research, and policy contexts. Moreover, assuming that teachers and other educational leaders uniformly believe in the ability of African American children is highly questionable.

In fact, research shows the opposite to be true, with many teachers having low expectations for African American children (e.g, Hilliard, 2003; Jackson, 2007; Oakes, 1985, 1990; Perry, 2003; Spencer, 2006). Research also shows that many white teachers, in particular, have very little, or impoverished, understanding of African American children's out-of-school lives and the cultural knowledge they bring with them (e.g., Gay, 2000; Ladson-Billings, 1994).

I would argue that, rather than reflecting deficiencies in African American children's premathematical knowledge, inability to connect their informal mathematical knowledge to school mathematics, or lack of effort and efficacy, it is the expectations and practices employed in their schools and classrooms, as well as the ways that mainstream research and policy are overlaid on their experiences, that result in the representation of African American children as lacking in mathematical knowledge.

Mainstream mathematics education research is only one context where African American children are constructed as less than ideal learners and inferior to white children. At the local level, entire school districts have adopted negative policy orientations toward African American children as evidenced by the very public discussions and rhetoric surrounding so-called racial achievement gaps. Cumulatively, these local discussions fuel and sustain an ongoing national conversation that allows the identity of African American children to be publicly disparaged. Along with other African American scholars, I have argued that the framing of schooling outcomes in terms of racial achievement gaps requires one to assume the intellectual inferiority of African American children as the starting point in these discussions. This policy framing also positions teachers and school officials to accept this belief as the starting point and motivating factor in their practices and interactions with African American children (Hilliard, 2003; Martin, 2007, 2009; Perry, 2003).

A November 1, 2007 article in the *Chicago Sun Times* illustrates how the public devaluation of African American children plays out at the school district level. The Chicago Public School system is the third largest in the United States. Forty-seven percent of the students are African American, 39% are Latino, and 8% are white. Against this backdrop, the major thrust of the article was to point out how African American and Latino student test scores lag behind the scores of white students in the district and state. Therefore, in a system where only 8% of the students are white and some of the system's best resources are often reserved for these students, the article's focus on the racial achievement gap made it clear that the education of African American and Latino students in the district is defined in terms of this very small group of white students rather than in terms of the particular needs of African American and Latino children. The normalization of white children and the standardization of their behavior are very apparent in the district's approach to educating African American and Latino children. This is particularly problematic for African American children, because it implies that the needs of these children are contingent on, and tied to, outcomes that are deemed appropriate for white children.

Two recent examples of this contingency in the national policy arena are *Mathematics for All* and *Algebra for All* (Damerow & Westbury, 1987; Keitel, 1987;

NCTM, 1989, 2000). Essentially, these efforts have been presented to the general public as mathematics education's attempt to provide African American, Latino, Native American, and poor students access to the same mathematical opportunities previously enjoyed by white middle-class and upper-class children. My critical analysis (Martin, 2003, 2009; Martin & McGee, 2009) of the deep structure of *Mathematics for All* and *Algebra for All* has shown that they are not focused on the specific needs of African American children but, instead, subsumes those needs under what is best for all students (e.g., NCTM, 1989, 2000; National Research Council, 2001; RAND Mathematics Study Panel, 2003). Workforce considerations and maintenance of U.S. international competitiveness, not a moral commitment, pervade much of the rhetoric associated with increased African American participation in mathematics.

Therefore, beyond their equity-oriented rhetoric, *Mathematics for All* and *Algebra for All* can be seen as part of a larger assimilationist agenda that attempts to standardize all children by countering heightened racial consciousness and minimizing attention to forces like racism. Within these movements, what is deemed best for white children is what is deemed best for African American children. As a consequence, I would argue that the quest for equality and sameness in such policies, rather than what is equitable, has the potential to further maintain the marginalization of African American children.

The early proponents of *Mathematics for All* and *Algebra for All* may have also ignored the possibility that once African American students were granted access to gatekeepers like algebra, new gatekeepers and processes (e.g., high school exit exams, multiple versions of what is called algebra, stricter university entrance requirements; resistance from white middle- and upper-class parents (e.g., Brantlinger, 2003) would emerge to maintain the status of these students relative to students from white middle- and upper-class backgrounds. In some states like California, this is precisely what has happened. Despite mandates for 8th grade algebra as a way to put more students on the college track, there has been no significant increase in African American enrollment throughout the University of California system and, at some campuses, African American student enrollment has decreased. In Los Angeles County, nearly 10,000 African American students graduated from high school in 2006. Of those, only 96 enrolled at UCLA in fall 2006. In total, only 210 African American freshmen were admitted to UCLA.

In my view, *Mathematics for All* and *Algebra for All* are emblematic of Derrick Bell's (1980, 1992) notion of *interest convergence,* which suggests that members of the dominant group will promote interests for African Americans only when they promote dominant group interests. The quotes presented above from *Everybody Counts* and *Final Report of the National Mathematics Advisory Panel* presented above are examples of how some policy-makers see the well-being of the nation and a productive, technologically powerful elite as being threatened by the mathematical illiteracy of African Americans and Latinos. Therefore, it is argued that increased levels of math literacy and participation among African Americans will help protect the interests of the nation and its elite.

Despite these implicit portrayals of African American children as mathematically illiterate, African American scholars have continued to point out that underachievement and illiteracy are not fundamental to the identities of African American children (e.g., Gay, 2000; Martin, 2000, 2006a, 2006b; Murrell, 2002; Perry, 2003; Shujaa, 1994). To begin with the premise that they are is highly problematic.

What is the Study of African American Children the Study of?

The discussion above can now be used to clarify and characterize the paradigmatic lens that has guided the study of African American children's mathematical development. In the 1991 edition of the book *Black Psychology* (Jones, 1991), developmental psychologist Vonnie C. McLoyd authored a chapter in which she critically examined these orientations by raising the question, *What is the study of African American children the study of?* This question referred not only to the content of research studies but also to the way that these studies were framed. Based on reviews of research published in several leading psychology journals, McLoyd (1991) concluded that the study of African American children in mainstream psychology research is often the study of how they differ from white children (McLoyd & Randolph, 1984; Washington & McLoyd, 1982). That is, a *race-comparative* paradigm has dominated the research orientations of scholars who engage in the study of African American children. Although she highlighted some of the merits of this approach, McLoyd (1991) offered the following critique:

> It should be clear that race-comparative studies *can* provide important information about the adverse affects of racism and economic oppression and the unique qualities of African American culture and behavior. This potential notwithstanding, it is no doubt the case that the dominance of the race-comparative framework has resulted in an impoverished body of knowledge about African American children and stymied the advancement of theory about development in these children. Sorely needed as a counterweight to the study of race and ethnic differences is study of African American children qua African American children. (p. 431, italics in original)

Contributing to her characterization of research based on the race-comparative approach, McLoyd (1991) cited several specific limitations, including: (a) the tendency to document the ways in which African American children do not behave rather than they how they do behave, (b) contributing to the belief that African American children are abnormal and incompetent based on the fact that differences between African American children and white children are attributed to cultural deficiencies on the part of African American children, and (c) promoting person-blame interpretations of social problems and outcomes rather than analyzing the roles of systemic and structural factors.

Gordon, Miller, and Rollock (1990), in writing about what they called *communicentric bias* in social science knowledge production, cited similar concerns with the nature of the knowledge that is produced about African Americans. They asserted that the social and educational sciences have "traditionally attempted to understand the life experiences of Afro-Americans from a narrow cultrocentric perspective and against equally narrow cultrocentric standards" (p. 15).

Given these concerns raised about psychological and social science research focused on African American children and the understanding of how discursive frames are used to support color-blind racism, I find it reasonable to ask, in the context is mainstream mathematics education research and policy is, *What is the study of African American children the study of?* I raise this question knowing that, in almost every other area of life, African Americans and African American identity have been the subject of scrutiny and scorn and that the value placed on Black life continues to diminish, not only in the collective psyche of the larger society but also in societal institutions like schools (National Urban League, 2007).

The questions that get asked about African Americans, the policies that get enacted on their behalf, and the practices that are employed in the contexts where they live and learn are all embedded with assumptions about their intelligence, competencies, motivations, and worthiness. The context of mathematics education offers no exception. It is fair to say that what has emerged as official knowledge and policy about African American students and mathematics has remained largely free of challenge and scrutiny within the mainstream math education community.

I also raise this question knowing that, over the last 25 years, mathematics education in the United States has undergone significant, and sometimes controversial, reform in the areas of curriculum, teaching, and assessment. Over this same time period, there have been paradigmatic shifts in how mathematics education researchers characterize the learning process, having moved from cognitivist to constructivist to situated cognition to sociocultural theories and perspectives. Despite the critical debate and reflection that these reforms and paradigm shifts have engendered, it is a remarkable fact that research and policy orientations and conclusions pertaining to mathematics education for African American children have remained relatively unchanged. In particular, little progress has been made on the nature of the research questions that have been asked about these children, the kinds of conclusions that are generated about their skills and abilities, or the aims and goals for their mathematical education.

Echoing McLoyd's (1991) critique of the research literature in psychology, I claim that the race-comparative approach in mainstream mathematics education research and policy has (a) resulted in an impoverished knowledge base about the mathematical development and experiences of African American learners in lieu of a narrow focus decontextualized skills, (b) contributed to the social construction of African American children as mathematically incompetent and mathematically illiterate, and (c) positioned these children not only at the bottom of the U.S. racial hierarchy but at the bottom of what I call the *racial hierarchy of mathematical ability* (Martin, 2009). This is a strong claim but one that can be supported by critical analyses of both research and policy.

As far back as the early 1980s, data from a wide rage of national assessments and achievement tests have been used as evidence to show that, collectively, students identified as African American score below those identified as white and Asian (e.g., Anick, Carpenter, & Smith, 1981; Johnson, 1984; Kenney & Silver, 1997; Lubienski, 2002; Secada, 1992; Strutchens & Silver, 2000; Tate, 1997; Treisman,

1985). A review of the articles published in the *Journal for Research in Mathematics Education*, the flagship journal of the field, shows that many of the articles relating to African American learners involved some form of comparative analyses between African American children and children from other groups (Anick, Carpenter, & Smith, 1981; Reyes & Stanic, 1988; Johnson, 1984; Tate, 1997).

During the same 25-year period of remarkable change in mathematics education research and policy, a damaging conventional wisdom emerged as part of the knowledge production process about African American learners and mathematics. In short, mainstream mathematics education research and policy converged with larger societal beliefs and ideologies to construct and reify African American children as mathematically illiterate and intellectually inferior to white and Asian American children. The examples presented earlier in this chapter from the *Final Report of the National Mathematics Advisory Panel* (U.S. Department of Education, 2008), *Everybody Counts* (National Research Council, 1989), and the *Second Handbook of Research on Mathematics Teaching and Learning* (Lester, 2007) bear this out.

Clearly, not every research study or policy can be characterized in this way. However, I would argue that the dominant and normal orientation of mainstream mathematics education research and policy stands in direct opposition to concerted efforts that attempt to conceptualize mathematics education for African American children in ways that are truly liberatory and emancipatory in nature. Whereas mainstream mathematics education research and policies conceptualize mathematics education for African American children in terms of increased course enrollments and workforce preparation, liberatory and African-centered (Madhubuti & Madhubuti, 1994; Murrell, 2002) orientations to mathematics learning and participation echo the sentiments made by Malcom X (1987) and, more recently, by Theresa Perry (2003):

> Read and write yourself into freedom! Read and write to assert your identity as human! Read and write as an act of resistance, as a political act, for racial uplift, so you can lead your people well into the struggle for liberation! (p. 19)

Culturally Sensitive Research Approaches

> Much of the minority scholar's time is consumed in efforts to refute or neutralize fallacious findings, questionable theories, and inappropriate interpretations . . . . Criticism is an essential and necessary role . . . . but critique and refutation are insufficient. We find ourselves in a reactive mode when a proactive stance is indicated. There are not enough of us doing the conceptual homework which is necessary to generate alternative paradigms. We must do the systematic observations and ethnographic analyses, which are the foundation for the development of alternative or parallel taxonomies more appropriate to the classification and investigation of our life conditions. (Gordon, Miller, & Rollock, 1990, p. 17)

What are the alternatives to mainstream approaches to mathematics education research and policy? My suggestions build on the work of a number of African

American scholars of education who have called for *culturally sensitive research approaches* that can provide richer characterizations of African American experiences in order to overcome the communicentric bias and hegemony inherent in mainstream research and policy (e.g., Akbar, 1991; Banks, 1993; Gordon, E. 1985; Gordon, B. 1990; Gordon, Miller, & Rollock, 1990; McLoyd, 1991; Tillman, 2002, 2006; Woodson, 1990).

Tillman (2006), for example, proposed a framework for conducting culturally sensitive research in African American communities. This framework consists of (a) culturally congruent research methods, (b) culturally specific knowledge, (c) cultural resistance to theoretical dominance, (d) culturally sensitive data interpretations, and (e) culturally informed theory and practice.

Culturally sensitive research *methods* include the use of qualitative methods such as individual, group, and life history interviews to capture "holistic contextualized picture of the social, political, economic and educational factors that affect the every day existence of African-Americans" (Tillman, 2006, p. 269). The use of *culturally specific knowledge* implies that the researcher relies heavily on the first-hand accounts of African Americans, what has been called Black self-representation. *Cultural resistance to theoretical domination* implies that there is an explicit effort to uncover and challenge "unequal power relations that may minimize, marginalize, subjugate or exclude the multiple realities and knowledge bases of African-Americans" (Tillman, 2006, p. 270) and to respond to claims of neutrality and objectivity. For example, Critical Race Theory (e.g., Lynn, 1999; Yosso, Parker, Solozano & Lynn, 2005) and Black feminist thought (Collins, 1990) are two approaches that have been used by African American scholars to resist theoretical dominance.

As I have argued throughout this chapter, the interpretation of data on African American children's mathematical behavior has been used to generate inadequate, but widely accepted, theories about their competence. The interpretation of data has often been in relation to norms based on the behavior or white children or with little understanding of African American children's cultural contexts of living and learning. Perhaps most troubling with respect to mathematics education research is the paucity of first-hand data collected from African American learners themselves. Very little is known about how African American learners make sense of their mathematical experiences and outcomes. According to Tillman (2006), culturally sensitive *data interpretations* can help:

> . . . position the experiential knowledge of African-Americans as legitimate, appropriate and necessary for analyzing, understanding and reporting data. Analysis and presentation that is appropriate to the research topic and the individual or group under study is co-constructed. Storytelling, family histories, biographies and narratives, as well as other forms of data presentation, may be used. The cultural standpoints of African-Americans provide "endarkened" analyses of their particular experiences in American society. An endarkened analysis emanates from an identity that is centered in African-American racial and cultural identity. (p. 270)

To illustrate, I draw from my research and teaching experiences with African American adolescents, adults, and parents (Martin 2000, 2006a, 2006b). This research has involved the use of qualitative methods (ethnography, participant observation, narrative analysis) and took a multilevel approach to understanding mathematics socialization and identity construction. Much of this work has focused on how African American learners co-construct their mathematics and African American identities through first-person, retrospective narrative accounts. In constructing their own theories on issues of mathematics achievement and persistence, I have found that the participants often offered accounts that challenged the truths produced by mainstream researchers and policy-makers. When interviewed and asked about their life experiences and experiences as learners of mathematics, many participants invoked contingency clauses that implicated their status and identity as African Americans. It was not unusual for participants to begin their responses with clauses like "Being Black," "As a Black man," "Because my children are Black," and "For Black people." These clauses were invoked not as excuses or causal explanations, but often served as precursors to extended narratives about the salience of their African American status and the salience of race and racism in their life, school, and mathematical experiences.

These narratives in my research have also provided me with a context to develop a conceptualization of mathematics learning and participation as *racialized forms of experience* (Martin, 2006a); that is, as experiences structured by the dominant ideologies and relations of race that exist in the larger society. In Martin (2009), I discuss how this perspective contrasts with mainstream cognitive and sociocultural theories in dealing with race. Table 1.1 offers a basic summary of some of these differences.

My research has shown that, to the degree that their African American status, identities, and prior knowledge are valued, devalued, or challenged in schools and by teachers, African American students respond by engaging in complex meaning-making practices and agency related behaviors in response to real and perceived racism and assaults on African American identity. Such a perspective does not stand in opposition to perspectives that view mathematics learning as cognitive or situated activities. Rather, it points out their weaknesses in addressing mathematics learning for African American learners and it centers race in the analysis.

Akbar (1991) also captured the necessity for culturally sensitive research approaches when he argued that it is necessary to carefully and critically evaluate the approaches to research and policy that have emerged about African Americans, particularly when those approaches are developed out of traditional Euro-American social science, psychological, and educational research perspectives. According to Akbar (1991), it is also important to "understand that methodology is not free of bias and in fact, methodology is a form of systematic bias. The application of that method or the outcome ... will only confirm the paradigm that gave rise to the methodology" (p. 723).

My own reading of mainstream mathematics education research and policy has shown that culturally sensitive research approaches and frameworks have not been utilized in discussions of African American children and mathematics (Martin, 2007; Martin & McGee, 2009). Increasingly, however, these methods as well as

Table 1.1 Contrasting Approaches to Race in Mathematics Education Research, Policy, and Practice

	Conceptualizations of race	Conceptualizations of learners	Research, policy, and practice orientations to race	Aims and goals of mathematics education research, policy, and practice
Mainstream mathematics education research, policy, and practice	Races as biologically determined. Race as a way to disaggregate data. Race as a causal variable for mathematics achievement.	Those who know mathematics. Those who do not. Those who are mathematically literate. Those who are mathematically illiterate. Students belong to a racial hierarchy of mathematical ability.	Resistance to realities of racism. Color-blindness. Racial apathy. Solution on demand. Interest convergence.	Close the racial achievement gap. Maintain white privilege and United States international competitiveness.
Mathematics learning and participation as racialized forms of experience	Race as a sociopolitical construction. Historically contingent nature of race. Consideration of racism and racialization.	Consideration of the negotiated nature of identity with respect to mathematics. Asks, What does it mean to be African American, Latino, Native American, white, and Asian American in the context of mathematics learning?	Consideration of everyday, institutional, and structural racism.	Empowerment and liberation from oppression for marginalized learners.

race-based research epistemologies are being used by African American and critical mathematics education scholars to better understand the mathematical experiences of African American students (e.g., Y. Johnson; Nasir et al.; Spencer; Stinson; Strutchens & Westbrook, this volume).

Reframing the Issues: What Should the Study of African American Children be the Study of?

In Martin (2007), I give particular attention to two discursive frames that have been used to inform mathematics education research and policy relative to African American learners. A critical analysis of the historically more dominant *achievement* lens showed how it has contributed to the social construction and representation of African American children as less than ideal learners. I also showed how the achievement lens, as it is applied to African American children, exacerbates the impact of ideologies that support color-blind racism (Bonilla-Silva, 2001, 2002, 2003; Gordon, 2005; Lewis, 2004). The second lens, which is equally informative and deserving of more attention, focuses on the ways that African American students *experience* mathematics in school contexts (e.g., Berry, 2003; Martin, 2000, 2006a, 2006b, 2009; Moody, 2001). What is most important about these lenses is that each gives rise to its own logic and approach to formulating research and policy characterizations of African American children and mathematics.

Given the power and privilege inherent in the knowledge production process and the power embedded in particular, negative framings of African American children relative to mathematics, I argue that there is a need to *re*frame issues in many of the most important areas of mathematics education research and policy. These reframings will result in more than a semantic shift in research and policy discussions but will also re-center the conversations about African American children to consider their needs *as African American children*, free of insidious comparisons to white children. Below, I outline a number of areas where these reframings might occur.

Reframing the Purposes of Mathematics Education for African American Children

The vast majority of mathematics education policy frames the purposes of mathematics education for African American in terms of increased course participation, access to higher education, and workforce preparation. Future policy efforts should be interrogated to ask if these purposes and goals for mathematics education are sufficient for African American children or if there are additional ways to frame mathematics education relative to the social realities of these children? In other words, how do we frame mathematics education policy to more effectively address the question, "Why should African American children learn *mathematics*?" In my own work (Martin & McGee, 2009), I argue for linking mathematics literacy to the notion of liberating African American children from various forms of oppression; that is, helping these children use mathematics to engage in sociopolitical critique and to change the conditions of their lives, not simply fitting into systems and structures that denigrate their African American identity (Potts, 2003). Clearly, participation in the larger opportunity structure will require that African American children simultaneously develop the mathematical skills called for in reform-oriented rhetoric.

Moreover, in reframing the purposes of mathematics education, future research and policy should more effectively address the question, "Why should *African American children* learn mathematics?" (Martin & McGee, 2009). I would argue that addressing this question requires a moral commitment to African American children that supersedes calls for increased workforce participation and increased course enrollment. Such calls represent a form of *interest convergence* (Bell, 1980), result in the commodification of African American children, and assume a bias-free social context outside of mathematics education. Policy that is ignorant of these facts will continue to have little relevance for African American children.

Countering Racial Achievement Gap Rhetoric

The very powerful notion of a *racial gap* in achievement and ability now drives a great deal of educational and social policy (Gutiérrez, 2008; Martin, 2009). As a framing strategy, this has been very effective in drawing attention to problematic educational outcomes for African American children. Gutiérrez (2008) has called this "gap-gazing." Yet, this particular framing also requires one to accept certain deficit-based characterizations of African American children at the outset. This framing also implies that mathematics education for African American children is contingent on, and driven by, educational outcomes of white children. This means that in some large urban public school districts, where the percentage of white students may be small and the percentage of African American children might be large, the educational outcomes of white students drive educational policy for African American children. Future research and policy efforts should develop and utilize alternative framings of differential schooling experiences and outcomes that do not require one to accept and put forth deficit-based characterizations of African American children and that do not create a contingency on white students (Hilliard, 2003; Perry, 2003). Hilliard (2003), for example, has suggested that we measures experiences and outcomes of African American children relative to *excellence* rather than white children. This would imply additional studies of mathematics success among African American children.

Mathematics for All and Algebra for All

These reform and policy discourses, or slogan systems, have been used to argue for increased access to mathematics for all children. They do so under the broad umbrellas of equity and diversity. Lacking in these broad formulations is a specificity that applies to the particular needs of African American children. The recently published *Mathematics Proficiency for All* (RAND, 2003) and *Adding it Up* (National Research Council, 2001) are examples of policy-oriented documents and texts that fail to consider the particular needs of African American children. Moreover, embedded in these policy discourses about *Mathematics for All* are arguments for assimilation that might be viewed as counter to a respect for diversity (Martin, 2003). In future policy initiatives, how do we continue to advocate for greater access to mathematics for all students but make particular kinds of arguments for African American children? In addition, given increased access to mathematics among African American children, how do policy-makers insure that new gatekeepers don't emerge to replace previous ones like algebra?

Highly Qualified Mathematics Teachers for Black Children

The *No Child Left Behind* Act as well as a growing knowledge base on mathematics teacher knowledge have converged to generate characterizations of highly qualified teachers based on the following: academic degree, certification, and strong mathematics content knowledge. Are these dimensions sufficient to characterize teachers who can be effective with African American children (Martin, 2007)? Alternatively, an emerging literature on *culturally relevant pedagogy*, as one example of an

African-centered pedagogy of liberation, posits another set of characteristics for teachers of African American children (Gay, 2000; Ladson-Billings, 1994; Matthews, 2003). In many of the studies and policies supporting this approach, while it is clear that these teachers address the social and cultural realities of African American students, what is often not clear is how much mathematics these teachers know (Martin, 2007). With respect to both of these approaches, are there specifications, in both research and policy contexts, that can be made in response to the question, *Who is a highly qualified mathematics teacher relative to the needs of African American children?* In Martin (2007), I suggest that, in addition to having mastery of the mathematics they will teach, teachers should (a) develop a deep understanding of the social realities experienced by African American students, (b) take seriously one's role in helping to shape the racial, academic, and mathematics identities of African American learners, (c) conceptualize mathematics not just as a school subject but as a means to empower African American students to address their social realities and life conditions, and (d) become agents of change who challenge research and policy perspectives that construct African American children as less than ideal learners.

Mathematics Socialization: Studying African American Children's Mathematical Experiences

In my previous research (Martin, 2000, 2006a, 2006b), I defined *mathematics socialization* as the experiences that individuals and groups have within a variety of contexts such as school, family, peer groups, and the workplace that legitimize or inhibit meaningful participation in mathematics. Documenting the ways that African American children actually experience mathematics in highly racialized contexts should be a goal for ongoing and future research in mathematics education (e.g., Berry, 2003; Nasir, Heimlich, Atukpuwu, & O'Conner, 2007; Jackson, this volume; Y. Johnson, this volume; Nasir, this volume; Stinson, 2004, this volume; Strutchens & Westbrook, this volume; Thompson & Lewis, 2005). These contexts could include classrooms, home, community, and informal peer group settings (e.g., Jackson, 2007, this volume; Nasir, 2002, this volume; Spencer, 2006).

I claim that studying the socialization experiences of African American children in mathematics will offer greater support to the idea that their achievement outcomes are indicators of the ways they experience mathematics learning and participation *as African Americans.*

Unlike research that simply documents achievement outcomes, research that is informed by the experience lens has the potential to make visible issues of racism and racialization in ways that mathematics educators may not have previously considered (e.g., Gutstein, 2003; 2006; Martin, 2006a, 2006b; Reed & Oppong, 2005; Stinson, 2004; Thompson & Lewis, 2005).

Mathematics Learning and Identity

Research on mathematics learning has been informed by shifting perspectives that have progressed from cognitivist to sociocultural theories. Within emerging sociocultural approaches, the importance of learning-identity connections is becoming well established. However, prior to the emerging interest in sociocultural theories of learning in mathematics education, African American scholars in other areas such as literacy have long pointed out that issues of identity are fundamental to understanding schooling experiences and outcomes among African American children. Mainstream mathematics education research has largely failed to incorporate African American perspectives on identity into sociocultural theories. A small number of scholars, however, have begun to examine issues pertaining to the co-construction of mathematics identity and racial identity so as to better understand the mathematical experiences, particularly success, of African American learners though their own voices (Berry, 2003; Martin, 2000, 2006a, 2006b; Moody, 2001; Nasir, 2000, 2002; Stinson, 2004; Thompson & Lewis, 2005). Additional studies are needed that merge research on racial identity with research on the learning of mathematics.

Theorizing Race and Racism in Mathematics Education Research and Policy

I claim that race and racism remain undertheorized in mainstream mathematics education research and policy (Diversity in Mathematics Education Center for Teaching and Learning, 2007; Martin, 2009; Powell, 2002). Within research and policy contexts, race is most often used as a way to disaggregate data and to create a racial hierarchy of mathematical ability (Martin, 2009). This hierarchy locates students identified as white and Asian American on top and those identified as African American on the bottom.

The normalization and privileging of whiteness also lies in the fact that most studies in mathematics education involving white students as the only group under study fail to mention *whiteness* as a consideration in these students' mathematical experiences and outcomes (Kumashiro, 2001; Lubienski & Bowen, 2000). On the other hand, in studies where African American children are included along with white children, the concept of race is frequently invoked, without definition, and used as an explanatory variable for observed differences in achievement or persistence (Kenney & Silver, 1997; Lubienski, 2002; Strutchens & Silver, 2000). Rather than asking how whiteness privileges students who are identified as white, the analyses, instead, tend to imply that *Blackness* explains problematic outcomes among African American students. The implicit message in both types of studies appears to be that white students do not experience mathematics learning and teaching through the ideological framework of race despite evidence from sociology that the concept of race serves as an organizing principle in almost every area of society for all social groups (Bonilla-Silva, 2001, 2003). In both types of studies, the advantages afforded to the concept of whiteness often go unanalyzed. Critical race scholars, on the other hand, have conceptualized whiteness as a form of property (Harris, 1995) that affords other material and non-material benefits to those identified as white.

A number of questions must be addressed in future research. How can we begin to theorize race and racism in ways that (1) move beyond race as a categorical variable used to disaggregate data to a consideration of the way this concept is a sociopolitical construction to create hierarchies among students and (2) allow us to better understand the role of racism in Black children's mathematical experiences in schools? Moreover, how do we define and center racism in our research and policy efforts knowing that this may engender negative responses from a largely white research and policy audience who may react as individuals and fail to understand structural racism as the greater concern? How do we utilize sociological perspectives that provide more sophisticated definitions of race and racism (everyday, institutional, structural) such as the one offered by Essed?

> ... race is an ideological construction with structural expressions (racialized or "ethnicized" structures of power), racism must be understood as ideology, structure, and process in which inequalities inherent in the wider social structure are related, in a deterministic way, to biological and cultural factors attributed to those who are seen as a different "race" or "ethnic" group. "Race" is an *ideological construction*, and not just a social construction, because the idea of "race" has never existed outside a framework of group interest. As part of a nineteenth pseudoscientific theory, as well as in contemporary "popular" thinking, the notion of "race" is inherently part of a "model" of asymmetrically organized "races" in which Whites rank higher than "non-Whites." Furthermore, racism is a *structure* because racial and ethnic dominance exists in and is reproduced by the system through the formulation and applications of rules, laws, and regulations and through access to and the allocation of resources. Finally, racism is a *process* because structures and ideologies do not exist outside the everyday practices through which they are created and confirmed. (p. 185)

How do we push sociocultural theories of learning, for example, to account for race and racism in students' mathematical experiences? What do perspectives that frame mathematics learning and participation as racialized forms of experience (Martin, 2006a, 2009) offer in the way of better understanding not only African American students' mathematical experiences and outcomes but other students as well?

It is my belief that expanded research and policy efforts in these areas will contribute to the production of a knowledge base that will move us beyond negative and harmful constructions of African American children and help us develop forms of mathematics education that are responsive to their social realities.

Conclusion

My goal in this chapter was to critically analyze the *nature* and *production* of knowledge about African American children and mathematics. It is through the knowledge production process, characterized by a continuing reliance on a race-comparative paradigm, that African American children come to be constructed as mathematically illiterate and that white children and their behavior come to be normalized. These constructions are supported by the use of particular discursive frames and the misapplication of mainstream theories, methods, and models to African American children. To counter this, future research should rely on culturally sensitive research methods and future policy should be constructed to respond to the needs of African American children *as African American* children in their specific and concrete positions in U.S. society. These are necessary steps in a process that will allow African American children to liberate themselves from the bonds of the oppressive knowledge that is produced about them.

Notes

1 One could argue that basic research into cognitive mechanisms need not take race (a sociopolitical construct) into account. However, one must consider the goals of such research particularly if it is used to justify or create hierarchies that support racist beliefs, practices, and policies.
2 It is worth noting, however, that Robert Moses does serve on the Mathematical Sciences Research Institute education advisory board.

References

Akbar, N. (1991). Paradigms of African American research. In R.L. Jones (Ed.), *Black psychology* (pp. 709–725). Berkeley, CA: Cobb & Henry Publishers.

Anick, C.M., Carpenter, T.M., & Smith, C. (1981). Minorities and mathematics: Results from the National Assessment of Educational Progress. *Mathematics Teacher, 74*, 560–568.

Banks, J. (1993). The canon debate, knowledge construction, and multicultural education. *Educational Researcher, 22*(5), 4–14.

Bell, D. (1992). *Race, racism and American law.* Boston: Little, Brown, and Company.

Bell, D.A. (1980). Brown V. Board of Education and the interest covergence dilemma. *Harvard Law Review, 93*, 518–533.

Berger, P.L. & Luckman, T. (1967). *The social construction of reality.* New York: Doubleday.

Berry, R.Q. (2003). *Voices of African American male students: A portrait of successful middle school mathematics students.* Unpublished doctoral dissertation, University of North Carolina. Chapel Hill, NC.

Berry, R.Q. (2005). Voices of success: Descriptive portraits of two successful African-American male middle school students. *Journal of African American Studies, 8*(4), 46–62.

Boaler J. (2000). *Multiple perspectives on mathematics teaching and learning.* Westport, CT: Ablex Publishing.

Bonilla-Silva, E. (2001). *White supremacy and racism in the post-civil rights era.* Boulder, CO: Lynne Reinner Publishers.

Bonilla-Silva, E. (2002). The linguistics of color blind racism: How to talk nasty about blacks without sounding "racist." *Critical Sociology, 28*(1–2), 41–64.

Bonilla-Silva, E. (2003). *Racism without racists: Color-blind racism and the persistence of racial inequality in the United States.* Lanham, MD: Rowman & Littlefield Publishers, Inc.

Brantliner, E. (2003). *Dividing classes: How the middle class negotiates and rationalizes school advantage.* London: Routledge.

Clements, D. & Sarama, J. (2007). Early childhood mathematics learning. In F. Lester (Ed.), *Second handbook of research on mathematics teaching and learning* (pp. 461–556). Charlotte, NC: Information Age Publishing.

Cobb, P. (1986). Concrete can be abstract: A case study. *Educational Studies in Mathematics, 17*(1), 37–48.

Collins, P.H. (1990). *Black feminist thought: Knowledge, consciousness, and the politics of empowerment.* London: Routledge.

Conley, D. (1999). *Being black, living in the red: Race, wealth, and social policy in America.* Berkeley, CA: University of California Press.

Damerow, P. & Westbury, I. (1985). Mathematics for all—Problems and implications. *Journal of Curriculum Studies, 17*(2), 175–184.

Delpit, L. (1986). Skills and other dilemmas of a progressive Black educator. *Harvard Educational Review, 56,* 379–385.

Delpit, L. (1988). The silenced dialogue: Power and pedagogy in educating other people's children. *Harvard Educational Review, 58,* 280–298.

Diversity in Mathematics Education Center for Teaching and Learning. (2007). Culture, race, power and mathematics education. In F. K. Lester (Ed.), *Second handbook of research on mathematics teaching and learning* (pp. 405–433). Charlotte, N C: Information Age Publishing.

D'Souza, D. (1991). *The end of racism.* New York: Free Press Paperbacks.

Education Trust. (2003). *African American achievement in America.* Washington, D.C.: Author.

English, L. (Ed.). (2002). *Handbook of international research in mathematics education.* Mahwah, NJ: Lawrence Erlbaum Associates.

Erlwanger, S. (1973). Benny's conception of rules and answers in IPI mathematics. *The Journal of Children's Mathematical Behavior, 1,* 7–26.

Ernest, P. (1991). *The philosophy of mathematics education.* London: Routledge Falmer.

Ernest, P. (2002). Empowerment in mathematics education. *Philosophy of Mathematics Journal, 15.* Retrieved April 18, 2003, from http://www.ex.ac.uk/~PErnest/pome15/contents.htm.

Essed, P. (2002). Everyday racism: A new approach to the study of racism. In P. Essed & D. Goldberg (Eds.), *Race critical theories* (pp. 176–194). Malden, Massachusetts: Blackwell Publishers.

Figueira-McDonough, J. (1995). Expendable children. *Journal of Progressive Human Services, 6*(2), 21–44.

Fordham, S. & Ogbu, J.U. (1986). Black students' school success: Coping with the "burden of 'acting White.'" *The Urban Review, 18*(3), 176–206.

Gay, G. (2000). *Culturally responsive teaching: Theory, practice, and research.* New York: Teachers College Press.

Ginwright, S. (2004). *Black in school: Afrocentric reform, urban youth and the promise of hip-hop culture.* New York: Teachers College Press.

Gordon, B. (1990). The necessity of African-American epistemology for educational theory and practice. *Journal of Education, 172*(3), 88–106.

Gordon, E. (1985). Social science knowledge production and the Afro-American experience. *Journal of Negro Education, 54,* 117–133.

Gordon, E., Miller, F., & Rollock, D. (1990). Coping with communicentric bias in knowledge production in the social sciences. *Educational Researcher, 19*(3), 14–19.

Gordon, J. (2005). Inadventent complicity: Colorblindness in teacher education. *Educational Studies, 38*(2), 135–153.

Grouws, D. (Ed.). (1992). *Handbook of research on mathematics teaching and learning.* New York: Macmillan.

Gutiérrez, R. (2008a). A "gap-gazing" fetish in mathematics education? Problematizing research on the achievement gap. *Journal for Research in Mathematics Education, 39,* 357–364.

Gutstein, E. (2003). Teaching and learning mathematics for social justice in an urban, Latino school. *Journal for Research in Mathematics Education, 34*(1), 37–73.

Gutstein, E. (2006). *Reading and writing the world with mathematics: Toward a pedagogy for social justice.* London: Routledge.

Hale, J. (2001). *Learning while Black: Creating educational excellence for African American children.* Baltimore, MD: Johns Hopkins University Press.

Harris, C. (1995). Whiteness as property. In K. Crenshaw, N. Gotanda, G. Peller, & K. Thomas (Eds.), *Critical race theory: The key writings that formed the movement* (pp. 357–383). New York: The New Press.

Herrnstein, R. & Murray, C. (1994). *The bell curve: Intelligence and class structure in American life.* New York: Simon & Schuster.

Hilliard, A. (2003). No mystery: Closing the achievement gap between Africans and excellence. In T. Perry, C. Steele, & A. Hilliard (Eds.), *Young, gifted, and black.* Boston: Beacon Press.

Jackson, K. (2007). *Under Construction: Learning mathematics across space and over time.* Unpublished doctoral dissertation, University of Pennsylvania. Philadelphia, PA.

Johnson, M. (1984). Blacks in mathematics: A status report. *Journal for Research in Mathematics Education, 15*(2), 145–153.

Jones, R. (1998). Proving blacks inferior: The sociology of knowledge. In J.A. Ladner (Ed.), *The death of white sociology* (pp. 114–135). Baltimore, MD: Black Classic Press.

Jones, R. L. (Ed.). (1991). *Black psychology.* Berkeley, CA: Cobb & Henry Publishers.

Keitel, C. (1987). What are the goals of mathematics for all? *Journal of Curriculum Studies, 19*(5), 393–407.

Kenney, P.A. & Silver, E.A. (Eds.). (1997). *Results from the sixth mathematics assessment of the National Assessment of Educational Progress.* Reston, VA: National Council of Teachers of Mathematics.

Kozol, J. (1992). *Savage inequalities.* New York: Harper Collins.

Kumashiro, K. (2001). "Posts" perspectives on anti-oppressive education in social studies, English, mathematics, and science classrooms. *Educational Researcher, 30*(3), 3–12.

Ladson-Billings, G. (1994). *The dreamkeepers: Successful teachers of African American children.* San Francisco, CA: Jossey-Bass.

Ladson-Billings, G. (2000) Racialized discourses and ethnic epistemologies. In N. Denzin & Y. Lincoln (Eds.), *Handbook of qualitative research* (pp. 257–278). Thousand Oaks, CA: Sage Publishing.

Leonard, J. (2008). *Culturally specific pedagogy in the mathematics classroom.* New York: Routledge.

Lesh, R., Hamilton, E., & Kaput, J. (Eds.). (2007). *Foundations for the future in mathematics education.* Mahwah, NJ: Lawrence Erlbaum Associates.

Lester, F. (Ed.). (2007). *Second handbook of research on mathematics teaching and learning.* Charlotte, NC: Information Age Publishing.

Lewis, A.E. (2004). "What group?" Studying whites and whiteness in the era of "color-blind-men," *Sociological Theory, 22*(4), 623–646.

Lomotey, K. (Ed.). (1990). *Going to school: The African-American experience.* Albany, NY: State University at Albany Press.

Lubienski, S. (2002). A closer look at Black-White mathematics gaps: Intersections of race and SES in NAEP achievement and instructional practices data. *Journal of Negro Education, 71*(4), 269–287.

Lubienski, S.T. & Bowen, A. (2000). Who's counting? A survey of mathematics education research 1982–1998. *Journal for Research in Mathematics Education, 31*(5), 626–633.

Madhubuti, H. & Madhubuti, S. (1994). *African-centered education.* Chicago: Third World Press.

Malcolm, X. (with the assistance of Alex Haley) (1987). *The autobiography of Malcolm X.* New York: Ballantine Books.

Martin, D.B. (2000). *Mathematics success and failure among African American youth: The roles of sociohistorical context, community forces, school influence, and individual agency.* Mahwah, NJ: Lawrence Erlbaum Associates.

Martin, D.B. (2003). Hidden assumptions and unaddressed questions in mathematics for all rhetoric. *The Mathematics Educator, 13*(2), 7–21.

Martin, D.B. (2006a). Mathematics learning and participation as racialized forms of experience: African American parents speak on the struggle for mathematics literacy. *Mathematical Thinking and Learning, 8*(3), 197–229.

Martin, D.B. (2006b). Mathematics learning and participation in African American context: The co-construction of identity in two intersecting realms of experience. In N. Nasir & P. Cobb (Eds.), *Diversity, equity, and access to mathematical ideas.* (pp. 146–158). New York: Teachers College Press.

Martin, D.B. (2007). Beyond missionaries or cannibals: Who should teach mathematics to African American children? *The High School Journal, 91*(1), 6–28.

Martin, D.B. (2008). E(race)ing race from a national conversation on mathematics teaching and learning: The national mathematics advisory panel as white institutional space. *The Montana Mathematics Enthusiast, 5*(2&3), 387–398.

Martin, D.B. (2009). Researching race in mathematics education. *Teachers College Record, 111*(2), 295–338.

Martin, D.B. & McGee, E. (2009). Mathematics literacy for liberation: Reframing mathematics education for African American children. In B. Greer, S. Mukhophadhay, S. Nelson-Barber, & A. Powell (Eds.), *Culturally responsive mathematics education* (pp. 207–238). London: Routledge.

Matthews, L. (2003). Babies overboard! The complexities of incorporating culturally relevant teaching into mathematics instruction. *Educational Studies in Mathematics, 53*(1), 61–82.

Matthews, W. (1983). Coloring the equation: Minorities and mathematics. *Journal for Research in Mathematics Education, 14*(1), 70–72.

McGee, E. (2007). *Race, identity, and resilience: Black college students negotiating success in mathematics and engineering.* Dissertation proposal, University of Illinois. Chicago, IL.

McLoyd, V. (1991). What is the study of African American children the study of? In R.L. Jones (Ed.), *Black psychology* (pp. 419–440). Berkeley, CA: Cobb & Henry Publishers.

McLoyd, V.C. & Randolph, S.M. (1984). The conduct and publication of research on Afro-American children: A context analysis. *Human Development, 27*, 65–75.

McWhorter, J. (2001). *Losing the race: Self-sabotage in Black America.* New York: Harper Perennial.

Moody, V. (2001). The social constructs of the mathematical experiences of African-American students. In B. Atweh, H. Forgasz, & B. Nebres (Eds.), *Sociocultural research on mathematics education* (pp. 255–278). Mahwah, NJ: Lawrence Erlbaum Associates.

Moore, W. (2008). *Reproducing racism: White space, elite law schools, and racial inequality.* Lanhan, MD: Rowman & Littlefield.

Murrell, P. (2002). *African-centered pedagogy.* Albany, NY: State University of New York Press.

Nasir, N. (2000). Points ain't everything: Emergent goals and average and percent understanding in the play of basketball among African American Students. *Anthropology & Education Quarterly, 31*, 283–305.

Nasir, N. (2002). Identity, goals, and learning: Mathematics in cultural practice. *Mathematical Thinking and Learning (2&3)*, 213–248.

Nasir, N., Heimlich, M., Atukpawu, G., & O'Conner, K. (2007, April). *Social constructions of race and identity in high school algebra classrooms.* Paper presented at the annual meeting of the American Educational Research Association. Chicago, IL.

National Council of Teachers of Mathematics (NCTM). (1989). *Curriculum and evaluation standards for school mathematics.* Reston, VA: Author.

National Council of Teachers of Mathematics (NCTM). (2000). *Principles and standards for school mathematics.* Reston, VA: Author.

National Research Council. (1988). *Everybody counts: A report to the nation on the future of mathematics education.* Washington, DC: National Academy Press.

National Research Council. (2001). *Adding it up: Helping children learn mathematics.* J. Kilpatrick, J. Swafford, & B. Findell (Eds.). Mathematics Learning Study Committee, Center for Education, Division of Behavioral and Social Sciences and Education. Washington, DC: National Academy Press.

National Urban League (2007). The State of Black America 2007. Silver Spring, MD: Beckham Publications Group, Inc.

Oakes, J. (1985). *Keeping track: How schools structure inequality.* New Haven: Yale University Press.

Oakes, J. (1990). Opportunities, achievement and choice: Women and minority students in science and mathematics. In C.B. Cazden (Ed.), *Review of research in education, 16,* 153–222. Washington, DC: AERA.

Perry, T., Steele, C. & Hilliard, A. (Eds.). (2003), *Young, gifted, and Black: Promoting high achievement among African-American Students.* Boston: Beacon Press.

Perry, T. (2003). Up from the parched earth: Toward a theory of African-American achievement. In T. Perry, C. Steele, & A. Hilliard (Eds.), *Young, gifted and Black: Promoting high achievement among African-American students* (pp. 1–108). Boston: Beacon Press.

Potts, R. (2003). Emancipatory education versus school-based prevention in African American communities. *American Journal of Community Psychology, 31*(1–2), 173–183.

Powell, A.B. (2002). Ethnomathematics and the challenges of racism in mathematics education. In P. Valero & O. Skovsmose (Eds.), *Proceedings of the 3rd international mathematics education and society conference* (Vol. 1, pp. 15–29). Copenhagen: Centre for Research in Learning Mathematics.

RAND Mathematics Study Panel. (2003). *Mathematics proficiency for all students: Toward a strategic research and development program in mathematics education.* Santa Monica, CA: RAND.

Reed, R.J. & Oppong, N. (2005). Looking critically at teachers' attention to equity in their classrooms. *The Mathematics Educator,* Monograph No. 1, 2–15.

Reyes, L.H. & Stanic, G. (1988). Race, sex, socioeconomic status, and mathematics. *Journal for Research in Mathematics Education, 19,* 26–43.

Secada, W. (1992). Race, ethnicity, social class, language, and achievement in mathematics. In D. Grouws (Ed.), *Handbook of research on mathematics teaching and learning* (pp. 623–660). New York: Macmillan.

Shujaa, M.J. (1994). Education and schooling: Can you have one without the other? In M. J. Shujaa (Ed.), *Too much schooling, too little education: A paradox in Black life in white societies* (pp. 13–36). Trenton, NJ: African World Press.

Silver, E. (1985). *Teaching and learning mathematical problem solving: Multiple research perspectives.* Mahwah, NJ: Lawrence Erlbaum Associates.

Silver, E., Smith, M., & Nelson, B. (1995). The Quasar project: Equity concerns meet mathematics education reform in the middle school. In W. Secada, E. Fennema, & L. Adajian (Eds.), *New directions for equity on mathematics education.* Cambridge: Cambridge University Press.

Spencer, J. (2006). *Balancing the equation: African American students' opportunities to learn mathematics with understanding in two central city middle schools.* Unpublished doctoral dissertation, University of California, Los Angeles, CA.

Steele, S. (1990). *The content of our character: A new vision of race in America.* New York: St. Martin's Press.

Steffe, L., Nesher, P., Cobb, P., Goldin, G., & Greer, B. (Eds.). (1996). *Theories of mathematical learning.* Mahwah, NJ: Lawrence Erlbaum Associates.

Stiff, L. (1990). African-American students and the promise of the *Curriculum and Evaluation Standards.* In T.J. Cooney & C.R. Hirsch (Eds.), *Teaching and learning mathematics in the 1990s* (Yearbook of the National Council of Teachers of Mathematics, pp. 152–157). Reston, VA: NCTM.

Stinson, D. (2004). *African American male students and achievement in school mathematics: A critical postmodern analysis of agency.* Unpublished doctoral dissertation, University of Georgia. Athens, GA.

Strutchens, M.E. & Silver, E.A. (2000). NAEP findings regarding race/ethnicity: Students' performance, school experiences, and attitudes and beliefs. In E.A. Silver & P.A. Kenney (Eds.), *Results from the 7th mathematics assessment of the National Assessment of Educational Progress* (pp. 45–72). Reston, VA: NCTM.

Tate, W.F. (1997). Race, ethnicity, SES, gender, and language proficiency trends in mathematics achievement: An update. *Journal for Research in Mathematics Education, 28*(6), 652–680.

Taylor, E.V. (2005). *Low-income African-American first and second grade students' engagement in currency exchange: The relationship to mathematical development.* Unpublished doctoral dissertation, University of California. Berkeley, CA.

Thernstrom, S. & Thernstrom, A. (1997). *America in black and white: One nation indivisible.* New York: Simon & Schuster.

Thernstrom, A. & Thernstrom, S. (2004). *No Excuses: Closing the racial gap in learning.* New York: Simon & Schuster.

Thompson, L. & Lewis, B. (2005). Shooting for the stars: A case study of the mathematics achievement and career attainment of an African American male high school student. *The High School Journal, 88*(4), 6–18.

Tillman, L. (2002). Culturally sensitive research approaches. *Educational Researcher, 31*(9), 3–12.

Tillman, L. (2006). Researching and writing from an African-American perspective: Reflective notes on three research studies. *International Journal of Qualitative Studies in Education, 19*(3), 265–287.

Treisman, P.U. (1985). *A study of the mathematics performance of Black students at the university of California, Berkeley.* Unpublished doctoral dissertation, University of California. Berkeley, CA.

Trepagnier, B. (2006). *Silent racism: How well-meaning white people perpetuate the racial divide.* Boulder, CO: Paradigm Publishers.

U.S. Department of Education. (2008). *Foundations of success: Final report of the national mathematics advisory panel.* Washington, DC.

Washington, E.D. & McLoyd, V.C. (1982). The external validity of research involving American minorities. *Human Development, 25,* 324–339.

Watts, R., Williams, N., & Jagers, R. (2003). Sociopolitical development. *American Journal of Community Psychology, 31,* 185–194.

White, J.L. (1991). Toward a black psychology. In R.L. Jones (Ed.), *Black psychology* (pp. 5–13). Berkeley, CA: Cobb & Henry Publishers.

Willie, C., Garibaldi, A., & Reed, W. (Eds.). (1991). *The education of African-Americans.* New York: Auburn House.

Woodson, C.G. (1990). *The mis-education of the Negro.* Trenton, NJ: African World Press (Original work published 1933).

Yosso, T., Parker, L., Solorzano, D., & Lynn, M. (2005). From Jim Crow to affirmative action and back again: A critical race discussion of racialized rationales and access to higher education. *Review of Research in Education, 28,* 1–25.

Section II

Pedagogy, Standards, and Assessment

2 Researching African American Mathematics Teachers of African American Students: Conceptual and Methodological Considerations

Lawrence M. Clark, Whitney Johnson, and Daniel Chazan

Introduction

There is a movement underway in the mathematics education research community that seeks to better understand students' mathematics schooling experiences by examining these experiences through sociocultural and historical perspectives (Atweh, Forgasz, & Nebres, 2001; Boaler, 2000; Martin, 2000, 2007; Nasir & Cobb, 2007; Secada, Fennema, & Adajian, 1995; Yackel & Cobb, 1996). A guiding tenet of this movement is the acknowledgement that the learning and teaching of mathematics is not "culture-free"; historical, political, and cultural forces determine that students at specific intersections of societal communities (racial, ethnic, economic, linguistic, geographical) *experience* mathematics differently than students positioned at other intersections, and these differential experiences contribute to differences in performance on measures of mathematics achievement and competence. A thread of this work focuses on examining teachers' mathematics instructional practices from sociocultural perspectives (Franke, Kazemi, & Battey, 2007) and seeks to conceptualize and study mathematics learning environments that are equitable and responsive to the needs and experiences of all learners, but particularly to U.S. mathematics learners from historically marginalized groups, namely African American and Latino students.

Without question, the work of exploring relationships between mathematics teaching and learning that foregrounds social and historical factors, particularly those related to race and racism, is daunting and wrought with tough choices. Researchers in this space must consider and respond to phenomena, trends, and characteristics within and between race- and class-defined groups (mathematics achievement and participation patterns, proposed learning styles, relevant instructional practices), yet resist essentializing and reducing both students' experience and teachers' practice in ways that oversimplify their complexities, despite the researcher's understanding of the ways in which these differences emerge from institutional and societal inequities. As researchers in this space put pen to paper, we must continuously maintain the awareness that our work is simultaneously describing and constructing our subjects and their practices (Foucault, 1972), constructions that inform the direction of subsequent inquiry and potentially influence mathematics education policy. Therefore extreme care must be taken in our efforts to clarify our positions, refine our conceptual frameworks, and, most importantly, resist falling into familiar traps of defining our subjects and phenomena in ways that perpetuate the conditions that create the very inequities we are attempting to expose, and in many ways, diminish.

The challenge can be no greater than in work attempting to document, interpret, and describe the ways in which African American mathematics teachers orchestrate classrooms and facilitate student–teacher interactions that promote their African American students' mathematics performance and achievement. There is a small but growing body of empirical evidence that suggests that students benefit educationally, particularly in mathematics, when matched with own-race teachers (Dee, 2004) and researchers have hypothesized as to why these benefits occur, such as role model effects (King, 1993; Clewell & Villegas, 1998), stereotype threat effect (Steele, 1997), and effects related to race-specific activity and belief patterns among teachers (Ferguson, 1998). The exploration of these hypotheses, however, demands acknowledgement of the complex nature of conceptualizing and studying relationships and interactions between African American teachers and their African American students. A short list of questions illustrating the complexities of conducting research in this area include:

- How do researchers determine, with some level of confidence, that shared African American group membership of mathematics teacher and student is "at play" in their interactions?
- If researchers are confident that this shared racial group membership is at play in mathematics teacher–student interactions, how does one determine when and how this shared racial group membership impacts students' mathematics learning?
- To what extent is African American mathematics teachers' pedagogy an effort to liberate their African American students from real or perceived oppressive forces? How do researchers know when and how this liberatory pedagogy is in effect?
- As members of a highly racialized society, how do researchers isolate/deconstruct their own personal viewpoints and biases when conceptualizing and studying the work of African American mathematics teachers?

Despite the evident challenges associated with these efforts, we view this work as a productive and, at times, agitating force—it further unmasks multilevel factors that contributes to our collective understandings and misunderstandings of relationships between mathematics teaching, learning, and experience (Martin, 2000) at all societal intersections, and complicates and extends traditional notions of the knowledge bases teachers draw on in their efforts to teach mathematics effectively.

In this chapter we will describe our approach to conceptualizing the role and work of African American mathematics teachers, particularly as they come in contact with African American mathematics learners. The ways in which we consider this complex experience is driven by data collected in the *Case Studies of Urban Algebra I Teachers Project*, described briefly below. Following is a brief discussion of conceptual and methodological dilemmas we explicitly acknowledge and attempt to address, a description of our conceptual and methodological framework, and "thumbnail" portraits of two teachers in our study, rendered through the conceptual framework described.

Case Studies of Urban Algebra I Teachers Project

In 2004, University of Maryland–College Park mathematics education faculty and graduate student researchers at the Mid-Atlantic Center for Mathematics Teaching and Learning (MAC-MTL)[1] embarked on an ambitious research effort titled the *Case Studies of Urban Algebra I Teachers Project.* The main purpose of the project was to document the practices and perspectives of "well respected" teachers of Algebra I in urban schools populated predominantly by African American and Latino students. Over a 3-year period, the project team conducted approximately eight interviews and 30 classroom observations (most of which were videotaped) for each of the six mathematics teachers in our study, all of whom are African American. Multiple goals related to the project have been established over time; however, for the purposes of describing the ways we have developed conceptual frameworks and methodological approaches in our efforts to responsibly study and articulate the roles African American mathematics teachers play in the lives of their African American students, two goals have come to play a central role:

- Identifying ways in which African American mathematics teachers in a specific academic and social context assist their African American students in negotiating identities that have historically been constructed in isolation or in opposition to one another–namely becoming and being an African American adolescent while simultaneously becoming and being a mathematics learner.
- Identifying the knowledge, resources, experiences, and rationales African American mathematics teachers draw on as they engage in this identity socialization work in this particular academic and social context.

Conceptual and Methodological Dilemmas

As alluded to earlier, researchers in this space confront numerous conceptual and methodological dilemmas (Milner, 2007; O'Connor, Lewis, & Mueller, 2007). Three dilemmas we consistently encountered and attempted to address in our work include 1) unmasking African American heterogeneity, 2) attending to researcher positionality, and 3) articulating sociocultural dimensions of knowledge mathematics teachers use in their practice.

Unmasking African American Heterogeneity

In the absence of thoughtful conceptualization and analysis, studies that attempt to examine, understand, and explain phenomena within and across groups of African Americans run the risk of "masking the heterogeneity of the Black experience" (O'Connor, Lewis, & Mueller, 2007, p. 543) and constructing Blackness as a static social category. Subgroups of African Americans, like all other U.S. residents, exist in distinct intersections of gender, social class, geography, and time. A subgroup of African Americans existing in one such intersection may hold a markedly different worldview and engage in noticeably different social practices than a subgroup of African Americans existing in a different intersection (Horvat & Lewis, 2003; O'Connor, 1997). Underconceptualization and underanalysis of variation in African American life in educational research can therefore lead to unsophisticated characterizations of African Americans that marginally reflect the complexities of becoming and being African American in the United States.

Notable scholars have produced exceptional work related to the role segregated schools played in the African American community prior to desegregation and the specific roles African American teachers played in their African American students' lives (Anderson, 1988; Siddle Walker, 1996). A handful of scholars have extended this work in their study of African American teachers of African American students in contemporary contexts (Foster, 1997; Ware, 2006). In many ways, these depictions of the roles African American teachers play in the lives of their African American students have established the beginnings of a critical historical and analytical record. However, despite considerable evidence of the persistence of residential segregation in the U.S. (Massey & Denton, 1989, 1993), African American community structures and interrelational practice change over time, inevitably influencing intergenerational relationships between African American teachers and their African American students. Changing conditions and contemporary contexts demand that we continue to examine the relationships between African American teachers and their students with an eye towards how the nature of these relationships differ and change across time and space. In reading existing literature and accessing the perspectives and conceptual tools that this work offers, we have concluded that the African American teachers in our study exist in geographical and temporal contexts that require us to conceptualize the practices (and factors influencing identified practices) of African American teachers somewhat differently than may be found in existing literature.

For example, existing literature often describes the role African American teachers play in their students' lives both inside the school and in settings outside of the school such as the neighborhood or church. The African American teacher therefore is rendered as having multiple points of contact with their African American students and these multiple points of contact are critical to providing a holistic educational experience for their African American students. Does this particular rendering of this relationship hold in contemporary settings? Should we expect it to hold in our setting? Should the conceptual framework (and resulting methodological approaches) for how and where we look for interactions between our participants in their students extend beyond the school boundaries? Analysis of our data, in fact, revealed that these multiple points of contact are few and far between. If, then, contemporary relationships between African American teachers and their African American students consist of fewer contact points, how then does the African American teacher assist their students in becoming intentional learners?

In our efforts to understand and describe the phenomena of African Americans teaching other African Americans in the United States, it is not uncommon for researchers and scholars to search for pedagogical commonalities across teachers. These efforts, however, may mask the wide range of experiences, local histories, perspectives, and instructional approaches that exist within the community of African American teachers. In fact, in our efforts to explicitly unmask heterogeneity of the six African American teachers in our study, we focus less on identifying pedagogical commonalities across our participants, and attempt to understand how and why our participants constructed strikingly different mathematics learning environments for their students.

Researcher Positionality

As researchers exploring issues of race and culture in U.S. mathematics classrooms, we must continuously examine our own life experiences and perspectives in relation to the ways we come to view and understand the participants in our study. The project team is diverse, including African American, European American, Asian American, Latino American, Catholic, Protestant, Jewish, and Latter-day Saints faculty members and graduate students. Furthermore, the project team members emerge from different U.S. social class strata. Some faculty and graduate students have experience teaching mathematics in exclusively urban or suburban schools, where other members have no secondary school teaching experience whatsoever. Lastly, some members of the research team have mathematics teacher education responsibilities while others do not. As a result of this variation of experience, our research team must stay attentive to our *positionality* (Milner, 2007) along two important dimensions: the dimension related to ways in which we view mathematics instruction (and assign the label "quality mathematics instruction") and the ways in which we interpret the presence of race and responses to racism in the interactions between the African American teachers in our study and their African American students.

As many of us on the project team exist in the dual roles of mathematics education researcher and mathematics teacher educator steeped in the literature of "best practice," we inevitably oscillate between observing/researching/analyzing teachers' mathematics practice and evaluating/correcting/critiquing teachers' mathematics practice. This duality finds its way into our conversations and analytical practice and, if not attended to explicitly, can prevent appropriate and thorough analysis of the pedagogical approaches of teachers in our study. For example, the mathematics teacher education literature encourages mathematics teachers to provide opportunities for their students to make sense and meaning of mathematics procedures or routinized solution strategies (NCTM, 2000; Swafford, Findell, & Kilpatrick, 2001). Implicit in these messages is the discouragement of the promotion of routinized solution strategies (such as step-by-step heuristics) that may lead the student to the correct solution yet not lead to student understanding. If, then, teachers in our study choose to use heuristics or routinized solution strategies, we as a research team must resist our inclinations to evaluate and critique the existence of such heuristics (our mathematics teacher educator perspective) and focus on an exploration of the social, cultural, and historical factors that contribute to teachers' decisions in choosing heuristics as pedagogical tools for use with their students and how teachers might use the heuristic to greater or lesser effect (our mathematics education researcher perspective). The quality of mathematics instruction in schools with high populations of students of color has been characterized as providing students with few opportunities to engage in cognitively demanding mathematics activities; therefore, as a research team, we must consistently stay attentive to our inclinations to define the instructional practices of our participants, urban mathematics teachers, as deficient or in need of improvement, regardless of what we may actually witness.

A second dimension we consistently remained attentive to was the ways we have all come to understand and view culture, race, and racism. As a racially heterogeneous group we brought a multitude of experiences and, consequently, a host of analytical stances—some members of the team could not or did not see where race and racism play a part in our participants' pedagogical approaches or interactions with their students; some members of the team see race and racism in most or all of what our participants did, yet oftentimes struggled to articulate this presence clearly. On many occasions, as research team meetings veered into discussions about the roles race, racism, and social class play in district and school structures, curricular offerings, instructional quality, and students' academic experiences, it was not uncommon for some research team members to fall silent whereas other research team members engaged fully. In an attempt to create a space for dialogue related to the ways race, racism, and social class appeared to influence what we were seeing in the schools and mathematics classrooms in our study, readings were distributed to research team members related to critical race theory, racial tracking, and mathematical experiences of students of color as a result of historical and contemporary discrimination and inequities. Unfortunately, the readings did not serve the purpose they were intended to; difficulties in articulating and comfortably discussing issues of race and racism persisted. Less-structured opportunities to explore research team members' views related to these issues and our positionality have emerged over time; opportunities that have provided us a space to better understand how our individual personal experiences shape directions of our inquiry. However, it is evident that we have to continue to press ourselves to establish an environment where team members can freely and comfortably air their perspectives and perceptions of the ways race, racism, and social class influence the experiences of the teachers and students in our study.

Articulating "Teacher Knowledge" in Mathematics Education

If the relationships between teacher knowledge, mathematics instructional practice, and students' mathematics achievement are viewed through sociocultural and sociohistorical lenses, "non-mathematical" dimensions of teachers' knowledge, namely knowledge of students' lived experiences and histories, as well as teachers' experiences and community memberships, must be examined side-by-side with more traditional dimensions of the knowledge teachers draw on to teach mathematics. Considerable activity is underway in an effort to measure, examine, and organize the mathematical knowledge teachers use in their practice, and there is considerable evidence that mathematics teachers in fact draw on a unique and sophisticated mathematical knowledge base (Hill, Rowan, & Ball, 2005; Hill, Schilling, & Ball, 2004). Despite these important advances in our understanding of the mathematical knowledge teachers draw on, there are concerns about how the insistent focus on the mathematical knowledge teachers use in their practice (no matter how specific to teaching the definition of mathematical knowledge might be) might blind us to the critical presence and importance of teachers capacity to engage students through knowledge of students' mathematical experiences (as well as the mathematics experiences of students' families, peer groups, and other relevant communities) (Martin, 2007).

We have been warned to avoid interpreting exemplary teacher characteristics (certification status, math courses completed, years of teaching experience, scores on mathematics competency assessments) for quality teaching practice (Hiebert & Grouws, 2007) and encouraged to acknowledge the *instructional dynamic* (Ball & Forzani, 2007) at play in mathematics classrooms that logically positions student mediation between teacher practice and student learning. It could be argued that much of the way students mediate the teaching-learning process may have little to do with the specific mathematical content under study and highly connected with students' perceptions, experiences, and histories. Yet, without clear conceptualization of the knowledge and skills mathematics teachers bring to and use in their practice that is not noticeably mathematical, it is difficult to articulate the specific nature of "knowledge of students lived experiences" or "cultural knowledge" to the mathematics education community. Researchers have made progress in this effort (González, Andrade, Civil, & Moll, 2001) yet conceptual models incorporating "non-mathematical" dimensions of the knowledge mathematics teachers use in their practice do not yet circulate in mathematics education research circles.

Our Conceptual Framework: Identity and Socialization in the Mathematics Classroom

In our effort to develop what we consider to be an appropriate and useful conceptual framework that is responsive to the dilemmas and challenges previously described, we draw on perspectives on identity formation and socialization. More specifically, our conceptual framework is designed to assist us in examining the role that African American mathematics teachers' presence and pedagogy play in their African American students' identity development as mathematics learners. Identity literature often describes identity development as the process of "becoming" a member of a community of practice (Wenger, 1998). Communities may come in many forms (ethnic, racial, familial, geographical), yet all communities of practice possess general characteristics, including mutual engagement of participants; a shared repertoire of actions, discourses, and stories; and a joint enterprise that is the "negotiated response to their situation" (Wenger, 1998, p.77). The growing interest in incorporating identity and community of practice constructs in mathematics education literature is motivated by the opportunities these constructs provide for analyzing and explaining affective aspects of mathematics learning central to student mediation of the teaching and learning process; aspects such as students' motivation, engagement, interest, anxiety, and participation (Cobb & Hodge, 2007).

Furthermore, identity development constructs are useful tools when attempting to understand and articulate what coming to know mathematics is and means for marginalized groups of students in the United States.

Learning, which is the goal of schooling, is characterized by Wenger (1998) as the interaction of practice and the formation of identity. The link between identity development and learning is described by Nasir (2007):

> The development of identity, or the process of identification, is linked to learning, in that learning is about becoming as well as knowing. It is my view that this issue of how learning settings afford ways of becoming or not becoming something or someone is central to understanding culture, race, and learning, particularly given the multiple ways that race (as well as social class) can influence both the kinds of practices within which one can "become," as well as the trajectories available in those practices. (p. 135)

In the school setting, therefore, learning mathematics is far more complex than "coming to know" mathematics concepts that were once unknown. Mathematics learning is not the process of simply "remembering and forgetting" mathematics concepts and procedures (Lampert, 2001). Learning mathematics is both taking on the label of "mathematics learner" and giving the label specific meanings through engagement in the practices of mathematics learners. It is doing what mathematics learners do (Lampert, 2001), being treated the way they are treated, forming the community they form, entertaining relations with other practices, and—in the details of this process—giving personal meaning to the category of mathematics learner (Wenger, 1998). Our interpretation of Wenger's view of learning therefore suggests that what mathematics students learn is inextricably bound to their practices as mathematics learners, the practices of other mathematics learners that surround them, their understanding of what it means to be a mathematics learner, and how their status as "mathematics learner" is perceived by others.

From an identity development perspective, *mathematics instruction* consists of both socializing students into the norms and discourse practices of the mathematics classroom (Yackel & Cobb, 1996), *and* influencing students' perceptions of themselves as members of a community of mathematics learners or "doers of mathematics" (Boaler, 1999, 2000). It is theorized that successful "doers of mathematics" have well-developed *mathematical identities* (Martin, 2000, 2007); an identity shaped by a student's perception of 1) their ability to perform in mathematical contexts, 2) the instrumental importance of mathematics, 3) constraints and opportunities in mathematical contexts, and 4) resulting motivations and strategies used to obtain mathematics knowledge. Although others have defined mathematics identity differently (Anderson & Gold, 2006), we found Martin's framework to be most useable and useful in our efforts. *Mathematics socialization* (Martin, 2000, 2007), therefore, describes the processes and experiences by which individual and collective mathematical identities are shaped in sociohistorical, community, school, and intrapersonal contexts.

African Americans in general, and African American students in particular, engage in a unique, continuous process of negotiating multiple traditions, cultural frames, and identities, some of which arguably have been perceived and/or constructed as incompatible, in an effort to function in U.S. society (Boykin, 1986; Du Bois, 1903). It is reasonable to believe, therefore, that teachers, particularly African American mathematics teachers, may play a role in assisting their African American students negotiate and reconcile (Wenger, 1998) real or perceived conflicts or dilemmas in their identity formation. If then, students "at the intersections of two important realms of experience: being African American and becoming doers of mathematics" (Martin, 2007, p. 147) are in the process of structuring identities in practice (Nasir, 2007), in what ways might African American mathematics teachers influence this process? In what ways might African American teachers influence their African American students' perceptions of themselves as "doers of mathematics"?

Our conceptual framework, therefore, is structured to acknowledge and consider the influence of individual teachers' distinct experiences and memberships in relevant communities (including but not limited to the African American community) on their African American students' mathematics identity formation. A modification of Martin's (2000) dimensions of mathematics identity[2] provides us a way of organizing and describing teachers' practices as potentially socializing acts that intentionally or unintentionally serve as opportunities to influence their students' mathematics identity development (i.e., a teacher gives a "speech" that seeks to provide a counter message to characterizations of African American students as being "less able"). We also conceptualize that African American mathematics teachers' pedagogy often takes on features of liberation pedagogy, although we conceptualize teachers' actions that could be considered liberatory as subtler and more nuanced than might be described by liberation pedagogy theorists (Freire, 1989, 2000) and writers and researchers of liberation pedagogy specifically related to mathematics instruction (Frankenstein, 1983; Gutstein, 2006; Gutstein & Peterson, 2005). The following sections describe components of our framework in more detail.

Teachers' Nexus of Multimembership in Relevant Communities of Practice

Wenger (1998) states that teachers are far more than "representatives of the institution and upholders of curricular demands" (p. 276); they are doorways into the adult world. Through implicit and explicit means, teachers communicate to their students what it means to construct healthy mathematical identities within this community. In terms of African American mathematics teachers of African American students, it is our stance that these messages and activities can, in many instances, be traced to teachers' experiences as African American mathematics learners and memberships in other relevant communities. In our efforts to resist essentializing and underanalyzing the experiences of African American mathematics teachers that contribute to their African American students' mathematics identity development, we deliberately explored additional communities of practice beyond the African American community that our participants hold membership. It is through this "nexus of multimembership" (Wenger, 1998) that we view our teachers. They are not simply African American and teachers; they are also young, middle aged, male, female, from the West and from the South, born into a range of social classes, Christian, schooled in large predominantly white institutions, or alumni of small historically Black colleges. Their unique paths towards their current status as African American mathematics teachers shaped their varied perspectives and practices related to mathematics teaching and learning. It is their experiences with, and responses to, issues of race and racism *within* these relevant communities of practice that shape the ways they interact with their African American students. Wenger (1998) states:

> Teachers, parents, and other educators constitute learning resources, not only through their pedagogical or institutional roles, but also (and perhaps primarily) through their own membership in relevant communities of practice. In other words, it is not so much by the specific content of their pedagogy as by their status as members that they take part in the generational encounter . . . teachers need to "represent" their communities of practice in educational settings. This type of lived authenticity brings into the subject matter the concerns, sense of purpose, identification, and emotion of participation . . . what students need in developing their own identities is contact with a variety of adults who are willing to invite them into their adulthood. (p. 276)

Ironically, the term "represent" is often used in the African American community to communicate that one is serving as a good example and showing respect for where one comes from (Friend 1: "Gotta go across town later. My Auntie wants me to come talk to her elementary class about me wanting to be a writer." Friend 2: "That's cool. *Represent.*"). The perspective we take in this exploration, therefore, is that the influences African American mathematics teachers have on their African American students' mathematics identities are highly influenced by the nexus of multimembership each teacher is situated in. Each teacher, however, has a unique nexus of communities in which he or she holds memberships, resulting in distinctly different histories, mathematics learning experiences, values, and approaches to mathematics instruction.

Teachers' Socialization Practices

In an effort to better understand teachers' practices that support (or inhibit) students' mathematics identity formation, we considered teachers' practices along three dimensions that parallel Martin's (2000) socialization framework. We contend that teachers engage in socialization practices that promote or inhibit students' processes of developing healthy and robust perceptions of 1) their ability to perform in mathematical contexts, 2) the importance of mathematics, and 3) the nature of mathematical activity. We also contend that history and context shapes the practices of African American mathematics teachers of African American students along these dimensions in unique and particular ways.

Students' Perceptions of their Mathematics Ability

It is our belief that teachers send students consistent messages and engage students in mathematical activity that influence students' perception of their capacity and ability to perform mathematically. Linkages between self-perceptions and achievement are an important assumption in theories of learning and academic achievement (Wigfield & Eccles, 2000), and a consistent finding in the ability research literature is that students' views of their academic abilities (i.e., academic self-concept) are associated with their levels of achievement in school, more so than are their more generalized views or feelings about themselves. It is not clear, however, in which direction this relationship flows; some researchers argue that student beliefs about their ability influence performance (self-enhancement model), whereas others contend that successful performance influences perceptions of ability (skills development model). Others argue the relationship is bidirectional and reciprocal—perceptions of ability builds on performance, which in turn builds a stronger perception of ability, which enhances performance, etc. The study of linkages between self-perception of ability and performance, however, would be incomplete without the consideration of sociocultural factors. Students receive messages and develop notions of their ability from multiple sources, including interactions with parents, community members, peers, and teachers (Martin, 2007).

It is plausible to contend that many African American mathematics teachers of African American students communicate messages to their students that are attempts to counter historical and contemporary portrayals of African Americans as less able in mathematics. Comparisons of the intellectual capacity of humans of African descent to the intellectual capacity of other racial and ethnic groups have been the center of an ongoing controversial debate rooted in numerous perspectives and interpretations, including theoretical orientations such as biological determinism, critiques and defenses of psychometric approaches to the measure of intelligence, and the relationships between inequities in societal structures (schooling, neighborhoods, etc.) and intellectual performance. In short, throughout history in general and U.S. history in particular, humans of African descent have consistently been portrayed as intellectually inferior to humans of European descent (Ehrlich & Feldman, 1977; Gould, 1996; Jenks & Philips, 1998). Measures of mathematical ability are often incorporated in broader measures of intelligence and intellect, therefore mathematical ability is often perceived to be a foundational component or proxy for intelligence. Furthermore, the current emphasis on accountability in U.S. schools as a result of *No Child Left Behind* legislation mandates to disaggregate student achievement data has given rise to considerable discourse around achievement gaps, their sources, and potential solutions. These achievement gap discourses may perpetuate images of African Americans as intellectually inferior and influence the ways African American students' perceive their ability to perform in mathematical contexts (Martin, 2007). African American mathematics teachers, therefore, may serve as bearers of counter-messages that challenge the historical and contemporary narrative of African American students as being "less able" than students in other racially defined groups in the United States.

Students' Perceptions of the Importance of Mathematics

It is our belief that teachers are instrumental in influencing their students' perceptions of the importance of mathematics as an academic discipline and useful tool. In and out of school environments, the general perception of mathematics as an important discipline is often due to its practical utility and cultural value (Gowers, 2002), although there is a contemporary push to view mathematics literacy as a civil right (Moses & Cobb, 2001). Mathematics undergirds a multitude of disciplines including engineering, physics, and computer sciences; disciplines central to technological innovation and economic progress. In recent years the importance of improving mathematics performance of U.S. students has been the focus of federal *No Child Left Behind* legislation and deliberations of high profile panels (Committee on Prospering in the Global Economy of the 21st Century, 2007). This focus is largely driven by the ongoing analysis of globalization trends that suggests that countries that develop large populations of well educated citizens prepared to pursue technologically oriented professions will rise in the ranks of world wealth and power (Friedman, 2005); those countries that lag behind in the development of this human capital will suffer. As most U.S. citizens develop their mathematical proficiency in U.S. public schools, the mathematical performance of U.S. students is central to the economic and technological competitiveness of the United States (Committee on Prospering in the Global Economy of the 21st Century, 2007). As the language of globalization continues to dominate political and economic discourses, and international comparisons of mathematics performance continue to consistently suggest U.S. students underperform relative to many other countries (Gonzales, 2004; National Center for Educational Statistics, 2006) the importance of U.S. school mathematics will only increase over time.

Marginalized citizens in the United States, particularly African Americans, have historically viewed educational access and the mastery of academic knowledge as keys to progress with higher paying jobs and better living conditions seen as the pay off. The importance of mathematics in the African American community is less clear, particularly because mathematics, apart from most other academic disciplines, has historically been viewed in the United States as the intellectual domain of white males (Campbell, Denes, & Morrison, 2000) and less accessible than other academic disciplines. It is our belief that African American mathematics teachers may serve as individuals in their African American students' lives that elevate and communicate the critical importance of mathematics to their African American students and how their African American students' success in mathematics may serve as an economically and politically empowering act.

Students' Perceptions of the Nature of Mathematical Activity

Without question, mathematics teachers and the mathematics learning environments they create are instrumental references and sources as their students form perceptions of what does and does not constitute mathematical activity. The extent to which mathematics teachers create opportunities for their students to engage in mathematical activities that demand any number of mathematical processes—computing, calculating, reasoning, communicating, higher order problem-solving, meaning making, developing an inquisitive mathematical disposition (Swafford, Findell, & Kilpatrick, 2001)—influence the extent to which students have narrower or wider views of the nature of mathematical activity. In recent years, researchers have conducted large-scale studies documenting mathematics instructional practices in U.S. classrooms (Stigler & Hiebert, 1999; Weiss, Banilower, McMahon, & Smith, 2001; Weiss, Pasley, Smith, Banilower, & Heck, 2003). Findings indicate that mathematics instructional practices in the United States are typically highly teacher-centered and directed, focused on basic skills acquisition, and provide limited opportunities for students to engage in reasoning and problem-solving, particularly as students advance through grade levels. It is evident that, on average, mathematics instructional practices in the United States are not focused on deliberately and strategically positioning opportunities for students to engage in cognitively demanding mathematics tasks or to develop an inquisitive stance towards mathematics. Furthermore, despite considerable energy expended by school districts, universities, and education policy organizations to "reform" mathematics classrooms, researchers have gathered evidence indicating that mathematics instructional practices in the United States are stubbornly stable and difficult to influence once established within the school culture (Stigler & Hiebert, 1999).

If mathematics instructional practices across the United States are cast as "traditional" (i.e., predominantly teacher-centered and skills-based), mathematics instruction in urban schools serving low income, high-minority communities tend to be perceived as chronically "traditional" (if not debilitating), and are particularly targeted for transformation (Knapp, 1995). There has been considerable investment in professional development and resources related to mathematics instruction in urban districts over the past two decades (i.e., NSF Systemic Initiatives); however, direct observation of mathematics instructional practices across the United States indicate that there appear to be persistent patterns of differential quality of instruction across types of communities (urban, rural, suburban), in classes with varying proportions of minority students, and in classes of varying ability levels (Weiss, Pasley, Smith, Banilower, & Heck, 2003). Although any generalized characterization of the quality of mathematics instruction African American students experience is inadvisable, it is plausible to suggest that large numbers of African American children, due to their positioning in intersections of SES and geography, are not consistently exposed to cognitively demanding mathematics tasks, and, in turn, do not have opportunities to expand their perceptions of the nature of mathematical activity in their school setting. Furthermore, as schools and teachers are increasingly held accountable for student performance on mandated assessments, low performing urban schools are increasingly incorporating pacing guides to provide students opportunities to be exposed to tested content, yet many teachers find such curriculum and pacing guides constraining and require that they prematurely move through narrowly defined mathematical content despite inclinations to broaden the nature of mathematical activity in their classrooms (Marsh et al., 2005).

If then it can be argued that large groups of African American students have historically and collectively experienced mathematics differently than other students in the United States, and those differences provide these students fewer opportunities to develop a rich perspective on the nature of mathematical activity, it is plausible that African American mathematics teachers may serve as architects of mathematics learning environments that consciously attempt to broaden and expand African American students exposure to the nature of mathematical activity in response to the historical and contemporary record of the limited experiences of African American students in mathematics classrooms.

Features of Liberation Pedagogy

Just as it is theorized that racism is an inescapable phenomenon in U.S. society (Ladson-Billings & Tate, 1995), we believe that features of liberation pedagogy are practically inescapable when African American mathematics teachers design learning environments for their African American students. There is a strong tradition of liberation for education in the African American community (Anderson, 1988; DuBois, 1903, 1975; Woodson, 1990), and, although perhaps more tacit and subtle than in prior decades, African American teachers of African American students continue to engage students in activities and discussions that provoke their students to identify and act on relevant inequities and oppressive forces that directly effect the quality of their students' present and future lives (Foster, 1997; Irvine, 2002; Murrell, 2007). It is our perspective, however, that this work is rarely done as a means of engaging students in examining and responding to large-scale social inequities such as overrepresentation of African Americans in prisons, racial profiling, and redlining in residential areas (Gutstein, 2006). The features and activities of liberation pedagogy we anticipated and identified in the practice of African American mathematics teachers were more subtle and interwoven in traditional classroom discourse. These activities and discussions encouraged African American students to critically examine a multitude of forces that press on students' capacity to appropriately engage in mathematical activity and perform on mathematics assessments. These features and activities include encouraging students to resist negative characterizations of African American youth, deliberately modifying the nature of mathematical activity in the classroom as a response to what they perceive as oppressive curricular offerings, and explicitly communicating messages of high expectations and beliefs in their students' mathematical ability despite students' mathematics history and prior experience.

Our Methodological Approach

In an effort to view our participants in ways that reflect our conceptual framework, it was critical that we designed data collection protocols and gathered multiple forms of data with distinctly different foci. As stated previously, teacher interviews (TI) and classroom observations (CO) made up the corpus of our data, however teacher interviews and classroom observations were designed to focus on one of five analytic themes: 1) biographical history, 2) concept map of algebraic and statistical concepts, 3) "sense of purpose" of teaching mathematics, 4) the teaching of specific topics in algebra and data analysis, and 5) race, racism, and identity formation of African American mathematics students.

Biographical Histories (TI)

In an effort to identify the nexus of multimembership each teacher in our study is situated in and draws on to promote students' mathematics identity development, a biographical interview was conducted with each teacher. Teachers reported their schooling locations, experiences as mathematics learners, and memberships in relevant communities of practice that they felt influenced their instruction.

Concept Maps (TI)

Teachers' mathematical knowledge is increasingly being conceived as a critical mediator between instructional mathematics goals and instructional mathematics practice (Ball, Hill, & Bass, 2005). Each teacher therefore constructed a concept map illustrating the ways in which they perceived the main ideas within the domains of algebra and data analysis, as well as the ways those ideas are connected within each domain.

Sense of Purpose (TI and CO)

Teachers' capacity to articulate and help students come to adopt a sense of purpose for learning mathematics in school is central to success with students who might be skeptical about schooling and its influence on their life chances. Teachers were interviewed and observed with a focus on the extent to which they communicated a sense of purpose of mathematics in general and several specific algebraic and statistical concepts.

The Teaching of Algebra and Data Analysis (CO)

Each teacher was interviewed and observed on multiple occasions in an effort to capture their perspectives and instructional practices of specific algebraic and data analysis concepts. Efforts were made to observe and videotape the same algebra and data analysis lessons across all six teachers for the purposes of illustrating the wide range of perspectives and approaches to instruction of the same mathematics topic.

Race, Racism, and Identity Formation (TI)

In our efforts to better understand teachers' perspectives on the role race, racism, and identity formation plays in their students' mathematics performance and achievement, teachers were interviewed and asked explicitly about their views related to these topics.

"Thumbnail" Portraits of Madison Morgan and Floyd Lee

Based on our conceptual framework and methodological approaches, we feel that we employ perspectives and identify relevant data that allows us to responsibly "render" our participants in ways that acknowledge the complexities of their work and the resources they draw upon to engage in their practice. The production of cases and portraits depicting the work of teachers in our study is underway (Birky, Chazan, & Farlow, 2008; Clark, Badertscher, & Napp, 2008; Johnson & Nyamekye, 2008). What follows are brief "thumbnail" portraits of two of our participants, Madison Morgan and Floyd Lee.

Madison Morgan

Madison Morgan is an African American female in her early 40s. At the time of the study she had been teaching for 13 years. Madison was born and raised in a large metropolitan city on the East Coast and attended public schools that were populated predominantly by African American students. Madison recalled having several African American teachers during her elementary school years, yet had no recollection of being taught by an African American teacher in high school. In fact, she had no memory of any African American teachers being employed in her high school during her enrollment there.

Madison stated that she performed well in mathematics in high school relative to her peers, yet described the mathematics learning environments in high school as unchallenging, heavily tracked, and, in retrospect, providing students very little preparation for the rigors of college level mathematics. She began her undergraduate studies at a predominantly white undergraduate institution in the Midwest confident in her academic abilities. Madison struggled in her freshman mathematics courses and, much to her shock and disappointment, found herself required to enroll in remedial mathematics classes during her freshman year. Madison's experiences in remedial mathematics classes in college caused her to develop feelings of resentment in relation to her academic preparation in high school. She believes that her lack of preparation for college-level mathematics is in part due to her segregated schooling experiences; she has memories as a child of visiting a white friend's predominantly white school and being struck by the exposure students in this school had to more complex, challenging mathematics relative to the exposure her peers in her school were receiving. As a result, Madison claimed that a central goal of her mathematics pedagogy is to provide her students, particularly her African American students, opportunities in high school mathematics classes that she maintains she did not have—opportunities to engage in authentic mathematical thinking, problem-solving, and sense-making—so that they may be better prepared for the rigors of college mathematics.

Madison was trained as a landscape architect and practiced professionally, but eventually shifted to mathematics teaching. Her commitment to her profession is profound; she successfully completed the requirements for certification by the National Board for Professional Teaching Standards. Due to her architecture and engineering training, Madison's typical teaching load was diverse and consisted of the mathematics courses for the engineering academy in the school, Algebra II, and Pre-Calculus. The first year of the research project was the second year she was assigned to teach Algebra I. Unsatisfied with the instruction that the Algebra I students were receiving in her school, Madison was delighted to teach the course for a second time and proposed to make great changes to it in her third year of teaching it. One goal she established for her Algebra I course for a third year was to eliminate the weeks dedicated to reviewing and practicing basic skills with students such as computing with integers and expending time on properties that she felt students knew well enough (distributive property, associative property, etc.) Instead, she wanted to immerse the students into activities that required them to find patterns and make generalizations from the first day of school.

Madison believes that all students are capable of high achievement in mathematics regardless of prior achievement in mathematics. She firmly believes that if you can engage students' interest in the doing of mathematics, then they will be motivated to learn the more mundane activities, adding fractions or finding the slope of a line, if it allows them to make progress on a larger task they are working on. She feels that her experiences as a mathematics student in high school and college, as well as her experiences as a practicing landscape architect have highly influenced her commitment to engaging students in rich, contextualized mathematics activities through which she teaches the mandated mathematics content. Although Madison attempted to follow the district's curriculum guide and pacing calendar, she consistently modified the content of the curriculum guide's lessons in an effort to integrate statistical concepts, data collection and analysis, and advanced algebraic concepts. For instance, during the period of time in which Madison was scheduled to introduce her students to solving linear equations in one variable (as encouraged by the district's curriculum guide and pacing schedule), she felt the time would be better spent having students gather data of the class members' height and weight, discuss multiple statistical and algebraic concepts related to patterns in the data, and algebraically and graphically identify the line that best fit for the student data. Through this experience students engaged in mathematical activity that served multiple purposes and provided a multitude of opportunities.

At research team meetings dedicated to discussing Madison's practice prior to interviewing Madison on the topics of race and mathematics identity development, most team members felt that Madison's mathematics pedagogy was not driven by the fact that both she and the majority of her students were African American. During these preliminary interviews and observations directly focused on her mathematics instructional practice, Madison never spoke of how her instructional decisions were made in part based upon the fact that her students were African American. Classroom obversational data indicate that she never made references in class to students' race, did not engage students in conversations about the mathematical history and legacy of people of color, nor did she engage students in mathematical activity that focused on societal inequities and injustices. Our probes during her interview related to race, racism, and student identity formation, however, revealed a drive and commitment to tenets of liberatory pedagogy, particularly in relation to her African American students. This commitment was somewhat surprising to the research team, in that we could not explicitly "see" these beliefs and commitments in her practice per se in her classroom. Yet, when asked directly, Madison spoke passionately about how and why her instructional choices are in a large part driven by her dedication to providing her African American students in particular meaningful, challenging, high quality mathematical experiences and opportunities so that they, in turn, can develop strong mathematics identities.

Floyd Lee

Floyd Lee is a 24-year-old Black[3] male and at the time of the study was in the first two years of his teaching career. Floyd attended school in the district in which he taught and also attended a local historically Black college for his undergraduate degree. As a young Black male, Floyd has firsthand experience with negotiating and rejecting public perceptions of his academic ability in general and mathematical ability in particular, and felt that he understood the tensions that his students regularly face. He credited his capacity to manage these tensions to his parents' insistence that he stay on a productive path and to their continuous support (although he readily admitted that he didn't always agree or understand why they were so demanding of him at times). Despite his young age, Floyd possessed a confident, "knowing" demeanor and believed that he could provide similar guidance to his students that his parents had provided him.

Floyd occasionally modified curriculum resources or mathematics tasks to increase cognitive demand, capture students' interest, and position mathematics differently for his students. However, the most unique and distinct dimension of his pedagogical approach was the content and flavor of the classroom discussions he led. Through employment of long speeches peppered with circumstances, language, and cultural referents very familiar to his students, Floyd explicitly advised his students to avoid actions and distractions—teenage sexual activity and pregnancy, alcohol and drug use, glorification of music and sports figures—that resulted in the very heavy consequence of doing poorly in school. In traditional mathematics education research analyses, these exchanges would more than likely be considered "non-mathematical" in nature, and therefore would not be identified as influences on students' capacity to perform mathematically. Floyd, however, did not feel that these topics were taboo or had no place in his mathematics classroom; in fact, he felt that, considering the power of these issues to deter students from committing fully to their study of mathematics, these topics and issues must be addressed frankly and publicly in his classroom. He used the experiences in his life, the choices he made, and the success he has had thus far as an example and a rationale for his students to perform to the best of their ability in his classroom. There were times when he explicitly engaged his students in mathematics by connecting to their personal interests or by transforming mathematics activities in ways that he felt increased engagement; however, he felt his role as a mathematics teacher and his experiences as a successful mathematics learner provided him with an additional opportunity. Explicitly and implicity, Floyd consciously and continuously conveyed the following message—*Look at me. I am not that much different than you. I successfully completed these same courses with this same mathematics content and I am making something out of my life. You can also if you choose to.*

Despite his continuous use of his mathematics classroom as a platform to engage in an oratorical style that could easily be interpreted as "preaching" or "sermonizing," a communication traditional firmly rooted in the Black community, Floyd did not consider his messages specifically tailored for his Black students. Floyd was conscious of the fact that he and most of his students shared the same racial group membership, yet he felt that this fact was not a major influence on his practice or the messages he communicated. His perspective on his practice seemed paradoxical to the research team—how could a Black teacher engage his mostly Black student population in an ongoing dialogue of self-empowerment, overcoming obstacles, and self-responsibility, yet not view these interactions as related to reactions to historical racism and contemporary inequities? His response to this was complex; Floyd felt that all students needed to hear what he had to say because all youth—Black, Latino, white—were susceptible to the same negative consequences of poor choices and were in the process of managing these choices. Floyd was conscious of the fact that the experiences and performances of his Black students are a result of contemporary and historical race-based inequities, yet he did not feel that the best use of his short time with his students should be committed to aiding students' feelings of powerlessness through discussions of factors that he perceived to be beyond their control. (A vivid example of this is a classroom exchange between Floyd and one his African American male students where Floyd becomes outraged when the student states that his failure to perform up to Floyd's expectations was due to the oppressive force of "the Man," suggesting his underperformance was directly attributable to white racism and its effects.) The tone and flavor of his discussion of his Black students, as well as his awareness of the challenges Latino and white youth face in their efforts to succeed academically, reflected a complex, simultaneous acknowledgement of his students' free will to make choices that best position them to succeed mathematically, and the presence of external forces and presses—many of which he had first hand knowledge of—that contemporary youth encounter in their everyday lives that distract them from their capacity to commit to the practices of successful mathematics learners. Floyd felt that his most important practice while in the role of their mathematics teacher was to serve as communicator and example of the message that, despite challenges, obstacles, and perceptions, his students are intellectually powerful and capable of successfully negotiating and reconciling social, racial, and academic identities.

Conclusion

Our efforts to frame, examine, interpret, and document the perspectives and pedagogical approaches of the African American mathematics teachers in our project have provided us the opportunity to understand their work in its totality and complexity. Portraits of our other participants in our project reveal a variety of experiences, histories, and instructional approaches that indicate that all participants in our study acknowledge and consider shared racial membership with their students, yet use this phenomena in considerably different ways. For example, as a result of being diagnosed with a learning disability as an adult, April Lincoln was highly sensitive to special needs students in her classroom and, through her interactions and mathematics practice, countered messages of the mathematical ability and capacity of students labeled with learning disabilities. In her efforts to provide students with a broad range of problem-solving tools, Dorothy Hicks relied heavily on technology and heuristics to create an environment where her students were free to draw on multiple resources to engage in mathematical activity. Penelope Jones, a young teacher with deep and extensive mathematical training, was excited about the prospects of building the same interest and love of mathematics in her students that she possessed, yet struggled in her efforts, in part due to what she perceived as obstacles related to students' affect—motivation, dedication, and engagement. Our interest in the variety and complexity of all of our participants' work has allowed us to consider an extremely important question central to our research project: *How do teachers draw on their experiences, the experiences of their students, their mathematical knowledge, and their pedagogical knowledge in the practice of teaching mathematics?*

We believe that our conceptual framework and methodological approaches in this project provide us the opportunity to appropriately explore this complex question. In summary, our conceptual framework and methodological approaches rest on the following tenets:

- Teachers are windows into the adult world; a world in which teachers are members of a community of mathematics doers as well as members of other relevant communities of practice that influence their classroom interactions with their students.

- As an intergenerational phenomenon, many African American mathematics teachers of African American students develop and maintain a pedagogy that is, in part, constructed as a response to the effects of historical and contemporary racism and oppression of African Americans. Therefore, with respect to African American mathematics teachers of African American students, incorporating liberatory features in their pedagogy is practically inescapable. These features may, however, be subtle and, in many instances, tacit.

- Given that many African American teachers practice, to some degree, features of liberatory pedagogy, we maintain that individual pedagogical approaches are distinctly and uniquely constructed and facilitated. This is due to the fact that we recognize that each African American teacher experiences life distinctly and uniquely differently while being African American, resulting in distinct and unique viewpoints, perspectives, values, and practices.

- This pedagogy is motivated by a confluence of teachers' historical knowledge of the African American experience, their personal experience as an African American mathematics learner, their mathematical knowledge, and their varied memberships in other relevant communities of practice.

- To understand and recognize the liberatory features of African American mathematics teachers' pedagogy, the researcher must be abreast of the history of African American teachers and their place in the history of liberatory pedagogy.

- Analysis and reporting of data must provide opportunities to describe the relationships between context, history, subjects' lives, and researcher positionality.
- As counter-narratives to prevalent depictions of instruction in high minority environments, the researcher must place considerable emphasis on research-ing and reporting the healthy, productive attributes of interactions between African American mathematics teachers and their African American students, yet not mask contradictions and complexities.

Notes

1 MAC-MTL is a multi-site partnership through which the University of Delaware, the University of Maryland, The Pennsylvania State University, and three public school sys-tems collaborate to work on critical tasks in mathematics education. MAC-MTL's research, development, and teaching projects are funded by a continuing grant from the National Science Foundation Centers for Learning and Teaching program.
2 For the purposes of simplifying our conceptual framework, we collapsed Martin's third and fourth dimension into one dimension titled "nature of mathematical activity."
3 The terms "African American" and "Black" are often used interchangeably in the United States to refer to American citizens of African descent; however, the terms hold distinctly different meanings to different people, and self-definition through use of either term is often viewed as an act of political and social empowerment. When describing our partici-pants individually, as through the thumbnail portraits, we employ the term each partici-pant preferred when describing himself or herself. In this case, Floyd Lee preferred the term "Black" versus "African American."

References

Anderson, D. & Gold, E. (2006). Home to school: Numeracy practices and mathematical identities. *Mathematical Thinking and Learning 8*(3), 261–286.

Anderson, J. (1988). *The education of Blacks in the South, 1860–1935*. Chapel Hill, NC: University of North Carolina Press.

Atweh, B., Forgasz, H., & Nebres, B. (Eds.). (2001). *Sociocultural research on mathematics education: An international perspective*. Mahwah, NJ: Lawrence Erlbaum.

Ball, D.L. & Forzani, F.M. (2007). 2007 Wallace Foundation distinguished lecture-What makes education "research educational"? *Educational Researcher, 36*(9), 529–540.

Ball, D.L., Hill, H.C., & Bass, H. (2005, Fall). Knowing mathematics for teaching: Who knows mathematics well enough to teach third grade, and how can we decide? *American Educator*, Fall, 2005, 14–46.

Birky, G., Chazan, D., & Farlow, K. (2008, April). Deliberately departing from the curricu-lum guide in search of coherence and meaning: Madison Morgan's mathematics instruc-tion in an urban high school. Paper presented at the Annual Meeting of the American Education Research Association, New York, NY.

Boaler, J. (1999). Participation, knowledge and beliefs: A community perspective on mathe-matics learning. *Educational Studies in Mathematics, 40*(3), 259.

Boaler, J. (2000). Exploring situated insights into research and learning. *Journal for Research in Mathematics Education, 31*(1), 113–123.

Boykin, A. W. (1986). The triple quandary and the schooling of Afro American children. In U. Neisser (Ed.), *The school achievement of minority children* (pp. 57–92). Hillsdale, NJ: Erlbaum.

Campbell, G., Denes, R., & Morrison, C. (Eds.). (2000). *Access denied: Race, ethnicity, and the scientific enterprise.* New York: Oxford University Press.

Clark, L., Badertscher, E., & Napp, C. (2008, April). *African American mathematics teachers as agents in African American students' mathematics identity formation.* Paper presented at the Annual Meeting of the American Education Research Association, New York, NY.

Clewell, B.C. & Villegas, A. M. (1998). Increasing the number of teachers of color for urban schools: Lessons from the pathways national evaluation. *Education and Urban Society, 31*(1), 42.

Cobb, P. & Hodge, L.L. (2007). Culture, identity, and equity in the mathematics classroom. In N.S. Nasir, & P. Cobb (Eds.), *Diversity, equity, and access to mathematical ideas* (pp. 159–171). New York: Teachers College Press.

Cobb, P. & Hodge, L. L. (2002). A relational perspective on issues of cultural diversity and equity as they play out in the mathematics classroom. *Mathematical Thinking and Learning, 4*(2 & 3), 249–284.

Cobb, P., Wood, T., Yackel, E., & McNeal, B. (1992). Characteristics of classroom mathematics traditions: An interactional analysis. *American Educational Research Journal, 29*(3), 573–604.

Committee on Prospering in the Global Economy of the 21st Century (2007). *Rising above the gathering storm: Energizing and employing America for a brighter economic future.* Washington, DC: National Academies Press.

Dee, T.S. (2004). The race connection: Are teachers more effective with students who share their ethnicity? *Education Next, 4*(2), 52–59.

Du Bois, W.E.B. (1903). *The souls of Black folk.* New York: Penguin Books.

Du Bois, W.E.B. (1975). *The education of Black people: Ten critiques, 1906–1960* (1st Modern Reader Paperback ed.). New York: Monthly Review Press.

Ehrlich, P.R. & Feldman, S.S. (1977). *The race bomb: Skin color, prejudice, and intelligence.* New York: Quadrangle/New York Times Book Co.

Ferguson, R.F. (1998). Teachers' perceptions and expectations and the Black–white test score gap. In C. Jencks, & M. Phillips (Eds.), *The Black-white test score gap* (pp. 217–317). Washington, DC: Brookings Institution Press.

Foster, M. (1997). *Black teachers on teaching.* New York: New Press.

Foucault, M. (1972). *The archaeology of knowledge and the discourse on language* [Archôlogie du savoir.]. New York: Pantheon Books.

Franke, M.L., Kazemi, E., & Battey, D. (2007). Understanding teaching and classroom practices in mathematics. In F.K. Lester (Ed.), *Second handbook of research on mathematics teaching and learning* (pp. 225–256). Charlotte, NC: Information Age Publishers.

Frankenstein, M. (1983). Critical mathematics education: An application of Paulo Freire's epistemology. *Journal of Education, 165*(4), 315–327.

Freire, P. (1989). *Education for critical consciousness.* New York: Continuum.

Freire, P. (2000). *Pedagogy of the oppressed* (30th anniversary ed.). New York: Continuum.

Friedman, T.L. (2005). *The world is flat: A brief history of the twenty-first century.* New York: Picador/Farrar, Straus and Giroux.

Gonzales, P.A. (2004). *Highlights from the trends in international mathematics and science study (TIMSS) 2003.* Washington, DC: National Center for Education Statistics, U.S. Dept. of Education, Institute of Education Sciences.

Gonzalez, N., Andrade, R., Civil, M., & Moll, L. (2001). Bridging funds of distributed knowledge: Creating zones of practices in mathematics. *Journal of Education for Students Placed at Risk (JESPAR), 6*(1 & 2), 115–132.

Gould, S.J. (1996). *The mismeasure of man* (Rev. and expand ed.). New York: Norton.

Gowers, T. (2002). *Mathematics: A very short introduction.* New York: Oxford University Press.

Gutstein, E. (2006). *Reading and writing the world with mathematics: Toward a pedagogy for social justice.* New York: Routledge.

Gutstein, E. & Peterson, B. (Eds.). (2005). *Rethinking mathematics: Teaching social justice by the numbers.* Milwaukee, WI: Rethinking Schools, Ltd.

Hiebert, J.S. & Grouws, D.A. (2007). The effects of classroom mathematics teaching on students' learning. In F.K. Lester (Ed.), *Second handbook of research on mathematics teaching and learning* (pp. 371–405). Charlotte, NC: Information Age Publishers.

Hill, H.C., Rowan, B., & Ball, D.L. (2005). Effects of teachers' mathematical knowledge for teaching on student achievement. *American Educational Research Journal, 42*(2), 371–406.

Hill, H.C., Schilling, S.G., & Ball, D.L. (2004). Developing measures of teachers' mathematics knowledge for teaching. *Elementary School Journal, 105*(1), 11–30.

Horvat, E.M. & Lewis, K.S. (2003). Reassessing the "burden of 'acting white'": The importance of peer groups in managing academic success. *Sociology of Education, 76*(4), 265–280.

Irvine, J.J. (2002). *In search of wholeness: African American teachers and their culturally specific classroom practices.* New York: Palgrave.

Jencks, C. & Phillips, M. (1998). *The Black-white test score gap.* Washington, DC: Brookings Institution Press.

Johnson, W. & Nyamekye, F. (2008, April). *The Case of Floyd Lee.* Paper presented at the Annual Meeting of the American Education Research Association, New York, NY.

King, S.H. (1993). The limited presence of African American teachers. *Review of Educational Research, 63*(2), 115–149.

Knapp, M.S. (1995). *Teaching for meaning in high-poverty classrooms.* New York: Teachers College Press.

Ladson-Billings, G. & Tate IV, W.F. (1995). Toward a critical race theory of education. *Teachers College Record, 97*(1), 47–69.

Lampert, M. (2001). *Teaching problems and the problems of teaching.* New Haven: Yale University Press.

Marsh, J., Kerr, K., Ikemoto, G., Darilek, H., Suttorp, M. Zimmer, M., & Barney H. (2005). *The role of districts in fostering instructional improvement: Lessons from three urban districts partnered with the institute for learning.* MG-361-EDU (available at www.rand.org/ publications/MG/MG361).

Martin, D.B. (2000). *Mathematics success and failure among African American youth.* Mahwah, NJ:Erlbaum.

Martin, D.B. (2007). Beyond missionaries or cannibals: Who should teach mathematics to African American children? *The High School Journal, 91*(1), 6–28.

Massey, D.S. & Denton, N.A. (1989). Hypersegregation in U.S. metropolitan areas: Black and Hispanic segregation along five dimensions. *Demography, 26*(3), 373–391.

Massey, D.S. & Denton, N.A. (1993). *American apartheid: Segregation and the making of the underclass.* Cambridge, Mass.: Harvard University Press.

Milner, R.I. (2007). Race, culture, and researcher positionality: Working through dangers seen, unseen, and unforeseen. *Educational Researcher, 36*(7), 388–400.

Moses, R.P. & Cobb, C.E. (2001). *Radical equations: Math literacy and civil rights.* Boston: Beacon Press.

Murrell, P.C. (2007). *Race, culture, and schooling: Identities of achievement in multicultural urban schools.* New York: Erlbaum.

Nasir, N.S. (2007). Identity, goals, and learning: The case of basketball mathematics. In N.S. Nasir, & P. Cobb (Eds.), *Diversity, equity, and access to mathematical ideas* (pp. 130–143). New York: Teachers College Press.

Nasir, N.S. & Cobb, P. (Eds.). (2007). *Improving access to mathematics: Diversity and equity in the classroom.* New York: Teachers College Press.

National Center for Education Statistics. (2006). *Comparing mathematics content in the national assessment of educational progress (NEAP), trends in international mathematics and science study (TIMSS), and program for international student assessment (PISA) 2003 assessments.* Washington, DC: United States Dept. of Education, National Center for Education Statistics, Institute of Education Sciences.

National Council of Teachers of Mathematics (NCTM). (2000). *Principles and standards for school mathematics.* Reston, VA: NCTM.

O'Connor, C. (1997). Dispositions toward (collective) struggle and educational resilience in the inner city: A case analysis of six African American high school students. *American Educational Research Journal, 34*(4), 593–629.

O'Connor, C., Lewis, A., & Mueller, J. (2007). Researching "Black" educational experiences and outcomes: Theoretical and methodological considerations. *Educational Researcher, 36*(9), 541–552.

Secada, W.G., Fennema, E., & Byrd Adajian, L. (Eds.). (1995). *New directions for equity in mathematics education.* New York: Cambridge University Press.

Siddle Walker, V. (1996). *Their highest potential: An African American school community in the segregated south.* Chapel Hill, NC: University of North Carolina Press.

Steele, C.M. (1997). A threat in the air: How stereotypes shape intellectual identity and performance. *American Psychologist, 52*(6), 613–629.

Stigler, J.W. & Hiebert, J. (1999). *The teaching gap: Best ideas from the world's teachers for improving education in the classroom.* New York: Free Press.

Swafford, J., Findell, B., & Kilpatrick, J. (Eds.). (2001). *Adding it up: Helping children learn mathematics.* Washington, DC: National Academy Press.

Ware, F. (2006). Warm demander pedagogy: Culturally responsive teaching that supports a culture of achievement for African American students. *Urban Education, 41*(4), 427–456.

Weiss, I.R., Banilower, E.R., McMahon, K.C., & Smith, P.S. (2001). *Report of the 2000 national survey of science and mathematics education.* Chapel Hill, NC: Horizon Research, Inc.

Weiss, I.R., Pasley, J.D., Smith, S., Banilower, E.R., & Heck, D.J. (2003). *Looking inside the classroom: A study of K–12 mathematics and science education in the United States.* Chapel Hill, NC: Horizon Research, Inc.

Wenger, E. (1998). *Communities of practice: Learning, meaning, and identity.* New York: Cambridge University Press.

Wigfield, A. & Eccles, J.S. (2000). Expectancy-value theory of achievement motivation. *Contemporary Educational Psychology, 25,* 68–81.

Woodson, C.G. (1990). *The mis-education of the negro.* Trenton, NJ: Africa World Press. (Original work published 1933).

Yackel, E. & Cobb, P. (1996). Sociomathematical norms, argumentation, and autonomy in mathematics. *Journal for Research in Mathematics Education, 27*(4), 458–477.

3 "This Little Light of Mine!" Entering Voices of Cultural Relevancy into the Mathematics Teaching Conversation

Lou Edward Matthews

Introduction

For centuries, the words of the Negro spiritual "This Little Light of Mine," have resonated loudly in the voices of churchgoers to boldly proclaim the spiritual "light" of transformed lives for all to see as witnesses. Historically, amongst the descendants of Africans who were displaced throughout the Americas and the Caribbean during slavery, especially important were the succeeding, repetitive, one-lined verses which often began with "All around the neighborhood, I'm gonna let it shine"; "Let it shine til Jesus comes, I'm gonna let it shine"; and, "Won't let Satan blow it out, I'm gonna let it shine." These verses represent powerful exhortations, typical of all Negro spirituals, framed to move participants and listeners to think individually and collectively about spiritual liberation, and to persevere through trying times. This liberatory discourse also served a dual political purpose in the Black diasporic experience. In this manner, spirituals were employed as hidden, coded messages in the fight for freedom from slavery. In contemporary times, these messages have been used openly as liberatory tools in civil rights movements, social protests, union rallies, war protests and political gatherings around the world.

As a mathematics education scholar, teacher, curriculum writer, consultant, and union representative in Bermuda's education system over the past 15 years of restructuring and reform, I have borne witness to what I have come to see as liberatory discussions about mathematics teaching, and the teaching, in general, of Black children. In union meetings, hallways, and street chats with former colleagues, the bulk of these conversations have extended far beyond content and method, into that which is decidedly political, racial, and cultural in nature, and very much focused on the collective hopes and dreams for citizenship and empowerment of Black Bermudians.

Reflecting on my own professional role as an agent of major reform initiatives in mathematics, I have realized that much of what is needed for improving mathematics teaching and learning for Black children cannot be simply gleaned from conventional wisdom found in workshops, methods classes, school meetings, and classrooms, etc. Rather, I have come to rely on the wisdom gained from my conversations with teachers "on the ground," who have an invaluable propensity for "keeping it real" when talking about successes and failures in the teaching and learning of mathematics for Black children. In addition to experiences regarding content and method, they often possess vital knowledge of pressing political, racial, and cultural issues that guide their thinking about Bermudian children in the context of education reform (Lipman, 1996; Matthews, 2003). The liberatory aspects of this wisdom include not only talk about achievement outcomes and possibilities, but also of heightened expectations, overcoming limited curricula, the ways in which culture can be used to make experiences relevant, and how school experiences can empower Black children to impact their communities.

Indeed, what has largely been absent in the restructuring in my island nation has been the content and contribution of conversations with teachers, many with high profile reputations for exemplary teaching of children in Bermuda's predominantly Black public school system. This is important to note because Shulman (2004) contended that education reform *should* draw from the "wisdom of practice" of successful, often influential teachers whose pedagogy could serve as models and whose potential school leadership would assist system efforts. Wisdom of practice as defined by Shulman, is the "reasoning and actions of gifted teachers into cases to establish standards of practice for particular areas of teaching" (p. 233). Even more pointedly, Lipman (1996) speaks to the potential impact of this wisdom of practice for Black children:

> The pedagogical knowledge, exemplary practices, and perspectives of successful teachers of students of color are resources for school change—and that these resources must be recognized, legitimized, and supported as essential components of transforming schools for all children.

In this chapter, I call on the revolutionary function of the Negro spiritual to draw out the "light" of hidden liberatory discourse about teaching, to rally mathematics educators and mathematics teachers of Black children in Bermuda, and elsewhere, toward excellence in teaching. More specifically, my purpose in this chapter is to examine the teaching perspectives of four middle school mathematics teachers with exemplary reputations in two predominantly Black middle schools in Bermuda, and further, to illuminate their practices utilizing a wisdom-of-practice perspective known as *culturally relevant pedagogy*. In consideration of this powerful contribution to knowledge, the first section begins with a brief introduction to the current conversation concerning education reform efforts for Black Bermudian children. This is followed by a discussion of culturally relevant pedagogy and the reporting of key findings of my work with the four teachers.

State of Affairs for Education Reform in Bermuda

Public education in the small self-ruled island nation of Bermuda has undergone monumental changes over the last 15 years. The bulk of large-scale structural changes have been implemented to shed vestiges of a colonial past with African, Caribbean, and British ties and to provide economic and social opportunities that were historically denied to Black Bermudians (Ministry of Education, 1993), who comprise 61% of the island-nation's approximately 63,000 citizens (Department of Statistics, 2007). In 2006, there were 10,364 students enrolled in Bermuda's schools, including 6,064 (59%) enrolled in public schools (Department of Statistics, 2007). Although race/ethnicity statistics on Bermudian students are not collected, the vast majority of the nation's public school students are Black. Private schools enroll 3,569 of the nation's students, which include the majority of white students on the island, and some Black Bermudians. The public education system currently consists of 12 pre-schools; 18 primary schools, for students aged 5 (P1) to 11 years (P6); five middle schools, for students aged 12 (M1) to 14 years (M3); and two senior secondary schools for students aged 15 (S1) to 18 years (S4).

Over 200 recommendations were given in a 1988 comprehensive review of the education system in Bermuda, which led to a massive restructuring plan (Ministry of Education, 1993). Breaking rank with its selectively tiered British-styled education system, these changes included: (a) adoption of a North American (i.e., styled after systems in United States and Canada) "comprehensive" schooling model involving the introduction of middle schools; (b) removal of policy and structural barriers restricting access for Bermudian students with special needs; (c) introduction of new modern curricula reflecting Western reforms in mathematics education and other critical areas; and (d) construction of new buildings and modernization of existing school facilities. The most significant of the changes were the introduction of middle and senior levels of education; a shift from a two-tiered primary/secondary model to the more North American-styled three-tier system (i.e., elementary, middle, and high school levels).

Fifteen years after the first reforms were implemented in the early 1990s, there is considerable debate as to whether the reforms have faltered and, in fact, compromised the nation's future. These concerns have dominated media circles (e.g., Johnson, 2004), public forums, and talk-circles over the last few years. The results of a 2007 comprehensive review of Bermuda's education system reported mostly unsatisfactory progress in mathematics and language arts in the middle schools, including: misalignment and confusion about curriculum, disgruntled and alienated teachers and students, ineffective systems and school leadership, and overall low achievement for many schools (O'Kelly-Lynch, 2007a, 2007b; Strangeways, 2007a, 2007b). Although some slight gains in mathematics and reading achievement for public school students were documented in the earlier years of reform (Matthews, 2001), more recent national consensus is that the "system" and its reforms are failing.

Mathematics Education Reform in Bermuda: A Familiar Conversation

Systemic efforts to impact the mathematics education of Black children in Bermuda have mirrored international efforts for mathematics reform. Promoted locally, nationally, and internationally, this movement has concentrated on helping school stakeholders build classroom communities in which mathematical ideas are explored and investigated actively by *all* students through collaborative discourse and meaningful mathematics tasks and activities (NCTM, 1991, 2000). Framed in a variety of settings (i.e., national and international conference meetings, professional development experiences, and rationales for systemic school initiatives), many of these reform perspectives ask teachers to "learn more challenging mathematics content and how to teach it" (Eisenhower National Clearinghouse for Mathematics and Science Education, 1999, p. 3). It is this mantra that forms the basis of professional reform conversation about the improvement of mathematics teaching (for example, see Ball, 1993; Carpenter, Fennema, Peterson, & Carey, 1988; Even, 1993).

Existing assessments of mathematics reform efforts for Black children elsewhere in the Diaspora, most notably in the United States, have continued to document systemic limitations in promoting equal access, opportunity, and outcomes (Ajose, 1995; Allexsaht-Snider & Hart, 2001; Anderson, 1990; Campbell, Voelkl, & Donahue 1997; Griffith, 1990; Tate, 1997; Zurawsky, 2004). Some mathematics educators have argued that the capacity for quality mathematics teaching and learning in districts serving Black children has been undermined. As to why this is so, I report elsewhere (see Matthews, 2005) on several fundamental forces identified by mathematics education researchers which work to limit the prospects of national reform:

a   Faulty notions about Black students and their experiences;
b   Resistance to equity notions in reform because of the protection of privilege;
c   Confusion about the nature of mathematics and mathematics teaching; and
d   Misinformation and miscommunication between the various stakeholders.

The first of these forces is particularly ominous because it points not only to the lack of practitioner knowledge regarding the experiences of Black children in mathematics, but also to the limited range of reform-oriented research efforts which might increase this knowledge. Another critical implication drawn is that failure to systemically account for practitioner wisdom on society, race, and culture can work to the detriment of reform's best efforts.

Culturally Relevant Pedagogy: A Wisdom of Practice Framework

A major reason that mathematics teaching and schooling are rarely talked about in ways that extend beyond content and method is that mathematics educators do not regularly frame their research and professional work to do so. A *culturally relevant pedagogy* framework offers a way to mine the wisdom-of-practice discussed above to develop excellence in mathematics teaching for Black children. Ladson-Billings (1994, 1995a, 1995b), in proposing a theory of culturally relevant pedagogy, argued that components of good teaching for Black students must (1) demonstrate an ability to promote academic success outside of explanations of cultural deficit (i.e., blaming Black students and their family characteristics for school failure), (2) locate excellence within the context of their community and cultural identities, and (3) challenge inequitable school and societal structures in the promotion of democratic citizenship.

Studies of culturally relevant pedagogy describe teachers who demonstrate skill in helping students achieve academic success while framing their teaching in such a way as to honor students' individual, community, racial and ethnic identities. The term *culturally relevant* is being used distinctively here, but not exclusively, to refer to the framing work of Ladson-Billings (1994, 1995a, 1995b). The term is often used interchangeably with *culturally responsive* in practice, and similarly framed (see Gay, 2000) to include the three elements outlined above. Nieto (1999) points out the shortcomings of other terms—*culturally compatible, culturally congruent* and *culturally appropriate*—arguing that they ignore more complex social and political power conflicts. Notwithstanding, the common thread of cultural approaches to teaching is that, together, they suggest as Nieto puts it, "culture and language can work in a mutual collaborative manner to promote learning rather than obstruct it." (p. 67).

Research on culturally relevant approaches to teaching has largely been concerned with illuminating the voices of successful teachers whose pedagogy draws on the intellectual, political, cultural and social aims of the diverse student groups they teach. Culturally relevant pedagogy has been used to address equity aims in a variety of communities that include the following: African American (Beauboeuf-Lafontant, 1999; Enyedy, Mukhopadhyay, & Danish, 2006; Ladson-Billings, 1997; Leonard & Guha, 2002; Lipman, 1995; Tate, 1995); African Canadian (Ladson-Billings, 1992); Bermudian (Matthews, 2003, 2008); Latino/Latina (Enyedy, Mukhopadhyay, & Danish, 2006; Gutstein, Lipman, Hernandez, & de los Reyes, 1997; Sheets, 1995); Maori (Airini, 1998); and West African (Maiga, 1995).

Ladson-Billings' work (1994, 1995b) has focused on the ways that teachers see themselves and others (Conceptions of Self and Others), how they view and engage general and content knowledge (Conceptions of Knowledge), and how they promote and organize social relationships in the schooling enterprise (Conceptions of Social Relations). This framework is depicted in Figure 3.1.

Academic Excellence
Cultural Competence
Critical Consciousness

Conceptions of Self and Others

Conceptions of Social Relations

Conceptions of Knowledge

Adapted from Ladson-Billings (1995b)

Figure 3.1 CRP Framework.

Conceptions of Self and Others

Culturally relevant teachers hold conceptions about themselves and students by placing academic success at the forefront of the realm of possibilities for all students. They see the act of teaching as artful, intimate, cultural, and political (Ladson-Billings, 1989, 1994, 1995b). These often-overlooked conceptions of self, which Beauboeuf (1999) argues are more representative of "psychological worldviews" (p. 4), stand in contrast to the pedagogy of teachers who see teaching as cultureless and detached, in which there are limited prospects for excellence. Beauboeuf's use of the term "politicized mothering" best encapsulates how culturally relevant teachers see teaching as an extension of their cultural selves yet decidedly political in nature (see also Beauboeuf, 1999; Powell, 1997; Trueba, 1993). With respect to students, these teachers reject traditional ways of labeling students such as "at-risk" and "gifted" (Sheets, 1995).

Conceptions of Knowledge

Ladson-Billings' framework (1989, 1995b; Trueba, 1993) also depicts exemplary teachers' conceptions of knowledge as both fallible and dynamic, placing emphasis on the central roles that students, teachers, culture, and community play in the construction of knowledge. This view of knowledge is seen in their critique of, and resistance to, textbooks and materials which limit the possibilities of excellence for all students (Ladson-Billings, 1995b). The conceptions of knowledge developed by teachers who engage in culturally relevant pedagogy are also evident in their actively reshaping classroom curriculum in order to align it with students' needs and experiences (Powell, 1997).

Conceptions of Social Relations

The conceptions of culturally relevant teachers lead them to build and foster empowering relationships with students, families and their communities while maintaining exceptionally high standards for academic learning (Beauboeuf-Lafontant, 1999; Lipman, 1995). Culturally relevant teachers believe that classroom and community relationships should be organized in ways that minimize traditionally competitive, teacher-centered approaches in favor of rich, collaborative, culturally centered learning environments (Ladson-Billings, 1989, 1995b). Deemphasizing academic competition, including peer teaching and decision-making, and promoting environments of "togetherness, unity, community and family" (Sheets, 1995 p. 192) are effective in helping students succeed.

Culturally Relevant Pedagogy in Mathematics Education

Recently, the NCTM Research Committee (2005) addressed the need to view equity not only as an end product of research, but as a lens through which to view reform efforts. The principles of culturally relevant pedagogy can be especially beneficial in this regard. In attempting to address equity concerns, a culturally relevant framework problematizes teaching with respect to achievement outcomes, cultural identity, and social justice. According to Ladson-Billings (1994), "a culturally relevant pedagogy is designed to *problematize* teaching and encourage teachers to ask about the nature of the student–teacher relationship, the curriculum, schooling, and society" (p. 483). Culturally relevant pedagogy holds great promise for mathematics education of Black children. It offers scholars a liberatory framing in the context of current teaching practice and ideology.

The stories of culturally relevant pedagogues in mathematics education illuminate teachers' experiences in framing mathematics instruction in liberatory ways and have helped to articulate how this kind of pedagogy builds on but transforms mathematics reform ideology beyond traditional concerns (Enyedy & Mukhopadhyay, 2007; Gutstein, Lipman, Hernandez, & de los Reyes, 1997; Ladson-Billings, 1997; Leonard & Guha, 2002; Matthews, 2003, 2008). For example, Tate (1995) discussed how one Southwestern middle school mathematics teacher's culturally relevant approach to teaching mathematics promoted collaborative communication and group work, learning through investigation, critical questioning, relevant rich problem-solving, and community action. In a similar way, Nelson-Barber & Estrin (1995) described how specific preferences for modeling and observation in the teaching of Native American students were "harmonious with constructivist notions of learning" (p. 175)—the predominant theory of learning underlying mathematics and science reform. Another important development has been the work of Gutstein et al. (1997) whose working model for the culturally relevant teaching of mathematics is framed around helping teachers to foster three reform connections: (1) connections between informal knowledge and cultural knowledge; (2) fostering critical mathematical thinking in students and the development of "critical approaches to knowledge and the tools they will need to be agents of social change" (p. 709); and (3) utilizing empowerment (versus deficit) orientations towards students and their communities.

Collectively, these studies represent a growing consensus that a culturally relevant pedagogy buoys math reform aims but also points toward a need for greater clarification of the notion of culturally relevant teaching of *mathematics* as it pertains to transforming teacher practice and development.

The remainder of this chapter will consider outcomes for a study conducted in 2001 and highlights the voices of four highly regarded teachers of mathematics in ways that illuminate liberatory, culturally relevant teaching for Black children. Doing so helps to clarify what culturally relevant pedagogy looks (or rather, sounds) like in practice. The study was conducted over the course of two 10-day visits to Bermuda while I was a doctoral student.

Teacher Selection: Community Nomination

I chose to explore the teaching perspectives of four Bermudian teachers using the *collective* case study method. As defined by Stake (2000), collective case study is a collection of *instrumental* case studies where the researcher's primary interests lie not in the cases themselves; rather, the cases serve as opportunities to learn more about a more general phenomenon or aim. That is, the cases are *instrumental* to learning about a bigger picture; in this case, the nature of liberatory pedagogy found in the perspectives of four teachers in Bermuda.

In attempting to learn from, and through, exemplary teachers in Bermuda, a method of teacher identification and selection, commonly employed in several other studies of culturally relevant teachers, called *community nomination* (Ladson-Billings, 1989, 1994; Tate, 1995), was utilized. Through this process, I was able to draw on local knowledge to locate participants. In the spring of 2000, different representatives of the education community with whom I was familiar were asked to nominate "good" middle school teachers who were exemplary in teaching mathematics and could participate in a study about exemplary mathematics teaching for Black children. In particular, I consulted several former teaching colleagues at the middle and high school levels, several principals, an education official, several parents, and community members. The process consisted mainly of informal street conversations, telephone calls, emails, and meetings.

During each of my interactions, I asked the nominators to first suggest the names of good teachers and, secondly, to explain why they felt the teachers were considered good teachers. As expected, the nominators offered varied explanations of their choices. For example, former colleagues who had experience teaching at both the middle and high school levels suggested teachers based on their professional reputations in the teacher community. Suggestions from this category seemed to emanate from "teacher talk" networks on the island (i.e., union meetings, staff rooms, etc.). Several parents also provided insight. Their reasons included what they noted about their children's attitudes towards mathematics, their personal feelings about the teacher, a known record of improvement in their child's performance or attitude, and even hearsay. Extensive conversations with the Ministry of Education's only mathematics education officer, the highest ranking official responsible for implementing mathematics education reform initiatives, were also helpful as she pointed to several persons based on past observations, as well as to informal and formal evaluations.

From the suggestions that were made, one teacher, Ms. Jackson,[1] from Evans Middle School, appeared at the top of the list with several colleagues, parents, and the education official having nominated her. She was often the first name mentioned. Several colleagues also recommended another teacher at her school, Mr. Hampton. I also worked with Mr. Hampton for two years in one of Bermuda's two high schools and was familiar with his reputation as an exemplary mathematics teacher. The education official also vouched for this selection, as did his principal. Two other teachers, Ms. Iris and Ms. Cole, were located at Wade Middle School. Several parents, the principal, as well as the mathematics education officer nominated these two.

Having narrowed the possible names to two schools, each having two of the teachers on the list, the principals of the two schools were then contacted. They corroborated the nominations using their own formal and informal evaluations, as well as standardized student test scores.

The Schools and the Teachers

Wade Middle School

The teachers in the study taught at two schools with very different historical traditions. Before the national push for restructuring, Wade Middle School had been a primary school. Physical modifications to the school were deemed necessary to accommodate its transition into a middle school. Located in the central part of the island, students who attended Wade have often been characterized as coming from "back-of-town (pronounced bak ah town)," a densely populated area in the most populous parish, Pembroke, which includes the capital city of Hamilton. In the minds of many Bermudians, the label back-of-town carries with it connotations of low-income, urban, and at-risk often found in other deficit conversations about Black students. There is also a heritage of great pride that emanates out of the "back-a-town" terminology, where its people have long engaged in struggles for political, economic and social equity. It is also where I grew up. Indeed, many of the residents in Central Pembroke live in harsher economic conditions than the rest of the country.

Evans Middle School

Situated towards the eastern end of the island, away from the city, Evans Middle School was recently converted from one of the more "academic" schools before restructuring, into one of the island's five middle schools. Although the school population is predominantly Black (as is Wade), the school was attended by large numbers of white students before the restructuring of schools. The population of the school became even more predominantly Black as large numbers of white students moved to the private school sector. The faculty was relatively mixed with several white faculty administrators, and board members. Despite having lived and taught in Bermuda for a number of years, this study represented my first "real" visit to the school.

Ms. Iris

Ms. Iris was a Black Bermudian woman in her early 30s whose primary and middle school teaching experience spanned 11 years in Bermuda. Interestingly enough, she had begun her teaching career at the nearby feeder primary school, where she was also educated, before coming to Wade Middle School to teach mathematics. Ms. Iris was educated at one of Bermuda's traditional academic schools where she was, according to her, "counted out" as not likely to succeed. At the time of study, she was serving as a grade-level team supervisor in addition to teaching mathematics at Evans.

Ms. Cole

Ms. Cole was an African American woman in her late 40s who had been teaching mathematics in Bermuda for 15 years. Originally from New York, her American accent was hardly detectable, having taken on somewhat of a Bermudian accent.

Ms. Cole actually began her career in nursing but later turned to teaching, which she maintains was an easy switch for her because she "always enjoyed working with people." She subsequently gained her certification license in junior high school mathematics to go along with a BS degree in elementary education and a Masters in curriculum and teaching.

Ms. Jackson

Ms. Jackson was a Black Bermudian woman in her early 30s who had been teaching mathematics at Evans Middle School for six years and was currently the head of mathematics at the school, supervising six other teachers. She was the youngest of a family of eight and described herself as being spoiled. She portrayed herself as a "hard worker" in a family that believed in a strong work ethic.

Mr. Hampton

The lone male in the study, Mr. Hampton, was in his first year of teaching at Evans and taught mathematics to all grade at the time of the study. Mr. Hampton was an African American in his early 30s who was married to a Bermudian and had been teaching in Bermuda for four out of his six-year teaching career. Upon earning a graduate degree in mathematics education, Mr. Hampton worked for two years as an underwriter before turning to teaching because he "wanted to help."

Interviews and Observations

Three of the teachers were interviewed twice, with each interview lasting approximately one hour. One teacher completed only one interview due to illness. One teacher fell sick and was unable to complete the last interview. In all, seven interviews were conducted. In total, 17 observations were conducted over the course of the study, with most of the teachers observed approximately four times each. Teachers were asked to reflect on the observed lessons and previous interviews.

My initial observations were to familiarize myself with the classroom, school setting, and the teachers' pedagogy. Subsequent observations were interspersed between the interviews. I wanted teachers to talk freely about teaching mathematics in Bermuda, so the initial interviews were loosely structured and included questions concerning teachers' background, philosophy of mathematics teaching, and challenges of teaching mathematics in Bermuda. In the second set of interviews, I posed further questions to the teachers utilizing Ladson-Billings' framework: (a) their conceptions of themselves and their students, (b) their ideas and stances toward knowledge, and curriculum, and (c) perspectives on Bermudian society and the nature of relationships between school and society. A general question on conceptions of themselves as teachers was:

> How do you see your role as teacher in your math class, and in your opinion, what are the most important challenges in ensuring that all students in Bermuda reach excellence in mathematics?

A question focused on conceptions of knowledge posed to one participant was:

> So you have talked about some of the pressures and challenges in teaching Bermudian kids and what they bring to the table. How is it, and I asked you how have you overcome this. How does all of that help or how is that influenced by the curriculum that you teach. What are your feelings about what you have to teach?

An example of a question asking one participant to discuss the relationship of schooling to Bermudian society was:

> I guess what I am asking [of] you is to compare what you just said to society at large. I mean, outside of education is there something that you are experiencing in Bermuda, period. Have you seen conflicts... do you have conflicts in any other aspect of Bermuda society that may influence how students are?

Synthesis and Illumination

In analyzing the data, I have employed what Shank (2001) terms *synthesis* and *illumination*. In contrast to analysis, which seeks to break phenomena into understandable parts, Shank argues that what we really see are facets, or different ways in which the phenomenon is seen. Thus, the researcher attempts to seek out ways in which the phenomenon is seen (rather than reduce its understanding to manageable parts) and then illuminates them for the reader. Illuminating the facets of teachers' perspectives was accomplished in several ways. From the interviews, I searched for ways in which the teachers' perspectives could be seen through the culturally relevant framework. In the "conceptions of self and others" category, I looked for how teachers perceived themselves as mathematics teachers, how they perceived the students they taught, and how they perceived the Bermuda community. Under "conceptions of knowledge," I explored teachers' conceptions about teaching as well as their conceptions of mathematics. I also focused on how teachers organized relationships: student–student, student–teacher, and classroom–community. Further, the observations allowed me to shed even greater light on what the teachers shared with me and helped focus the interviews that followed.

I corroborated what I heard and saw in the course of the study with education officials, teachers, parents of middle school students, and friends in the community. Their comments helped in the illumination process. In this manner, I accessed and affirmed community wisdom in exploring culturally relevant pedagogy.

The Culturally Relevant Nature of Teachers' Perspectives on Teaching Mathematics

The general purpose of this chapter is to explore the pedagogy of four highly regarded teachers in the hope of better understanding how the wisdom-of-practice perspectives of these teachers in Bermuda might shape mathematics reform for Black children. It is important for the reader to recall the spiritual metaphor upon which this chapter is encased, the Negro spiritual, *This Little Light of Mine*. Accordingly, each section that follows includes a declarative statement about culturally relevant mathematics teaching and learning for Black children as seen through the collective voices of the four teachers.

The perspectives of the four teachers represented three powerful ideas about culturally relevant teaching of mathematics for Black Bermudian children: (a) the extended role of the mathematics teacher in the context of racial, community, and cultural identities; (b) creative and critical approaches by teachers to current mathematics curricula; and (c) the centrality of relationship building in the mathematics teaching/learning enterprise. Each of these ideas is preceded by a declarative amplification of these perspectives, followed by actual excerpts and discussion from conversations, which serve to illuminate their ideas as succinctly and powerfully as possible.

Extended Roles of the Mathematics Teacher

Good mathematics teaching requires that teachers see themselves in extended roles, as interconnected with the realities of their students, their racial identities and life struggles. Centered in this connectedness, mathematics is taught for understanding of both concepts and these realities. Teachers believe that all students can learn mathematics with success.

"Everybody Being Able to Get It."

On one occasion, as I entered Ms. Jackson's class, students were involved in a warm-up game involving mental computations with integers. Ms. Jackson would later characterize them as her "low achieving" class. As she began the lesson on solving simple equations, I watched as students shared verbal strategies for solving equations, with Ms. Jackson continually posing questions aimed at getting students to rethink or modify when necessary. The students appeared motivated and engaged.

I thought the lesson went well in that the session represented the kinds of problem-solving focus and reasoning promoted in current reform standards (NCTM, 2000) where students validate their own mathematical thinking and communicate their reasoning in multiple ways. I was genuinely surprised after an ensuing conversation with Ms. Jackson, during which she suggested otherwise. When I asked Ms. Jackson if she thought her lesson was a success, she hesitantly responded:

> I don't think [so]. I think the majority, everybody liking it, everyone enjoying it, everybody being able to get it, that's what I [like to] see. When I see five and six and seven [referring to the number of students], then I know that is not a successful lesson.

Admittedly, Ms. Jackson's answer was not what I had hoped she would say. Yet, she continued, saying, "Because I find that if they did not get it, then you have to go over it again, so at least to try to grab more, try to grab them, to understand." I remembered thinking that she was particularly hard on herself in this regard, but I also recalled Ms. Jackson's non-chalant attitude toward her status as an exemplary teacher. It was only subsequent to our conversation, that I learned from her principal that her class's achievement outcomes consistently surpassed the national test averages in mathematics.

It was the second part of her statement, which helped to clarify her perspective on teaching mathematics for understanding—that *all* students should "get it" and that she could "grab" it from them. In this way she echoed reform ideas (NCTM, 2000) of teaching mathematics for understanding (i.e., NCTM Teaching Principle) and that all students can learn mathematics (i.e., Equity Principle) but in a way where equity becomes a precondition for establishing excellence in teaching.

Further, Ms. Jackson's insistence on grabbing was similar to that expressed in the stories of other culturally relevant teachers, where teaching is viewed as a mining endeavor (Ladson-Billings, 1994). In this manner, all students possess the capacity for learning challenging mathematics and can do so when artfully and eclectically engaged by teachers.

Ms. Jackson's powerful views on "teaching by grabbing" were also echoed by Ms. Iris:

> What I learned the other day is not to just give a child back a test for corrections. I find it more successful sitting down with them and pulling it out of them and I get a lot more out of them.

She said this after I had visited one of her classes where she was going over corrections to a test in which several of her students did not perform well.

You Have to "Put Something into It!"

Another aspect of my conversations with the teachers revealed how "good" teachers might navigate the teaching of mathematics for students with particularly difficult backgrounds. It was not surprising that teachers at Wade, located in central Pembroke, articulated much harsher opinions regarding students' circumstances and backgrounds than did teachers at Evans. Despite expressing great concern and care for students, as Mr. Hampton and Ms. Iris did, none of the teachers accepted students' circumstances as excuses for failure. On the contrary, each demanded that students rise above difficulties by being personally accountable. This was especially true for the teachers at Wade who articulated working with greater numbers of students with "baggage." This was evidenced by Ms. Iris's comments:

Ms. I: Well, you ask any of my students, my first expectation is you always give 110%, okay? I tell them "Once you step down and refuse to work, I can't work with you. So take a seat at the back and knock yourself out until you are ready to open back up and I can help you."

I: Why is that?

Ms. I: Because these kids come with a lot of baggage. And I never make excuses for them. I don't say what society has dealt to them is why you can't go home and do your homework . . . I don't make excuses for them, but I know it is there. It is a reality to them, you know. They don't have any parents at home [or] they are working two jobs and all that stuff.

I understood more about the expectations of the teachers in the face of their students' realities after talking with Ms. Jackson. Ms. Jackson's expectations for her students mirror what was expected as she was growing up. Therefore, I was not surprised by her response when I asked her about her expectations from her students in light of some of the personal, home, and societal challenges they faced. Ms. Jackson responded: "[I expect] that they've put something into it, you know. That they've learned something, you know. That they've learned something." The emphasis is on personal contribution and accountability as a precondition for class membership.

Common equity-oriented language espouses the idea of high expectations and support as critical to mathematics success. In practice, teachers often articulate high expectations but are left wondering about the kinds of scaffolding to move *expectations* towards *actualization*. What often transpires is dissonance between the two with the latter being discussed as difficult to achieve due to deficits in student behavior, parental support, etc. What Ms. Jackson intimates is the *connection* between high expectations, classroom management, and mathematics learning by attaching to high expectations a personal condition for engagement as central to the learning enterprise.

Ms. Iris further elaborated on how one might attempt to bridge this potential dissonance as she saw students' circumstances as strengths rather than deficits:

Ms. I: The funny thing is, these kids are awesome problem solvers. Awesome. They may not have the fancy formula to go along with it and all of that but they can tear apart some problems, which is good because the Terra Nova [standardized assessments] requires them to do a process and are not just interested in end results.

I: What makes you realize that they are awesome problem solvers?

Ms. I: Because they are street smart.

In recognizing students' difficulties from their backgrounds as opportunities for actualization rather than deficits, Ms. Iris's focus on strengths represents the kind of empowered orientations called for in culturally relevant mathematics teaching (e.g., Gutstein, Lipman, Hernandez, & de los Reyes, 1997).

Critical and Creative Stances Toward Mathematics Curriculum

Good mathematics teaching requires that teachers must often employ both creative and critical stances toward mathematics curriculum. In doing so, teachers seek to incorporate students' experiences; view mathematics teaching and learning as dynamic, student and community centered; and challenge limitations of problematic curriculum issues.

"I Want You to Come in This Room and Teach It!"

All four teachers echoed a view of learning mathematics as a student-*generated* endeavor. They emphasized this view from different vantage points but, nevertheless, expressed ideas that supported students constructing knowledge for themselves, the importance of explaining their mathematical thinking, and utilizing activities which promote *doing* mathematics. I note one comment from Ms. Jackson that illustrated her ideas about students' contributions to knowledge-making:

> *I:* So are you saying that the knowledge doesn't always come from you?
> *Ms. J:* No! It doesn't. Not at all! . . . From me doing that scenario [reflecting classroom episode] . . . it shows me some things I don't even mention, but yet they're asking it.

Ms. Jackson described instances where students took on the shared role of researchers during teaching. She commented: "Like the research they do. 'Like, okay this is your topic. I want you to research that topic and I want you to come in this room and teach it.' And the ideas they come up with are amazing." Additionally, Ms. Cole stressed the need for students to be able to explain and justify their understanding by saying:

> I like for them to be able to explain in their own words what they are learning or what the concept is, you know. So I have an understanding that they know what they are talking about and they understand what they are doing.

Ms. Cole also stressed the importance of doing and understanding mathematics versus more traditional views of teaching mathematics by transmission. When asked how learning took place, she stated:

> I am not going to say you have to pile a whole lot of work on them, give them 50 questions just to understand that A plus B equals C. No, you do a few of one kind and a few of another, but they learn by doing, not just by lecturing. Or they work on a few examples themselves.

The importance of fostering critical thinking in teaching mathematics was evident in how Ms. Iris responded to my question on defining "mathematics." She replied:

> Pure critical thinking whether it is number-related [or something else] it still boils down to being able to make the better choice of a given situation and that could be in written form or represented numerically. Looking at that is fine but what does that tell you? Do you add or subtract?

The teacher comments and insights presented above revealed consistency with reform ideas in the sense of fostering critical mathematical thinking and a focus on doing mathematics. The tone for these teachers was emphatic that these are necessary experiences for all students.

"To Hell with the Curriculum!"

Beyond their talk and perspectives on mathematics learning, all of the teachers had strong, even conflicting concerns about national mathematics curriculum. Without exception, the teachers talked at length about their concerns and challenges in covering a curriculum they described as "intense," "wordy," "too much," or "not good." In response to sweeping changes and modifications that have taken place concerning curriculum, Ms. Jackson reflected the collective stance of the teachers when she said, "Let's just work with what we have," feeling that reform would involve more than mere curricula changes. Similarly, I encountered several critical and creative approaches to meeting the challenges of curriculum during my interviews with teachers. The strongest critical stances came from Ms. Jackson, the experienced head of the department:

> Oh, I only do what I can do and if it is not mastered I'll make sure that they do know it. Now, not every student will get it but, I am a person that . . . any curriculum . . . to hell with the curriculum . . . this is what we are going to do. And that is what I think Bermudian teachers fail to do.

Ms. Cole echoed these pacing challenges—making choices between coverage versus mastery—but also preferred to focus on excellence in learning:

> It's not a problem for me, in the fact that, what the children learn, when they learn it, they learn it well. It is just that they don't always get everything that's supposedly done in a given year, and of course end up moving to the next year.

Ms. Iris described a creative approach for addressing the challenges:

> I have become very creative because there is a lot of overlapping in the document itself. So when I am looking at addition or decimals and fractions with same denominator at the same time, because you are still doing the same thing—you're adding, right? And you just . . . do perimeter . . . okay, so you become very creative when you start doing a lot of this.

What is amazing about Ms. Iris's response is that she later claimed that 75 out of the 102 students in the year group she taught at the time were identified with special education needs, and that she was operating without a learning support teacher, who left earlier in the school year. I was unable to verify the accuracy of Ms. Iris's claim.

I did not realize until I had finished the interviewing how awkward it might have seemed for teachers to talk about incorporating the experiences of Bermudian students into their mathematics teaching. For Ms. Jackson, it just seemed like the natural thing to do. I remember thinking that, because of their expressed connectedness and commitment to the island, they might have considered doing so as part of a natural process, and not something to be explicit about. Nevertheless, after several roundabout attempts by me to discuss it, Ms. Jackson talked about incorporating student experiences in order to foster academic excellence. She referred to the eclectic manner in which this takes place:

> I relate everything that we basically do. Before I start a topic, I always relate it to a real-life situation. Even if I do problem-solving questions and stuff like that, I relate it to a situation that is happening here, so they can actually see the connection. We do newspaper work . . . that's something else that we do, where we take the newspaper and we look for statistics and stuff like that . . . and we decipher information, so they're learning mathematics, but they are learning in the context of Bermuda.

"Everything's Money!"

What is interesting is that none of the teachers revealed anything significant in their teacher preparation that focused on relating mathematics teaching to the experiences of Bermudian students. Yet, they all revealed a rather robust perspective on the nature of the mathematics they taught. For them, mathematics was more than mere subject matter—it was about life itself. Cognizant of this, the teachers were adamant about the need to incorporate some political and economic realities into their mathematics teaching. "I am a person who always talks about money," stressed Ms. Jackson. "Everything's money," she repeated making sure I noted that point. In a similar way, Ms. Cole discussed a project that incorporated a money focus with help from the local community. She commented, "One year we did a project on the stock market. Not saying that I had any money to invest. But you know, just expose them to different things." For her the use of money was also to help better facilitate the teaching of the lesson. She added, "Well at the time we were working with fractions and decimals and that was just an easy way."

A recent project assigned by Mr. Hampton involved students tackling some of the current issues in one of Bermuda's main industries, tourism. He explained: "We just finished a project on tourism, actually, and what we were looking at is why tourism is having the amount of trouble it is having and what can we do to improve it." In earlier comments, he offered his rationale for believing that teaching should tap into the political and economic realities of Bermudian students which, itself, brought new challenges:

> Well I think that being that it is a small location, there is definitely a stronger sense of the politics on the island. They definitely come to the classroom knowing what's happening and knowing that certain things are not equitable.

In my conversations with education officials, I became aware of a national initiative to improve the literacy of public school students. In addition to seeking the integration of mathematics curriculum with national literacy goals, a focus on literacy was a mandatory part of school policy at Evans. Both Ms. Cole and Ms. Jackson talked about incorporating these foci into the mathematics classroom. Ms. Jackson explained:

Ms. J: I find Bermudian students are very weak when it comes to [pauses and trails off] . . . and I am [linking] Math to English when it comes to reading, and just that reading alone allows them not to comprehend [pause] properly, you know what I mean. Because somebody may read a passage and somebody else reads the passage differently. Even though it is the same concept, but you can see the difference . . . [pause] Like, "Oh, but you didn't stress that."

I: What do you get them to read . . . you mean mathematics problems?

Ms. J: Mathematics problems. Textbooks . . . get them used to seeing words that are [pause] uh [pause] mathematically related.

In general, there was a tendency among the teachers to not only talk about class-room practice, but to frame mathematics teaching in the context of a national understanding of Bermudian children, their needs, and communities. This was most evident in the conversations with Ms. Jackson. In this regard, her talking about mathematics always deferred to a broader societal conversation.

Communities of Relationships in the Mathematics Classroom

Exemplary mathematics teaching is committed to organizing classrooms and instruction in ways that stress relevance, by fostering empowering relationships with students. The mathematics classroom is a place where larger community and societal goals are achieved.

"You Have to Relate!"

In speaking to how mathematics classrooms are organized, the teachers often talked about the importance of structuring environments that are relevant for Bermudian students. One particular aspect of relevance that stood out in my con-versations with several of the teachers centered on the extent of teacher authority. Ms. Jackson understood her authority, but also recognized that the authority role would have to be modified. She commented:

You have to relate and you have to put yourself on a level . . . you know . . . with them . . . Like you are on that same level and you are learning together. They know you already know, but let's take it from the very beginning . . . Just imag-ine we [teachers] don't know this information . . . You have to . . . you have to do things . . . you have to create an environment that's not strict.

Even Mr. Hampton, a foreign teacher and admittedly more authoritarian in his view of the teacher role, realized that a more effective approach for teaching Bermudian students required a more non-traditional approach to the role of the teacher:

Each first year that I started in a new school . . . each first year I started at Howard and at Evans, it was the same problem that I came in from a strong authoritar-ian type of role, and they all run away from it. The next year at Howard, I was more relaxed, I kind of knew the feel of the kids and they could accept me more because I think the atmosphere here is much more "laid back". . . It is a very fine line when you have the discipline but you also have to know that they need some leeway, and that seems to be found in my first year in each of the different schools here in Bermuda—that the authoritarian role does not work.

Mr. Hampton, although he was relatively new to the school and the Bermuda community, viewed himself as a role model—a "Black male figure"—for the students in his class. He talked of his desire for "getting to the students" through his personal life:

> Through their personal life, through their personal ritual actions, and having them understand who I am, and being I can relate to them as a younger Black American, served much better. A lot of the music that they listened to, I listened to, so we could relate on that level.

This interconnectedness with students represented a common thread among the teachers as they shared much of their own history. For example, Ms. Iris talked of her interest in the welfare of students when she referred to her own school experiences. She reflected: "That is why I am more of a child advocate and more sensitive because I see kids here and I am like, 'don't give up on them now' because if someone gave up on me you know, heavens!" In talking of her own life, I recalled how she had earlier revealed that she was classified as a low achiever, largely because of her behavior and did not do well in high school, despite attending one of Bermuda's premier academic high schools.

The idea of relating not only involved immediate classroom relationships, but also extended to include other people and contexts that impact students' futures. There were some practical realities revealed by the teachers concerning the classroom environment. For example, Ms. Jackson revealed her rationale for group and individual work in the classroom:

Ms. J: Group work is very, very important. But then we have to understand, and, I have them understand: "Now it's time for an independent exercise. Now, I want to see how much you know." You and your partner got together, you discussed it, everybody got that information, now let's see how much you [emphasized] know." And they know . . . after that group [work], it's always independent [work].

I: So you are saying they need to be able to do things on their own. Why?

Ms. J: Because we live in a world where you have to, you have to know how to work with people . . . but you also live in a world that [pause] you have to do quite a few things by yourself, you know, and in order to do that you have to have a lot of knowledge in a lot of areas.

The focus on the mathematics classroom as a community rather than a collection of individuals is another reform idea which reflects a shift away from traditional teaching (NCTM, 1991, 2000). Here, Ms. Jackson recognizes this shift but also holds on to what she views as an essential rationale for student competence as individuals. Her rationale reflects a somber acknowledgement of the workplace realities for Bermudian children. So, in addition to group learning, she stresses individual accountability.

The voices of the teachers represent views toward mathematics that, at their best, extend teacher roles to include interconnectedness, understanding, and engagement of student identities; and require active resistance, competence, and creativity regarding mathematics curriculum. Represented here, also, are views about the mathematics classroom as a site where the practice of relating content while fostering empowered social interactions is central to instructional planning and structure. As Ladson-Billings (1995) maintains, ". . . a culturally relevant pedagogy is designed to problematize teaching and encourage teachers to ask about the nature of the student-teacher relationship, the curriculum, schooling, and society" (p. 483).

Conclusion: Entering Voices of Cultural Relevancy Into Mathematics Reform Conversation

Drawing on the wisdom-of-practice of the teachers in this study has led to several important considerations for conversations on the mathematics excellence of Black children in Bermuda and elsewhere in the Diaspora. In this section, I wish to expound on these considerations in order to underscore what I believe is the potential of the teachers' perspectives to "witness" to conventional conversations on mathematics teaching and learning.

The first consideration represents a discussion of the extent to which the perspectives of these teachers are no different from the conventional conversations currently taking place in mathematics education reform. Second, in line with theme of this book, how does the wisdom of the teachers presented here contribute to our understanding of mathematics teaching and learning in the context of the liberation of Black children?

Considered together, and amplified, these perspectives are presented in Figure 3.2. Portraying them as amplified messages exemplifying culturally relevant

---

Extended Roles of the Mathematics Teacher

Good mathematics teaching requires that teachers see themselves in extended roles, as interconnected with the realities of their students, their racial identities and life struggles. Centered in this connectedness, mathematics is taught for understanding of both concepts and these realities. Teachers believe that all students can learn mathematics with success.

Critical and Creative Stances Toward Mathematics Curriculum

Good mathematics teaching requires that teachers must often employ both creative and critical stances toward mathematics curriculum. In doing so, teachers seek to incorporate students' experiences; view mathematics teaching and learning as dynamic, student and community centered; and challenge limitations of problematic curriculum issues.

Mathematics Communities of Relationships

Exemplary mathematics teaching is committed to organizing classrooms and instruction in ways that stress relevance, by fostering empowering relationships with students. The mathematics classroom is a place where larger community and societal goals are achieved.

Figure 3.2 Amplified messages for the culturally relevant teaching of mathematics.

mathematics teaching is critical as it draws on the function of the Negro spiritual to utilize the wisdom of these teachers to "witness," or move others to engage in similar kinds of conversations. The messages also serve a dual function of not only representing what might have been seen and heard, but also what *should be* with regard to the mathematics excellence and liberation for Black Bermudian children and children elsewhere in the Diaspora.

Amplified Messages for Culturally Relevant Mathematics Teaching

The first message (Extended Roles of the Mathematics Teacher) is important because it asks teachers to consider the orientations that they possess toward Black children. This is also necessary to move beyond talk of parent and community deficits or discussions of low teacher expectations. The message here serves a clarifying role. An important way this was brought to light was in the ways teachers engaged challenging aspects of students' backgrounds. None of the teachers sought to ignore the challenges faced by Bermudian students, in and out of school. Rather, they were decidedly deliberate, often unorthodox and unapologetic, in the very direct ways in which they engaged students' personal lives as a central part of their pedagogy. The teachers suggested that nothing short of active, deliberate engagement with students and community, and redefining their challenges as strengths, will suffice. Current equity ideology for reformers advocates high expectations, strong support, and understanding students' diverse needs (NCTM, 2000). As such, current equity conversation is vague, even unhelpful, in addressing the broader cultural and societal aspirations of students and their communities, as practitioners are left to interpret just what this means (Matthews, 2005). As discussed earlier in this chapter, fundamental faulty notions about Black children and their communities have undermined the impact of mathematics reform initiatives.

The second message (see Figure 3.2) captures the practical difficulties experienced while encountering and resisting the hegemony of school mathematics curriculum. I refer to these as *challenges* in Matthews (2008); others (Enyedy & Mukhopadhyay, 2007) have labeled them as *tensions*. A key challenge for each of the teachers involved getting through a mathematics curriculum they believed to be overloaded and unforgiving (in terms of pace) for Bermudian children. For the teachers, their approaches to the official mathematics curriculum reflected an attitude of resistance, and, in at least one view, resulted in deliberate counteraction in framing instruction so that students had greater opportunities to succeed.

Current professional development experiences in most contexts are more focused on helping teachers understand and implement mathematics reform than on assisting teachers in developing meaningful counteraction when district reform goals clash with their liberatory notions of student development. In doing so, mathematics educators may, in fact, serve as agents of conformity and be less likely to move in solidarity with movements of resistance that can benefit Black children.

The mathematics classroom as a site for liberatory action is in itself a very different conversation from those that reformers routinely suggest. As articulated in the third message, and for the teachers in this study, this meant a determined focus on

"relating" in term of content, building relationships, and focusing on empowerment. When reflected back onto the literature, these actions are less liberatory when
measured against a major element of culturally relevant pedagogy, critical consciousness. That is, how teachers challenged inequitable societal structures through
the teaching of mathematics was hard to assess. This difficulty in articulating critical notions of their work is also consistent with previous examination of culturally
relevant teaching of mathematics (see Enyedy & Mukhopadhyay, 2007; Leonard &
Guha, 2002; Matthews, 2003).

It should be cautioned against viewing these amplified messages as exhaustive or
mutually exclusive, and therefore taken as a representative of what culturally relevant mathematics teaching might look like for all students, or in all contexts. There
is no need to arrive at some generalizable truth about culturally relevant pedagogy
or mathematics teaching in the context of liberation. Such expectations about generalizability are not consistent with the research methodology employed here nor
do they do justice to the complexity of utilizing pedagogy of this kind in varying
contexts.

Moving Conversations Toward Liberation

The key endeavor here has been to illuminate the conversation that occurs when
research is framed in such a way that allows for mathematics teaching to be viewed
beyond its privileging of content to include broader societal and critical perspectives which are more relevant to the outcomes of Black children. It was also clear
how difficult it is to capture this conversation. In the purest sense of what has been
argued as culturally relevant, culturally relevant pedagogy represents liberatory
pedagogy. Drawn from a tradition of critical theory and oppositional pedagogy,
culturally relevant pedagogy allows us to talk about good mathematics teaching to
the extent that it also connects with the liberatory aspirations of students and communities. In talking about themselves, their students, the sociopolitical context of
Bermuda, and teaching and learning mathematics, the teachers in this study have
helped us to see this.

Perhaps what can be taken from this study has as much to do with the nature of
liberatory conversations, as it has to do with the *production* of such conversations.
They might be seen as framing points from which educators might approach professional development in mathematics teaching, particularly where equity aims are
deeply imbedded into school and district missions. In my current experiences with
practicing teachers, I have come to appreciate the importance of helping teachers
grow through the examination of daily teaching dilemmas arising through the
teaching of mathematics.

The power of the Negro spiritual rests in the belief that persistent, powerful discourse can work effectively to support change and hope in the most challenging of
circumstances. This has always been true in the liberation struggles of Blacks in the
Diaspora. That is, what you sing about and, in this sense, talk about, can work to
inform and shape the future. The conversations illuminated and amplified in this
chapter offer ways of talking about mathematics that need not ignore the pressing
social, political, and cultural realities of our current day. If embraced, movements

of reform that build from the wisdom of liberatory pedagogy can actively support these aspirations.

Notes

1 All names of teachers and schools are pseudonyms.

References

Airini, C. (1998). What is good teaching? Lessons from Maori pedagogy. Paper presented at the Annual Conference of the New Zealand Association for Research in Education (Dunedin, New Zealand, December 1998).

Ajose, S.A. (1995). Mathematics education research on minorities from 1984 to 1994: Focus on African American Students. Paper presented at the Annual Meeting of the North American Chapter of the International Group for the Psychology of Mathematics Education (17th, Columbus, OH, October 21–24, 1995). 81.

Allexsaht-Snider, M. & Hart, L.E. (2001). "Mathematics for all": How do we get there? *Theory Into Practice, 40*(2), 93–101.

Anderson, B.J. (1990). Minorities and mathematics: The new frontier and challenges of the nineties. *Journal of Negro Education, 59*(3), 260–272.

Ball, D.L. (1993). Subject matter knowledge and pedagogical content knowledge: Prospective secondary teachers and the function concept. *Journal for Research in Mathematics Education, 24*(2), 94–116.

Beauboeuf, T.M. (1999). "Politicized mothering": Evidence of a relational and extended self-concept among culturally relevant women educators. Paper presented at the Annual Meeting of the American Educational Research Association (Montreal, Quebec, Canada, April 19–23, 1999).

Beauboeuf-Lafontant, T. (1999). A movement against and beyond boundaries: "Politically relevant teaching" among African American teachers. *Teachers College Record, 100*(4), 702–723.

Campbell, J.R., Voelkl, K., & Donahue, P. (1997). *NAEP 1996 trends in academic progress.* Washington, DC: National Center for Education Statistics, U.S. Department of Education.

Carpenter, T.P., Fennema, E., Peterson, P.I., & Carey, D.A. (1988). Teachers' pedagogical content knowledge of students' problem-solving in elementary arithmetic. *Journal for Research in Mathematics Education, 19*(5), 385–401.

Department of Statistics. (2007). *Facts and figures 2007.* Hamilton, Bermuda: The Cabinet Office, Government of Bermuda.

Enyedy, N. & Mukhopadhyay, S. (2007). They don't show nothing I didn't know: Emergent tensions between culturally relevant pedagogy and mathematics pedagogy. *The Journal of the Learning Sciences, 16*(2), 139–174.

Enyedy, N., Mukhopadhyay, S., & Danish, J. (2006). At the intersection of statistics and culturally relevant pedagogy: Potential and potential challenges of learning statistics through social activism. Paper presented at the International Conference on the Teaching of Statistics (Salvador, Bahia, Brazil, July 2–7, 2006).

Even, R. (1993). Subject-matter knowledge and pedagogical content knowledge: Prospective secondary teachers and the function concept. *Journal for Research in Mathematics Education, 24,* 94–116.

Gay, G. (2000). *Culturally responsive teaching: Theory, research and practice.* New York: Teachers College Press.

Griffith, J.B. (1990). Developing more minority mathematicians and scientists: A new approach. *Journal of Negro Education, 59*(3), 424–438.

Gutiérrez, R. (2002). Enabling the practice of mathematics teachers in context: Toward a new equity research agenda. *Mathematical Thinking and Learning, 4*(2&3), 145–187.

Gutstein, E., Lipman, P., Hernandez, P., & de los Reyes, R. (1997). Culturally relevant mathematics teaching in a Mexican American context. *Journal for Research in Mathematics Education, 28*(6), 709–737.

Johnson, A. (2004, June 15). Bridging the education gap. *The Royal Gazette [Online edition]* Retrieved September 1, 2008, from http://www.royalgazette.com/siftology.royalgazette/Article/article.jsp?articleId=7d4678e3003000b&sectionId=60

Ladson-Billings, G. (1989). A Tale of two teachers: Exemplars of successful pedagogy for Black students. Paper presented at the Educational Equality Project Colloquium "Celebrating Diversity: Knowledge, Teachers, and Teaching" (New York, NY, May 4–5, 1989).

Ladson-Billings, G. (1992). Liberatory consequences of literacy: A case of culturally relevant instruction for African American students. *Journal of Negro Education, 61*(3), 378–391.

Ladson-Billings, G. (1994). *The Dreamkeepers: Successful teachers of African American children.* San Francisco: Jossey-Bass, Inc.

Ladson-Billings, G. (1995a). But that's just good teaching! The case for culturally relevant pedagogy. *Theory Into Practice, 34*(3), 159–165.

Ladson-Billings, G. (1995b). Toward a theory of culturally relevant pedagogy. *American Educational Research Journal, 32*(3), 465–491.

Ladson-Billings, G. (1997). It doesn't add up: African American students' mathematics achievement. *Journal for Research in Mathematics Education, 28*(6), 697–708.

Leonard, J. & Guha, S. (2002). Creating cultural relevance in teaching and learning mathematics. *Teaching Children Mathematics, 9*(2), 114.

Lipman, P. (1995). "Bringing out the best in them": The contribution of culturally relevant teachers to education. *Theory Into Practice, 34*(3), 203–208.

Lipman, P. (1996). The missing voice of culturally relevant teachers in school restructuring. *Urban Review, 28*(1), 41–62.

Maiga, H.O. (1995). Bridging classroom, curriculum, and community: The GAO School Museum. *Theory Into Practice, 34*(3), 209–215.

Matthews, L.E. (2001). A selected analysis of mathematics assessment data in Bermuda public schools, 1992–2000. Unpublished report prepared for the Ministry of Education.

Matthews, L.E. (2003). Babies overboard! The complexities of incorporating culturally relevant teaching into mathematics instruction. *Educational Studies in Mathematics, 53*(1), 61–82.

Matthews, L.E. (2005). Towards design of clarifying equity messages in mathematics reform. *The High School Journal, 88*, 46–58.

Matthews, L.E. (2008). Lessons in "letting go": Exploring constraints on the culturally relevant teaching of mathematics in Bermuda. *Diaspora, Indigenous, and Minoritiy Education (DIME), 2*(2), 115–134.

Ministry of Education. (1993). *Ministry of Education Restructuring Implementation Plan (Section 100.1).* Hamilton, Bermuda: Ministry of Education.

National Council of Teachers of Mathematics (NCTM). (1991). *Professional standards for teaching mathematics.* Reston, VA: Author.

National Council of Teachers of Mathematics (NCTM). (2000). *Principles and standards for school mathematics.* Reston, VA: Author.

NCTM Research Committee. (2005). Equity in school mathematics education: How can research contribute? *Journal for Research in Mathematics Education, 36*(2), 92–100.

Nelson-Barber, S. & Estrin, E.T. (1995). Bringing Native American perspectives to mathematics and science teaching. *Theory Into Practice, 34*(3), 174–185.

Nieto, S. (1999). *The light in their eyes: creating multicultural learning communities.* New York: Teachers College Press.

O'Kelly-Lynch, R. (2007a, May 8). Public education has turned into a political football, says expert *The Royal Gazette.* Retrieved December 17, 2007, from http://www.royalgazette.com/siftology.royalgazette/Article/article.jsp?sectionId=60&articleId=7d7523330030005

O'Kelly-Lynch, R. (2007b, May 4). The ten point plan to improve our public schools. *The Royal Gazette.* Retrieved December 17, 2007, from http://www.royalgazette.com/siftology.royalgazette/Article/article.jsp?sectionId=60&articleId=7d7523330030005

Powell, R. (1997). Then the beauty emerges: A longitudinal case study of culturally relevant teaching. *Teaching and Teacher Education, 13*(5), 467–484.

Shank, G.D. (2001). *Qualitative research: A personal skills approach.* Upper Saddle River, New Jersey: Pearson Education.

Sheets, R.H. (1995). From remedial to gifted: Effects of culturally centered pedagogy. *Theory Into Practice, 34*(3), 186–193.

Shulman, L.S. (2004). Knowledge and teaching: Foundations of the new reform. In S.M. Wilson (Ed.), *The wisdom of practice: Essays on teaching, learning, and learning to teach/Lee S. Shulman* (pp. 219–250). San Francisco: Jossey-Bass.

Stake, R.E. (2000). Case Studies. In N.K. Denzin & Y. S.Lincoln (Eds.), *Handbook of qualitative research* (2nd ed.). Thousand Oaks: Sage Publications, Inc.

Strangeways, S. (2007a, May 4). Education's failing grade. *The Royal Gazette [electronic version].* Retrieved December 17, 2007, from http://www.royalgazette.com/siftology.royalgazette/Article/article.jsp?sectionId=60&articleId=7d7520d300300ab

Strangeways, S. (2007b, May 4). "Teachers did not come out unscathed." *The Royal Gazette [electronic edition].* Retrieved December 17, 2007, from http://www.royalgazette.com/siftology.royalgazette/Article/article.jsp?sectionId=60&articleId=7d7523330030005

Tate, W.F. (1995). Returning to the root: A culturally relevant approach to mathematics pedagogy. *Theory Into Practice, 34*(3), 166–173.

Tate, W.F. (1997). Race-ethnicity, SES, gender, and language proficiency trends in mathematics education: An update. *Journal for Research in Mathematics Education, 28*(6), 652–679.

Trueba, H.T. (1993). From failure to success: The roles of culture and cultural conflict in the academic achievement of Chicano students. Chapter 6. *In Chicano School Failure and Success: Research and Policy Agendas for the 1990s.* (ERIC Document Reproduction Service No. ED 182 465). Retrieved January 15, 2008 from http://eric.ed.gov/ERICDocs/data/ericdocs2sql/content_storage_01/0000019b/80/14/2d/b3.pdf.

Zurawsky, C. (2004). *Closing the gap: High achievement for students of color* (Vol. 2). Washington, DC: American Educational Research Association.

4 Instructional Strategies and Dispositions of Teachers Who Help African American Students Gain Conceptual Understanding

Carol E. Malloy

No challenge has been more daunting than that of improving academic achievement of African American students. Burdened with a history that includes the denial of education, separate and unequal education, and relegation to unsafe, substandard inner-city schools, the quest for quality education remains an elusive dream for the African American community. However, it does remain a dream—perhaps the most powerful for the people of African descent in this nation. (Gloria Ladson-Billings, 1994, p. ix)

Introduction

Motivated by the lack of empirical research about how African American students who become proficient in mathematics have been taught, my purpose in this chapter is to present the instructional strategies and dispositions of teachers who helped African American middle school students gain conceptual understanding in mathematics. Before presenting data on these teachers, I feel compelled to share a brief case that represents what happens to many African American students in mathematics classrooms. I chose this case because it does not represent a student who continually struggled to understand mathematics or who was in a lower track mathematics class; it presents what happened to a student in a ninth-grade honors geometry class.

One of my student teachers had been a participant observer in her mentor teacher's classes for six hours a week for three months. On this day, she was teaching a trial lesson prior to student teaching on determining when angles formed by two lines cut by a transversal are congruent. Her mentor teacher and I were observing her lesson. She asked her students to work in groups of two or three to complete an activity that would help them discover that select pairs of angles formed by parallel lines have the same measure. Standing in the front of the room, she watched her students work on the activity, but did not move around the room to observe student progress. Because I did not want to instruct her in front of her class, I walked around looking at student work to encourage appropriate behavior. Then she began walking around the classroom to check her students' progress. Of the 17 students in the class, one was African American, one was mixed race, two were Asian, and 13 were Caucasian. Only one student in the class did not appear to have a group of students working with him, the African American student. When I asked him where his group members were, he pointed to the two boys sitting in front of him. Neither of the boys in his group nor the teacher interacted with him during the class period. He also chose not to interact with the two boys in his group. Therefore, I asked the student leading questions to help him complete the activity. He smiled and said thank you.

In the reflection period after the lesson, I asked both my student and the mentor teacher about the African American student who worked alone. They both told me that he was not at the same level as the rest of the students in the class. I was disheartened. Here was a ninth-grade African American boy in an honors geometry class that was left to languish because he was seen as not being at the level of the rest of the class. His two teachers had contributed to his being *invisible* in their mathematics classroom. I quickly pointed out that the other students were working together, supporting each other as they tried to complete the activity. I explained that it was understandable that he was not at the level of the other students, since he had no group to interact with and they, as teachers, did not approach him to support his learning. Only then did they realize what had occurred. They were shocked and embarrassed because they had allowed their preconceived notions about his capacity to learn, unintentionally or even intentionally, isolate this young man from the class and learning.

The mentor teacher and student teacher both were aware and thought that they believed in educating all students in their classroom. As evidenced from the activity used in the lesson, they were knowledgeable about the power of constructivist theories on learning in mathematics classrooms. Lacking was knowledge of how their instructional decisions could impact individual students, causing them to fail to comprehend vital mathematics and to become *invisible* as mathematics learners.

Because many African American students are invisible in mathematics classrooms, evidenced in their lack of opportunity to learn, in this chapter I intend to describe instructional strategies and dispositions of teachers who have reversed the trend of African American students receiving less than adequate instruction in mathematics. The question guiding this investigation is: What are the instructional strategies and dispositions of teachers who help African American middle grades students gain conceptual understanding in mathematics? I accomplish this through a secondary analysis of data (observation narratives, teacher interviews, quantitative scores from an observation protocol, and quantitative scores from surveys of student perceptions of teacher instruction) collected as a part of a three-year longitudinal study, *Mathematics Identity Development and Learning* (MIDDLE).

The purpose of MIDDLE was to examine the ways in which mathematics reform—defined as a teacher's use of instructional practices and curricular materials that are aligned with the NCTM *Curriculum and Teaching Standards* (1989, 1991) and the *Principles and Standards for School Mathematics* (2000)—shapes students' development as *knowers* and *learners* of mathematics during the middle grades years. In particular, the study documented changes in students' learning during the middle grades years as well as the processes by which those changes occur. It focused on several important aspects of students' mathematical development with a particular interest in students' success in mathematics as assessed by standardized achievement tests and grades. However, this study went beyond traditional measures of achievement to examine students' conceptual understanding of mathematics.

Perspectives

Instructional practices of teachers are recognized as important mediators of student learning (Gutiérrez, 2000; Miller & Hudson, 2007; Wenglinsky, 2004). This premise does not exclude the influence of society, self, family, or other forces in students' mathematical development. Even considering students' backgrounds, the learning experiences mathematics teachers offer have a direct impact on students' understanding of mathematics, their ability to solve problems (Boaler, 1998), and their confidence in, and disposition toward, their personal mathematics learning (Grouws & Lembke, 1996). The argument put forth in this chapter uses two perspectives that I believe are important in the learning of African American students in mathematics making them visible in the classroom. The first is that the cognitive development of African American students is supported by the use of instructional strategies grounded in learning preferences of African Americans. The second is that students' opportunities to learn mathematics should be tied to their cultural experiences and social justice in their communities.

Instructional Strategies and Dispositions

The broader spectrum of early literature on the learning of African American students reveals important characteristics of successful teachers which include both instructional strategies and dispositions (Delpit, 1995; Gay, 2000; Hooks, 1994; Irvine, 1992; Ladson-Billings, 1994). Additionally, the research on learning preferences from the late twentieth century had the goal of aligning instruction to learning processes.

Learning processes that support African American students' mathematics learning based on their preferences have been identified in learning preferences literatures (Malloy & Malloy, 1998; Malloy, 1997). Students should be allowed to focus on the whole (Dance, 1997; Willis, 1992), use improvisational intuitive thinking (Hale-Benson, 1986; Shade, 1989; Willis, 1992), recall relevant verbal ideas, engage in human and social content material (Shade, 1989), respond to extrinsic motivation, focus on interests, learn from informal class discussion, achieve interdependently (Hale-Benson, 1986; Hilliard, 1976; Willis, 1992), and narrate human concepts (Willis, 1992). This does not mean that these students should not be exposed to mathematics teaching that focuses on skill-based instruction. It means that students should be given multiple methods of teaching that will allow them to choose the method that suits their learning preferences and that students learn new ways of thinking and learning that are not necessarily their primary preference.

Harris (1994) explains the contextualization of instruction to African American students' learning preferences is a process that requires accommodation of the teacher; "This does not mean that allegiance to or identification with anyone's individual culture is denied or denigrated. It does mean, however, that a common ground is created wherein interaction can occur that is meaningful to those involved" (p. 78). Based on the preferences summarized above, accommodating instruction for all students requires that the teacher (a) acknowledges and uses individual student preferences in the acquisition of knowledge; (b) develops activities that promote mathematical discourse within the classroom among students and between the students and teacher, (c) values student discourse and verbal knowledge, (d) creates interdependent learning communities within the classroom, and (e) encourages, supports, and provides feedback to students as they learn (Malloy, 2004). Previously, I showed that the alignment learning processes for African American students and these accommodations can result in the outcome goals of the NCTM standards documents (see Malloy, 2004).

Culturally relevant pedagogy of Ladson-Billings (1994) and the culturally responsive pedagogy of Irvine (1992) are specific pedagogies that are important to this process. "The primary aim of culturally relevant teaching is to assist in the development of a relevant Black personality that allows African American students to choose academic excellence yet still identify with their African and African American culture" (Ladson-Billings, 1994, p. 17). Ladson-Billings presents successful teachers of African American children as having specific qualities in the areas of their conceptions of self and others, social relations, and knowledge.[1] Irvine (1992) states that effective teachers (a) are competent in subject matter, (b) provide all students with high-level knowledge regardless of previous categorization or labeling, and (c) have appropriately high standards and expectations for their students (Irvine, 1992). Further, speaking to effective teachers of African American students, she explains that they "need to be more than effective teachers, they need to be culturally responsive teachers who contextualize teaching by giving attention to immediate needs and cultural experiences of their students" (p. 83).

The aforementioned literature highlights instructional strategies and dispositions of teachers whose African American students achieve success across varied content areas. Several studies focusing on mathematics instruction have investigated the impact of instruction on students' achievement by examining teachers' instructional practices and classroom norms. Research in middle grades mathematics classrooms demonstrate that building teachers' capacity improve and reform instruction (Silver & Stein, 1996) resulted in improvement in student learning, and Boaler (1998) found that open-ended mathematics instruction rather than procedural, skill-based approaches resulted in stronger achievement. Hamilton et al. (2003) employed NCTM reform practices at the high school level, which resulted in improved student achievement in mathematics. Additional mathematics reports and research that have focused on African American students propose culturally relevant and responsive pedagogies, specific strategies, and processes as methods to improve the education of these students (Cousins-Cooper, 2000; Smith, Stiff, & Petree, 2000). In related research, Hill, Rowan, and Ball (2005) found that teachers' mathematical knowledge was significantly related to student achievement at the elementary level. Missing from these reports is research that identifies teachers who were more successful in helping their African American students gain conceptual understanding, specifically research that looks into classrooms using teachers' self reports, and student perceptions, and classroom observations to extract specific strategies and dispositions.

Community and Social Justice

Another area of research that appears in limited research addressing strong instructional strategies for African American students is democratic education and social justice (Gutstein, 2003; Moses & Cobb, 2001). Education where students have access to mathematics through a lens of democracy can result in students having the tools and learning conditions to develop mathematical skills, knowledge, and understanding to become educated and effective citizens. Is it possible that students would use the power of mathematics to address ills in our society—for emancipation? Education of this sort addresses social justice and political aspects of democratic schooling. If students lack the ability to think numerically, they will not be able to understand or participate in the processes necessary for democratic governments (Orrill, 2001). Furthermore, democratic education can also provide students an understanding of democracy and its traditions of (a) a Socratic commitment to questioning of ourselves, authority, dogma, parochialism, and fundamentalism; (b) the prophetic commitment to justice for all people; and (c) the shield and inner strength of the tragicomic commitment to hope (West, 2004, p. 16).

Moses and Cobb (2001) make a compelling argument that African American students' access to mathematics in the United States, especially algebra and advanced mathematics is a human right in our technologic society just as the vote in the United States is a human right. However, all African American students still do not experience that human right because many students, families, and teachers establish educational goals focusing on learning for intellectual growth or learning for personal benefits rather learning for the good of others. Using a social justice frame propelled through democratic education, mathematics classrooms can address issues of race and inequities that result in student learning and achievement (Gutstein, 2003; Moses & Cobb, 2001). Democratic education is a process where

> teachers and students work collaboratively to reconstruct curriculum to include everyone. Each classroom will differ in its attributes because the interactions of democratic classrooms are based on student experiences and community and educational context. Just as this occurs in democratic classrooms, it occurs in mathematics classrooms. There is no one way or context through which mathematics is taught. There are concepts, topics, and processes that must be taught and learned, but individual teachers and learners will approach mathematics based on their needs, preferences, and experiences. Democratic education—accessible to all students—rests on the assumption that all students can learn, given the right circumstance, provides students with an avenue through which they can learn substantial mathematics, and, at the same time, can help students become productive and active citizens. (Malloy, 2008)

The literature on democratic education consistently identifies distinguishing qualities of democratic classrooms to include: (a) problem-solving curriculum, (b) inclusivity and rights, (c) equal participation in decisions, and (d) equal encouragement for success (Beyer, 1996; Pearl & Knight, 1999; Wilbur, 1998). As an example, Vithal (1999) proposed a lens through which mathematics educators and researchers can think about the dual concept theme of democracy and authority in mathematics classrooms. In Vithal's research, her students after Apartheid were able to conceptualize authority, both in the classroom and schools. It was her thought that these students would use their mathematical knowledge not only in mathematics learning but for the common good of their school and community. A concurrent skill developed by students in such classrooms is proficiency in mathematics.

Conceptual Understanding

Student proficiency in mathematics not only involves a facility with factual and procedural knowledge; more important, it also includes having the ability to use knowledge flexibly and to apply what is learned to new situations (Bransford, Brown, & Cocking, 1999; Carpenter & Lehrer, 1999; NCTM, 2000). Proficiency in mathematics also requires more than connecting new and prior knowledge, it requires a structuring of knowledge so that new knowledge can be accessed and used (Skemp, 1987). Kilpatrick, Swafford, and Findell (2001) extend mathematical proficiency to include five interwoven and interdependent strands: conceptual understanding, procedural fluency, strategic competency, adaptive reasoning, and productive disposition. They describe conceptual understanding as comprehension of mathematical concepts, operations, and relations (p. 5). In MIDDLE conceptual understanding was defined as students' demonstrated ability (a) to apply concepts to new situations; (b) to connect new concepts with existing information; and (c) to use mathematical principles to explain and justify problem solutions. These dimensions are directly related to the five forms of mental activity of Carpenter and Lehrer (1999) and are important in attaining conceptual understanding of mathematics.[2]

In facilitating Carpenter and Lehrer's (1999) generative process of students understanding mathematics, the teacher must make instructional decisions about curriculum and pedagogy that facilitate student development of conceptual understanding. Teachers committed to developing students' conceptual understanding use pedagogically appropriate instructional practices, materials, and assessment methods that promote students' conceptual development (NCTM 2000, Stein, Smith, Henningsen, & Silver, 2000). They provide students with problem-solving opportunities using valuable and meaningful mathematical tasks, where students learn mathematics through a socio-cultural approach that requires that students share, question, challenge, and explore mathematics together (Boaler, 2002; Grouws & Lembke, 1996; Van Haneghan, Pruet, & Bamberger, 2004). Such teachers also provide a learning environment that is non-threatening and where students' ideas are valued (Skemp, 1987; Sowder & Phillipp, 1999).

My Approach

The current investigation is a secondary analysis of qualitative and quantitative data from the MIDDLE cross-sectional data set. In this section, I include research results using this same data set and essential contextual information from

MIDDLE. The goal of the prior research was to examine the relations between the instructional practices of middle grades mathematics teachers, whose instruction represented a continuum of reform practice, and the conceptual understanding of their students. Findings documented that the teachers who used reform instructional practices improved student learning in mathematics, even when students' prior achievement on state tests are taken into account. Controlling for ethnicity, prior ability, and grade level, the results showed that classroom differences in levels of reform-oriented teaching explained 27% of between-classroom differences in students' scores on the conceptual understanding measure. Gender and characteristics of the home environment, including parental education as reported by students, were not significantly related to students' performance on the conceptual understanding measure.

The School District

MIDDLE research was conducted in middle schools located in a medium size urban school district in southeastern United States with a student population of about 30,500. The district serves a diverse student population that was 54% African American, 24.3% white, 15.7% Hispanic, 3.4% multiracial, 2.4% Asian, and 0.2% Native American. The student population was also diverse in terms of family income levels; district records indicate that 49% of student received free or reduced lunch.

Teachers and Students

The cross-sectional data set includes information from 126 classrooms of 44 teachers whose experience ranged from 1 to 30 years, with an average of 10 years. Based on school district criteria, classrooms in the study were designated as non-gifted and non-inclusion. Two-thirds of the teachers were female, and 70% were Caucasian, 25% were African American. A total of 946 students are included in the data set. Upon entry into middle school, the majority of the students in total sample were at or above grade level (approximately 85%), based on fifth-grade statewide assessments. The purposeful sample of students for this study was drawn from the 431 African American students in the cross-sectional data set, which included 159 students in sixth-grade (mean age = 11.7), 190 students in seventh-grade (mean age = 12.7), and 82 students in eighth-grade (mean age = 13.6).

Materials

Using mixed methods, the dependent variables were student conceptual understanding and student end-of-grade test scores, and the independent variable was teacher instruction drawn from classroom observations and student perceptions of instruction. Variables used to inform mathematics teachers' instructional decisions and the instruments are pedagogy, content, tasks, assessment, and mathematical interaction. *Pedagogy* is the focus of instruction lesson plans and the resulting flow of the lesson. Pedagogy included how students were given opportunities to learn, how discourse was pursued, and how tools were used in lessons (Carpenter & Lehrer, 1999; Gay, 2000). *Content* includes the objectives of the lesson, including where the student is being led and allowed to advance and the mathematical knowledge, both procedural and conceptual, that students should learn (NCTM, 2000). *Tasks* represent the mathematical work that students were engaged in during class, and the opportunity students had to internalize and connect mathematical ideas. Of particular interest were characteristics of classrooms and instructional level of cognitive demands afforded students (Stein, Smith, Henningsen, & Silver, 2000). *Assessment* includes the ways that the teacher determined what students had learned, specifically, evidence of student performance, the relation of student understanding to content being taught, feedback to students, and student involvement in critique (Shafer, 2001). *Mathematical interaction* is the mathematical discourse that resulted from the instruction planned and modified by the teacher and initiated by students (Malloy & Meece, under review). The five variables were operationalized into observable actions.

Teacher Instruction

The *Reformed Teaching Observation Protocol* (RTOP), developed by Sawada et al. (2000) at the University of Arizona, was selected as the observation instrument for this research. The RTOP consists of 25 Likert-scale items that are rated from 0 (not observed) to 4 (very descriptive). These scales corresponded well with four variables in our model for reform instruction: pedagogy, content, tasks, mathematical interaction. There are two limitations to the use of the RTOP in the secondary analysis: (a) reform instruction was not a requirement for this analysis and (b) the instrument did not measure teacher use of instruction related to students' histories or culture. To counter these limitations, in identifying the practices of teachers who were successful in teaching African American students, in my analysis I relied heavily on classroom observation and interview data supported with the RTOP data.

Conceptual Understanding

The MIDDLE conceptual understanding instruments measure the broad spectrum of middle grades curriculum including developmental items on measurement, proportion, and problem-solving. The topics were selected because they were major mathematical ideas stressed in middle school content strands of the *Principles and Standards of School Mathematics* (NCTM, 2000), the *State Course of Study for Mathematics* (State Department of Public Instruction, 2000), and the participating district's pacing guides for middle grades mathematics. Items were selected from national assessments, by reviewing a pool of released items from the TIMSS 1994 and the NAEP 1990 and 1992. Four conceptual understanding items per year were used in this analysis. Items were grade level specific. Students completed these items in the fall and spring of each year. (See Appendices D and E for sample items and a rubric.)

To ensure that our definition of conceptual understanding[3], which informed our assessment rubrics, yielded the necessary information, we conducted a pilot test on the items using students from a university pre-college program for minorities and females. The majority of the students were African American.

Student Perception Survey

The MIDDLE student survey was constructed to assess students' perceptions of instruction. Survey items were worded to parallel the five dimensions of instructional practices: Pedagogy, Content, Tasks, Mathematical Instruction, and Assessment. A total of 49 items were generated from descriptors of the five variables, existing classroom climate measures, and from rewording items from the RTOP. For each item, students were asked their opinions and feelings about their mathematics classes. Using a six-point Likert scale students indicated whether the actions outlined almost never occurred, sometimes occurred, or very often occurred. Our exploratory and confirmatory factor analyses on the learning opportunities students perceive in their classrooms opportunities had dimensions: discourse, mastery of math content, meaningfulness, and authority with math content. Across all scales, teachers with higher reform level ratings were perceived by their students as promoting discourse, mastery, meaningfulness, and authority in their classrooms. Additionally, student perceptions of their teachers' instruction correlated with observer ratings on the RTOP across three dimensions of pedagogy, tasks and mathematical interactions (Ellis, Malloy, Meece, & Sylvester, 2007).

Looking into Classrooms

Teacher observation and interview data, student conceptual understanding, and classroom perception data were collected in the fall and spring from sixth-grade classrooms in Years 1 and 2, seventh-grade classrooms in Years 2 and 3, and eighth-grade classrooms in Year 3. Each teacher in MIDDLE was observed in each classroom and interviewed from four to ten times during the three years depending on their level of participation. Four teachers a year also participated in at least one in-depth interview about their instructional practice and dispositions. Selection was based on levels of reform practice.

The observation and conceptual understanding teams were made up of trained principal investigators and graduate students. Prior to, and after, each observation, teachers answered pre- and post-interview questions that focused on assessment. The pre- and post-interviews also reduced misinterpretations and alerted the observer to important moments of the lesson content and/or context. During classroom observations, the observers took detailed notes on teacher instruction and student participation, based on our five variables of reform practice. At the end of the class, observers completed the RTOP as directed by the developers of the protocol. Within 48 hours of the class session, observers used data from the RTOP and notes to write detailed narratives of the class session, describing the pedagogy, content, task, mathematical interaction, and assessment that occurred in lessons. The interviews and narratives also provided insight into the ways in which the teachers believed they assessed student progress.

To ensure that teachers would not teach to our materials, conceptual understanding items were administered by MIDDLE staff. Observation inter-rater reliabilities (ICC >0.75), scoring agreement on conceptual understanding items (Kappa from 0.75 to 0.90), construct validity on RTOP, and content validity on conceptual understanding and survey measures were documented.

Selection of Teachers

To select teachers whose African American students achieved the greatest growth in conceptual understanding, I computed, by teacher, the percent increase from fall to spring of students' conceptual understanding scores on four grade-based items for African American students in the data set based on mean student scores. Next a two-tailed t-test was performed to compare the mean scores for differences and to see if any scores differed significantly from the others. The selection criteria for teachers were: (a) the teacher had greater than 15 African American MIDDLE students in classes, and (b) the average of student growth on conceptual understanding items was greater than 10% or significant at the $p<0.05$ level. Four teachers who qualified on both criteria taught 107 MIDDLE African American students[4] who demonstrated an average percent increase of over 16% on conceptual understanding items with p values $0.000 < p<0.040$ (see Table 4.1). The instruction of all four teachers who qualified was observed at the highest two levels (from four) of reform instruction.

The first teacher of those who qualified was Mr. Johnson,[5] an African American lateral entry teacher with eight years' experience. He taught sixth-grade mathematics at Greenleaf Middle School. Greenleaf had an enrollment of 450 students with 56% receiving free or reduced lunch. Based on mathematics end-of-grade test scores, 23% of African American students at Greenleaf were at, or above, grade level. Mr. Johnson taught 30 African American students in four MIDDLE classes, who as a whole demonstrated 15% increase in conceptual understanding.

Two teachers, Ms. Spears and Ms. Codd, were from Lakeland Middle School which had 700 students; 67% of the students received free or reduced lunch. Thirty-nine percent of the African American students at Lakeland were at or above grade level based on end-of-grade mathematics test scores. Ms. Spears, a Caucasian female, was a lateral entry teacher with five years' experience, and taught seventh-grade mathematics. Prior to teaching, Ms. Spears had been employed for five years as an engineer. She taught 37 African American students in two MIDDLE classes, who demonstrated 11.2% growth on the conceptual understanding items during the school year. Ms. Codd, a Caucasian female with 15 years' experience, taught

Table 4.1 Student Increase in Conceptual Understanding by Teachers

Teacher	African American Students	Classrooms	P value	Percent increase
Johnson	30	4	.000	15%
Spears	37	2	.040	11.2%
Codd	21	2	.014	19%
Winston	19	3	.001	19.4%

sixth-grade mathematics. She taught two MIDDLE sixth-grade classes that contained 21 African American students who participated in the project. These African American students demonstrated 19% growth on the conceptual understanding items.

Ms. Winston, a Caucasian female with 17 years' teaching experience, taught eighth-grade mathematics at Sampson Middle School which had an enrollment of 600 students; 39% of the students received free or reduced lunch. She taught 19 African American MIDDLE students in three classes who demonstrated 19.4% growth on conceptual understanding items.

The process of determining teachers' specific instructional practice and dispositions was four-pronged, allowing triangulation of data from four sources: observation narratives, teacher interviews, quantitative scores from the observation protocol, and quantitative scores from student surveys. First, I reviewed the teacher classroom observation narratives looking for specific instructional strategies that each teacher used based on the five variables: pedagogy, content, tasks, interaction, and assessment. As a part of this process, I read and coded the in-depth interviews[6] with each of the teachers to glean information regarding their stated dispositions. I reviewed narratives and the RTOP for further information about the observed dispositions of the teachers. Second, I totaled instructional strategy descriptors from the RTOP for each teacher. Third, using the constant comparative method (Glaser, 1965), I was able to determine the similarities among the instructional strategies and dispositions of the four teachers. Finally, I calculated the sum of students' scores on the items of the perception instrument for each of the four teachers to determine the instructional strategies and dispositions that students identified as occurring often and very often in their classes.

Instructional Strategies and Dispositions of Teachers

Using the data described above, I present cases of the four teachers to describe their instructional strategies and dispositions that contributed to their students demonstrating the greatest gains in conceptual knowledge followed with a composite of the common strategies and dispositions of the four teachers. Finally, a synthesis of common instructional strategies and dispositions is compared to student perceptions of teacher practices.

Mr. Johnson: "They don't realize they know before I teach them."

Instructional Practices

Mr. Johnson described his instruction as using entertainment and contextual mathematics through models, graphs, and activities. He stated that he uses students as teachers in the instruction process and assessed students learning through recitation, writing, student questioning, and body and facial reactions. Our observations concurred with his description and revealed that Mr. Johnson often established communities of learners, which created a family atmosphere where students had voice and authority in the classroom. We saw evidence for learning both in participatory groups and as a whole class where they were involved, taught each other, and made presentations about what they learned. Students were comfortable challenging each other and justifying their mathematical positions. It was evident that students knew that they did not have to be perfect and that it was acceptable to be wrong. In our observations, Mr. Johnson generally accomplished his instructional goals. We also saw that Mr. Johnson was very concerned about his students scoring well in the end-of-grade tests as he constantly referred to the test items when he presented tasks to his students.

Teaching Dispositions

In his interview, Mr. Johnson was reflective of his practice, talking at length about his continuing struggle with providing the best instruction for his students. He explained how he questioned and modified his instruction because he believes that mathematics is inside of students but they do not realize it. He stated, "They don't realize they know [the mathematics] before I teach them." Believing that students are tired of being told mathematics and learning through hands-on activities with repetition, he sees himself as a facilitator with a student-oriented classroom that gives students "power to do the work." Mr. Johnson was a caring teacher who was patient, as he created a climate of respect for what others had to say. He established classroom norms for group work because "it takes time and effort for students to learn to work together," and rescued students who were disruptive and those who were affected by disruption. Students were independently responsible for their contributions, involvement and respectful behavior in groups and also interdependently responsible to the members of their groups through sharing their knowledge and understanding. He demonstrated in classes that he valued student independence with interdependence.

A clear example of his care of students and his disposition independence with interdependence philosophy was seen in an observation where he rescued a disruptive class. In his first period class, Mr. Johnson had his students use a protractor activity to identify acute, right, and obtuse angles. They had not used a protractor prior to this lesson. When he started the same lesson with his second period class, a teacher came to Mr. Johnson's room and explained that his first period class was "out of control" in a classroom with a substitute teacher. Instead of calling the principal, Mr. Johnson went to the substitute's classroom and brought his first class back to his classroom. Because both classes were small, there were only 24 students in the double class. After he had firmly explained to his first period students that their behavior was hurtful and an unacceptable way to treat a substitute who wanted to help them learn, he re-revamped his lesson, placing students in groups of two with one student from each class. Following a brief introduction about angle size where Mr. Johnson made his arms, legs, and torso into angles, he instructed his first period students to use the activity sheet to teach the second period students to use the protractor to measure angles. The solution worked for both groups. Students who were teachers were able to solidify their use of protractors, and each of the second period students had an individual tutor. This was a mathematically and behaviorally successful effective solution.

Ms. Spears: "I'd rather they'd be working."

Instructional Practices

Ms. Spears struggled to find her style but moved to an investigative approach rather than an algorithmic emphasis because she said, "I'd rather they'd [students] be working because the conversations they have are very nice . . . . I want them to get into a problem and understand it. Go beyond just the math itself application-wise. I think a lot of kids can memorize algorithms, but their answers don't make sense." She explained that she instructed through group work over individual work, and with children working with each other using models, graphs, activities, and peers as teachers. Her assessment was accomplished through group investigations more than through tests, and through application projects—building models. Formatively, she assessed their understanding by talking to students, listening to questions they asked, and watching their facial expressions. Ms. Spears used student mathematical "talk" discussions to help develop concepts. Based on our observations and interviews, she was successful in meeting her instructional goals. Students were involved, taught each other, played games, solved problems together, challenged each other, and explained their mathematical positions. She was adept at establishing communities of learners and, in our observations, usually accomplished her instructional goals.

A lesson where students were exploring the area of a circle, by using their knowledge of the area of parallelogram and the circumference of a circle, showed how she created a learning community even when she was leading the discussion. Her students knew that the area of a parallelogram could be found by multiplying the height times the base. Ms. Spears asked students to cut a circle into small pie-shaped sectors and then rearrange the sectors into shapes for which they knew the area formula. Working in groups, the students arranged the sectors into a parallelogram that resembled a rectangle. Ms. Spears allowed her students to complete their assignments with limited teacher support and did not discipline students if they talked as they worked. When her students understood that the height of the parallelogram was the radius of the circle and that the base of the parallelogram was half of the circumference, she brought them together for a discussion of how to find the formula for the area of a circle. She gave students an opportunity to think and talk out loud about their ideas. Thus, students were encouraged to become a part of the class and work toward their own understanding along with their classmates. Ms. Spears used students' voices rather than her voice to teach. Leading the discussion, she had students build on comments of other students to extend their knowledge. Her students were able to see that $bh = r(2\pi r)/2$ or πr^2. During the discussions, she acted as a resource person to her students.

Teaching Dispositions

Ms. Spears was reflective on her practice. She wanted students to do the work rather than listen to the teacher, believed that students learn mathematics in different ways, and believed that learning is not consistent across different mathematics content. She saw herself as a facilitator—a leader who gets them started and lets them take the leadership. Her verbalized belief that all students want to be successful was demonstrated in our observations. Ms. Spears was a caring teacher who wanted her students to do well. She established classroom norms for working together (i.e., talking low, staying on task, being responsible). She felt that her students were motivated, involved, and showed effort and respectful behavior. Ms. Spears also valued independence with interdependence.

Ms. Codd: "Let the kids learn and generalize and see things."

Instructional Practices

Ms. Codd stated in her interview that her teaching style was investigative—students explore and investigate mathematical phenomena, either with patterns or making generalizations which are then tested. She stated, "I want to facilitate the mathematics learning. I don't want to be the one. I'm not a lecturer. I want to keep it going, and keep discussions going, and let the kids learn and generalize and see things." In our observations, Ms. Codd used mathematical discussion as the major instructional strategy. Within classroom discussions, we observed active student involvement where students taught each other through challenge and justification of answers.

Ms. Codd assessed through student participation more than through tests. She also assessed through projects. She felt that students' mathematical explanations and their ability to explain procedures and relationships to the teacher and other students were strong indicators of what students knew. An example of her assessment occurred during a discussions with students regarding magnitude of negative numbers. She stated, "And then they, like today, they put some integers in order from least to greatest and I said, 'Well how do you know that negative 1.9 is less than negative 1.8?' And they were like, 'I don't know. I just know.' And I said, 'Well, you've got to tell me how you know?' And then one student said, 'Well, negative 1.9 is further from zero.' And well, that's reasoning."

Teaching Dispositions

Ms. Codd believed deeply that students should learn to reason by listening to each other as they explain thinking, and having others repeat their explanation. As a caring teacher, she also was reflective on her practice. She believed that all students need to see how mathematics works, not just learn a procedure or algorithm. She valued student motivation, involvement, effort, success, reasoning, independence with interdependence, and established classroom norms in group works at the start of the year. Ms. Codd spoke of her use of instructional reflection as she talked about situations where her students did not engage in the lesson. She stated, "I would go back to a prerequisite; or was the way I presented it just not clear? But how do I change? It depends on what I'm doing how you change your teaching. A lot of times I just take a different approach. You know, if a manipulative doesn't work, maybe a model will work." She did not place blame on the students for their lack of participation; she reflected on her instruction to revamp her lessons.

Her confidence in her students' ability was seen in her requirement that, if a student disagreed with another person, they had to pursue and understand each other's reasoning to see if they still disagreed. Additionally, she required them to select partners for teaching and learning pairs that were accountable for their learning. In our observations she always accomplished her instructional goals.

Ms. Winston: "I try to do what is best for the students."

Instructional Practices

Ms. Winston explained that, in her many years of teaching, she "developed a style of 'teaching for understanding,' but had to make adjustments" as she and her students encountered high-stakes testing. She stated, "I think I fluctuate somewhere between the traditional teachers who tell students how to do it and the more investigative." Ms. Winston wanted her students to understand mathematics and how it connected to other mathematics. She started a new lesson by asking herself, "What is it I want them to get out of this? What is the point of this? Where are we headed with this? What is the big picture? And then what do I want the students to do?" Ms. Winston's description of her practice concurred with our observations. She assessed through asking students what they understood, by looking at student work, by talking with students, and by asking higher-level questions to guide them to better conceptual understanding of the mathematics. She was adept at using student "mathematical talk" with challenge and justification to help develop concepts. Based on our observations and interviews she was successful in meeting her instructional goals. Her students worked in groups with varied levels of dedication and enthusiasm. Even though she was challenged with establishing group norms that would work throughout the school year, Ms. Winston continued to use instructional groups where students struggled together to find out why the mathematics worked as it did. In her interview, she described a situation where she learned about her instructional decisions and students by changing group composition when three African American boys were disruptive in separate groups:

> I had three boys and they ended up being good friends. All year I fought keeping them separate, and they wouldn't work, and I'd call home, and they just weren't going to do. So finally I just said, "OK, you all three just sit together. You're smart. You know what you're supposed to be doing, and me sitting here fussing at you and separating you, it's not going to do a bit of good." They sat over there and they worked together, and they would call each other at night, and they'd do the work. And, you know, I just quit fighting the battle of them. I think that has been real interesting, you know, watching that dynamic.

She learned that, as these students learned in their new group, they were involved, taught each other, and became a learning community where they could struggle with mathematics.

Teaching Dispositions

Ms. Winston tried to do what was best for her students and was reflective of her practice. She believed that students learned best blending traditional and reform instructional approaches, and respected different learning styles "if some students cannot see it, they do not know what they are doing." Respecting varied approaches to problem-solving, she encouraged student recitation, group projects, and individual assignments. She explained how she changes her teaching to capture students' understanding and interest saying:

> Sometimes . . . it depends on really what it is a lot. Because if there is something I can grab, something they need to see, if they don't understand, that's what I'll do. If it's more they're not engaged . . . one little boy, he will not do anything until he thinks he can come up to the front and explain it. So a lot of times I say, "Let me just ask Mark to come up and explain it," then when it just kind of changes and shifts around, they'll become a little bit more engaged then.

Not only did Ms. Winston allow Mark, who was an African American boy, to process information orally—which was the manner in which he learned best—she also valued student motivation, involvement, effort, respectful behavior, and independence with interdependence.

Common Instructional Strategies and Dispositions

Instructional Strategies

It is clear that, although the four teachers in this study saw themselves as facilitators of student understanding, they varied in their approach of teaching. Mr. Johnson used entertainment to help his students relate mathematics to a context. Ms. Spears wanted students to do the work of learning mathematics. Ms. Codd wanted her students to investigate mathematical phenomena. Ms. Winston used a mixture of "telling" and student investigations to help her students learn.

The brief narratives of teachers above give a synopsis of their instructional practices and dispositions. The specific common instructional practices of the four teachers listed below fall into three areas of practice: (a) Reflecting on Practice, (b) Building Communities of Learners, and (c) Giving Students Voice.

Reflecting on Practice

- Blended memorization, procedural, and conceptual tasks
- Involved fundamental concepts of the subject in lessons
- Respected students' prior knowledge and preconceptions
- Were knowledgeable about content
- Listened and responded to students to anticipate their understanding and/or misunderstanding

Building Communities of Learners

- Encouraged students to generate conjectures, alternative solution strategies, and ways of interpreting evidence
- Created a climate of respect for what others had to say
- Valued intellectual rigor, constructive criticism, and the challenging of ideas
- Encouraged elements of abstraction when important

Giving Students Voice

- Acted as a resource person, working to support and enhance student investigations
- Saw knowledge and authority in both teachers and students
- Encouraged and valued active participation of students
- Used learning communities that promoted student–teacher and student–student mathematical interaction

Even though the areas of practice have some overlap, reflecting on practice includes the pedagogy teachers planned for their students, their knowledge of the content and their use of formative assessment practices. Building communities of learners show actions teachers used to establish learning communities that enabled student-to-student conversations about mathematics. Giving students voice captures the spirit of the classrooms regarding authority and interdependence. The question remains, How does the instruction of these teachers compare to the recommended learning processes for African American students and those of culturally relevant and congruent pedagogies?

The information in Table 4.2 is a compilation of areas of practice above, the recommended learning process recommended for African American students, the recommended instruction of culturally relevant pedagogy (Ladson-Billings, 1994), and the recommendations of culturally responsive pedagogy (Irvine, 1992), and composite teacher actions. A fourth area of practice, Recognizing Cultural Experiences and Communities, is included in the table because it is essential to the recommendations for African American student learning. The teachers matched up well in the reflecting on practice, building communities of learners, and giving students voice; however, the area they did not compare favorably in was in recognizing and using cultural experiences of their students and their communities. Only one teacher occasionally accessed his African American students' culture and community as a part of his instruction.

Dispositions

The overarching shared disposition was that the teachers *cared* about the learning and welfare of their African American students. The following dispositions are reflective of their care of their students.

- Believed that all students could learn mathematics
- Valued student motivation, involvement, effort, respectful behavior, and responsibility

Table 4.2 Comparison of Areas of Practice, Pedagogies and Composite Teacher Actions

Area of Practice	Learning Preferences and Culturally Relevant and Congruent Pedagogies	Composite Teacher Actions
Reflecting on Practice	Focus on the whole Use improvisational intuitive thinking	Presented memorization, procedural, and conceptual tasks Involved fundamental concepts of the subject in lessons
	Help students develop necessary skills Provide all students with high-level knowledge regardless of previous categorization or labeling Competent in subject matter Demonstrate a connectedness with all students	Encouraged to generate conjectures, alternative solution strategies, and ways of interpreting evidence Encouraged elements of abstraction when it was important to do so Were knowledgeable about content Blended procedural and conceptual knowledge
Building Communities of Learners	Recall relevant verbal ideas Narrate human concepts	Encouraged and valued active participation of students Valued intellectual rigor, constructive criticism, and the challenging of ideas
	Learn from informal class discussion Encourage students to learn collaboratively	Created a climate of respect for what others had to say Encouraged and valued active participation of students Respected students' prior knowledge and preconceptions Encouraged to generate conjectures, alternative solution strategies, and ways of interpreting evidence
Giving Students Voice	Respond to extrinsic motivation Demonstrate a connectedness with all students	Acted as a resource person, working to support and enhance student investigations Listened and responded to their students to anticipate their understanding and/or misunderstanding
	Achieve interdependently Teacher–student relationship is fluid, humanely equitable Encourage a "community of learners" Expect students to teach each other and be responsible for each other Encourage a community of learners	Saw knowledge authority in both teachers and students Used learning communities Promoted student–teacher and student–student mathematical interaction Saw the authority in classroom as both students and teachers
Recognizing Cultural Experiences and Communities	Focus on interests Engage in human and social content material Focus cultural experiences of their students	Not Evidenced in two or more teachers

- Demonstrated concern to address the varied learning styles of their students and accommodated instruction-based student learning preferences
- Demonstrated that knowledge their students brought into the classroom should be shared
- Helped their students feel safe in their classrooms and cared about their students and their learning
- Were reflective about their practice

Because the strategies and dispositions listed above were common to three or more teachers, the four teachers were more similar than they were different. The information in Table 4.3 compares the culturally relevant and responsive dispositions of the teachers to those of the teacher in this study. It shows that the four teachers were generally successful in accomplishing the instructional dispositions but, as in instruction, failed to approach the community and cultural experiences of their students within their mathematics classrooms.

Comparison of Teacher Practice to Student Perceptions

Data from the perception survey provide instructional and dispositional context of teacher actions within the classroom from students' classroom experiences. The information in Table 4.4 shows how student reports of instructional practices compare to interview and observation data. This table merges instructional strategies and dispositions and provides the number of teachers who required students to complete specific tasks. The perceptions of students confirm most actions of their teachers in the classroom, both in teacher dispositions and in instructional strategies. There are two major differences. The first difference is that observational data indicated all teachers used exploration to begin lessons, but students of three teachers disagreed. Most students believed most teachers began a new topic by explaining the rules and definitions. The second difference is in the area of mathematical tasks offered to students. Observations and teachers agreed that students were often given tasks that required them to recall, extend, and apply mathematical relationships, and they used a variety of means to represent phenomena. However, only two of four teachers were consistent in requiring and valuing intellectual rigor, constructive criticism, and the challenging of ideas. This process could be described as mathematizing or "doing mathematics" (Stein et al., 2000). In contrast, these students felt that their teachers pushed them to mathematize problem situations through inventing or coming up with new ways to solve problems, talking about why an answer was not correct, and figuring out things for themselves.

Students of all teachers reported that their teachers helped them to understand how procedures work in math and improved their understanding of math, and they were asked to think about how they solve problems. Working in groups means that everyone shares our ideas was reported by most students. Based on student reports, the majority of teachers also asked students to use different strategies to work out problems, understand what they did to solve problems, and asked them questions that made them think. Students stated that they were asked to talk about mathematics and look at mathematics in different ways. They indicated that teachers

Table 4.3 Comparison of Culturally Relevant and Congruent Dispositions with Composite Teacher Dispositions

Culturally Relevant and Congruent Pedagogies[a]	*Composite Teacher Dispositions*[b]
Believes all students can succeed	Believed that all students could learn mathematics
Believes knowledge is continuously recreated, recycled, and shared by teachers and students	Valued student motivation, involvement, effort, respectful behavior, and responsibility Demonstrated that knowledge their students brought into the classroom should be shared
Sees teaching as pulling knowledge out, like mining	Demonstrated concern to address the varied learning styles of their students and accommodated instruction based student learning preferences
Has appropriately high standards and expectations for their students	Cared about their students and their learning Believed that all students could learn mathematics
Sees excellence as a complex standard that may involve some postulates but takes student diversity and individual differences into account	Created learning communities Helped their students feel safe in their classrooms
Sees herself as an artist, teaching as an art achieved interdependently	Were reflective about their practice
Knowledge is not static or unchanging, and it is viewed critically	Not Evidenced by three or more teachers
Sees herself as a part of the community and teaching as giving something back to the community, encourages students to do the same, believes all students can succeed	Not Evidenced by three or more teachers
Helps students make connections between their community, national, and global identities	Not Evidenced by three or more teachers
Extends interactions beyond the classroom into the community	Not Evidenced by three or more teachers

a From Ladson-Billings & Irvine
b Evidenced in three or more teachers

taught for both procedural and conceptual understanding. Students also described teachers who cared about their understanding of and their comfort with mathematics (Table 4.4).

Thoughts, Challenges, and Questions

The question driving this research was, What are the instructional strategies and dispositions of teachers who help African American middle grades students gain conceptual understanding in mathematics? Findings indicate that there are common instructional strategies and dispositions shared by the four teachers in this research and that students in most cases concur with teacher and observational data. The similarities and differences are important because limited prior research has used empirical data to investigate instructional strategies and dispositions of mathematics teachers of successful African American students. Rather than restating findings as expressed in the previous section, I will pursue two areas in the discussion: differences in observational and student perceptions of instruction and the differences in the instructional practices and dispositions of these teachers as compared to recommended practices for African American students.

Differences in Observational/Teacher Reported Instruction and Student Perceptions

The differences in student perceptions of teacher instruction are both significant and encouraging. The first difference is that observational data indicated teachers used exploration to begin lessons, but students believed most teachers began a new topic by explaining the rules and definitions. Researchers often depend on the observation skills of their researchers to describe teacher practice. However, the practice of teachers is complex in conception and delivery, resulting in the creation of numerous methods and tools to capture what teachers do such as teacher-reported information, judgement of experts within the school system without the use of a standard protocol (Briars & Resnick, 2000; Supovitz, Mayer, & Kahle, 2000; Walker, 1999). Here, students were able to reveal significant differences in teacher practice from those than observations yielded. The fact that students' views of instruction generally matched the views of trained observers and their teachers reinforces the need for multiple views of classroom instruction. Looking into classrooms is a complex process. This finding points to the voices of students, who are in the classroom every day, as an important tool to describe the practice of their teachers.

The second difference is that observations revealed that students were often given tasks which required them to recall, extend, and apply mathematical relationships, but most did not ask students to use complex and non-algorithmic (original) thinking as they solved non-routine problems. The students of only two teachers, those whom students stated were consistent in requiring and valuing intellectual rigor, constructive criticism, and the challenging of ideas, indicated that their teachers encouraged them to invent methods and come up with new ways to solve problems. Doing mathematics as these teachers encouraged, is a process

Table 4.4 Comparison of Observed Teacher Instructional Strategies with Student Perceptions of Instruction

Variables	Teachers' Instructional Strategies (Number of teacher less than 3)	Student Perceptions (Number of teacher less than 3)

Pedagogy	**Student exploration preceded formal presentation**
	
	Instruction was inquiry-based, teacher directed, and student discussion
	Teachers
	  accommodated instruction based on student learning
	  respected students' prior knowledge and preconceptions
		New lessons began by having the teacher explain rules and definitions
		
		Teachers
		  asked questions that make us think
		  built on math we already knew (2)
		Students
		  used different strategies to work out problems

Content	Teachers
	  blended procedural and conceptual knowledge by requiring students to memorize and recall facts, use procedures, and apply procedures to develop deeper understanding of mathematical ideas
	  strongly pressed for procedural knowledge and moderately pressed for conceptual knowledge
	  were knowledgeable about content
	  involved fundamental concepts of the subject in lessons
	  encouraged elements of abstraction when it was important
		Teachers
		  helped us to understand how procedures work in math
		  improved our understanding of math
		  gave rules to solve problems (2)
		Learned to solve sets of similar problems (2)
		Procedures make sense (2)
		Students used a calculator and math equipment (2)

Tasks	Teachers
	  presented memorization, procedural, and conceptual tasks **valued intellectual rigor, constructive criticism, and the challenging of ideas**
	  required students be reflective about their learning (2)
	  required student justification (2)
	  offered solution method in inquiry group (2)
	Students used a variety of means to represent phenomena
		Teachers encouraged us to
		  try to understand why formulas work
		  invent ways to solve math problems (2)
		  come up with new ways to solve problems (2)
		  figure out things for ourselves (2)
		  talk about why answer is not correct (2)

Assessment	Teachers
	  assessed through student participation, recitation, writing, projects, questions students asked, and responses to higher level questions
		Teachers
		  asked us to think about how we solve problems
		  helped us to understand what we are doing to solve problems

Table 4.4 Continued

Variables	Teachers' Instructional Strategies (Number of teacher less than 3)	Student Perceptions (Number of teacher less than 3)
	listened to their students to anticipate their understanding or misunderstanding assessed understanding by the level of scaffolding students needed for understanding (1)	Teachers comments help us to understand our errors (2)
Interaction	Teachers created an atmosphere where learning communities promoted student–teacher and student–student mathematical interaction knowledge authority seen in both teachers and students there was a climate of respect for what others had to say active participation of students was encouraged and valued acted as a resource person, working to support and enhance student investigations was patient with students The metaphor "teacher as listener" was very characteristic of this classroom There was a high proportion of student talk and a significant amount occurred between and among students Students were encouraged to generate conjectures, alternative solution strategies, and ways of interpreting evidence	Working in groups means that everyone shares our ideas Feels safe asking questions about math when something does not make sense (2) Work together to understand new math ideas (2)

where students may have to find a pathway to the solution; it is often symbolic and abstract. Having students participate in learning mathematics by actually "doing mathematics" requires students to pursue and understand the underlying structure of mathematics and enables students to own the mathematics (Carpenter & Lehrer, 1999; Stein et al., 2000).

Students who do mathematics by reflecting on, talking about, and articulating mathematical ideas, as these students were encouraged to do, develop a sense of involvement and autonomy, moving them to mathematical understanding (Carpenter & Lehrer, 1999). This finding is noteworthy because, again, the students described a process of learning—missed by observers—that gave them the opportunity to think about, and do, mathematics at a deeper, more complex level. Moreover, students were able to develop a sense of agency, commitment, and authority in their mathematics learning. In survey responses, students described the opportunity for *agency* over their own learning, through opportunities to define their own goals, to submit and justify their own mathematical ideas, and to experience challenge with appropriate tasks. They reported opportunities to attain *competency* and *commitment* through their teachers' insistence on engagement in complex problems and opportunities for reflection on their mathematical thinking, and they recognized their opportunities to experience their *authority* through lessons that required them to take an active role in the creation and verification of mathematical ideas. Are the voices of these students telling us that we have to use their voices to look more deeply into the instruction of their teachers and their mathematical experiences?

Teacher Differences with Recommended Instruction for African American Students

Though not a primary but a related focus of this research, the findings encouragingly reveal that teachers displayed many instructional strategies and dispositions suggested for teachers of African American students listed earlier in this chapter. They embodied the characteristics of Irvine's (1992) effective teachers, most instructional characteristics of Ladson-Billings' (1994) culturally relevant teachers, and many of the areas listed from the work of Dance (1997), Hale-Benson (1986), Hilliard (1976), Shade (1989), and Willis (1992) as seen in Table 4.2. However, these teachers fell dramatically short in Ladson-Billings' (1995) criteria of culturally relevant teaching where she states that culturally relevant teachers must have "an ability to develop students academically, a willingness to nurture and support cultural competence, and the development of a sociopolitical or critical consciousness" (p. 483). Findings show that most of these teachers did not intend to develop cultural competence or sociopolitical and critical consciousness. Nor did most teachers consider the experiences and cultural needs of their students implored by Irvine (1992) who stated, "they need to be culturally responsive teachers who contextualize teaching by giving attention to immediate needs and cultural experiences of their students" (p. 83). In observations and interviews, they did not demonstrate or talk about approaching mathematics teaching and learning as Moses and Cobb (2001) describe, an issue of civil rights, or as students whose teachers are involved in social justice and/or critically radical mathematics would require.

These teachers have academic competence and dispositions to encourage students to learn and understand mathematics. They established classroom norms that reflected democratic education by using a problem-solving curriculum, inclusivity and rights, equal participation in decisions, and equal encouragement for success (Beyer, 1996; Pearl & Knight, 1999; Wilbur, 1998). They discussed the importance of learning mathematics to do well on their end-of-grade tests, enroll in courses that will allow them to enter college, and to obtain options for careers of their choices. Unlike the teachers in the opening case, these teachers ensured that African American students in their classes were very visible. They began the process of emancipation by giving their African American students a sense of agency, commitment and competence, and authority in their mathematics learning; but they could not see or perhaps understand the need to go further.

Could it be that these teachers were so influenced by the need to improve the academic achievement of their students measured by high-stakes standardized test that they were not aware of the importance of using mathematical instruction as an emancipating tool? The teachers in this study did not appear to understand that teaching and learning of mathematics is political and can be emancipating for students and their communities. In re-analyzing this data of teachers who were more successful than others in educating African American students using a political/emancipation lens, it is very clear that they did not appear to help students make connections among their community, national, and global identities. They did not extend interactions beyond the classroom and into the community or engage in human and social content material.

It is important to think about how this could occur in the middle grades classroom. Consider the important work of Vithal (1999), where South African sixth-grade students after Apartheid were able to conceptualize authority both in the classroom and in schools. She used a critical perspective informed by critical mathematics education and ethnomathematics, with concerns about dimensions of diversity in mathematics education, and developments in people's mathematics in South Africa. Vithal moved beyond rhetoric and policy to classroom-based research in order to elucidate the potentials and challenges of democracy in a mathematics classroom on three domains: whole class, group work, and teacher/student and teacher/researcher interactions and found oppositional themes of authority and democracy in teacher actions within a mathematics class. Her assumption in this research was that if students could learn about, and through, democracy in a mathematics classroom, they would learn to act critically in their own democratic society. She found that students in her study had to negotiate between authority of the teacher and the authoritarianism of the school as they spoke out against authoritarian and undemocratic practices.

Vithal's work showed that giving students access to democratic mathematical ideas can result in students having the tools and learning conditions to develop mathematical skills, knowledge and understanding to become educated and effective citizens. They see the power of mathematics and understand that they can use mathematical power to address ills in our society. Education of this sort addresses social justice and political aspects of democratic schooling, the social systems of nations, and often has as its focus the social betterment of nations and the world

(Beyer, 1996). Teachers I describe in this chapter recognize and value the authority of their students in their mathematics classes, and they were very successful in teaching their students to learn mathematics. Yet they have not yet moved that authority beyond the teaching of the school curriculum in mathematics. Is it possible that these teachers do not realize that learning mathematics and gaining authority in the learning processes are not in opposition and can create students' social empowerment? It is my challenge and the challenge of other mathematics educators to help teachers extend their instruction to include social justice issues in their students' communities through democratic mathematics education instruction so that their students can experience personal and collective liberation using mathematics for the betterment of their communities.

Conclusion

This research was completed as a secondary analysis of data collected in a school district that had groups of students from different ethnic and racial groups. My intent was to find answers about mathematics instruction that could emancipate and liberate African Americans from falling short of their expectations in mathematics learning. I wanted to find a way to help African American students' learning to be very visible in mathematics classrooms by looking at the practice of teachers of successful African American students. This research shows that these four teachers accomplished making the learning of their African American students both important and very visible.

It is difficult to make a conclusion about the students' feelings about emancipation or liberation gained from their teachers' instruction; but it is clear from student survey responses that they knew their teachers gave them the mathematical knowledge to learn mathematics and that many students gained agency, commitment and competence, and authority in their mathematics classrooms.

The question remains, Is this enough? In my view it is not. Emancipation in mathematics includes both the learning of mathematics to be success and using that mathematics for the better good—to change the injustices that plague our communities. We are not in a position to be incomplete in the mathematics education of African American students.

Author Note

The research reported in this article was funded by a grant (REC 01–25868) from the National Science Foundation to the authors. The opinions expressed are those of the authors and do not reflect the position of the National Science Foundation.

Acknowledgements

The author gratefully acknowledges the generous support of the teachers and students who participated in this three-year study and the reviewers whose insightful comments and suggestions greatly improved this chapter.

Notes

1 Based on self, the teacher sees herself as an artist, teaching as an art, sees herself as a part of the community and teaching as giving something back to the community, encourages students to do the same, believes all students can succeed, helps students make connections between their community, national, and global identities; and sees teaching as pulling knowledge out, like mining (Ladson-Billings, 1994, p. 34). Successful teachers reveal social relations with students through being fluid, humanely equitable, extending interactions beyond the classroom into the community. The teacher demonstrates a connectedness with all students, encourages a community of learners, and encourages students to learn collaboratively. Students and the teacher are expected to teach each other and be responsible for each other (Ladson-Billings, 1994, p. 55). Related to knowledge Ladson-Billings (1994) states that the teacher believes knowledge is continuously recreated, recycled, and shared by teachers and students. Knowledge is not static or unchanging, and it is viewed critically. Passionate about content, the teacher helps students develop necessary skills, and sees excellence as a complex standard that may involve some postulates but takes student diversity and individual differences into account (p. 81).

2 They characterize understanding not as a static attribute but as emerging in learners as they engage in the following activities: (a) constructing relationships, (b) extending and applying mathematical knowledge, (c) reflecting about experiences, (d) articulating what one knows, and (e) making mathematical knowledge one's own and thus available for use in future situations (p. 20).

3 Students demonstrated ability (a) to apply concepts to new situations; (b) to connect new concepts with existing information; and (c) to use mathematical principles to explain and justify problem solutions.

4 The total does not represent all the African American students in a teacher's classroom. Our research required 40% of the students in a class as participants to qualify as a MIDDLE classroom.

5 All teacher and school names are pseudonyms.

6 Each of the four teachers had been selected for an in-depth interview at least once during their participation in the research.

References

Beyer, L.E. (Ed.). (1996). *Creating democratic classrooms: The struggle to integrate theory and practice.* New York: Teachers College Press.

Boaler, J. (1998). Open and closed mathematics: Student experiences and understandings. *Journal for Research in Mathematics Education, 29*(1), 41–62.

Boaler, J. (2002). Learning from teaching: Exploring the relation between reform curriculum and equity. *Journal for Research in Mathematics Education, 33*(4), 239–258.

Bransford, J.D., Brown, A.L., & Cocking, R.R. (Eds.). (1999). *How people learn: Brain, mind, experience, and school.* Washington, DC: National Academy Press.

Briars, D.J. & Resnick, L.B. (2000). Standards, assessments—and what else? The essential elements of standards-based school improvement. National Center on Education, Standards, and Student Assessment (CRESST).

Carpenter, T.P. & Lehrer, R. (1999). Teaching and learning mathematics with understanding. In E. Fennema & T.A. Romberg (Eds.), *Mathematics classrooms that promote understanding* (pp. 19–32). Mahwah, NJ: LEA.

Cousins-Cooper, K.M. (2000). Teacher expectations and their effects on African American students' success in mathematics. In W.G. Secada, M.E. Strutchens, M.L. Johnson, & W.F. Tate (Eds.), *Changing the faces of mathematics: Perspectives on African Americans* (pp. 15–20). Reston, VA: NCTM.

Dance, R. (May 1997). Modeling: Changing the mathematics experience in post-secondary classrooms. Paper presented at The Nature and Role of Algebra in the K-14 Curriculum: A National Symposium, Washington, DC.

Delpit, L. (1995). *Other people's children: Cultural conflict in the classroom.* New York: W.W. Norton & Co., Inc.

Ellis, M.E., Malloy, C.E., Meece, J.L., & Sylvester, P.R. (2007). Convergence of observer ratings and student perceptions of reform practices in sixth-grade Mathematics Classrooms. *Learning Environments Research, 10*(1), 1–15.

Gay, G. (2000). *Culturally responsive teaching: Theory, research, and practice.* New York: Teachers College Press.

Glaser, B.G. (1965). The constant comparative method of qualitative analysis. *Social Problems, 12*(4), 436–445.

Grouws, D.A. & Lembke, L.O. (1996). Influential factors in students motivation to learn mathematics: The teacher and classroom culture. In M. Carr (Ed.), *Motivation in mathematics* (pp. 39–59). Cresskill, NJ: Hampton Press.

Gutiérrez, R. (2000). Advancing African-American, urban youth in mathematics: Unpacking the success of one math department. *American Journal of Education, 109*(1), 63–111.

Gutstein, E. (2003). Teaching and learning mathematics for social justice in an urban, Latino school. *Journal for Research in Mathematics Education, 34*(1), 37-73.

Hale-Benson, J. *Black children: Their roots, culture, and learning styles.* Baltimore, MD: Johns Hopkins Press, 1986.

Hamilton, L.S., McCaffrey, D., F., Stecher, B.M., Klein, S.P., Robyn, A., & Buglairi, D. (2003). *Educational Evaluation and Policy Analysis, 25,* 1–29.

Harris, O.D. (1994). Equity in classroom assessment. In H. Roberts, J.C. Gonzales, O.D. Harris, D.J. Huff, A.M. Johns, R. Lou, & O. L. Scott (Eds.), *Teaching from a multicultural perspective* (pp. 77–90). Thousand Oaks, CA: Sage.

Hill, H.C., Rowan, B., & Ball, D.L. (2005). Effects of teachers' mathematical knowledge for teaching on student achievement. *American Educational Research Journal, 42*(2), 371–406.

Hilliard, A.G. (1976). Alternatives to IQ testing: An approach to the identification of gifted minority children. Final Report to California State Department of Education.

hooks, b. (1994). *Teaching to transgress: Education as the practice of freedom.* New York: Routledge.

Irvine, J.J. (1992). Making teacher education culturally responsive. In M.E. Dilworth. (Ed.), *Diversity in teacher education* (pp. 79–92). San Francisco, CA: Jossey-Bass Publishers.

Kilpatrick, J., Swafford, J., & Findell, B. (Eds.). (2001). *Adding it up: Helping children learn mathematics.* Washington, DC: National Academy Press.

Ladson,-Billings, G. (1994). *The dreamkeepers: Successful teachers of African American children.* San Francisco, CA: Jossey-Bass.

Ladson-Billings, G. (1995). Toward a theory of culturally relevant pedagogy. *American Educational Research Journal, 32*(3), 465–491.

Malloy, C.E. (1997). Including African American students in the mathematics community. In J. Trentacosta (Ed.), *Multicultural and gender equity in the mathematics classroom: The gift of diversity* (pp. 23–33). Reston, VA: National Council of Teachers of Mathematics.

Malloy, C.E. (2004). Equity in mathematics education is about access. In R. Rubenstein & G. Bright (Eds.) *2004 NCTM yearbook: Effective mathematics teaching* (pp. 1–14). Reston, VA, NCTM.

Malloy, C.E. (2008). Looking throughout the world for democratic access to mathematics. In L.D. English (Ed.), *Handbook of international research in mathematics education* (pp. 20–31). London: Taylor and Francis/Routledge.

Malloy, C. & Malloy, W. (1998). Issues of culture in mathematics teaching and learning. *The Urban Review, 30*(3), 245–257.

Malloy, C.E. & Meece, J.L. (under review). The relations between reform instruction and student learning in middle grades mathematics classrooms.

Miller, S.P. & Hudson, P.J. (2007). Using evidence-based practices to build mathematics competence related to conceptual, procedural, and declarative knowledge. *Learning Disabilities Research and Practice, 22*(1), 47–57.

Moses, R.P. & Cobb, Jr., C.E. (2001). *Radical equations: Math literacy and civil rights.* Boston: Beacon Press.

National Council of Teachers of Mathematics. (1989). *Curriculum and evaluation standards for school mathematics.* Reston, VA: Author.

National Council of Teachers of Mathematics. (1991). *Professional standards for teaching mathematics.* Reston, VA: Author.

National Council of Teachers of Mathematics. (2000). *Principles and standards for school mathematics.* Reston, VA: Author.

Orrill, R. (2001). Mathematics, numeracy, and democracy. In L. A. Steen (Ed.), *Mathematics and democracy* (pp. xiii–xx). National Council of Education and the Disciplines. Retrieved June 8, 2006 from http://www.maa.org/Ql/mathanddemocracy.html

Pearl, A. & Knight, T. (1999). *The democratic classroom: Theory to inform practice.* Cresskill, NJ: Hampton Press.

Sawada, D., Piburn, M., Falconer, K., Turley, J., Benford, R., & Bloom, I. (2000). *Reformed teaching observation protocol (RTOP)* (ACEPT Technical Report No. IN00–1). Tempe, AZ: Arizona Collaborative for Excellence in the Preparation of Teachers.

Shade, B. (1989). The influence of perceptual development on cognitive style: Cross-ethnic comparisons. *Early Child Development and Care, 15,* 137–155.

Shafer, M.C. (2001, April). Instructional quality in the context of reform. Paper presented at the Research Pre-session of the annual meeting of National Council of Teachers of Mathematics Teachers, Orlando, FL.

Silver, E.A. & Stein, M.K. (1996) The QUASAR Project: The "revolution of the possible" in mathematics instructional reform in urban middle schools. *The Urban Review, 30*(4), 476–521.

Skemp, R.R. (1987). *The psychology of leaning mathematics.* Hillsdale, NJ: Lawrence Erlbaum Associates.

Smith, L.B., Stiff, L.V., & Petree, M.R. (2000). Teaching mathematics to the least academically prepared African American students. In W.G. Secada, M.E. Strutchens, M.L. Johnson, & W.F. Tate (Eds.), *Changing the faces of mathematics: Perspectives on African Americans* (pp. 89–96). Reston, VA: NCTM.

Sowder, J.T. & Phillipp, R.A. (1999). The value of interaction in promoting teaching growth. In J.T. Sowder & B.P. Schappelle (Eds.), *Providing a foundation for teaching mathematics in the middle grades* (pp. 223–250). Albany, NY: State University of New York Press.

State Department of Public Instruction (2000). Retrieved July 17, 2007 from www.statepublicschools.org/curriculum/mathematics/scos/2003/k-8/.

Stein, M.K., Smith, M.S., Henningsen, M.A., & Silver, E.A. (2000). *Implementing standards-based mathematics instruction: A casebook for professional development.* New York: Teachers College Press.

Supovitz, J.A., Mayer, D.P., & Kahle, J.B. (2000). Promoting inquiry-based instructional practice: The longitudinal impact of professional development in the context of systemic reform. *Educational Policy, 14*(3), 331–356.

Van Haneghan, J.P., Pruet, S.A., & Bamberger, H.J. (2004). Mathematics reform in a minority community: Student outcomes. *Journal of Education for Students Placed at Risk, 9*(2), 189–211.

Vithal, R. (1999). Democracy and authority: A complementarity in mathematics education? *Zentralblatt für Didaktik der Mathematik, 98*(6), 27–36.

Walker, C.M. (1999). The effect of different pedagogical approaches on mathematics students' achievement. Paper presented at the Annual Meeting of the American Educational Research Association, Montreal (ERIC Document Reproduction Service No. ED 431011).

Wenglinsky, H. (2004). The link between instructional practice and the racial gap in middle schools. *Research in Middle Level Education Online, 28*(1), 1–18,

West, C. (2004). *Democracy matters.* New York: Penguin.

Wilbur, G. (1998). Schools as equal cultures. *Journal of Curriculum and Instruction, 13*(2), 123–147.

Willis, M.G. (1992). Learning styles of African American children: Review of the literature and interventions. In A.K.H. Burlew, W.C. Banks, H.P. McAdoo, and D.A. Azibo (Eds.), *African-American psychology* (pp. 260–278). Newbury Park, CA: Sage.

Appendix A: Observation Protocol

Reform Teaching Observation Protocol (RTOP)

Daiyo Sawada   Michael Piburn
External Evaluator   *Internal Evaluator*
Kathleen Falconer, Jeff Turley, Russell Benford, and Irene Bloom
Evaluation Facilitation Group (EFG)
Technical Report No. IN00–1
Arizona Collaborative for Excellence in the Preparation of Teachers
Arizona State University

BACKGROUND INFORMATION

Name of teacher _____   Announced observation?_____
        (yes, no, or explain)

Location of class _____
        (school and room)

Subject observed _____   Grade level_____

Observer _____   Date of observation_____

Start time _____   End time_____

CONTEXTUAL BACKGROUND AND ACTIVITIES

In the space provided below please give a brief description of the lesson observed, the classroom setting in which the lesson took place (space, seating arrangements, etc.), and any relevant details about the students (number, gender, ethnicity) and teacher that you think are important. Use diagrams if they seem appropriate. (space removed)

I. PEDAGOGY

	Never Occurred	Very Descriptive
1. The instructional strategies and activities respected	0 1 2	3 4

students' prior knowledge and the preconceptions inherent therein.

2. The lesson was designed to engage students as members of a learning community.   0 1 2 3 4

3. In this lesson, student exploration preceded formal presentation.   0 1 2 3 4

4. This lesson encouraged students to seek and value alternative modes of investigation or of problem solving.   0 1 2 3 4

5. The focus and direction of the lesson was often determined by ideas originating with students.   0 1 2 3 4

II. CONTENT

6. The lesson involved fundamental concepts of the subject.   0 1 2 3 4

7. The lesson promoted strongly coherent conceptual understanding.   0 1 2 3 4

8. The teacher had a solid grasp of the subject matter content inherent in the lesson.   0 1 2 3 4

9. Elements of abstraction (i.e., symbolic representations, theory building) were encouraged when it was important to do so.   0 1 2 3 4

10. Connections with other content disciplines and/or real world phenomena were explored and valued.   0 1 2 3 4

III. TASKS

11. Students used a variety of means (models, drawings, graphs, concrete materials, manipulatives, etc.) to represent phenomena.   0 1 2 3 4

12. Students made predictions, estimations and/or hypotheses and devised means for testing them.   0 1 2 3 4

13. Students were actively engaged in thought-provoking activity that often involved the critical assessment of procedures.   0 1 2 3 4

14. Students were reflective about their learning.   0 1 2 3 4

15. Intellectual rigor, constructive criticism, and the challenging of ideas were valued.   0 1 2 3 4

17. The teacher's questions triggered divergent modes of thinking.   0 1 2 3 4

IV. INTERACTIONS

16. Students were involved in the communication of their ideas to others using a variety of means and media.   0 1 2 3 4

18. There was a high proportion of student talk and a significant amount of it occurred between and among students.   0 1 2 3 4

19. Student questions and comments often determined the focus and direction of classroom discourse.   0 1 2 3 4

20. There was a climate of respect for what others had to say.   0 1 2 3 4
21. Active participation of students was encouraged and valued.   0 1 2 3 4
22. Students were encouraged to generate conjectures,   0 1 2 3 4
    alternative solution strategies, and ways of interpreting
    evidence.
23. In general the teacher was patient with students.   0 1 2 3 4
24. The teacher acted as a resource person, working to support   0 1 2 3 4
    and enhance student investigations.
25. The metaphor "teacher as listener" was very characteristic   0 1 2 3 4
    of this classroom.

Appendix B: Perception Survey Items

Pedagogy
> Talk about why answer is not correct
> Talk about why an answer is correct
> Working in pairs/small groups
> It's okay to make an error
> Teacher encourages us to ask questions about math

Content
> Procedures we learn make sense
> Teacher relates math to other subjects
> Learn how math is used to solve real-life problems
> Learn how math ideas are related
> Understand how procedures work
> Connect math to everyday lives
> Improve understanding of math

Tasks
> Try to understand why formulas work
> Come up with new ways to solve problems
> Encouraged to invent ways to solve problems
> Teacher encourages us to make conjectures, predictions, and estimations
> Think about how to solve problems
> Allowed to use different strategies to solve problems correctly

Assessment
> Teacher asks us to understand problems
> Explain understanding of math concepts
> Teacher's comments help understand errors

Interactions
> Working in groups means everyone shares ideas
> Discuss ideas of students to understand math
> Teacher encourages group work
> Talk with classmates about how to solve problems
> Work together to understand new math ideas

Ask one another to share thinking about math
Do problems in small groups
Talk with other students to figure out right answers

Feel safe about asking math questions when something does not make sense

Appendix C: Teacher Interview Questions

Pre Observation

1. Tell me about your class (type of class, students, etc.).
2. What do you plan to do in class today?
3. Describe how this lesson is related to what students already know.
4. What do you hope students will learn as a result of what you have planned?
5. What instructional materials will you be using?
6. What are the important mathematical ideas in the lesson?
7. How will you determine if students understand the mathematical ideas presented in the lesson?
8. Please describe the unit within which this lesson will take place.

Post Observation

9. Overall, how do you think the lesson went?
10. Were there any ways that the lesson was different than what you had planned?
11. Would you say that today was a typical day for this class? Why or why not?
12. What did you use as evidence of students' understanding in the lesson?
13. What did the lesson tell you about what your students are learning and/or still need to learn?

In Depth Interview

1. Describe your role as a teacher.
2. Describe your teaching style.
3. How do students learn mathematics?
4. What does it take for a student to be successful?
5. To what extent and in what ways do you have students work together?
6. How do you establish expectations (norms)?
7. What are the advantages and disadvantages of having students work together?
8. How are you satisfied with student progress?
9. Are student conversations and mathematical ideas important?
10. How do you assess student learning?

Appendix D: Sample Conceptual Understanding Items—Topic Number

Sixth-Grade

Using the circle below, shade in approximately the same fraction that is shaded in the rectangle above.

Concepts Assessed

    Understand faction as a part-to-whole relationship.

    Understand how to make equivalent fractions.

    Understand how to interpret and create area models for fractions.

Seventh-Grade: Which is the smallest number?

    A. 0.625

    B. 0.25

    C. 0.375

    D. 0.5

    E. 0.125

Concepts Assessed

    Understand place value.

    Understand that decimals represent part of a whole.

Eighth-Grade: If the price of a can of beans is raised from 60 cents to 75 cents, what is the percent increase in price?

    A. 15%

    B. 20%

    C. 25%

    D. 30%

Concepts Assessed

    Understand the meaning of percent as parts of a hundred.

    Understand how to estimate a percentage by using appropriate strategies.

Appendix E: Specific Rubric for Eighth-Grade Item—Number

If the price of a can of beans is raised from 60 cents to 75 cents, what is the percent increase in price?

A. 15%
B. 20%
C. 25%
D. 30%

Concepts Assessed

Understand the meaning of percent as parts of a hundred.
Understand how to estimate a percentage by using appropriate strategies.

Score	Indicator	Student Response
0	• No work or states they do not understand with no answer given.	• "I don't understand."
1	• Selected an answer (correct or incorrect) but gives unrelated or no explanation. • No evidence of understanding of proportional relationships.	• A; "I think this is correct because when I subtract 60 from 75 I get 15. And because cents are in 100 to make a dollar it would be 15%." (8942) • C; "Not sure. I guessed." (8917)
2	• Limited understanding of percent as parts of a hundred. • Describes a correct method to start the problem but fails to carry through to find the correct answer.	• A; "I multiplied .25 by 60." (8933) • C; "I was taught this rule in 7th grade (to find percent of change you put the change over the 2nd #) and I used that and got the answer." (8935)
3	• Demonstrates mechanical understanding of percent as parts of a hundred. • Does not provide sufficient explanation of strategy used in solving problem.	• C; "It is C because I figured 15, 20 and 30 and none worked." (8949) • C; "25% × 60=15" (8962)
4	• Demonstrates understanding of percent as parts of a hundred beyond mechanical computation. • Explains why the method they chose works in this case.	• C; "Because 25% of 60 is 15 and if you add 15 to 60 you get 75." (8954) • C; "I found the amount of increase and by dividing it by the original price, I came up with the increased percent." (8944)

5   Contrasting Pedagogical Styles and Their Impact on African American Students

Robert Q. Berry III and Oren L. McClain

Introduction

Ms. Canady[1] is a white woman with 14 years of teaching experience. Ms. Canady grew up in the community in which she teaches and all of her teaching experiences have been at Spartan Middle School. Spartan Middle School (SMS) is located in a rural county in a southeastern state. This rural county is geographically large with a population of about 12,200 people. Warehousing, trucking, and textile are the primary industries for employment in this county. Ms. Canady has an undergraduate degree in middle school education with an emphasis in mathematics and a master's degree in mathematics education. At the time that observations of Ms. Canady took place, 514 students were enrolled at the school: 258 Black, 248 white, 3 Hispanic, 4 Asian, and 1 unspecified. Two hundred and eighty-nine students (56%) at SMS received free or reduced lunch.

Ms. Canady's pedagogy can be described as an aggregate of high-demanding structure and a disciplined environment coupled with instruction that builds on students' experiences and realities. Irvine and Fraser (1998) used the term "warm demanders" to describe teachers like Ms. Canady. Ms. Canady described her teaching style by stating:

> Knowing the backgrounds, family issues, and struggles of many students helped me to develop empathy and understanding and to want to reach my students.... This community has gone through some tough times. It is my job to make sure my kids can be successful ... Over the years I've become creative in my teaching. My classroom has changed dramatically over the past years ... from a class with me as the instructor to a community of learners with me as the facilitator. Students really enjoy this environment and typically do well.

Observation of Ms. Canady's classroom also showed that she had developed a strong rapport with her students. She expected them to work hard by making sure the students were engaged while at the same time connecting with the students by asking questions about their families, discussing their hobbies, and discussing larger community issues.

Ms. Canady began a seventh-grade unit on addition and subtraction of integers by presenting students with contextual problems she found in the newspaper.

These problems included issues surrounding the local drought conditions, temperature, football, and debt/income relationships. One problem she presented was, "In Friday night's football game the Spartans lost eleven yards on first down then gained five yards on second down. What was the total yardage for these two plays?" This problem was appropriate for Ms. Canady's class because, in the small rural county where her school is located, high school and youth football are revered. The arrangement of the desks allowed students to work in groups of four.

Donovan, Shonda, and Cheri worked together. Donovan and Shonda are African American and Cheri is white. In attempting a solution to the problem, Donovan shared with his group a picture he drew that resembled a football field showing that the team started on the 20 yard line and ended on the 14 yard line. He stated the answer was 14. Shonda looked at Donovan's pictures and stated, "Yeah, they lost six yards." Ms. Canady asked, "Supposed the Spartans started on the 50." Donovan stated quickly the answer would be 44; Shonda stated "minus six." During whole-class discussion, Marcel, an African American student working in a different group, presented a picture similar to Donovan's with exception that the starting point was 0 and the ending point was –6. Donovan made a connection with Marcel's strategy by stating to his tablemates that, "... it does not matter where they start, they lose six yards." In Ms. Canady's classroom, the use of context along with sharing strategies in small groups provided Donovan and his classmates with the necessary opportunities to make connections with different representations of integers.

Ms. Able

Ms. Able is a white woman with 12 years of teaching experience and teaches a different section of the grade-level seventh-grade mathematics course at Spartan Middle School. Ms. Able attended the same undergraduate institution as Ms. Canady and was enrolled in a master's degree program in mathematics education, having completed all requirements with the exception of one course. Ms. Able also grew up in the community and graduated from the same high school as Ms. Canady.

Ms. Able's pedagogy can be described as authoritative. The desks in her class were arranged in rows facing the front and she claimed authority on all classroom interactions by requiring students to use her prescribed problem-solving techniques. Ms. Able described her teaching style as "professional." Observations of Ms. Able's classroom showed that her interactions with students were focused primarily on the mathematics content and the steps students must demonstrate to get a right answer. Ms. Able's goals for her teaching focused primarily on students achieving high scores on the state mandated assessment. In order for students to achieve on the test, she stated "... my students need discipline. I need to know that they can do what is asked of them when testing comes around." It appeared that she maintained distance from her students, both emotional and physical. Motivating contexts for doing mathematics were not discussed.

Ms. Able started a unit on addition and subtraction of integers by demonstrating to students how to solve $5 + (-3)$ using colored counters. She demonstrated five

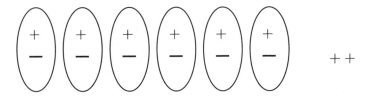

Figure 5.1 Jamal's representation of 8 + (–6).

addition problems, emphasizing the concept of zero pairs. She defined a zero pair as "A counter representing a positive integer and a counter representing a negative integer constitutes a zero pair." She then gave the students a worksheet and two colored counters. As the students worked on their problems, Ms. Able circulated throughout the class making sure the students set up the problems prior to finding the sum. Setting up the problem meant that students were required to represent the positive counters on paper with the "+" symbol and negative counters with the "–" symbol. Students were allowed to discuss their work with a partner. The lesson ended with three students demonstrating how to do three problems on the overhead. To demonstrate 8 + (–6), Jamal, an African American boy, drew a representation on the whiteboard as depicted in Figure 5.1. Jamal described the representation of the circle around "+" and "–" symbols as a zero pair. He concluded that he had six zero pairs and stated that the answer was "plus two."

Contrasting Pedagogical Styles

While the vignettes of Ms. Canady's and Ms. Able's classrooms are snapshots in time, they provided an interesting contrast to introducing addition and subtraction of integers to similar classrooms of students. Ms. Canady's classroom appeared to be student-centered where context is provided to connect the students' backgrounds to the mathematics and where students can share and evaluate each other's strategies. In contrast, Ms. Able's classroom appeared to be teacher-centered, where emphasis was placed on students mimicking the strategies presented by the teacher.

Interestingly, these remarkably different approaches to mathematics teaching and learning produced similar results as measured on the state mandated assessment in mathematics. Both teachers' students achieved pass rates higher than that of the state average over the past three years. Both teachers cited their classroom environments and teaching styles as reasons for the high pass rate on the state assessment. Given the contrast in pedagogy and classroom environments, questions arise concerning the long-term impact of these different approaches on students' mathematical understanding and identities.

Therefore, this chapter examines two contexts of mathematics teaching and learning with a focus on how these contexts influenced mathematical outcomes for African American students. The teachers in the vignettes described earlier were participants in a larger research project focusing on contextualizing mathematics teaching and learning. The hypothesis for the larger study was that incorporating a contextual approach to mathematics teaching and learning would have a positive impact on students' outcomes. This hypothesis was informed by a review of the literature, which revealed that students of color, students in the lower socio-economic strata, and rural student populations benefited positively from experiencing mathematics teaching and learning in a context that allowed them to make mathematical connections. While the larger study included all students, this chapter focuses on seventh-grade African American students.

Mathematics Teaching

The most dominant mathematics classroom teaching pattern in American schools is the initiation–response–evaluation (IRE) pattern (Hiebert & Stigler, 2000). IRE is a teacher-centered pattern of teacher-initiated questions, student response, and teacher evaluation (Cazden, 2001). In IRE mathematics classrooms, students typically listen and remember what teachers say and demonstrate. Little emphasis is placed on students explaining their thinking, working through mathematical ideas publicly, making conjectures, or coming to consensus about mathematical ideas (Franke, Kazemi, & Battey, 2007). The IRE pattern is well documented in mathematics classrooms that serve African American students (Lubienski, 2002; Lubienski, McGraw, & Strutchens, 2004; Strutchens, Lubienski, McGraw, & Westbrook, 2004; Strutchens & Silver, 2000). According to the National Assessment for Educational Progress (NAEP) data, African American middle school students have made significant gains in mathematics achievement (Tate, 2005). However, African American students are more likely to be enrolled in lower-level mathematics courses and are more likely to experience a mathematics curriculum that emphasizes basic skills (Tate, 2005). Because African American students are more likely to be in lower level courses, they are more likely to use computers for drill and practice than for simulations, demonstrations, or application of concepts (Lubienski, McGraw, & Strutchens, 2004) and they are more likely to use worksheets on a daily basis (Strutchens, Lubienski, McGraw, & Westbrook, 2004). Simply put, African American middle school students are not experiencing instructional practices consistent with the standards-based recommendations suggested by the National Council Teachers of Mathematics (NCTM) (Lubienski, McGraw, & Strutchens, 2004) and their teachers are less likely to emphasize reasoning and problem-solving during instruction (Strutchens & Silver, 2000). The standards-based approach emphasizes conceptual understanding, reasoning, student engagement with mathematical ideas, use of multiple representations, collaborative investigations, and discussion and writing (Goldsmith & Mark, 1999).

Mathematics educators have suggested that an IRE teaching pattern limits students' ability to fully understand and appreciate the complexities of mathematics understanding because there is an emphasis on the use of school-learned methods and rules (Boaler, 2000; Malloy & Malloy, 1998; Tate, 1995). Tate (1995) uses the descriptor "foreign pedagogy" (p. 166) to describe teaching parallel to the IRE teaching pattern. Tate states that this "foreign pedagogy" has negative effects on African American students because it is attributed to: (a) African American students being tracked into remedial mathematics; (b) low numbers of African American students in college preparation or advanced mathematics courses; and (c) fewer opportunities for African American students to use technology in school mathematics. Schoenfeld (2002) argues that teaching methods similar to the IRE teaching pattern encourage the development of procedural knowledge that is of limited use in non-school situations. Boaler (2000) uses the term "cue-based" behaviors, which is analogous to the IRE teaching pattern, to describe how students receive cues that influence their choice of mathematical methods. For example, in cue-based classrooms, students are expected to use the procedures demonstrated by the teacher; they expect questions in the textbook to become progressively more difficult; they expect to use all the numbers given to them in a mathematics question; and they do not expect to use any knowledge that was gained outside the mathematics classroom, such as real-world knowledge. Boaler (2000) contended that students become proficient at finding and interpreting different cues within their mathematics textbooks and use these cues to help them proceed through mathematics exercises.

Franke, Kazemi, and Battey (2007) present an alternative view to the IRE teaching pattern by stating that mathematics teaching is relational and multidimensional. Mathematics teaching is relational in the ways that teachers coordinate the mathematics content, representation of the mathematics, and the students in the classroom in relation to one another. This viewpoint situates mathematics teaching as building relationships between (a) students and teachers; (b) among students themselves and mathematics; and (c) engagement among students and teachers to develop mathematical understanding (Lampert, 2004). Mathematics teaching as relational means knowing students' identities, histories, experiences, and social and cultural contexts (Boaler, 1998; Gutstein, 2003). Mathematics teaching is multidimensional in that there are interactions among (a) teachers' pedagogical content knowledge, (b) teachers' beliefs about mathematics teaching and learning, (c) teacher understandings about students' social and cultural contexts, and (d) creating an environment for mathematics learning (Lampert, 2004; Moschkovich, 2002). These interactions influence the ways teachers of mathematics structure mathematical experiences for students. A teacher who situates mathematics teaching and learning as relational and multidimensional will structure mathematical experiences that are highly contextual and provide opportunities for students to exchange strategies and share mathematical ideas.

Mathematics, like all other forms of knowledge, is situated in a cultural context (Lave & Wenger, 1991). The use of context can help students understand mathematics and how it can apply to everyday life. Context in mathematics teaching and learning is capable of helping students determine the choice of mathematical procedures and can impact students' performance on mathematical tasks (Boaler, 1998). While a relational and multidimensional approach to mathematics teaching suggests the use of context, teachers must be still be cautious. Boaler (1993) suggested that random insertions of context into mathematics teaching ignores the complexity, range, and degree of students' experiences. Such insertions could lead to the development of misconceptions and the overgeneralization of ideas. Consequently, the use of context in mathematics teaching must be purposeful and teachers must thoughtfully consider the experiences of students and the mathematical goals to be learned.

Boaler (1993) contends the degree to which context affects students' performance is underestimated. She challenges the belief that mathematics in "everyday" context is easier than the abstract equivalent; rather, context provides broader links to the mathematics to be learned. Two tasks involving fractions provide an example of the broader connections. One task asked the fraction of a cake each child would get if it were shared equally among six children. The other task asked the fraction of a loaf of bread shared equally between five children (Boaler, 1993). The use of cake and loaf of bread influences approaches to problem-solving in that the word *cake* implies a single entity, whereas a loaf of bread can be regarded as something that is already divided into slices. These examples challenge the belief that abstract calculations provide higher-level skills than calculations in context (Boaler, 1993). Rather, the context in which the mathematics is placed is a factor in determining mathematical procedures and performance.

We contend that, for African American students, experiencing mathematics learning and teaching as relational and multidimensional requires knowing and understanding these students' cultural background, prior experiences, and contexts. In doing this, we give credence to culturally relevant pedagogy. Ladson-Billings (1995) defined culturally relevant pedagogy as a pedagogy that fosters meaningful classroom experiences that affirms students' backgrounds and prior knowledge. Culturally relevant pedagogy provides a framework for using contextual situations for mathematics teaching and learning, connecting to students' experiences, and linking mathematics to students' social and cultural ways of knowing.

Culturally relevant pedagogy rests on three guiding principles: (a) students must experience academic success; (b) students must develop and/or maintain cultural competence; and (c) students must develop a critical consciousness. Culturally relevant teaching requires teachers to attend to students' academic, social, and cultural understandings (Ladson-Billings, 1994, 1995, 2000). Consequently, mathematics teachers must demand, reinforce, and produce excellence in their students. Achieving excellence requires mathematics teachers to use students' social and cultural contexts as a bridge for developing mathematical understanding; thus, teachers are acknowledging and supporting cultural competence. Cultural competence is also supported through the use of curriculum content selections that connect to students' social realities and cultural backgrounds (Ladson-Billings, 1994, 1995, 2000). Culturally relevant teaching allows students to use mathematics to critique the cultural norms, values, mores, and institutions that produce and maintain social inequities (Ladson-Billings, 1994, 1995, 2000).

Matthews (2003) presented ways of evidencing the incorporation of culturally relevant pedagogy into mathematics instruction. Matthews found that culturally relevant pedagogy in mathematics requires teachers to formally and informally use mathematics to critically examine community and social issues; students were encouraged to use social and cultural contexts to discuss and justify their mathematics understandings. The notion of building on students' cultural knowledge was seen in the ways teachers used the local newspaper, menus of local restaurants, and magazines as a source of cultural knowledge. Matthews also found that culturally relevant pedagogy in mathematics requires that teachers build a classroom environment in which teachers press students for justifications, require students to defend their thinking; allow students to struggle with the mathematics; and nurture a classroom community that demands excellence and engagement among the students.

Culturally relevant teachers identify the resources that students bring to the mathematics classroom and these teachers find ways to build on these resources to construct meaningful mathematical understanding (Gutiérrez, 2002). Hence, effective, culturally relevant mathematics teachers of African American students have strong mathematics content knowledge, pedagogical skills, and knowledge of African American cultural style and learning preferences. For this research, we used culturally relevant pedagogy as the foundation for examining the impact an IRE teaching pattern and a relational and multidimensional teaching pattern have on African American students.

African American Students' Learning Preferences

In order to engage in pedagogy culturally relevant for African American students, mathematics teachers must have some understanding of the African American culture and accept that the African American culture is a significant socializing force for African American students. African American students' mathematics identities are shaped by culture, learning preferences, and experiences with mathematics (Berry, 2003). Martin (2007) refers to mathematics identity as one's belief about (a) their ability to do mathematics, (b) the significance of mathematical knowledge, (c) the opportunities and barriers to enter mathematics fields, and (d) the motivation and persistence needed to obtain mathematics knowledge. The development of a positive mathematical identity is essential to help students sustain an interest in mathematics and develop persistence with mathematics. Culturally relevant pedagogy keeps African American students' experiences with mathematics in the forefront and has "the potential to highlight the ways in which African American students experience mathematics *as* African Americans and how these social realities impact mathematics learning and participation among these students" (Martin, 2007, pp. 24–25).

Knowledge about African American cultural experiences provides educators with a means for interpreting students' thoughts, feelings, and actions, while raising expectations for student success (Bennett, 2001). It is essential that mathematics teachers understand African American learning preferences if they are to have a positive impact on African American students' mathematical identities. African American learning preferences are connected to African American cultural experience. Boykin (1986) identified nine interrelated dimensions of the African American cultural experience:

a Spirituality is the conviction that non-material forces influence people's lives.
b Harmony addresses the notion that people are interrelated with other elements.

c   Movement emphasizes the interweaving of pattern, rhythm, music, and dance.
d   Verve is a propensity for high levels of stimulation, to action that is energetic and lively.
e   Affect focuses on emotions, feelings, and nurturing.
f   Communalism is an awareness that social bonds and responsibilities transcend individual privileges.
g   Expressive individualism is the cultivation of a distinct personality and a preference for novelty, freedom, and personal distinctiveness.
h   A social time perspective is an orientation in which time is treated as passing through a social space.
i   Oral tradition is a preference for oral modes of communication in which both speaking and listening are treated as performances (Boykin & Toms, 1985, p. 41).

Although African Americans share common cultural, historical, and social experiences, not all cultural characteristics uniformly apply to all African Americans. Having an understanding of research associated with the African American culture can help increase student learning when pedagogy is compatible with the cultural style of African American learners (Bennett, 2001).

Shade (1997) described the African American learning preference as an aggregate of holistic, relational, and field-dependent learning styles. Holistic learners seek to synthesize divergent experiences in order to obtain the essence of experiences. They thrive on content tied into a larger whole, and perceive cause and effect as separate entities. The kinesthetic mode is the primary mode of information induction; thus, concreteness is needed to facilitate new learning (Shade, 1997). Relational learning preference is characterized as freedom of movement, variation, creativity, divergent thinking, inductive reasoning, and focus on people. Learners who have a relational learning preference approach object relations in a global manner (Shade, 1997). Field-dependent learners need cues from the environment, prefer external structure, are people oriented, are intuitive thinkers, and remember material in a social context (Shade, 1997).

Irvine and York (1995) suggested that the research on learning preferences and culturally diverse populations should be interpreted cautiously. They asserted that research on learning preferences of culturally diverse students is based primarily on the cultural anthropological literature. Additionally, Irvine and York stated:

> Although it is clear that culture, particularly ethnicity, is a powerful force that influences students' predisposition toward learning, it must be emphasized that cultural practices are learned behavior that can be unlearned and modified. Culture is neither static nor deterministic; people of color are not solely products of their culture. Consequently, culture affects individuals in different ways.

Culture and ethnicity are frameworks for the development of learning preferences; however, other factors play a significant role in cultural and learning preferences (Irvine & York, 1995).

The learning preferences of African American students suggest that mathematics instruction for these students should include not only opportunities to learn mathematics in an abstract manner, but must also embed contextual contexts, use concrete imagery, and provide experiences based on how mathematics concepts are related to each other. Teachers need to understand the structures of students' experiences; consequently, this understanding may lead to doing things with students that are not mathematics, such as interviewing them, having them write autobiographies, and discussing their interests (Ladson-Billings, 1997).

NCTM Process Standards

The NCTM Process Standards complement the learning preferences of African American students. Berry (2003) theorized the overlap between the NCTM Process Standards and African American learning preferences. The NCTM Process Standards are: Problem Solving, Reasoning and Proof, Communication, Connections, and Representation (NCTM, 2000). The five NCTM Process Standards focus on how students should learn and use mathematics. The Problem Solving Standard is consistent with the learning preferences of African American learners because it recommends that students build mathematical knowledge through problem-solving, solve problems in context, apply and adapt a variety of problem-solving strategies, and reflect on the problem-solving process. This standard supports the notion that African American learners should have opportunities to experience mathematical problem-solving in a social context and utilize various strategies to solve problems. By experiencing problem-solving in a social context, African American learners can connect abstract mathematical concepts to a situation or context. The use of creativity, experimentation, and improvisation to test, monitor, and reflect on the problem-solving process can broaden the pool of problem-solving strategies for African American learners.

The Reasoning and Proof Standard suggests that students make and investigate conjectures, develop and evaluate mathematical arguments, and select and use various types of reasoning and methods of proof (NCTM, 2000). If African American learners are given opportunities to develop and justify their own reasoning in mathematics, this expectation would complement expressive individualism, experimentation, and divergent thinking. By employing expressive individualism, African American learners can use their preference towards divergent thinking to develop mathematical arguments and investigate mathematical conjectures as they relate to content tied into a larger whole.

The Communication Standard proposes that students organize and consolidate their mathematics thinking, coherently communicate their mathematical ideas to others, analyze and evaluate the mathematical thinking and strategies of others, and use the language of mathematics to express mathematical ideas (NCTM, 2000). Because African American learners have a person-to-person orientation, preference towards oral expressions, social and affective emphasis, and are attuned to non-verbal communication (Boykin, 1986; Shade, 1997), the propositions proposed by the Communication Standard correspond well with their cultural styles and learning preferences. When the oral learning preference is emphasized, the teacher can monitor students' use of oral reasoning and justifications, assist them in organizing their thoughts, and help them develop critical thinking and problem-solving skills. In addition, teachers can model writing in mathematics as an equally important approach in learning mathematics.

The Connections Standard recommends that students interconnect mathematical ideas within mathematics and outside of mathematics, and understand how mathematics ideas interconnect and build on one another to produce a coherent whole (NCTM, 2000). In addition, the Connections Standard recommends a holistic view of mathematics that contextualizes mathematical ideas and concepts. Shade (1997) observed that African American learners need an understanding of the interconnectedness and interdependence among ideas, items, and experiences for optimal learning to exist. African American learners need contextual experiences that connect mathematical ideas within and outside of mathematics. Teachers would do well to consider students' daily experiences and cultural ways of knowing when designing mathematical tasks. These experiences should consider the interweaving and connecting abstract mathematics concepts with patterns, rhythm, pulsation, music, and movement—all part of the African American cultural experience.

The Representation Standard suggests that students create and use representations to organize, record, and communicate mathematical ideas; select, apply, and translate among mathematical representations to solve problems; and use presentation to model and interpret physical, social, and mathematical phenomena (NCTM, 2000). Since African American learners have a propensity for verve, mathematics learning and teaching should be stimulating and interesting as well as offer opportunities for hands-on experiences that promote interactivity. Mathematics can be represented in multiple ways: it can be viewed through students acting out problem-solving situations; it can be talked about, listened to, written about, graphically represented, and represented by building models.

The alignment between pedagogical practices and the classroom environment with the lived experiences and cultural backgrounds of students positively influences student performance (Berry, 2008; Franke, Kazemi, & Battey, 2007). Mathematics classrooms are cultural and social spaces where students shape their mathematics identities through the experiences which they encounter. For African American learners, this means teachers provide opportunities that allow them to capitalize on their strengths as well as compensate for their weaknesses.

Revisiting Ms. Canady and Ms. Able's Pedagogical Styles

Earlier we presented vignettes to show a contrast of Ms. Canady's and Ms. Able's pedagogical styles. We would characterize Ms. Canady's teaching style as being closely related to relational and multidimensional and Ms. Able's teaching style as being closely related to IRE. Table 5.1 illustrates the teachers' pedagogical style using the NCTM Process Standards as the framework.

Ms. Canady and Ms Able's school adopted Holt, Rinehart, and Winston's (2004) *Middle School Math: Course 2* textbook for seventh-grade mathematics and used a pacing guide that is parallel with the textbook. The school had two mathematics

Table 5.1 Ms. Canady's and Ms. Able's Pedagogies using the NCTM Process Standards

Ms. Canady	Ms. Able
Problem Solving • Open-ended problems • Problems presented in contextual situations • Acting out problems	Problem Solving • Closed problems • Problems devoid of context
Reasoning and Proof • Developed reasoning for adding and subtracting integers based on experimentation • Students justified and defend ideas • Created and modified rules for adding and subtracting integers from a running list keep throughout the unit	Reasoning and Proof • The teacher gave the rules for adding and subtracting integers to the students to memorize and practice
Communication • Students justified ideas with each other orally • Student wrote mathematical ideas in writing, through drawings, and with mathematical symbols • Students developed lyrics and performed a song based on the rules for adding and subtracting integers • A class list of ideas was displayed and modified by the students • Student to student interactions • Student to teacher interactions	Communication • Students wrote mathematical ideas using mathematical symbols and drawings. • Student to student interactions • Student to teacher interactions
Connections • Students connected mathematics with issues found in the local newspaper • Multiple contexts were used to connect the mathematics	Connections • No contexts were used
Representation • Virtual and hands-on manipulatives were used • Used the local newspaper to find representations of the mathematics	Representation • Hands-on manipulatives

tracks, an on grade-level track and an advanced track. With two mathematics tracks, the school adopted an inclusion model; this meant that all mathematics classes were collaboratively taught with a special educator. Observations of both classes revealed that the special educators worked to support the teachers rather than taking the lead to teach any lessons. The special educators moved about the classroom supporting any student that needed help. It was not apparent which students had special needs and the students with special needs were not identified to the authors.

As stated earlier, Ms. Canady and Ms. Able were participants in a research study. These teachers were selected for the study because observations of their classrooms revealed that these teachers had contrasting pedagogical styles. Ms. Canady incorporated context, students' interests, and multiple representations in her mathematics pedagogy and Ms. Able's pedagogy was primarily rules focused. Below are descriptions of Ms. Canady's and Ms. Able's units.

Ms. Canady's Unit

The authors collaborated with Ms. Canady to develop an addition and subtraction of integers unit that incorporated students' learning preferences, the NCTM process standards, and context to represent and teach the mathematics. Collaborating with Ms. Canady was an intervention for the research project that focused on incorporating the learning preferences of students. Three of Ms. Canady's classes participated in this study. There were 51 students total in these classes; 33 were African Americans and 18 white. Table 5.2 illustrates Ms. Canady's unit; a primary NCTM process standard was denoted, each activity incorporated multiple process standards.

Providing a context at the beginning of the unit was essential because it set the tone for students to make connections between abstract mathematics and contexts relevant to the students. The contexts were derived from the local newspaper. On day one of this unit, students worked on word problems that included the contexts of drought, temperature, football, and debt/income relationships. The context of drought was particularly relevant for these students because the area in which they live was experiencing severe drought conditions, which were a topic in print and television news reports. Additionally, the drought had a negative impact on a large lake in the county. An example problem was, "The newspaper reported the normal monthly precipitation is about 22 inches. The total precipitation for this month is 3 inches below normal. What is the actual precipitation for this month?" Football as a context was also appropriate because, in this county, high school football is revered. In addition, the teacher was able to incorporate debt/income relationships by using the increase of payday lending businesses in the county.

While context is important, the unit also included elements that connected to students learning preferences, incorporated critical thinking, and included the use of hands-on and virtual manipulatives. Table 5.3 shows the daily activities of the unit and how they are correlated with the NCTM process standards and with African American students' learning preferences. It should be noted that the NCTM process standards and the African American learning preferences correlated across multiple activities rather than across one or two.

One of the goals for the unit was to not provide students with a list of rules for adding and subtracting integers. Students were expected to develop the rules themselves. Consequently, several experiences were developed so that students could conceive the rules with understanding. On day two, students had experiences with two colored counters in which they explored the notion of zero pairs. This task allowed students to discuss their thinking in small groups. Students were given opportunities to represent and solve words problems with two colored counters. For example, students were asked to solve, "Tiki Barber lost 7 yards on first down but rushed for 3 yards on second down. What was his total yardage for the two

Table 5.2 Ms. Canady's Seventh Grade Mathematics Unit on Adding Integers

Lessons			
Lesson 1 (1 day) Providing a context for addition and subtraction of integers	Solving word problems involving integers • Problem-solving strategies included drawing pictures, acting out, and small group discussions (**Problem-Solving**)	After solving word problems using integers, students created words problems involving integers and solved each others problems in small groups (**Representation**)	• Headline news: Adding integers in the newspaper (**Connections**)
Lesson 2 (1 day) Two colored counters	• Solved problems using two colored counters (**Problem Solving**) • Making zero pairs (no other "rules" were discussed) (**Representation**)	When given an integer, students created three representations of that integer using two colored counters (**Representation**)	• Represent words problems using the two colored counters, and then solving (**Representation**)
Lesson 3 (1 day) Virtual Manipulatives and Negotiation of Rules	• The classes generated a list of rules for adding and subtracting integers then the classes edited the rules to create a final list (**Reasoning and Proof**) • Color Chip-Addition Applet: Computer generate problems (http://nlvm.usu.edu/en/nav/frames_asid_161_g_1_t_1.html) (**Representation**)	Color Chip-Addition Applet: User Generated Problems and Free Play (http://nlvm.usu.edu/en/nav/frames_asid_161_g_1_t_1.html) (**Representation**)	
Lesson 4 (1 day) Song or Rap	Develop a song or rap that incorporated the rules for adding integers (**Communication**)	Small group newspaper search for integer use (**Connections**)	
Lesson 5 (1 day) Analysis and Performance	Analysis of lyric across small groups (**Reasoning and Proof**)	Performance of songs and raps (**Communication**)	

The words in parentheses are the NCTM Process Standards

Table 5.3 The NCTM Process Standards and African American Learning Preferences in a Seventh Grade Mathematics Unit on Adding Integers

Lessons	Problem-Solving • Social context • Experimentation • Improvisation	Reasoning and Proof • Divergent thinking • Holistic perspective	Communication • Oral expression • People Oriented • Affective emphasis	Connections • Interconnectedness • Authentic	Representation • Concrete imagery • Hands-on experiences
Lesson 1 (1 day) Providing a context for addition and subtraction of integers	Solving word problems involving integers				Create word problems involving integers and solved each others' problems in small groups
Lesson 2 (1 day) Two colored counters	Solved problems using two colored counters			Headline news: Adding integers in the newspaper	• Represent word problems using the two colored counters, and then solving. • When given an integer, students created three representations of that integer using two colored counters • Color Chip-Addition Applet
Lesson 3 (1 day) Virtual Manipulatives and Negotiation of Rules		The classes generated a list of rules for adding and subtracting integers then edited the rules to create a final list			
Lesson 4 (1 day) Song or Rap			Develop a song or rap that incorporated the rules for adding integers	Small group newspaper search for integer use	
Lesson 5 (1 day) Analysis and Performance		Analysis of lyric across small groups	Performance of songs and raps		

downs?" Also, on day two students worked on "naked numbers" problems like –8 + 3. The lessons were structured such that students could develop and understand processes for adding integers. The use of contexts and abstract symbols allowed the students to broaden their representations of integers.

The use of virtual manipulatives allowed for further exploration prior to whole-class discussions on rules. The students used the Color Chip Addition applet found on the National Library of Virtual Manipulatives website. This applet presented various individual problems for students to solve. Students then represented the problems with two-color chips, and solved each problem after representing it concretely. After working on computer-generated problems, the students generated their own problems using the color chip applet. Students were told that they had to develop rules for adding integers and to generate problems that would help them develop rules. The last portion of day three focused on whole-class discussions for generating and editing rules for adding integers. All classes developed and agreed upon similar rules. Below is an example of a group of African American students generating rules.

Amber: When you have a negative and positive, you subtract; if the negative is higher, then the answer is negative; if the positive is higher, then the answer is positive.

Angelic: OK, put it on the list. Here is mine: if there are two negatives, add them together and the answer is negative.

The group: Alright, yeah, and OK.

Shawon: If both are positive, then the answer is positive.

Tony: When adding opposites, you come out with zero.

During whole-class discussion, Tony posed the following question: "Suppose you have a problem with two positives and one negatives?"

Ms. Canady: Can you give me an example?

Tony: Seven plus six plus negative ten.

Many students in the class either drew representation of the problem or used two colored counters to explore this problem. They concluded that this problem would have a positive answer.

Ms. Canady: Can you develop a rule for problems with multiple addends.

Jasmine: I would add all of the positives number, then all of the negative numbers; if the positive is higher, then the answer is positive, if the negative is higher then the answer is negative.

All of the students in the class appeared to agree with Jasmine.

On day four of the unit, the students developed a song or a rap that incorporated the rules for adding integers. The students worked in groups or pairs to develop lyrics that met the following requirements: (a) describe situations involving adding two positive integers; (b) describe situations involving adding two negative integers; (c) describe situations adding one positive and one negative integer; and (d) describe situations adding opposite integers. Most of the students wrote or adapted lyrics for existing rhythm and blues songs, country songs, or hip-hop raps. Additionally, some students worked out dance routines or movements for their songs. The movements/dances not only complement the songs but also complement the mathematics. For example, one group situated themselves as a "human number line" and their movements/dances complemented the rules as one move up or down the number line. In addition, on day four, the students continued the newspaper searches for integer use. The activity was parallel to the headline news activity on day one; the major difference was that the students searched for integer use rather than the teacher providing the context.

The final day of the unit consisted of student performances of their songs, an analysis of some lyrics, and a review of the unit. While the performances were entertaining, the goal was for students to come to know the rules for adding and subtracting integers and for them to develop a context for memorizing and understanding the rules. The analysis of the lyrics consisted of the teacher writing the lyrics that conveyed similar rules and having the students compare and contrast their meanings. In addition, the teacher reviewed adding integers in the "naked numbers" context.

Ms. Able

The authors did not collaborate with Ms. Able. Rather, one of the authors observed Ms. Able's class to document her pedagogical style. Three of Ms. Able's classes participated in this study. There were 49 students in total in these classes; 30 were African Americans and 19 white. Ms. Able followed the textbook and pacing guide closely. On day one, the students worked on "naked numbers" problems with two colored counters. The students used worksheets that had pictures of the colored counters that represented problems. The worksheets revealed to the students rules for adding integers and Ms. Able's instruction supported learning and following the given rules. She made statements such as, "If there are more red counters than yellow counters, then you know the answer is positive . . . so all you need to do is subtract to get the answer." On day two, the students worked on "naked numbers" problems without two colored counters and Ms. Able reminded students of the rules for adding integers. On day three, the students worked on word problems from the textbook and discussed changing subtraction problems to addition problems. Ms. Able introduced a rule called "copy–change–change." The example below describes the "copy–change–change" rule.

> Ms. Able: For this problem [6– (–7)], you copy the six, then change the subtraction to addition, then change negative seven to a positive seven.

On the board, she wrote the new problem as 6 + 7. After demonstrating two more problems using the "copy–change–change" rule, the students worked on a worksheet. On day four, the students reviewed adding with "naked numbers" problems.

Pre- and Post-Tests

To understand the impact of the Ms. Canady's and Ms. Able's pedagogical styles on students' learning, pre- and post-test were given to both groups of students. The tests were constructed from released items on the mandated state assessment. The tests were designed to be parallel; that is, they had the same number and types of items. The tests were each composed of ten items involving a combination of multiple-choice and open-ended problems. The tests were reviewed by a mathematics educator, a mathematics education doctoral student, and a high school mathematics teacher for face validity.

The six multiple choice items were adapted from the state assessment released items. The state assessment gave students choices of solution to a "naked numbers problem." The pre- and post-test were adapted by giving students choice of whether the solution would be positive, negative, neither, or unsure. In addition, the students were asked to explain their thinking. Figure 5.2 is representative of the multiple-choice items with directions.

On both the pre- and post-tests students analyzed the thinking of three persons who solved "naked numbers" problems. These problems were adapted from multiple choice items among the released items of the state assessment; the choices were reduced from five to three choices and were put into a context of solutions found by three students. Figure 5.3 represents an adapted problem that appeared on the pre- and post-tests.

Two open-ended items were on both tests. On the post-test, students were asked to solve, "Sam the snake slithers forward 4 feet and backwards 2 feet everyday. How many days will it take Sam to reach a rock 25 feet away from his starting point?"

The pre- and post-test measures were scored by two raters—one mathematics educator (one of the authors) and a high school mathematics teacher. The pre- and post-test measures were scored after the instructional units were completed. The raters used a 16-point rubric to rate the overall quality of the open-ended responses. If a multiple choice item was correct, then the raters used a five-point rubric to rate the quality of the explanation. Prior to scoring the measures, the raters discussed the rubrics and discussed expectations of quality for each item; this helped to establish a reliable coding scheme. For the items that required subjective ratings on the pre-test, the mean inter-rater correlation was 0.92. On the post-test, the mean

---

Using mental mathematics
- circle **positive** for the problem(s) that will result in a positive answer,
- circle **negative** for the problem(s) that will result in a negative answer,
- circle **neither** for the problem(s) that will result in neither negative nor positive answer, or
- circle **unsure** for the problem(s) that you do not know what the result will be.
- Explain your answers.

1   a. Positive   b. Negative   c. Neither   d. Unsure
Explain your answer.

Figure 5.2 An example of a multiple choice item with directions.

The class was given the problem.

- Oren stated the answer is 5 because he subtracted.
- Robert stated the answer is −19 because it is an addition problem but he put the negative in front because of −12.
- Joe stated the answer is −5 because he said there are five more negatives than positives.

Who is right? Why?

Figure 5.3 Post-test Analytical problem.

inter-rater correlation was 0.96. These correlations were considered sufficiently high to provide reliable assessments of students' performance on these measures. The scores on each item were added together to determine the students' individual scores on the pre- and post-tests. A score of 100 was considered a perfect score.

Findings

A one-way analysis of covariance (ANCOVA) was used to investigate the effectiveness of the two methods of instruction, controlling for group differences. Students were administered a pre-test before the units were taught and a post-test after units were completed. The effect size was obtained to measure the amount of variance accounted for in achievement by the two types of teaching methods.

Prior to evaluating the different methods of instruction on student achievement, several assumptions underlying the one-way ANCOVA were examined. Observations of skewness values and normal probability plots indicated that normality was satisfied. In addition, within group box-and-whisker plots indicated students' post-test scores were normally distributed. Levene's test of homogeneity of variance indicated that the variances of the two groups were not significantly different; $F(1, 61) = 0.005, p > 0.05$. Linearity between the covariate and dependent variable was shown to be satisfied by a linear regression of post-test scores on pre-test scores. Also, interaction between the group and pre-test variables indicated the interaction term was insignificant ($p > 0.05$), supporting the assumption of homogeneous regression slopes.

Tables 5.4 and 5.5 summarize a one-factor ANCOVA and the descriptive statistics. A one-way ANCOVA indicated that the method of instruction students

Table 5.4 One-Factor Analysis of Covariance Summary Table

Source	SS	df	MS	F
Pre-test	7188.585	1	7188.585	75.629
Group	661.939	1	661.939	6.964
Error	5703.032	60	95.051	
Total	13553.556	62		

a. R Squared = .579 (Adjusted R Squared = .565)

Table 5.5 Post-test Descriptive Statistics

Group	N	Mean	SD	Variance
Control	30	77.043[a]	15.432	252.860
Intervention	33	83.537[a]	13.497	182.172
Total	63			

a. Covariates appearing in the model are evaluated at the following value: Pre-test = 54.67.

were exposed to had a statistically significant influence on their achievement, $F(1, 60) = 6.96$, $p < 0.05$. Parameter estimates indicate that, given two students with similar pre-test scores, you can expect the student in the intervention group to have a score of 6.5 points higher then the student in the control group. Furthermore, the adjusted r-squared indicates that 57% of the variance can be accounted for by group assignment.

Discussion and Conclusion

The findings using snapshots of Ms. Canady's and Ms. Able's classrooms have limited generalizability. However, we cannot discount the fact that Ms. Canady's class appeared to have a strong impact on African American students' learning of addition and subtraction of integers. The reasons for this impact are hard to isolate but we speculate that the use of contexts for teaching addition of integers, students sharing and justifying their thinking, and Ms. Canady's "warm demandering" disposition positively impacted students' motivation to do mathematics. Furthermore, observations of both classrooms revealed that Ms. Canady's classroom was more engaging. Perhaps, the difference might be found in the level of engagement of the students. In other words, the activities and engagement of Ms. Canady's pedagogy are strongly correlated to relational and multidimensional teaching, which appears to be strongly suited for African American learners.

The knowledge required for effective teaching is substantial. Teachers need not only know mathematics content, but must also be able to understand students' understanding of the mathematics content, and understand curricular goals (Schoenfeld, 2002). This means they must know, and be able to teach, problem-solving skills, represent mathematical concepts in multiple ways, connect mathematical concepts within mathematics and to other subject areas, and be able to analyze students' thinking about mathematics. Schoenfeld (2002) contended that this is a gross underestimation of the knowledge and skills required to be effective mathematics teachers. While the aforementioned knowledge for teaching mathematics is essential, we argue that this knowledge is shortsighted when teaching mathematics to African American students. Knowledge of content, teaching, and curriculum are effective components of teaching mathematics and can positively impact on the mathematics teaching and learning of African American students. This knowledge alone, however, will not have the sustaining impact necessary for long-term effects on the mathematics teaching and learning of African American students (Martin, 2007).

Effective mathematics teachers of African American students must not only have knowledge of content, curriculum, and teaching, but must also possess the tenets of culturally relevant pedagogy. These teachers must be "warm demanders," that is, they must demand academic excellence from their students, while being culturally competent. Mathematics teachers of African American students must have knowledge of the African American cultural style and learning preferences and know how to use this knowledge to develop effective learning experiences in mathematics for African American students.

Notes

1 All names of people and places are pseudonyms.

References

Bennett, C. (2001). Genres of research in multicultural education. *Review of Educational Research, 71*(2), 171–217.

Berry III, R.Q. (2003). Mathematics standards, cultural styles, and learning preferences: The plight and the promise of African American students. *The Clearing House, 76*(5), 244–249.

Berry III, R.Q. (2008). Access to upper-level mathematics: The stories of African American middle school boys who are successful with school mathematics. *Journal for Research in Mathematics Education, 39*(5), 464–488.

Boaler, J. (1993). The role of contexts in the mathematics classroom: Do they make mathematics more real? *For The Learning of Mathematics, 13*(2), 12–17.

Boaler, J. (1998). Open and closed mathematics: Student experiences and understandings. *Journal for Research in Mathematics Education, 29*(1), 41–62.

Boaler, J. (2000). Exploring situated insights into research and learning. *Journal for Research in Mathematics Education, 39*(1), 113–119.

Boykin, A.W. (1986). The triple quandary and the schooling of Afro-American children. In U. Neisser (Ed.), *The school achievement of minority children: New perspectives*. Hillsdale, NJ: Lawrence Erlbaum Associates.

Boykin, A.W. & Toms, F.D. (1985). Black child socialization: A conceptual framework. In H.P. McAdoo & J.L. McAdoo (Eds.), *Black children: Social, educational and parental environments* (pp. 33–51). Newbury Park, CA: Sage.

Cazden, C (2001). *Classroom discourse: The language of teaching and learning*. Portsmouth, NH: Heinemann.

Franke, M.L. Kazemi, E. & Battey, D. (2007). Mathematics teaching and classroom practices. In F. K. Lester (Ed.), *Second handbook of research on mathematics teaching and learning* (pp. 225–256). Charlotte, NC: Information Age Publishing.

Goldsmith, L. & Mark, J. (1999). What is a standards-based mathematics curriculum? *Educational Leadership, 57*(3), 40–44.

Gutstein, E. (2003). Teaching and learning mathematics for social justice in an urban, Latino school. *Journal for Research in Mathematics Education, 23*(1), 37–73.

Guttiérrez, R. (2002). Beyond essentialism: The complexity of language in teaching Mathematics to Latina/o students. *American Educational Research Journal, 39*(4), 1047–1088.

Hiebert, J. & Stigler, J. (2000). A proposal for improving classroom teaching: Lessons from the TIMSS Video Study. *The Elementary School Journal, 101*, 3–20.

Irvine, J. & Fraser, J. (1998, May 13). "Warm demanders:" Do national certification standards leave room for the culturally responsive pedagogy of African American teachers? *Education Week*, p. 56.

Irvine, J.J. & York, D.E. (1995). Learning styles and culturally diverse students: A literature review. In J.A. Banks & C.A.M. Banks (Eds.), *Handbook of research on multicultural education* (pp. 484–497). New York: Macmillan.

Ladson-Billings, G. (1994). *The dreamkeepers: Successful teachers of African American students*. San Francisco: Jossey Bass Publishers.

Ladson-Billings, G. (1995). Toward a theory of culturally relevant pedagogy. *American Educational Research Journal, 32*, 465–491.

Ladson-Billings, G. (1997). It doesn't add up: African American students' mathematics achievement. *Journal for Research in Mathematics Education, 28*(6), 697–708.

Ladson-Billings, G. (2000). Fighting for our lives: Preparing teachers to teach African American students. *Journal of Teacher Education, 51*, 206–214

Lampert, M. (2004). When de problem is not the question and the solution in not the answer: mathematical knowing and teaching. In T.P. Carpenter, J.A. Dossey, J.L. Koehler (Eds.), *Classics in mathematics education research*, (pp. 152–171). Reston, VA: NCTM.

Lave, J. & Wenger, E. (1991). *Situated learning: Legitimate peripheral participation*. Cambridge: Cambridge University Press.

Lubienski, S.T. (2002). A closer look at Black–White mathematics gaps: Intersections of race and SES in NAEP achievement and instructional practices data. *Journal of Negro Education, 71*(4), 269–287.

Lubienski, S.T., McGraw, R., & Strutchens, M. E. (2004). NAEP findings regarding gender: Mathematics achievement, student affect, and learning practices. In P. Kloosterman & F.K. Lester (Eds.), *Results and interpretations of the 1990 through 2000 mathematics assessments of the National Assessment of Educational Progress* (pp. 305–336). Reston, VA: NCTM.

Malloy, C.E. & Malloy, W.W. (1998). Issues of culture in mathematics teaching and learning. *The Urban Review, 30*, 245–257.

Martin, D.B. (2007). Beyond missionaries or cannibals: Who should teach mathematics to African American children? *The High School Journal, 91*(1), 6–28.

Matthews, L.E. (2003). Babies overboard! The complexities of incorporating culturally relevant teaching into mathematics instruction. *Educational Studies in Mathematics, 53*(1), 61–82.

Moschkovich, J. (2002). A situated and sociocultural perspective on bilingual mathematics learners. *Mathematical Thinking and Learning, 4*(2&3), 189–212.

National Council of Teachers of Mathematics (NCTM). (2000). *Principles and standards for school mathematics*. NCTM (Ed.), Reston, VA: Author.

Schoenfeld, A. (2002). Making mathematics work for all children: Issues of standards, testing, and equity. *Educational Researcher, 31*(1), 13–25.

Shade, B. (1997). Culture and learning styles within the African American community. In B. Shade (Ed.), *Culture, style, and the educative process: Making schools work for racially diverse students* (pp. 12–28). Springfield, IL: Charles. C. Thomas.

Strutchens, M. & Silver, E. (2000). NAEP findings regarding race/ethnicity: Students' performance, school experiences, and attitudes and beliefs. In E.A. Silver & P.A. Kenney (Eds.), *Results from the seventh mathematics assessment of the National Assessment of Educational Progress* (pp. 45–72). Reston, VA: NCTM.

Strutchens, M., Lubienski, S.T., McGraw, R., & Westbrook, S.K. (2004). NAEP findings regarding race and ethnicity: Students' performance, school experiences, attitudes and beliefs, and family influences. In P. Kloosterman & F. Lester (Eds.), *Results and interpretations of the 1990–2000 mathematics assessments of the National Assessment of Educational Progress* (pp. 269–305). Reston, VA: NCTM.

Tate, W.F. (1995). Returning to the root: A culturally relevant approach to mathematics pedagogy. *Theory into Practice, 34*(3), 166–173.

Tate, W.F. (2005). *Access and opportunities to learn are not accidents: Engineering mathematical progress in your school.* Greensboro, NC: SERVE.

6 More than Test Scores: How Teachers' Classroom Practice Contributes to and What Student Work Reveals About Black Students' Mathematics Performance and Understanding

Erica N. Walker

Introduction

Assessment has been a key component of mathematics reform in the USA, driven by reformers' emphasis on deepening students' conceptual understanding of as well as improving their procedural fluency in mathematics. In this chapter, I argue for a multi-dimensional approach to assessment, suggesting that standardized test scores do not adequately capture the extent of Black students' mathematical knowledge and performance. This chapter reports results from the implementation of an intervention around elementary mathematics with a group of elementary teachers and their African American students in an ethnically and socioeconomically diverse school district, Joytown. Although the intervention had a positive effect on mathematics performance (participating students outperformed non-participating students), so-called low scoring students on standardized assessments demonstrated mathematical knowledge that, at times, was nuanced and sophisticated, but may not have been adequately measured by these assessments. In this chapter, the impact of implementing lessons with multiple assessment opportunities on African American mathematics achievement is discussed, and the mathematics performance and conceptual understanding of a sample of African American students are analyzed, using pre- and post-standardized test data as well as instructional tasks given throughout the academic year. The importance of providing rich formative as well as summative assessment opportunities for students is discussed in the context of enhancing classroom practice, deepening these students' knowledge of mathematics, and reframing the discussion about Black students' mathematics achievement from one of deficit to one of excellence and potential.

By the most common measure of mathematics achievement, standardized test scores, the performance of US students, particularly of students of color and those from low socioeconomic status backgrounds, is cause for concern among many educators (Allexsaht-Snider & Hart, 2001; Schoenfeld, 2002; Strutchens, Lubienski, McGraw, & Westbrook, 2000; Tate, 1997). Yet many have suggested that these static assessment measures cannot adequately capture the mathematics knowledge held by students labeled as underachieving; in short, there is much more potential and expertise than meets the eye, particularly among Black students (Martin, 2000). Further, others have suggested that the key means of determining mathematics achievement—standardized testing—is flawed and cannot accurately assess many important aspects of students' mathematics knowledge (Boaler, 2003; Hilliard, 1997). Relying solely on standardized tests to tell us about student knowledge is a flawed proposition, many argue. In some cases, tests are biased, lack validity, and/or are not appropriately linked to curriculum or instruction. Further, that socioeconomic status, opportunities to learn, and other school factors are directly related to students' achievement suggests that we have much work to do in terms of equalizing the resources and capacity of teachers at our most challenged schools (Darling-Hammond, 2004).

These issues are particularly salient for African American students. Despite the numerous reform efforts to improve elementary mathematics student outcomes (National Research Council, 2001), and in particular, to address the racial/ethnic disparities in elementary mathematics outcomes (National Council of Teachers of Mathematics, 2000), differences in mathematics achievement between African American and Latino/a students and Asian American and White students, on average, still persist (NCES, 2004; Tate, 1997). In addition to school funding inequities, differential placement of highly qualified and experienced teachers, and patterns of discrimination that all contribute to continuing opportunity, equity, and achievement gaps, researchers and educators have pointed out that there are critical differences in the quality of instruction that students from different ethnic groups receive (Schoenfeld, 2002; Walker, 2003). Yet many studies that report on Black students' achievement in mathematics do so without examining closely the links between their achievement, their teachers' instructional practices, their opportunities to learn, and the nature of teacher–learner interactions in classrooms. Often, these studies solely re-document the lower average achievement of Black students on standardized assessments, without examining other evidence about their mathematics knowledge, potential, and learning. Further, this work serves to attach a stigma to Black children as chronically underachieving in mathematics.

In this chapter, I report results from an intervention, Dynamic Pedagogy, developed for elementary teachers and students, that was designed to address these issues and improve the performance of elementary students of color in an ethnically and socioeconomically diverse school district. After describing key components of Dynamic Pedagogy briefly, I focus on examining more deeply teacher practice and student performance in classrooms where Black students excel and demonstrate mathematical understanding. In doing so, I seek to challenge dominant discourses that serve to reify low expectations of Black children, based on the common discussions of their average "rank" relative to others which contributes to a "racial hierarchy of mathematical ability" (Martin, this volume). I seek to answer two key questions: What are characteristics of teachers' practice in classrooms where Black students are achieving at high levels in mathematics? What kinds of mathematical knowledge do Black students—whether "high" or "low" achieving—demonstrate?

The Dynamic Pedagogy Model

Colleagues and I at the Institute for Urban and Minority Education at Teachers College, Columbia University (Armour-Thomas, Gordon, Walker, & Hurley, 2002; Walker, 2007; Walker, Armour-Thomas, & Gordon, in press) developed an intervention, Dynamic Pedagogy (DP), to address the issue of instructional quality for underserved students. We developed DP in response to questions about how instructional quality could be improved for African American and Latino/a children in school. In particular, we sought to address teachers' low expectations, which are often enacted in the classroom through their providing low-level, repetitive mathematical tasks, and further, the assumptions that children from Black and Latino/a backgrounds have little worthwhile mathematical knowledge.

Undergirding DP is a four-pronged theoretical framework that comprises Sternberg's triarchic theory of intelligence (1988); Vygotsky's sociocultural perspective of cognitive development (1978); Feuerstein's (1979) mediated teaching-learning experiences; and Artzt and Armour-Thomas's (1999) model of teaching as problem-solving. While these were not specifically developed for African American students, we believe that these theories and their emphasis on interconnectedness, collaboration, and flexibility would be appropriate for an intervention designed to increase teachers' abilities to enhance classroom instruction techniques for, and to interact productively with, children from diverse backgrounds.

Sternberg's theory of intelligence (1988, 1998) posits that there are three kinds of abilities—analytic, creative and practical—that draw upon a number of metacognitive and cognitive processes. We surmise that the development of these capacities in students is enabled when students engage in curriculum tasks requiring the use of these mental processes. We assume that students have some skill in one or more of these modalities, and thus, teachers should develop activities and provide options for students to develop expertise in a variety of modalities.

The second, from Vygotsky's sociocultural perspective of cognitive development (Vygotsky, 1978), contends that complex mental processes are first used in social activities through conversations and collaborations among individuals, and that cognitive growth and learning occur when children engage in activities within their zone of proximal development (ZPD). This challenges the notion that learning, and learning mathematics in particular, is an isolated endeavor.

The third is informed by Feuerstein's (1979) concepts of cognitive potential of individuals and the role of mediated learning experiences to help build new and effective cognitive structures. Vygotsky's and Feuerstein's ideas suggest that teachers should use scaffolding and other mediating instructional strategies in helping students to access their nascent and developed prior knowledge and skills and to use them in the construction and consolidation of new knowledge and skills. In particular, the nature and quality of questioning in teacher–student interactions (Campione, 1989; Gickling & Havertape, 1981; Slavin, 2001) are paramount. I take the position that teachers must think carefully about how to engage students in learning new concepts, and further, that the judicious use of assessment strategies during classroom instruction plays a critical role in stimulating children's thinking in ways that enable their learning.

Finally, the fourth element of DP derives from Artzt and Armour-Thomas' (1999) suggestion that teachers implement carefully organized and crafted lessons that comprise three phases—initiation, to spark students' thinking and elicit their prior knowledge about a particular concept; development, the instructional component of the lesson, based on students' responses, needs, and knowledge; and closure, during which students reinforce and/or extend their learning of a particular concept. (To learn more about these elements of DP, particularly the role of professional development for teachers (which I designed), see Walker, 2007 and Walker, Armour-Thomas, & Gordon, in press.)

Major components of the intervention were developed using this theoretical framework as a basis and included on-site professional development[1] targeting teachers' lesson planning, implementation, and reflection; the development of mathematics lessons and tasks targeted to students' strengths and needs in different, but not necessarily disjointed, cognitive modalities (creative, practical and analytical); and the effective of questioning (or probing) in instruction to gauge students' prior knowledge of a mathematics concept, to evaluate their readiness for new content knowledge, and to activate student interest in mathematics. The underlying purpose of the intervention was to ensure that mathematics teaching in the elementary school is not a static, solely teacher-directed enterprise but rather a dynamic exchange where teachers and students explore mathematics together (NCTM, 1989, 2000; Walker, 2007). Further, as Ladson-Billings (1997) points out, "school mathematics is presented in ways that are divorced from the everyday experiences of most students, not just African American students" (pp. 700–701). Thus, we also wanted to ensure that students became exposed to mathematics experiences in the classroom in ways that resonated with their everyday experiences.

In short, Dynamic Pedagogy integrated curriculum, instruction, and assessment components in an effort to provide elementary students with mathematics experiences that, instead of emphasizing basic skills acquisition, focus on students attaining computational fluency, procedural skill, conceptual understanding, and problem-solving skills (Armour-Thomas, Gordon, Walker, & Hurley, 2002; AMS, 1999; NCTM, 1989, 2000). As we developed the intervention, we suggested, as do many in the education and mathematics education communities (Fennimore, 1997; Wiliam, 2007), that assessment practices be embedded in all components of DP instruction, as demonstrated in Table 6.1. In this way, we hoped to expand teachers' capacity for eliciting and responding to students' mathematical potential. These

Table 6.1 Selected Dynamic Pedagogy Elements and Indicators

DP Element	Indicators
Curriculum	In a lesson, the teacher provides a variety of tasks encompassing analytical, practical, and creative modalities as well as tasks that require memory recall for students to demonstrate their knowledge.
Instruction	The teacher engages in the following instructional behaviors in interactions with students consistently throughout lesson: scaffolding, modeling, explaining, modeling, and regulating.
Assessment	The teacher asks students questions in a variety of modalities: declarative, procedural, conceptual, and metacognitive.

components make clear that assessment of students' knowledge, skills, and dispositions is critical to designing curriculum, implementing instruction, and developing tasks and activities that evaluate students' mathematical knowledge and enhance mathematics performance.

Overview of Black Student Performance in Joytown's DP Classrooms

After developing the intervention, we worked with a group of 11 third-grade teachers and their students in an ethnically and socioeconomically diverse school district, Joytown, to implement DP in 2003–2004, and a follow-up group of eight teachers in 2004–2005. Two years of data on third-grade students in this district revealed that overall, dynamic pedagogy had a positive effect on students' achievement in both years of the implementation of DP in Joytown schools. Results showed significant differences in the performance of students in the intervention classes when compared to their peers in comparison classes (Gordon & Armour-Thomas, 2006).

However, one of the key determinants for use of DP success is its effectiveness with underserved students, particularly those who are Black and Latino/a. We found that DP was effective for these students; and in particular, as will be described, some DP teachers experienced very strong results. Table 6.2 shows the results of nine teachers who participated in Dynamic Pedagogy in 2003–2004.[2] While it is clear that students

Table 6.2 DP Teachers[3] and Their Students' Mathematics Achievement

DP Teacher (number of Black students)	Average mathematics achievement score, start of 3rd grade(standard deviation)	Average mathematics achievement score, end of 3rd grade (standard deviation)	Average pre-test/post-test gains (percent change)	Teacher rank (beginning of 3rd grade average score, end of 3rd grade average score, positive change in absolute score)
Serena (n=12)	552.09 (32.19)	610.83 (42.05)	58.74 (10.6%)	5th, 7th, 8th
Ophelia (n=11)	538.36 (33.52)	609.80 (22.28)	71.44 (13.3%)	7th, 8th, 3rd
Lorraine (n=9)	536.00 (34.85)	646.56 (31.13)	110.56 (20.6%)	8th, 1st, 1st
Martha (n=10)	585.89 (33.12)	637.00 (43.44)	51.11 (8.7%)	1st, 2nd, 9th
Davinia (n=13)	557.08 (41.02)	619.92 (40.26)	62.84 (11.3%)	4th, 5th, 6th
Stephanie (n=12)	563.50 (36.95)	623.00 (27.71)	59.5 (10.6%)	3rd, 4th, 7th
Ellen (n=8)	531.25, (25.63)	598.14 (52.51)	66.89 (12.6%)	9th, 9th, 4th
Nicole (n=10)	548.00 (24.81)	619.70 (24.73)	71.70 (13.0%)	6th, 6th, 2nd
Isabel (n=11)	564.50 (31.7)	630.36 (21.89)	65.86 (11.7%)	2nd, 3rd, 5th
Average of 9 DP teachers	552.96	621.70	69.99 (12.4%)	

in all classrooms, on average, improved their performance from the beginning to the end of the year, in some classrooms student performance was significantly greater than in others. Overall, the range of scores at the start of third grade on the standardized assessment was between 482 and 640, with a mean of 554.51 (36.62); at the end of third grade, the range of scores was between 529 and 712, with a mean of 620.05 (35.18).

At the beginning of third grade, the three teachers whose African American students had the highest scores were Martha, Isabel, and Stephanie. The teachers whose students had the lowest scores were Ophelia, Lorraine, and Ellen. What is particularly interesting about these initial indications is that Martha and Lorraine work closely together as third-grade teachers in the same school, and Isabel and Ellen team teach their students.

Yet by the end of third grade, while some teachers hold the same rank in terms of students' scores among this group of teachers, others shift up or down noticeably. For example, Ellen's students are the lowest scoring students at the beginning of the year and they remain so at the end of the year. Davinia's students hold steady in the "middle of the pack." Lorraine's students, who were near the bottom of the group in the beginning of the year, are now the top scorers, on average, outscoring Martha's students (but only slightly, as Martha's students hold the second spot).

What is also of interest is the growth of students' test scores. As expected, because of their leap from eighth place to first, Lorraine's students gained the most (110.6 points, or 20.6%), followed by Ophelia (71.4 points, or 13.3%), then by Nicole (71.7 points, or 13.0%). The teachers whose students gained the least were Stephanie (59.5 points, or 10.6%), Serena (58.7 points, or 10.6%), and Martha (51.1 points, 8.7%). While Stephanie and Martha's relative positions did not change substantially, Serena moved from fifth place to eighth place among the teachers in terms of absolute achievement. Although Ophelia's, Lorraine's, Ellen's, and Nicole's students started out with test scores below the sample average of 552.96, by the end of the year Lorraine's students were among the top scorers. In addition, among the teachers whose students were at the average or above the average (Serena, Davinia, Isabel, and Stephanie) at the start of third grade, only Serena's were noticeably performing at a lower level.

We believe that DP contributes to improving students' performance level as measured by students' performance levels (Level 1 being the lowest, and Level 4 being the highest) on the standardized assessment. At the start of the year, 37.8% of DP's Black students were scoring at Level 1 and only 4% were scoring at Level 4. By the end of the year, 14% of DP students were scoring at Level 1, and 15.2% of students were scoring at Level 4 (Table 6.3).

Table 6.3 further demonstrates the effectiveness of some DP teachers. Notably, only one of Lorraine's five students was still scoring at Level 1 by the end of the year, and five of Martha's students were now scoring at Level 4. Of Davinia's and Ophelia's 11 students who scored at Level 1, only 1 (in Ophelia's class) remained at that level. However, of Serena's five students who were at Level 1 in second grade, four remained at that level.

What might explain these differential results for teachers participating in DP? We found that teachers had varying levels of quality in implementing DP

Table 6.3 Number of Students Scoring at Each of Four Levels of Achievement on Standardized Examinations in 2nd and 3rd Grade, by Teacher

DP Teacher	Number of students scoring at level 1		Number of students scoring at level 2		Number of students scoring at level 3		Number of students scoring at level 4	
	Beginning of grade 3	End of grade 3	Beginning of grade 3	End of grade 3	Beginning of grade 3	End of grade 3	Beginning of grade 3	End of grade 3
Serena	5	4	3	3	3	4	0	1
Ophelia	5	1	5	7	1	2	0	0
Lorraine	5	1	1	4	2	3	0	1
Martha	1	1	1	2	7	2	0	5
Davinia	6	0	2	6	3	3	2	3
Stephanie	4	1	3	4	4	4	1	2
Ellen	4	2	4	5	0	0	0	0
Nicole	2	2	4	5	1	2	0	1
Isabel	2	1	5	6	3	3	1	1
Total	34	13	28	42	24	23	4	14
(percentage)	(37.8%)	(14%)	(31.1%)	(45.7%)	(26.7%)	(25.0%)	(4.0%)	(15.2%)

instructional practices (see list in Table 6.5). In the next section, we turn to an examination of these teachers' practices to illuminate some of the patterns we see in student performance. As part of our research about the effectiveness of DP, we collected data about teachers' practices. We obtained four portfolios from participating teachers for each DP unit (number sense, fractions, geometry, and measurement). In each portfolio, teachers submitted a representative lesson pre-planning template, lesson plan, samples of student work, and teacher self-assessment worksheet. In addition, members of the research team observed lessons during each unit and took field notes. For two units, we also obtained a videotaped lesson for each teacher as part of the portfolio for that particular unit.

Although we discuss some general trends in DP teachers' mathematics instructional practice, we examine three teachers' practice most closely, especially as it relates to the embedding of assessment throughout instruction, selected because their students underperformed, overperformed, or maintained their level of achievement. We examine the work of Lorraine, because of Lorraine's students' notable performance gains, and the work of Davinia and Serena. Davinia we describe because her students performed near the average in both years, although she was also very effective at moving students from Level 1 to higher levels. Further, she was Serena's counterpart at the same school, and she and Serena developed lessons together and often implemented the same lesson. Contrasts between her teaching and Serena's will thus be illustrative of how teachers who have the same lesson plans and materials may implement their work very differently. Further, we examine Serena closely because her students substantially underperformed relative to their starting position at the beginning of the year. It should be noted that Lorraine and Davinia both used high levels of DP instructional strategies, while Serena used significantly fewer. While it is true that other factors (such as mathematics content knowledge, pedagogical skill, and years of experience) undoubtedly contributed to these results, the next section will show that the quality of teacher–learner interactions—particularly among teachers who use a high level of DP strategies—appears to contribute to students' mathematics knowledge and performance.

Teacher Practice and Student Learning

Teaching elementary mathematics requires both considerable mathematical knowledge and a wide range of pedagogical skills. For example, teachers must have the patience to listen for, as well as the ability to hear the sense . . . in children's mathematical ideas. They need to see the topics they teach as embedded in rich networks of interrelated concepts, know where, within those networks, to situate the tasks they set their students and the ideas these tasks elicit. In preparing a lesson, they must be able to appraise and select appropriate activities, and choose representations that will bring into focus the mathematics on the agenda. Then, in the flow of the lesson, they must instantly decide which among the alternative courses of action open to them will sustain productive discussion. (American Mathematical Society, 2001, p. 55)

The American Mathematical Society (AMS) and Mathematical Association of America's (MAA) (2001) emphasis on mathematical and pedagogical knowledge for elementary teachers has been underscored by the research literature documenting that elementary mathematics teaching and learning in the United States has too often been limited to rote, didactic experiences that do not propel mathematics thinking (Ball, 1996; National Research Council, 2001).

In this section, we focus on an important and practical aspect of teaching—how teachers select activities appropriate for what their students need to learn. One way to discern teachers' understanding of mathematics and their instructional practice is to analyze the kinds of tasks that teachers provide and the kinds of questions that teachers ask students during mathematics lessons (Tirosh, 2000). As Sullivan and Clarke (1991) stated:

> Good questions have more than one correct mathematical answer; require more than recall of a fact or reproduction of a skill; are designed so that all students can make a start; assist students to learn in the process of solving the problem; and support teachers in learning about students' understanding of mathematics from observing/reading solutions. (p. 337)

In the three descriptions that follow, we examine the work of Davinia, Serena, and Lorraine, in a unit on fractions that comprised one of the DP professional development foci. We explore their use of instructional tasks, the questions they posed of students, and we provide some analysis of the effective strategies they used. Further, we provide some explanations for why Davinia and Lorraine were more effective teachers for African American students than Serena.

Davinia

In a lesson about equivalent fractions, Davinia began the lesson by asking students to think of the multiple ways we use equivalence in mathematics and the "real world." She elicited ideas from multiple students, from both genders as well as across ethnic groups. In doing so, she helps students make connections between mathematics and "real world" experiences, underscores the value of all students' contributions, as well as linking the idea of equivalence to fractions and integers. This grasp of equivalence is particularly important when students begin to engage in algebraic thinking in the later grades. In asking students to think about whole numbers as well as fractions, she is making connections between two (or more) mathematics topics that will be useful to supporting student thinking about number.

We include here several instances during Davinia's lesson when she helped students to think about connections between fractions and their lives, as well as connections between mathematical terms and everyday terms.

> "Let's think . . . If someone has a name, let's say James, but people also call him Jimmy, is he the same person?"
> "We talked about the number on the clock as 12 pm, and we called it noon . . ."

"Another way to think of six is as $3 + 3$ ... what are other ways?"

"All of these are different ways of representing the same amounts..."

"Let's talk about fractions and see if we can figure out what equivalent fractions are."

"So now we are making fractions that are the same size but have different names."

In addition, she provided opportunities for students to engage in thinking about fractions through multiple representations of this concept.

Davinia: Look at your fraction strips—who can tell me what other fractions would be equivalent to $\frac{1}{2}$?

Keith: $\frac{4}{8}$

Davinia: Let's see if he is right, Keith, come up and show us. [Davinia places the new fraction strip on the blackboard; Keith comes up to the blackboard to explain. He is allowed to change the positioning of the strip in order to present his explanation.]

Davinia: Who has another way to make $\frac{1}{2}$? [Most of the students raise their hands.]

Art: I used $\frac{2}{4}$. [*Art* comes up to the blackboard to demonstrate that the fractions are equal.]

Davinia: Are we making fractions of the same size that have different names?

Davinia: [Using pattern blocks] So, if I exchange the trapezoid for those green, what am I saying?

Student: $\frac{3}{6}$ are equivalent to $\frac{1}{2}$.

Throughout the lesson, Davinia interspersed attention to students' emerging, re-emerging, and/or lingering misconceptions about fractions while working with the fraction strips and pattern blocks. Her closing activity asked students to generalize from concrete materials to see if her lesson on equivalence was successful: Do students understand how equivalent fractions, an important building block for future computation and algebraic problem-solving, operate? Her closing question to the students about who ate more of a pizza pie relates to her thinking about how to get third graders to understand that $\frac{2}{8}$ of a pizza is not more than $\frac{1}{4}$ of the same pizza:

Brian ate $\frac{2}{8}$ of a pizza pie. Michelle ate $\frac{1}{4}$ of the pie. Brian says that he ate more. Michelle claims that they ate the same amount. Who is right? Explain. You may draw a picture.

Students' work on this problem reveals that they use a variety of strategies to answer the problem. For example, Jane wrote:

Michelle is right because I mesured [sic] $\frac{2}{8}$ and $\frac{1}{4}$, and I found out that $\frac{2}{8}$ is the same as $\frac{1}{4}$. I found that out because I put one fraction strip that said $\frac{1}{4}$ under another fraction strip that had $\frac{2}{8}$, and that how I knew they were equivalent.

Lance wrote:
Michelle is right because when I crossed multiply I found out the fractions were equal.

Joy wrote:
Michelle is right because $\frac{1}{4}$ is the same as $\frac{2}{8}$ just like one eighth is half of one forth [sic]. Then if one eighth is half of one forth then two eighths must be one fourth.

And finally, Chris wrote:
Michelle is right because when I put my fraction strips together I relized [sic] that $\frac{2}{8}$ is equal to $\frac{1}{4}$. I also relized Michelle was right by drawing two pies the same size, one with four pieces one with eight pieces. When I colored the right amount in I realized they were the same amount just like Michelle had said. They are equivalent fractions.

Although it is clear that students have various levels of understanding and various strategies of solving the problem, they all have arrived at the correct answer. Lance uses cross-multiplication to solve the problem, although Davinia has not explicitly taught this process. Joy's process reveals some sophisticated thinking about fractions as fractional parts of other fractions. Chris uses two methods: his fraction strips and drawing to check his answer. What is unclear is if students like Jane and Chris can expand their thinking beyond fraction strips to answer questions about equivalence without relying on concrete manipulatives.

Serena

In a lesson about equivalent fractions observed at the same point in the unit as Davinia's, Serena used a game with pattern blocks as the focal point of her lesson. Her questions posed at the beginning of the lesson, designed to pique students' interest in learning about equivalent fractions, seemed perfunctory. For example, the question "When do you use fractions in your everyday life?" was met with some enthusiasm by students but Serena did not follow up on their responses. In addition, her questions, which were originally designed to introduce the idea of equivalence, were generally not connected to the concept of equivalence, unlike Davinia's:

> "Does anyone know what the shorter name is for Robert? . . . Elizabeth?"
> "How many one half strips equal a whole strip?"

Throughout the lesson, Serena most often asked questions like "How many triangles would cover the entire hexagon?" and "How many blue pieces cover the hexagon?" which focused on the procedural aspects of working with pattern blocks instead of conceptual questions like "What fraction is one of those blue shapes of the hexagon?". When she and her students revisited the game during the close of the lesson, Serena's questions had more to do with the game ("What did you think of this game?" "What was fun about it?") instead of the conceptual or metacognitive aspects of the mathematics of the game. While it was clear from the observation that

Serena's students were enjoying the game, it was not clear that this significant amount of instructional time was providing students with opportunities to discover new mathematics concepts, or even review old ones in a significant way. At the end of the lesson, Serena emphasized the fun/difficult aspects of the game, but the portion of the discussion about what they learned about equivalent fractions or about themselves was less than a minute. In fact, one student responded that she had learned that she was bad in math. Instead of addressing this comment, Serena chuckled. Another adult in the room followed up on this question, emphasizing what this child was able to do in the game, making this student feel like a success and not a failure.

Many of Serena's lessons focused on the use of mathematical games and/or interesting activities, an excellent strategy when coupled with opportunities for students to explore the mathematical concepts underlying the game or activity. However, Serena's students rarely had the opportunity to do this. Often, Serena's tasks, while compelling and interesting for third graders, were time consuming and provided little opportunity for students to delve as deeply as they could into the mathematics of the task. For example, during a unit on measurement, Serena's students were given the prompt and questions in Figure 6.1.

The stated goals of the lesson, according to Serena's lesson plan and de-briefing conversation following the lesson with two of the researchers, were to add pounds and ounces together and to give students practice in converting ounces to pounds, and vice versa. However, the task is much richer than Serena allowed. The questions that follow the prompt do not provide opportunities for students to make

---

You are going on a trip. You can fill a backpack with everything you need for the trip, but the bag cannot weigh more than 15 pounds. Please choose from the following items. Your bag must weigh close to 15 pounds without going over this weight.

Item	Weight
Backpack	2 lb.
Camera	8 oz.
Clothing	3 lb.
Coat	4 lb.
Sneakers	2 lb.
Books	8 oz. each
Video game player	1 lb.
Video games	8 oz. each
Baseball bat	3 lbs.
Baseball mitt	1 lb.

1. Create a list of items that you will pack for your trip. You cannot pack a backpack that weighs more than 15 lbs. What will the total weight of your backpack be when you pack all of your items.
2. When you added pounds to ounces together, how did you convert ounces to pounds? Explain.
3. Explain why you chose the items that you packed.

Figure 6.1 Serena's activity for measurement unit.

predictions about how many items they can take along or to estimate the weight of a backpack with certain items in it. The last two questions could provide some opportunity for students to explore how they can most efficiently add ounces to pounds or convert pounds to ounces. However, because students worked on the assignment individually, they did not get an opportunity to hear thinking strategies from their classmates that could have helped everyone to explore the fact that all of the items that are in "ounces" are in units of 8 ounces, which is $\frac{1}{2}$ a pound. This is an opportunity for students to revisit fractional relationships and/or to recognize by doubling the amount of an 8 ounce item they arrive at a pound.

At the close of the lesson, Serena could have asked students to think about a question that revisited the relationship between 8 oz and 1 lb. She could also have given students a problem that involved a number of ounces that was not a multiple of 8 and sparked students to think about division, especially remainders. She could have linked the work that students were doing on this day to their work on fractions. Instead, Serena's questions during the close of the lesson focused on the procedural and peripheral:

> How do you add pounds and ounces?
> How did you decide what to bring on the trip? ·
> How do you convert ounces to pounds?

Lorraine

At the start of her lesson on equivalent fractions, Lorraine used graham crackers to spark students' thinking about fractions. Figure 6.2 shows an exchange from the start of the lesson that demonstrates Lorraine's range of questioning, her ability to use questions to encourage students to think mathematically and express their

---

Lorraine:	Now, what we're going to do first, boys and girls, is we're going to see how good you are at sharing something fairly . . . Each pair of students is going to share one cracker, fairly. Who can tell me one way they might do it?
Student A:	You can break it in half because there's two people.
Lorraine:	Okay. Now I want each of you to break each of the two pieces in half. Break it in half now. So now how many pieces do you have that are equal?
Student B:	$\frac{2}{4}$
Lorraine:	She has $\frac{2}{4}$. Who can explain what she means by that? That was very smart, but I don't understand what she means. Who can explain it to me?
Student C:	Out of 4 pieces you have 2 equal ones, so it's $\frac{2}{4}$.
Lorraine:	But I thought I had $\frac{1}{2}$.
Student C:	That's because when it was together that made it one. But when you break it in half that.takes one part of each other and it makes 2.
Lorraine:	Does that mean that I have more now than before?

Some students reply "yes" and others "no". A few say they are equal.

Figure 6.2 Lorraine's opening interaction with students during an equivalent fractions lesson.

thinking, and her responses to what students have to say about the problem she has posed.

Lorraine used this discussion to motivate students' thinking about the concept of equivalent fractions. What is interesting about Lorraine's class is that the students are in disagreement about whether or not $\frac{2}{4}$ is more than $\frac{1}{2}$. To resolve this misapplication of the size of whole numbers to fractions, Lorraine asked the students to compare the size of the sets of broken graham crackers and to evaluate which set was larger. This underscores the concept of equivalence for students.

On many occasions, Lorraine's tasks encompassed several modalities at the same time. Further, her tasks encompassed a number of levels of difficulty. For example, for the unit on equivalent fractions, Lorraine provided these activities (Table 6.4).

As shown in Table 6.4, Lorraine provided tasks that allowed students to demonstrate their knowledge of fractional concepts but also to use their creative problem-

Table 6.4 Selection of Lorraine's Equivalent Fraction Tasks

Task prompt	Selected sub-tasks	Modalities addressed
1 You have been asked to help decorate a bulletin board in your classroom. It is almost Halloween and the teacher gives you 12 decorations to put on the bulletin board. Come up with a creative plan for decorating the board using the exact amount of the different pumpkins, ghosts, and black cats as shown below.	a $\frac{2}{3}$ of the decorations are pumpkins; $\frac{1}{4}$ of the decorations are ghosts; $\frac{1}{12}$ of the decorations are black cats.	Memory, analytical
2 A cake is missing. Solve the clues to figure out the mystery of the missing cake. Use the blanks beside each clue to fill in the letters.	a Take the first $\frac{1}{3}$ of the letters in **though** and the last $\frac{1}{3}$ of the letters in **ate**. b Take the last $\frac{2}{3}$ of the letters in **bit**.	Memory, analytical
3 Use your set of crayons [16] to answer the following questions.	a Write the number that is $\frac{1}{2}$ of your set. ____ Write this number as a fraction of the whole set. ____ Explain why this fraction is equivalent to $\frac{1}{2}$.	Memory, analytical, practical
4 Imagine you had to give a cup of soda to one friend and a cup of milk to another friend, but you do not have a one-cup measure.	a How would you measure one cup of soda using the $\frac{1}{4}$ cup?	Memory, practical, analytical
However, you do have a set of measuring cups ($\frac{1}{4}$ cup $\frac{1}{2}$ cup and $\frac{1}{3}$ cup).	b How would you measure one cup of milk using both the $\frac{1}{3}$ cup and $\frac{1}{6}$ cup?	Memory, practical, analytical, creative

solving abilities. The tasks require that students understand what fractions represent, using a variety of models (e.g., set, unit) and to work with fractions in a number of different contexts, tapping into their analytical abilities. The tasks also have motivational appeal: they are designed to pique the interest of third grade students: decorating a bulletin board for Hallowe'en, giving beverages to friends, solving a mystery, and using concrete items with which students may have a great deal of experience (measuring cups and crayons). The tasks vary in difficulty, and subtasks within the tasks can also have differing levels of difficulty. For example, in Task #4, Subtask A is an easier question than Subtask B. Further, Subtask B allows students to report several different answers, which provides an opportunity for rich class discussion and also underscores that, in mathematics, there can be more than one correct solution.

Lorraine also asked questions to further her instructional goals to help her students master mathematics concepts. At the beginning of her lessons, Lorraine probed students to elicit their *prior knowledge* of a particular mathematics concept. Sometimes, Lorraine used questions to provide a *transition* from one topic to another; often, she uses a question as a predictive measure, to help students think about where the next lesson will lead them. Lorraine also used questions that tap into students' ability to describe a concept in their own words or using their own methods, especially to probe how much students comprehend about a certain topic using different media ("Can anyone draw a picture to explain what a fraction is?" "Can anyone tell me a little story that uses fractions"). In doing this, Lorraine tapped into students' creative and analytical modalities and provides some opportunity for students to demonstrate what they know in a variety of ways.

Lorraine often used metacognitive questions to engage students in explaining their responses or elaborating on their own or others' thinking. She would ask students to explain each other's work ("Who can explain what she means by that? Can you explain it another way?") and often had them explain their thought processes and alternative solutions. Lorraine was clearly interested in developing her students' mathematical problem-solving ability as independent thinkers, and so she often allowed students to try problems on their own. Occasionally, Lorraine asked questions that refocus students or encourage them to stay on task, as do many classroom teachers who demonstrate good classroom management.

I argue that DP's focus on continual informal assessment of all students, regardless of their prior achievement levels—and how to respond with curricular, instructional, and assessment activities that develop and enhance understanding—is key to the success of Davinia and Lorraine. We worked with teachers during professional development to develop ways to conduct ongoing assessment of students' knowledge prior to the lesson and their grasp of mathematics concepts during the lesson. Probing was one way in which teachers were to gauge students' learning before, during, and after instruction. Lorraine's and Davinia's questions to students during instruction showed that they paid attention to what students were thinking and were interested in hearing their thinking about mathematics. Often, Serena's questions to students during instruction were procedural; she asked students to explain how to do mathematical computations, but rarely invited them to explain their thinking about a problem.

We saw that Lorraine and Davinia used questioning throughout her lessons for a variety of assessment purposes, while Serena used questions mainly to elicit basic knowledge or facts. Very commonly, as do many teachers, Lorraine, Davinia, and Serena asked declarative or procedural questions to get information from students about a particular problem, operation or concept ("How do I divide this equally into three groups?"). However, Lorraine and Davinia also frequently asked conceptual questions ("What's the pattern you notice here?"). In analyzing Serena's video-taped lessons, we found that she very rarely asked students to explain their answers. Most of her questions were declarative or procedural in nature and were related directly to the materials or games she was using, rather than to the mathematical concepts underlying them. Further, Lorraine, and to a lesser extent, Davinia, provided several examples of activities that encompassed the analytical, creative and practical modalities and memory activities that are associated with Dynamic Pedagogy (Armour-Thomas, Gordon, Walker, & Hurley, 2002; Sternberg, 1988). Serena, on the other hand, often focused on memory tasks and activities that encompassed low-level practical and analytical modalities.

While all of the teachers had excellent classroom management skills, presented a variety of mathematical tasks, and used DP strategies that were effective for student mathematics learning, we found that Serena's instructional practice was more

Table 6.5 Lorraine's, Davinia's, and Serena's Use of Dynamic Pedagogy Instructional Strategies

DP instructional strategies	Davinia	Lorraine	Serena
Tasks provided for students encompass several modalities (analytical, creative, and practical)	*	*	
Questions posed to students encompass several modalities (analytical, creative, and practical)	*	*	*
Activities for students vary in difficulty	*	*	
Students' misconceptions are explicitly addressed in the lesson and activities designed to correct them are provided to students	*	*	
Tasks provided for students have substantial motivational appeal	*	*	*
Students are asked to justify and explain their thinking throughout the lesson, verbally and in written form	*	*	
Various games, media, and/or manipulatives are used throughout lessons	*	*	*
Questions posed to students vary in difficulty and type (procedural, declarative, conceptual, metacognitive)	*	*	*
Questions posed to students about tasks, games, and/or activities are mathematically focused	*	*	
The bulk of instructional time during lessons is devoted to mathematics content rather than to the procedure of a game or activity		*	
Questions are used throughout the lesson to assess students' knowledge and understanding of a mathematics concept or topic	*	*	

limited in scope than Lorraine's or Davinia's. Table 6.5 shows the DP strategies that these three teachers used. Despite her use of some effective strategies, however, a key difference in Serena's lessons we observed was the quality of the tasks she gave and the scope and rigor of the questions she asked.

We have shared the work of these three teachers participating in our DP project to illustrate the point that teachers who share professional development experiences and similar goals for the mathematics learning of their students may enact mathematics instruction in very different ways. In examining Lorraine's, Davinia's, and Serena's work, we found that, while the teachers all incorporated Dynamic Pedagogy strategies in their teaching, Lorraine's and Davinia's use of the strategies was more developed and extensive than Serena's. In terms of curriculum, Lorraine used a wide variety of tasks to engage students and develop their conceptual understanding of mathematics concepts, in addition to the games that Davinia and Serena provided.

Lorraine's African American students, many of whom had been identified as low performing at the beginning of the year, were able to demonstrate that they learned much more mathematics content over the course of the school year than Serena's, and somewhat more content than Davinia's. Although we think all of these teachers have strengths and limitations in their teaching, Lorraine, in using a wide range of DP strategies, essentially provided more opportunities for her students to learn more mathematics in the course of the school year. Davinia's and Serena's emphasis on mathematical games and practical activities was somewhat detrimental, in that, at times, the games and activities used a great deal of instructional time but did not allow for much mathematical discussion. However, Davinia was much more adept than Serena at engaging students and focusing the discussion about the games and activities on mathematics content. Overall, Lorraine consistently asked more meaningful questions, used shorter, more relevant mathematics tasks and activities, and engaged in more meaningful teaching and learning interactions with her students. In contrast, Serena provided engaging activities, but these were not necessarily rich in mathematics and were limited in scope. They often focused on memorization or practical applications without tapping into students' creative and analytical strengths.

What Students Know: Analyzing Student Work on Mathematical Tasks

In Joytown, third-grade teachers, with the assistance of mathematics coaches and supervisors, largely develop their own materials, drawing from numerous textbooks, workbooks, and other curricular items to meet district and state instructional standards. (There is no official adopted third-grade mathematics textbook.) As part of Dynamic Pedagogy, I developed two assessment tasks for students so that we would have a common task to evaluate that all DP students would complete. Teachers were given these tasks ("Cookies," about fractions, and "Bulletin Board," about area and perimeter) to give to students. Teachers were asked to give these as "stand-alone" tasks, without any instruction. These tasks were designed to illuminate for teachers, during professional development sessions, that students could have a lot of knowledge that goes untapped by traditional assessments. Further, we discussed in professional development sessions that these tasks could be used to determine what additional instruction might be needed in particular mathematics content domains.

I designed these tasks in accordance with DP principles and NCTM standards. Both tasks address concepts that are often difficult for third grade students, fractions and area and perimeter. The tasks were open-ended and required that students respond to two prompts. They also tapped into students' creative, analytic, practical, and memory modalities, and were designed to be engaging and interesting to students. Students were asked to draw on each task and explain their answers. The tasks were given in April and May of the school year.

Although we have no information about whether or not teachers helped students with the tasks, the results are illustrative. We present here the work of selected African American students from several teachers' classes, but focus on students from Lorraine's, Davinia's, and Serena's classes to show how their students performed on mathematical tasks.

Students' Understanding of Fractions

Sam's work in Serena's class was consistently excellent; and this is reflected in the fact that he was one of the top scoring students in her class. He scored 651 on the end-of-year assessment and began and ended the year as a Level 3 student (Figure 6.3).

In contrast, Sandra was one of the lowest scoring students in Serena's class (569, nearly 100 points less than Sam on the end-of-year assessment), and a Level 1 student at the start and end of the year. Her work on the fraction task is illustrative. While she could answer part 1 (which asked students to divide the three cookies among six children), part 2 stymied Sandra (Figure 6.4).

However, Sandra's answer makes some sense. She suggests that two cookies be shared by dividing them in half, and the third cookie be "saved." Another student, Sara, suggested a similar approach, as did several students in Davinia's, Ophelia's, and

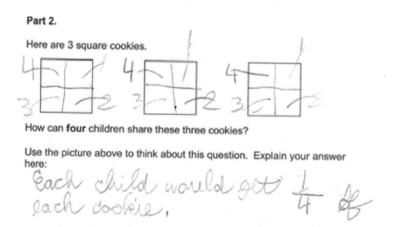

Figure 6.3 Sam's solution to the fraction problem.

Part 2.

Here are 3 square cookies.

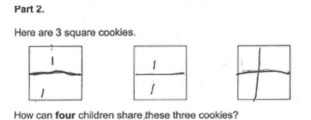

How can **four** children share these three cookies?

Use the picture above to think about this question. Explain your answer
here: *you Just   need   brak   two*

cookies   and   save   the   last   cooke,

Figure 6.4 Sandra's solution to the fraction problem.

Nicole' classes. Despite their not coming up with the expected answer, it is clear that
Sara and Sandra (as well as the other students) have some understanding of fractions
(by their correct answers in part 1) and have a reasonable strategy for sharing
three cookies among four children. Sara and Sandra, with some prompting about
that last cookie—in short, how they might split the last cookie if they had to distrib-
ute all of the cookies right now—probably could have come up with a correct answer.

Another one of Serena's students, Solomon, who scored 608 at the end of the year
(and was a Level 2 student), was able to draw the division correctly and explain
fairly accurately an approach to the problem, but was unable to come up with the
correct fraction (Figure 6.5).

Solomon clearly understands fractions from a representation standpoint, but
seems to have difficulty with understanding how to convert graphic representations
of fractions into their numerical representation.

Part 2.

Here are 3 square cookies.

How can **four** children share these three cookies?

Use the picture above to think about this question. Explain your answer
here: *You have to split a lin and then sh the third
cookie you have to split there in to four.*

$$\frac{2}{3}$$

Figure 6.5 Solomon's solution to the fraction problem.

Part 2.

Here are 3 square cookies.

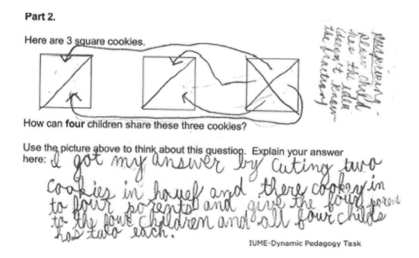

How can **four** children share these three cookies?

Use the picture above to think about this question. Explain your answer here: *I got my answer by cuting two cookies in hovel and there cookey in to four porents and give the four porent to the four children and all four child has two each.*

IUME-Dynamic Pedagogy Task

Figure 6.6 Danielle's solution to the fraction problem.

In Davinia's class, Danielle had a very interesting approach to part 2 of the cookies task (Figure 6.6).

Danielle is a relatively low scoring student (scoring 551 on the end-of-grade assessment, a gain of only 13 points from her start-of-year score; Level 1 at the start of the year, and Level 2 at the end of the year). But her work in part 2 suggests a very creative and sophisticated approach, that may not be valued by teachers who have low expectations for students who have performed at low levels on standardized assessments. Because Danielle doesn't report a fraction, Davinia noted in the professional development session that "she has the idea but doesn't know the fraction." Danielle's mathematical language is also less than fluent: she says "there [three]" when she means the third cookie and spells "parts" as "parents." But the explanation is correct: give each of the four children one of the four parts of the third cookie. Although she doesn't say this explicitly, each of the four children gets one of the $\frac{1}{2}$ cookies; thus they have "two" pieces each. Compare Danielle's response with Denise's—the top scoring student in Davinia's class (675; Level 4 at beginning of year, Level 3 at end of year): "give $\frac{1}{4}$ of each cookie to one child, every child will have $\frac{3}{4}$." Denise's fluent response and her accompanying drawing makes clear that she understands fractions in representational and numerical forms. Yet, I argue that all that separates Danielle from Denise—at least on this task—is more work on conceptual understanding of what fractions mean.

We saw this kind of understanding of division among most DP teachers' low- and average-scoring students frequently, but their command of fraction notation and terminology often prevented their giving the "correct" solution to the Cookie task. However, this was surprisingly not the case for students in Ophelia's class. Most of the low scorers did not draw anything on the pictures of cookies and, when they did, they did not attempt to divide them evenly as the overwhelming majority of the students in the other teachers' classes did. One student, Charlene, who scored 531 at the beginning of third grade (and at Level 1) and 580 at the end of third grade (remaining at Level 1), was able to subdivide the three cookies into four parts, and her explanation—"They can share this cookie if the[y] cut the [cookie] into four pieces"—demonstrates that she has some understanding of how to start out the problem. Other students, however, were simply stymied, with one student pointing out that "there would be an extra [cookie]!" The highest scoring students in Ophelia's class, while able to subdivide the cookies, were often unable to represent fractions correctly ($\frac{1}{2}$ was represented as $\frac{2}{1}$, for example, by the top scoring student, Ora) and they were unable to generate a reasonable explanation for part 2. The exception was Ora (Level 3 at start and end of year), who wrote, "Each child will get $\frac{1}{4}$ of each cookie" and showed each cookie divided into fourths.

Lenny is a student in Lorraine's class, who scored 586 at the beginning of the year, and 698 at the end of the year, and also moved from Level 3 to Level 4 by the end of the year. Consistently, during professional development sessions, Lorraine shared Lenny's work as an exemplary student. His work on the fraction task shows his clear understanding of fractions. In addition, Lenny's work on other assignments in Lorraine's class reveals that he has a strong and well-developed sense of numbers and how they operate. As mentioned before, Lorraine's instructional tasks often encompassed several representations of single concepts. One task involved using grid paper to create rectangles with the same area (36 square units) but with different dimensions. As students created these rectangles, they were to draw the rectangles and document the different dimensions. In response to the question "What patterns do you notice?" in terms of the charts of different dimensions, Lenny wrote: "They [the lengths and widths] are all multiples [sic] of 36."

Although Lenny really means the dimensions of the rectangles are all factors, not multiples, his answer to this question reveals his understanding of mathematical concepts on more than one level.

One of Lenny's classmates, Lance (519 score and Level 1 at the start of year, 649 and Level 2 at the end of the year), was able to successfully create several rectangles (including a square), but also created non-rectangles with area of 36 square units. This meant, in terms of dimensions and patterns, that Lance was unable to see the link between the dimensions of the length and width of the rectangles with the area. However, Lance is able to conceive of unusual figures and create polygons with areas of 36 square units. This reveals some sophisticated understanding of area, although it is not directly related to the assignment.

Students' Understanding of Area and Perimeter

The bulletin board problem, like the fraction problem, consisted of two parts. The first question asked students to determine how much wrapping paper in square feet was needed to cover the board. The second question asked students to determine if a string 9 feet long was long enough to make a string border for the bulletin board.

What the answers to "Bulletin Board" reveal is that students in general have a fairly good understanding of area, although low scoring students struggle a bit with this concept, as Sara, a student in Serena's class reveals (Figure 6.7).

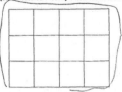

TASK 2.
Jeffrey and Maria are helping their teacher, Ms. Richards, decorate a bulletin board in their classroom. The bulletin board is made up of squares. Each square measures 1 foot by 1 foot. The bulletin board looks like this:

1. Ms. Richards is going to buy wrapping paper to cover the board. How much wrapping paper does she need to cover the board, in square feet? Explain your answer.

Ms. Richards needs 4 feet of rapping paper because the the buletin bord is 9 feet long

2. Ms. Richards wants to put a string border around the **outside** edges of the bulletin board. With your pencil, draw in the string on the bulletin board. Maria and Jeffrey have a roll of string that is 9 feet long. Is this enough string to make the border? Explain your answer.

No Because the string is to short.

Figure 6.7 Sara's solution to the bulletin board problem.

Sara's work is illustrative of many low scoring students—she does not understand the relationship of area and square feet to the board. Thus, she only considers one dimension (the width—4 feet), but does recognize, as evidenced in her drawing, that a 9 foot long string would be too short for the border.

One of the top scoring students, Diane in Davinia's class, presented the following argument (Figure 6.8).

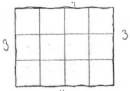

1. Ms. Richards is going to buy wrapping paper to cover the board. How much wrapping paper does she need to cover the board, in square feet? Explain your answer.

She needs 12 square feet to cover the board because three time 4 equals 12.

2. Ms. Richards wants to put a string border around the **outside** edges of the bulletin board. With your pencil, draw in the string on the bulletin board. Maria and Jeffrey have a roll of string that is 9 feet long. Is this enough string to make the border? Explain your answer.

The string is not enough to make the border because 4 plus 3 is 7 and 7 times 2 equals 14 and nine feet is not enough to fit in 14 feet.

Figure 6.8 Diane's solution to the bulletin board problem.

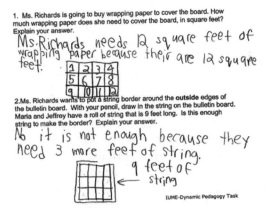

Figure 6.9 David's solution to the bulletin board problem.

Another student, David, understands the concept of perimeter but makes a computational error (Figure 6.9).

Generally, students across achievement levels struggled with the concept of perimeter. While many students agreed that a string 9 feet long was not long enough for the border, they based this answer on the *area* rather than the perimeter, writing for example, that Ms. Richards needs "12 feet of string." Sam, a top scoring student in Serena's class wrote, "The answer is no. I found my answer because a 9 square foot piece of string cannot fit around a 12 square foot board."

Danielle's answer, again, is very interesting (Figure 6.10).

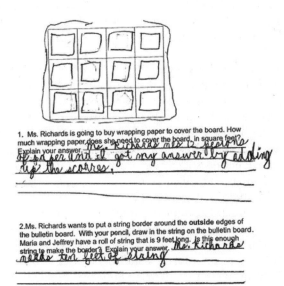

Figure 6.10 Danielle's solution to the bulletin board problem.

Danielle understands how to answer the area question, and, as requested, has drawn in the string, but suggests that Ms. Richards needs 10 feet of string instead of the 14 she really requires. In this sense, she actually demonstrates more practical knowledge than Sam, who conflates square feet and feet in an effort to make the dimensions fit the requirements of the second question.

If this had been a multiple choice assessment, by and large, many of these students would have done quite well, because they can calculate the area and would be able to point out that the string was "too short" for the border. However, in asking them to explain their answers, their explanations reveal hidden misconceptions about the meaning of perimeter, area, and dimensions.

These results reveal that there is more than meets the eye in terms of students' achievement levels—low scoring students may reveal sophisticated solutions to problems and in fact, may be on the right track but in need of prompting or brief additional instruction to clarify misconceptions and procedural errors. Teachers have to be responsive to these issues, and this is too often not the case for elementary teachers in general, and for elementary teachers who teach African American children in particular.

Conclusion: What We Can Learn From Black Students and Their Teachers in Joytown

DP suggests that the use of multiple assessment strategies, use of questions to elicit students' interests, mathematical knowledge, and dispositions, as well as a meaningful variety of tasks across modalities and tasks that present concepts in multiple representations are critical to improving student achievement. Further, DP teachers and their African American students in Joytown reveal several key issues to be considered when examining African American student achievement. First, it is important to consider where and with whom African American students are excelling. What are characteristics of classrooms and schools where students are achieving at high levels?

Second, it is clear from these results that so-called low scoring students on standardized assessments demonstrate mathematical knowledge that, at times, is nuanced and sophisticated but may not be measured by these assessments. Why these students may be unable to translate their obvious mathematical knowledge to success on standardized assessments should be explored. It may be that they have little experience with translating their verbal and graphical fluency to a multiple choice or rigidly defined question; there also may be a mismatch between the types of experiences demonstrating their knowledge in a typical classroom session and the ways in which students are expected to report their solutions to mathematical questions on standardized assessments. Instructional practices that give students multiple opportunities to develop and enhance strengths in mathematical skills and processes such as reasoning, justification, and procedural fluency, should be hallmarks of teacher practice with these students.

Third, the implementation of DP (or any initiatives around curriculum, instruction, and/or assessment targeting mathematics teaching) relies on the skills, adaptability, and effectiveness of teachers. Although overall, DP was effective in improving student achievement, the qualitative data reported here about teacher practices reveal that different teachers had differing levels and quality of implementation. Further, the content, pedagogical, and pedagogical content knowledge of teachers implementing such initiatives are keys to its success: as teachers may be stymied when students present solutions or questions that they don't understand. This is most visible in Serena's lessons in comparison to those of Davinia, her counterpart at the same school, and Lorraine. While she implemented some of the same activities as the two other teachers, in some cases the students did less and learned less because of her inability to extend questions and respond meaningfully to student ideas. The impact of such initiatives on student learning and performance depends directly on the quality of implementation.

Fourth, it is important for teachers to provide rich, rigorous opportunities to learn mathematics for *all* students. Lorraine is most illustrative here; despite the fact that a substantial proportion of her students were low scoring at the beginning of the year, her instructional activities were consistently at a high level and were of high quality. It is clear from her questions and interactions with students that she believed they were competent and knowledgeable and that it was her responsibility to provide them with opportunities to demonstrate this competence (Ladson-Billings, 1997). This resulted in the outstanding achievement gains of her students. While it is beyond the scope of this chapter to examine if there were differences in how teachers interacted with students of different ethnic backgrounds, there is evidence that suggests that teachers teaching Black or low-income students often provide less rigorous activities and overwhelmingly focus on drill and rote activities (Walker, 2007).

Strengthening Black students' achievement in mathematics depends a great deal on teachers who have high expectations for students and who do not allow students' prior achievement levels to influence the opportunities to learn mathematics they offer in their classrooms. The most effective DP teachers provided rigorous and multi-dimensional mathematics tasks and their classrooms were characterized by high levels of student engagement. These teachers built on students' strengths and interests in designing curriculum, instructional activities, and assessment practices, and further, the best teachers ensured that these activities also had meaningful and high levels of mathematical content. Such practice should be the norm in classrooms and schools populated by African American students.

Author Note

The work reported herein was supported under the Educational Research and Development Centers Program, PR/Award Number R206R000001–04, as administered by the Institute of Education Sciences, U.S. Department of Education. The findings and opinions expressed in this report do not reflect the position or policies of the Institute of Education Sciences or the U.S. Department of Education.

Notes

1 Two teachers participated and their students were omitted from these analyses because one teacher taught IEP students (four) and the other teacher joined the study mid-year.

2 Elements of these analyses appeared in Walker (2007) and Walker, Armour-Thomas, and Gordon (in press).
3 All names of teachers and students are pseudonyms.

References

Allexsaht-Snider, M. & Hart, L.E. (2001). Mathematics for all: how do we get there? *Theory into Practice, 40*(2), 93–101.

American Mathematical Society (AMS) and Mathematical Association of America (2001). *The mathematical education of teachers.* Rhode Island: Author.

Armour-Thomas, E., Gordon, E.W., Walker, E.N., & Hurley, E.A. (2002). A conceptualizing of Dynamic Pedagogy: A social-constructivist teaching model. Working Paper prepared for the Institute for Urban and Minority Education, Teachers College, Columbia University.

Artzt, A. and Armour-Thomas, E. (1999). A cognitive model for examining teachers' instructional practice in mathematics: A guide for facilitating teacher reflection. *Educational Studies in Mathematics, 40*, 211–235.

Ball, D.L. (1996). Teacher learning and the mathematics reforms: What we think we know and what we need to learn. *Phi Delta Kappan, 77*, 500–508.

Boaler, J. (2003). When learning no longer matters: Standardized testing and the creation of inequality. *Phi Delta Kappan, 84*(7), 502–506.

Campione, J.C. (1989). Assisted assessment: A taxonomy of approaches and an outline of strengths and weaknesses. *Journal of Learning Disabilities, 22*(3), 151–165.

Darling-Hammond, L. (2004). The color line in American education: Race, resources, and student achievement. *DuBois Review, 1*(2), 213–246.

Fennimore, B.S. (1997). Moving the mountain: Assessment and advocacy for children. In A.L.Goodwin (Ed.), *Assessment for equity and inclusion: Embracing all our children* (pp. 241–260). New York: Routledge.

Feuerstein, Reuven. (1979). *The dynamic assessment of retarded performers.* Baltimore: University Park Press.

Gickling, E. & Havertape, J. (1981). *Curriculum-based assessment (CBA).* Minneapolis: National School Psychology In-service Training Network.

Gordon, E.W. & Armour-Thomas, E. (2006). *The effects of dynamic pedagogy on the mathematics achievement of ethnic minority student: Final Report.* New York: Institute for Urban and Minority Education.

Hilliard, A.G. (1997). Language, culture, and the assessment of African American children. In A.L.Goodwin (Ed.), *Assessment for equity and inclusion: Embracing all our children* (pp. 229–240). New York: Routledge.

Ladson-Billings, G. (1997). It doesn't add up: African American students' mathematics achievement. *Jounal for Research in Mathematics Education, 28*(6), 697–708.

Martin, D.B. (2000). *Mathematics success and failure among African American youth: The rôles of sociohistorical context, community forces, school influence, and individual agency.* Mahwah, NJ: Erlbaum.

National Center for Education Statistics (NCES). (2004). *The condition of education.* Washington, D.C.: U.S. Department of Education.

National Research Council. (2001). *Adding it up: Helping children learn mathematics.* J. Kilpatrick, J. Swafford, & B. Feindell (Eds.). Mathematics Learning Study Committee, Center for Education, Division of Behavioral and Social Sciences and Education. Washington, D.C.: National Academy Press.

National Council of Teachers of Mathematics (NCTM). (1989). *Curriculum and evaluation standards for school mathematics.* Reston, VA: Author.

National Council of Teachers of Mathematics (NCTM). (2000). *Principles and standards for school mathematics.* Reston, VA: Author.

Schoenfeld, A.H. (2002). Making mathematics work for all children: Issues of standards, testing, and equity. *Educational Researcher, 31*(1), 13–25.

Slavin, R.E. (2001). *Educational psychology: Theory and practice.* New York: Allyn & Bacon.

Sternberg, R.J. (1988). *The triarchic mind: A new theory of human intelligence.* New York: Viking.

Sternberg, R. (1998). Principles of teaching for successful intelligence. *Educational Psychologist, 33*(1), 65–72.

Sullivan, P., & Clarke, D. (1991). *Communication in the classroom: The importance of good questioning.* Geelong, Victoria: Deakin University.

Tate, W.F. (1997). Race-ethnicity, SES, gender and language proficiency trends in mathematics achievement: An update. *Journal for Research in Mathematics Education, 28*(6), 652–679.

Tirosh, D. (2000). Enhancing prospective teachers' knowledge of children's conceptions: The case of division of fractions. *Journal for Research in Mathematics Education, 31*(1), 5–25.

Vygotsky, L.S. (1978). *Mind in society.* M. Cole, V. John-Steiner, S. Scribner, & E. Souberman (Eds.), Cambridge, MA: Harvard University Press.

Walker, E.N. (2003). Who can do mathematics? In B. Vogeli and A. Karp (Eds.), *Activating mathematical talent* (pp. 15–27). Boston: Houghton Mifflin and National Council of Supervisors of Mathematics.

Walker, E.N. (2007). Rethinking professional development for elementary mathematics teachers. *Teacher Education Quarterly,* Summer, 113–134.

Walker E.N., Amow-Thomas, E., & Gordon, E.W. (in press). *Dynamic pedagogy in diverse elementary classrooms: A comparison of two teachers instructional strategies.* National Council of Teachers of Mathematics (NCTM) Mathematics for AU Book Series.

Wiliam, D. (2007). Keeping learning on track: Classroom assessment and the regulation of learning. In F.K. Lester (Ed.), *Second handbook of research on mathematics teaching and learning* (pp. 1053–1098). Charlotte, NC: Information Age Publishing.

Wilson, L.D. (2007). High-stakes testing in mathematics. In F.K. Lester (Ed.), *Second handbook of research on mathematics teaching and learning* (pp. 1099–1110). Charlotte, NC: Information Age Publishing.

Section III

Socialization, Learning, and Identity

7 The Social Construction of Youth and Mathematics: The Case of a Fifth-Grade Classroom

Kara J. Jackson

"The Dumb Denominator"

It is mid-February, and Ms. Ridley (T/R),[1] a fifth-grade math teacher at Johnson Middle School, introduces addition and subtraction of fractions with like denominators (e.g., $\frac{2}{4} + \frac{1}{4}$) for the first time. She tells the students, "Raise your hand and tell me what dumb people might do. Tell me some stuff people do at Johnson that's dumb." The students make comments such as "not studying for a test," "making stupid noises," "talking in the cafeteria from table to table," "starting a food fight," and "chewing gum." Ms. Ridley then asks, "What do smart people do?" The students suggest the following: "thinking before you speak," "raising hands for every question," "paying attention in class," and "not making the same mistakes again."

With her students' rapt attention, Ms. Ridley says quietly:

T/R:	I have another little secret to tell you . . . . The denominator in our fraction is dumb. Since it's dumb, it never studies for the test. It comes time for the test—
	T/R writes on the board: $\frac{1}{3} + \frac{1}{3}$
T/R:	Think about a dumb decision. If you didn't study for the test.
M/St 1:[2]	Leave your answers blank.
T/R:	No, think about what happens on test day.
	. . .
M/St 2:	I just write down any answer, almost.
F/St 1:	Cheat.
T/R:	Yes! If the denominator's dumb, what do you think it's going to do? It's going to copy! The denominators copy because they're dumb, the numerators are smart, what are they going to do?
F/St 2:	Add.

(FN, 2/14/06)[3]

Ms. Ridley returns to the example on the board. She tells the students to add the numerators $(1 + 1 = 2)$ and that the denominator "copies" and remains a 3. Ms. Ridley exclaims, "Yes, let's try another one!"

However, before moving to another example, Ms. Ridley places a transparency on the overhead that contains "Rules for Adding and Subtracting Fractions" (see Figure 7.1).

Rules for Adding and Subtracting Fractions

Fact #1: When we add and subtract fractions, the denominators must be the same.

Fact #2: The denominators copy.

Fact #3: The numerators follow the rules.

Figure 7.1 Notes on adding and subtracting fractions (FN, 2/14/06).

After the children have copied the three facts into their notebooks, Ms. Ridley announces, "If you want, you can put Johnson students in place of numerators. Almost like numerators are good Johnson students, they follow the rules. Denominators are like bad Johnson students, they break the rules." The students remain quiet, as usual. The class moves on to another example.

Social Construction of Youth and Mathematics

In this excerpt from a fifth-grade math classroom, both mathematics and youth are constructed in particular ways. The addition of fractional parts of numbers is constructed as a procedural task to be carried out with little understanding of the meaning of numerators, denominators, or the addition of parts of wholes, not to mention the multiple meanings that numerals represented as fractions may have (e.g., Thompson & Saldanha, 2003). Simultaneously, Johnson Middle School students are constructed as "good" and "bad." The talk in this segment both reifies what it means to be "good" and "bad" Johnson students and potentially identifies particular students as "good" or "bad," depending on their typical behaviors.

In this short segment of classroom instruction, we are forced to grapple with the reality that mathematics instruction is not a socially or culturally neutral process. Rather, as others have argued, mathematics instruction, like any type of instruction, is laden with social and cultural norms, expectations, and practices (Baker, Street, & Tomlin, 2003). However, in part because the discipline of mathematics is often constructed as an "objective science" (Dossey, 1992), the social and cultural assumptions and implications of instructional practices in mathematics classrooms have been less explored in comparison to humanities classrooms (for examples of such research in humanities classrooms, see Heath, 1983; Wortham, 2006).

In this chapter, I show how mathematics instruction involves the social construction of mathematics and of youth. As alluded to in the Dumb Denominator excerpt above, how children are constructed informs how mathematics is constructed and vice versa. Furthermore, I argue that the way that both children and mathematics were constructed in this school drew on discourses about poor children of color that circulate beyond the classroom. As a case in point, I illustrate how one instructional practice was consequential to how two students, Nikki and Timothy, and mathematics were simultaneously constructed in Ms. Ridley's class.

Nikki Martin and Timothy Smith were both African American youth from the same low-income neighborhood, attended the same schools, and were in the same fifth-grade math classroom. On the one hand, Nikki and Timothy were restricted mathematically in similar ways because of institutional discourses about poor, urban children of color as related to discourses about mathematics that circulated in Johnson Middle School. On the other hand, social construction is an interactive, dynamic process (Holstein & Gubrium, 2008), and Nikki and Timothy illustrate that individuals negotiate discourses about youth and mathematics in unique ways. As a result, their social and academic trajectories varied.

Mathematical Socialization and Social Identification

There is a rich tradition of attention to processes of socialization and social identi-fication in studies of learning to speak, read, and write (e.g., Heath, 1983; Street, 1993). For example, it is well established that children engage in two concurrent, related processes when learning to speak: "*socialization through the use of language* and *socialization to use language*" (Schieffelin & Ochs, 1986, p. 163, italics in origi-nal). Children not only learn to speak the language around them (socialization to use language); they also learn about the role that language plays in socially and cul-turally organized ways of acting, and they use language as an entrée into mastering those ways of acting (socialization through the use of language). Furthermore, lan-guage socialization is an "interactive process," and "the child or novice . . . is not a passive recipient of sociocultural knowledge but rather an active contributor to the meaning and outcome of interactions with other members of a social group" (Schieffelin & Ochs, 1986, p. 165).

Sociocultural theorists argue that learning is as much about individuals experi-encing a change in their understanding of some content as it is about changing who one is with respect to the community to which that content is central (Lave & Wenger, 1991; Packer & Goicoecha, 2000). Over the past 15 years, there has been an increasing number of scholars who have drawn on sociocultural theories of learn-ing to understand students' learning of mathematics (e.g., Boaler, 1997, 2000; Cobb, Stephan, McClain, & Gravemeijer, 2001; deAbreu, 1999; Greeno & Middle School Mathematics Through Applications Project Group, 1998; Kieran, Forman, & Sfard, 2001; Martin, 2000; Nasir, 2002). Recent work has shown that, as with lit-eracy, mathematics is embedded in social and cultural practices that are inextrica-ble from power relations (Baker, Street, & Tomlin, 2003; Street, Baker, & Tomlin, 2005). Such situated accounts of learning mathematics have illustrated how math-ematical practices are related to the development of "mathematical identities" (Boaler, 1999; Martin, 2000, 2006b; Nasir, 2002). In turn, mathematical identities afford and constrain different opportunities for learning and participation in wider contexts (Anderson & Gold, 2006; Martin, 2000, 2006a, 2006b).

Horn (2007) explicitly investigates the relationship among the construction of mathematics, students, and teaching practices. In a study of two high school math-ematics departments in the midst of a detracking reform, Horn found that teachers' constructions of students hinged upon their construction of mathematics. Teachers who tended to construct mathematics knowledge as a "sequential" series of topics to be mastered tended to construct students in terms of their motivation, which in turn limited the pedagogical actions the teachers might take if students did not achieve at expected levels (p. 43). Alternatively, teachers who tended to construct mathematics as a body of connected ideas had more latitude in how they identified their students, and therefore, if students were not achieving at expected levels, they had more latitude in the pedagogical actions they might take.

Horn's work, as well as the body of situated accounts of learning mathematics mentioned above, has illuminated the need to attend to the social processes of learning mathematics. However, this body of work has been less attuned to how such social processes within local settings, like classrooms, are connected to discourses that circulate outside of local settings. An exception is the work of Martin (2000). Martin developed a model of "mathematics socialization" based on research of high- and under-achieving African American mathematics students in a low-performing middle school. Martin found that he could not explain (under)achievement in school mathematics among African American youth without attending to broader socio-historical and community forces. This led him to explore discourses about racially based differential access to mathematics that circulated among the communities and homes in which these students lived. Through interviews with students, parents, and community members, Martin found that individuals' experiences with mathematics were intricately connected to their cultural and social identification as African American. Significantly, Martin's work captured the relationship between culturally and socially organized discourses about mathematics, race, and individual achievement.

Martin contends that (under)achievement in mathematics, particularly for African Americans, but likely for other groups of students as well, is best understood as a dynamic interplay between processes of socialization and identity formation. According to Martin (2006b),

> *Mathematics socialization* refers to the experiences that individuals and groups have within a variety of contexts such as school, family, peer groups, and the workplace that legitimize or inhibit meaningful participation in mathematics. *Mathematics identity* refers to the dispositions and deeply held beliefs that individuals develop about their ability to participate and perform effectively in mathematical contexts and to use mathematics to change the conditions of their lives. A mathematics identity encompasses a person's self-understandings and how they are seen by others in the context of doing mathematics. (p. 150)

Martin's work raises an important issue—namely, there are various contexts in which socialization and social identification happen. For the purposes of my analyses, I investigate processes of socialization and social identification that happen in and across institutional and local contexts. In particular, I focus on the prevalence and deployment of particular discourses. I draw from the work of Jim Gee (1990/1996), in which he defines discourses as "ways of behaving, interacting, valuing, thinking, believing, speaking, and often reading and writing that are accepted as instantiations of particular roles (or 'types of people') by specific *groups of people*. ... They are 'ways of being in the world'" (p. viii, italics in original). Discourses, for example regarding who is "good" at mathematics, regiment thought and action in that they shape (but do not determine) how individuals get recognized as particular sorts of people at any given moment given their actions (e.g., speech, behavior, dress).

In my work, then, when I discuss processes of social identification and socialization that operate at institutional contexts, I focus on discourses that circulate throughout institutions, like schools. By local contexts, I mean the discourses that circulate in particular classrooms, like Ms. Ridley's fifth-grade math classroom at Johnson Middle School. Institutional and local contexts are by no means isomorphic. Rather, discourses that circulate at broad, institutional contexts are inflected in particular ways in local contexts, like classrooms (Wortham, 2006). There was a distinctly local character regarding mathematics and youth evident in Ms. Ridley's classroom, as reflected in the Dumb Denominator excerpt above. However, I argue below that more widely circulating institutional discourses about poor children of color, particularly African American children, and their ability to do mathematics, shaped the local approach to mathematics. In other words, the peculiar way in which Ms. Ridley introduced the addition of rational numbers was not merely a product of idiosyncratic pedagogy.

Research Context

The data presented are from a 14-month study of how two African American 10-year-olds (Nikki Martin and Timothy Smith) and their families learned mathematics within and across home, school, and occasionally neighborhood contexts. The overarching goal of the study was to understand how individuals learn mathematics across distinct contexts and over time. I used ethnographic methods (e.g., participant observation, interviews, document collection) to document how the participants experienced, and made sense of, their participation in, across, and exclusion from, a variety of mathematical practices. There were four major sources of data for this study: fieldnotes based on more than 300 hours of participant observation in multiple sites; 35 hours of interview data; document collection at all of the sites; and 36 hours of video-taped recordings of 18 parent math classes held in the neighborhood that at least one of the focal children's parents attended. Although I began data collection when Nikki Martin and Timothy Smith were in fourth grade at their local elementary school, for the purposes of this chapter, I am only drawing on the data of the children's participation in the fifth-grade math classroom at Johnson Middle School, including fieldnote, document, and interview data. (For more detail on the research design of the study, see Jackson, 2007.)

My analyses for the larger study focused on how individuals interacted with other individuals and resources in particular events, as embedded in social practices. I traced contingent events to understand how strings of events amounted to longer time-scale (Lemke, 2000) processes of mathematical socialization and social identification. Because of space limitations, I have chosen to represent my analysis in the form of abbreviated narratives in this chapter. Rhetorically, I have organized these narratives around one key classroom practice, Math Royalty, which I explain below. I have chosen to focus on Math Royalty because it illustrates a daily practice in which personhood and academic understandings of mathematics were at stake.

(For evidence of other events and practices upon which both a construction of youth and mathematics were simultaneously contingent, see Jackson, 2007.)

This study grew out of my work with an Educational Scholarship Program (ESP) in a predominantly African American, low-income neighborhood in a large, Northeastern city in the United States. ESP provided full-tuition college scholarships to groups of low-income students upon successful completion of high school. In an effort to increase the chances that the students would graduate from high school, ESP provided academic and social support to the students and their families. Caregivers were given an opportunity to further their own education, and ESP children's siblings were given partial tuition to colleges of their choice.

My initial introduction to ESP was through a university-supported research project with ESP families, intended to provide parental support in mathematics. I continued to work part-time for ESP as a summer program mathematics coordinator and tutor for four years. Through this work, I developed close relationships with several mothers and children, including the families of Nikki Martin and Timothy Smith. I describe Nikki and Timothy in more depth throughout the chapter.

My researcher identity was central to my relationships with the families, the schools, the data I collected, and how I analyzed the data. I am a white woman, who at the time of the study was completing a doctoral degree in education. I differed from the families of Nikki and Timothy—racially, educationally, and otherwise. I intentionally discussed my analyses with the families through member check interviews and informal conversations on a regular basis. On the other hand, I did not differ racially from the majority of the teachers with whom I interacted. In both cases, the information that was provided to me, as well as how I made sense of it, was shaped by who I am and how the participants in this study made sense of me.

Discourses of Deficit and Change: Fifth Grade Mathematics at Johnson Middle School

Johnson Middle School was part of a national middle school reform network of charter schools in urban areas in the United States. The network's mission was to serve populations of students that they claimed were not being served in traditional neighborhood schools; it aimed to provide a rigorous, college preparatory education for predominantly poor children of color, who they described as "under-served" and "under-resourced." Johnson Middle School served students in grades five to eight. When I began my fieldwork, there were three classrooms of 30–35 students for grades five and six, and two classrooms of seventh graders at Johnson. (Eighth grade was added the year after I finished my fieldwork.) Because Johnson Middle School was a charter school, students were admitted by lottery.[4] Students traveled from all parts of the city to come to Johnson.

Sixty-nine percent of students in grades five through seven were African American, and 31% were Hispanic.[5] However, in fifth grade alone, 88% of the students were African American, and 11% were Hispanic. In the class I regularly observed, there were two Hispanic students out of 33, and the rest were African American. Eighty-six percent of Johnson's students qualified to receive reduced-price or free meals, and 15% of Johnson students received special education services. Of the 33 students in the mathematics class that I regularly observed, seven, including Timothy, received special education services.

Although Johnson's student body was majority African American, and all the students were of color, the staff was majority white. Of the 18 administration and teaching staff at the time of the study, 13 were white. To be hired to teach at Johnson, teachers had to have at least two years of teaching experience. Of the 15 full-time teaching staff, six were considered "highly qualified teachers," as determined by the state in which the study took place.[6] Most teachers were under the age of 30, and only the principal, a secretary, and a few teachers had worked at the school since its opening two years before I began my fieldwork.

Ms. Ridley was a white woman in her mid-20s. She taught math in a neighborhood middle school just 15 blocks from Johnson for two years prior to joining the staff. The year I conducted fieldwork was her first year at Johnson. She had an undergraduate degree in communications and a master's degree in education.

As I describe below, Johnson Middle School officials (e.g., administrators, teachers) were explicit about the school's mission to *change* incoming fifth graders, academically and socially, in particular ways over the course of the three years that they were likely to attend Johnson. Of course, all schools are in the business of changing students, in some way or another. However, Martin (2006a, this volume) argues that there are particular, racialized ways in which school officials often characterize African American students as change-worthy or as problems in need of solutions. Martin argues for the need to understand how it is that representatives of institutions, like university researchers and school officials, frame African American students in relation to mathematics. For example, drawing from the work of sociolinguists and sociologists on "framing," Martin (2007) convincingly shows how African American students are often constructed as less able than their white peers in mathematics through discussions (written and oral) of the "achievement gap." This frame, or way of understanding achievement discrepancies, focuses societal attention on African American students as the "problem" in need of fixing and away from the racialized social structures and practices that have created a system of inequitable opportunities for access to high-quality mathematics instruction for the majority of African American youth. In the case of this chapter, framing refers to the ways in which school officials characterized, categorized, and positioned the needs and accomplishments of the student body in relation to how mathematics was characterized, presented, and enacted in classroom practice. Below, I describe how fifth graders and fifth-grade mathematics were framed at Johnson Middle School.

Framing Students

In public relations documents, conversations with the principal and teachers, and in classroom talk, it was clear that Johnson staff framed incoming fifth graders in particular ways, rooted in their assumptions about, and experiences with, low-income, children of color educated in neighborhood, urban schools. Throughout the school, emphasis was placed on changing the "academics, behavior, and character" of the students. Underlying Johnson's focus on changing the students' "academics, character, and behavior" was an assumption that fifth graders did not arrive at Johnson with the necessary academic content knowledge, values, or behavioral norms. Fifth grade was framed as a year of "remediation."

All schools assume that students need to learn academic knowledge. However, the principal and teachers at Johnson repeatedly referred to the incoming fifth graders as "below grade level." Their judgement was not based on empirical data. The staff did not test the new entrants, nor did they use their district and state test scores or report cards as resources for evaluating the children's academic backgrounds. The principal and fifth-grade math teacher both told me that they "didn't trust the report cards of the neighborhood schools." Most of the staff had taught in the city's neighborhood schools for at least two years and held a view that "there was little learning" happening in the classrooms, and so little could be predicted from the children's previous grades.

In addition to an assumed deficit of academic knowledge, the staff also assumed the children arrived with behavioral deficits. Johnson held a three-week summer intensive "initiation" to the norms of Johnson for incoming fifth graders. The principal and teachers told me that they did this because the children were used to "being out of control" in schools where "teachers didn't care what the children did." In the words of one Johnson staff member, the children were "in need of discipline."

A focus on behavior went hand-in-hand with a focus on "building the children's character." Johnson Middle School drew on a popular six-stage theory of moral development (Kohlberg, 1984) to design its approach to "character building." The theory claims that children initially make moral decisions for purely extrinsic reasons. As they develop a sense of "right" and "wrong," they move "up" the stages to where they eventually make moral decisions for purely intrinsic reasons. Moral decisions were framed in terms of "good" and "bad choices" at Johnson. The staff believed that, in fifth grade, external motivation was necessary to get the majority of the children to make "good choices." As the fifth-grade math teacher explained to me, "We know that a few students, like Nikki, came to Johnson knowing how to act," but most of the fifth graders needed to be taught to make "good choices." Several practices were instituted to assist the students to move up the stages of moral development, including a monetary system of rewards and sanctions that governed all of the teachers' disciplinary actions.

Johnson Middle School was decidedly committed to securing a path to college education for its students. It was assumed that college attendance would lift students out of poverty, a common trope in educational interventions and programs aimed at poor children of color. Johnson's public relations documents reflected a "college prep" mission, and within the school there were several ways in which a focus on college attendance was reinforced. For example, all the homerooms were named after colleges and universities, and teachers and students identified one another by college/university names. Cohorts of students were identified by the year they were expected to graduate from high school and enter their first year of college. The youth I followed closely were the class of 2013. Every teacher had to display her college diplomas on her classroom wall, there were several days throughout the year when students were allowed to wear college t-shirts rather than their usual Johnson uniform shirts, and students occasionally took field trips to visit colleges and universities in the area.

Framing Mathematics

Related to the framing of the students as academically, behaviorally, and morally deficient, the approach to fifth-grade mathematics at Johnson Middle School reflected and constituted a deficit framing of the students. According to Ms. Ridley and administrators, fifth-grade mathematics was designed to "give the children basic skills." The staff acknowledged privately that the mathematics curriculum was at the fourth-grade level, but they did not share this with parents or the students. They said it "had to be low" because the children "didn't have basic skills." The assumption was the children were not able to do mathematics at grade level. Ms. Ridley offered that most of the students arrived to Johnson with limited mathematics knowledge.

> With fifth grade I have kids that are coming in [with] no times tables, no nothing. But then somebody like Nikki, she probably knew her times tables. So when we do times table chants, that's just review. You know what I mean? That's the, that's the struggle, is that with fifth grade we know we're going to be remediating and we're gonna do a lot of things that they should already know. (INT, 10/04/05)

Johnson Middle School used a fifth-grade mathematics curriculum created by members of the charter school network. It was not publicly available, although the fifth-grade teacher shared parts of it with me. The curriculum laid out lesson plans for each curricular topic. In sequential order, topics included memorization of multiplication times tables; addition, subtraction, multiplication, and division of multi-digit numbers; four operations on fractions and decimals; identification of geometric figures (including angles, lines, rays, and polygons); patterns (arithmetic and geometric sequences); solving simple algebraic equations (addition and subtraction); conversion of fractions, decimals, and percents; statistics (including finding mean, median, mode, and range and creating line and bar graphs); and simple probability. Although these topics are common in commercially packaged fifth-grade mathematics curricula, the pedagogy associated with them was somewhat unique to this curriculum and network of schools.

Ms. Ridley emphasized that her goal was to "make math fun." This goal rested on assumptions that some students were "scared of math" and that some were "frustrated" by math. Subsequently, Ms. Ridley believed if math was fun, students would do math "without realizing what they're doing."

> I think math has this negative stigma on it and it sucks because I love math. I think a big part of my battle, getting them in fifth grade, is that they've already been exposed to either possibly bad math teachers, possibly frustration with math where they don't understand it. So anything related to math is confusing, even if they don't try it. So you kind of have to break that up. Which is why

Johnson is designed the way that it is, the math curriculum, because it's this idea that times tables can be fun. It doesn't have to be this idea of sitting there going 1 times 2 is 2, 2 times 2 is 4. It can be fun. So making math fun, so that they're doing it without realizing that they're doing it. Like subtraction, they don't even realize what they're doing. They're saying this little chant thing. But they're getting the right answer because they're having fun and they are able to scream stuff out. So I guess my philosophy [is] if you make it fun, it will be fun, and if you make it fun and it is fun, they will understand it. (INT, 10/04/05)

Ms. Ridley's pedagogical practices reflected this stance towards the teaching and learning of mathematics. As evident in the Dumb Denominator excerpt above, Ms. Ridley taught most of the content in a procedural manner. Children were expected to mimic steps that Ms. Ridley showed them. Emphasis was placed on producing a correct answer. There was little discussion of the reasonableness of answers or of alternative solution strategies. This pedagogy was suggested by the fifth-grade mathematics curriculum.

Ms. Ridley acknowledged her emphasis (as suggested by the curriculum) on developing a procedural understanding of mathematics:

The one flaw in the Johnson fifth-grade math is that it's not conceptual. It's just drill and kill. But at the same time, because we know that sixth grade, seventh grade is not drill. They will do investigations, they will have to discover stuff. I prefer this kind of math myself. I was always the kind of math student, my teacher did not need to prove to me why base times height divided by two gave the area [of a triangle]. And that's very much how this is. There's a few things I've explained, like area. I showed them how that was like cutting a rectangle in half. But much beyond that, no. It's more just getting them to get the concepts and skills down, so that when they do go to [the sixth-grade teacher] she can have them understand it. (INT, 3/29/06)

The theory of learning described by Ms. Ridley and reflected in the curriculum, namely that a procedural understanding, needed to precede the development of conceptual understanding, was bolstered by the school's assumption that the children arrived without "basic skills." Ms. Ridley saw her job as providing the "missing" skills so that they could go on to "understand" the mathematics in a conceptual manner.

Emphasizing a procedural understanding of mathematics is not unusual in United States middle school mathematics classrooms; it is the norm rather than the exception (Stigler & Hiebert, 1999). Mathematics educators' analyses of classrooms that promote procedural understanding argue that children who learn mathematics procedures as disconnected from their underlying meanings will not be equipped to apply their understandings in novel situations (Boaler, 1998; Hiebert, 2003). However, how discourses about particular populations, like low-income children of color, that circulate at institutional levels are related to pedagogies that promote procedural understanding has been relatively unexplored.

Math Royalty

One daily practice that had significant academic and social outcomes for students was known as Math Royalty. Math Royalty, a practice suggested in the curriculum, was intended to lead to "mastery of basic skills" and altogether, it took about 25 minutes out of every 90-minute class period. It consisted of five math problems. Figure 7.2 is an example of a typical problem set.

The students worked individually on a new problem set at the beginning of every class period. Once a student believed that she had the correct answers to all five problems, she announced, "Done." In turn, Ms. Ridley assigned each student a number, from 1–33, to represent the order in which the students finished. However, by November, once she assigned numbers in the 20s, Ms. Ridley typically stopped whoever was still working and checked the answers with the students. Typically, between eight and ten students did not finish the five problems before the class checked the answers.

After the class had checked their answers, Ms. Ridley asked the children, starting with the first student to finish, to share publicly how many problems she or he had completed correctly. The first student to get all five correct was then crowned Math Queen or King. The Queen or King had to come to the front of the room and choose a tiara or crown that she or he wore for the rest of the period and then turn to the class and yell, "I RULE!" The other students in the class were expected to respond loudly and in unison, "YOU RULE!" The Queen or King wrote her or his name on the front board for the other classes to see throughout the day and added a tally mark to a poster hanging in the classroom that tracked how many Queens versus how many Kings were crowned throughout the year. In the class that I observed, there was a group of three students who routinely came to occupy the position of Queen or King, two girls (Nikki and Angela) and one boy (Terrence).

How does this practice of Math Royalty both reflect and constitute the construction of mathematics and learners in this particular setting? First, it is clear that quickness was valued, and to be successful in this mathematical practice, one must be both quick and accurate. Second, when checking answers, there was usually one valued solution strategy to a math problem. Third, the teacher provided the problems, and

---

February 15, 2006

1) $\underline{5} + \underline{10} =$
   25   25

2) Reduce the sum in #1.

3) Compare 176 + 54 ◯ 1,234 − 975

4) Draw parallel line segments.

5) Find median: 5, 3, 0, 8, 11, 0

Figure 7.2 Math Royalty problem set (FN, 2/15/06).

the students solved them. Students were not expected to ask questions about the problems, nor were they positioned as problem creators. This practice publicly recognized a "top" math student every day; the corollary was that it also made public those who were not "top" math students. In fact, those who did not finish quickly enough were not given numbers and effectively excluded from this daily ritual.

Math Royalty was a central practice in Ms. Ridley's classroom and was certainly central to the paths that Nikki and Timothy's learning of mathematics took in fifth grade. Importantly, as I show below, different students negotiated this practice in distinct ways, implying that processes of mathematics socialization and social identification are not monolithic. In other words, although institutionally the staff at Johnson Middle School tended to characterize all of their students in similar ways, the students experienced the same practice in distinct ways. Nikki and Timothy's trajectories were decidedly different in Ms. Ridley's class.

I acknowledge that the case presented here may appear "extreme," in that Math Royalty is not a staple of all middle school math instruction. However, the analytical points raised by this case implicate the importance of considering both what models of mathematics are being furthered by, and through, instructional practice and, simultaneously, how youth are constructed by and through their participation in those practices.

Nikki's Negotiation of Royalty

Nikki was quickly identified as a "model" and "top" student in Ms. Ridley's fifth-grade mathematics class and maintained this social identity throughout the year. Within the first two months at Johnson, Ms. Ridley identified Nikki as one of her "top" students. Nikki "followed the rules" at Johnson. She participated regularly in class, her homework was almost always complete, and she regularly received As on tests and quizzes. Nikki was awarded the fifth-grade female Johnson Student of the Year award and achieved "straight As" each quarter, earning her a special recognition of "high honors" at the end-of-year school-wide ceremony. Importantly, Nikki was not the only student to perform well on tests, complete her homework, and arrive on time at school. Yet, she managed to secure a social identity that, in Ms. Ridley's class, was granted to only a few students. The primary vehicle to achieving this identity was through Math Royalty. Even though Nikki was socially identified as "successful" and a "top" student, as I show and discuss below, the negotiation of this identity was not straightforward. Moreover, Nikki's success has to be understood against the prevailing model of mathematics in the room. This, I will argue, has implications for how we construct and assess success in mathematics.

Inheriting the Throne

During the three-week summer initiation program and most of September, Nikki was usually between the fifth and tenth student to finish Math Royalty. She often had all of her problems correct, but other students were quicker than her to finish. In late September, Nikki won the title of Math Queen for the first time. She finished fifth that day; however, the students who finished before her had answered at least one problem incorrectly. Ms. Ridley announced that Nikki had won. She approached the front of the room. With a grin and her head tilted slightly to the right, she shouted, "I RULE." The class screamed back, "YOU RULE." Nikki placed the pink tiara on her head and returned to her seat.

Over the next two months, Nikki regularly occupied the first, second, or third slot in terms of when she finished Math Royalty. And, her work was almost always perfect. As Nikki continued to win Math Royalty, she assumed other roles in the classroom that positioned her as a "top" math student, but simultaneously positioned her tenuously with respect to her peers. Ms. Ridley framed Nikki as teacher-like and regularly evaluated Nikki's responses in class positively.

Twice, Ms. Ridley had Nikki teach the class. During class on November 1, Ms. Ridley came over to where I was sitting in the back of the room and said, "Kara, I under-planned. I didn't expect this [lesson] to go so quickly." The class was working on three-by-two digit multiplication. To pass time, Ms. Ridley asked the class, "Anybody think they can stand up here and do it [go over the problem on the board] and I'll sit in your seat?" Several students raised their hands, including Nikki. Ms. Ridley chose Nikki to come to the front and asked her to go through the steps to solve 837×37 with the class.

Nikki went to the front. She faced the class and took a deep breath. She asked the class to join with her as they went step-by-step through the procedures for multiplying the numbers. She mimicked exactly how Ms. Ridley went over multiplication problems with the class. At one point, Nikki forgot to say one of the rhymes that Johnson used when multiplying. Ms. Ridley called out, "Teacher, teacher you forgot to say—" and Nikki said the rest of the rhyme with Ms. Ridley. Ms. Ridley then said to the class, "Tell Ms. Martin what to do next." At the end of every computation problem, Ms. Ridley asked, "Who can read me this number [answer]?" A student told Nikki that was what she should say next. Nikki smiled and asked, "Who can read me this number?" She called on a student who was raising his hand, and he read the product. Nikki commented, "Very good." Ms. Ridley announced to the class, "Round of applause for Nikki. Hard work, very nice." The class clapped for Nikki, and she took her seat. Ms. Ridley resumed her spot at the front of the classroom.

Both Nikki and Angela, another female student who won Math Royalty as often as Nikki, occasionally corrected Ms. Ridley's mathematics, which contributed to their positioning as knowledgeable and as teacher-like. When corrected, Ms. Ridley thanked them and apologized to the class. Ms. Ridley occasionally checked her answers against Nikki's and Angela's before sharing them with the class. For example, in mid-October, Ms. Ridley placed the answers to the homework from the night before on the overhead projector. Several students raised their hand to question the answer to a particular problem. Ms. Ridley said to the class, "So, if Nikki and Angela get the same answer, it must be right." Ms. Ridley then asked Angela what she got. "Nikki, did you get the same answer?" Nikki nodded in agreement. Ms. Ridley told the class that what she had written on the overhead projector was correct, since both Angela and Nikki had the same answer as she did.

Nikki had more control over how she was positioned in some of the practices than in others. For example, Nikki had little control over how Ms. Ridley explicitly positioned her in the classroom. Of course, had she chosen to disobey classroom rules, it is likely that Ms. Ridley would have identified her differently. I tracked the social identification of other students, including those who regularly disobeyed classroom and school rules, in the classroom over the course of fifth grade, and Ms. Ridley did not position them favorably. Ultimately, Ms. Ridley chose to praise Nikki for her work habits and to position her as teacher-like, in part because Nikki's approach to mathematics was in alignment with what Ms. Ridley expected. On the other hand, Nikki had a great deal of control over whether she won Math Royalty. I now return to Nikki's public identification as a consistent Math Queen; the discussion illustrates how complex it was for Nikki to negotiate and maintain an identity of a successful mathematics student in the context of the classroom.

Nikki's Abdication of the Throne

By December, Nikki wore the tiara nearly every day. She regularly occupied the first or second spot in terms of when she finished the five Math Royalty problems. Not only was Nikki accurate, she also increased her speed. However, by late January, the boys in the class began to react to Nikki's repeated success in Math Royalty.

In late January, some of the male students who rarely won the crown began to accuse Nikki of "cheating." They claimed she would say, "Done," and then make some changes on her paper. Nikki denied this. She said that occasionally she forgot to write her number down at the top of the paper, so she would go back and do this. My observations confirmed this. Ms. Ridley also maintained that Nikki was not cheating, and she told the boys who made this claim that they were jealous and that they should work harder to win. As Nikki continued to win, some of the boys began to make "sss" noises as she said, "I RULE." Nikki, in turn, began to turn away from the class and mumble, "I rule." The girls loudly responded, "YOU RULE," but many of the boys did not join them. Ms. Ridley did not acknowledge these behaviors.

On February 8, when Nikki said, "Done," other students said, "Dang!" indicating their surprise at how quickly she finished. Nikki was then crowned Math Queen for the fifth day in a row. Nikki mumbled, "I rule." Only the females responded with, "You rule." The males were silent. One male student told Ms. Ridley, "It's not fair that she always gets to be Math Queen." One of the male students said, "Come on boys. We got to pull it together." Ms. Ridley responded, "Don't give [Nikki] garbage. You all need to increase your skills so you can beat her. Don't be haters just because she's got skills." Nikki continued to win for the next several days. She continued to mumble, "I rule," and the boys continued to abstain from congratulating her.

On February 15, a critical event in Nikki's trajectory of participation occurred. Math Royalty was structured as usual. Angela finished first; a few seconds later Nikki announced she was finished. After the class checked answers, and it was established that Angela had completed all five of the problems correctly, Ms. Ridley announced that Angela was the Math Queen. The entire class, girls and boys, clapped and cheered when Ms. Ridley announced this. Angela came to the front to pick up her crown and complete the "I RULE!" and "YOU RULE!" ritual. She then wrote her name on the board, added a tally to the chart for Queens versus Kings, and took her seat. Ms. Ridley then turned to Nikki, and the following exchange ensued:

T/R:	Nikki, what was the running streak?
Nikki:	I don't know.
T/R:	You could look in your book, I bet it's 10 days.
Tanya:	She did it on purpose.
T/R:	You're just jealous.
Tanya:	No, she stopped and she didn't want to win so she waited for Angela to say one and then [she] said two.
T/R:	Nikki, is this true?
	Nikki nods her head yes. She begins to write on her paper.
Angela:	Should Nikki be number one?
T/R:	No, you won. Nikki, you're putting Angela in an awkward position. Stop writing.
	Nikki stops writing on her paper.
T/R:	What I'm saying, Nikki, is you're making her feel bad. In my mind, Angela, you won fair and square. Nikki, if you don't want to win, that's your decision. But I think that sucks that you don't want to win. I think you need to say something to Angela.
Nikki:	I don't know what to say.
T/R:	You're making her feel really bad.
Nikki:	(murmurs) Sorry.
T/R:	I could hardly hear that.
Nikki:	I'm sorry.
T/R:	Tanya, you're part of the problem. This is a waste of time. We should be going over homework.
T/R to Angela:	I don't want you to feel bad. You won fair and square.

After this brief exchange, Nikki began to rip up pieces of her binder. She did not raise her hand the rest of the class.

Later that evening, I called Nikki and asked if I could come interview her about what had happened in class that day. She agreed. We talked about this event; she was still very upset by it. She said she had actually informed Ms. Ridley the day before that some of the boys had been teasing her for repeatedly becoming Math Queen. Maurice, another student in her class, had given a "shout out" (praise) in Science the day before for a male student who had beaten Nikki a while back. Nikki's decision to lose the contest was intentional. She said she did not want to be teased any more by the boys in her class. She also said that she told Ms. Ridley several times that Maurice, in particular, had been teasing her for continuing to win, but that each time she told her, Ms. Ridley said she was too busy to deal with it at the time but to remind her again at a different time.

This event, namely Nikki's "abdication of the throne," was contingent on a local model of gender, "boys versus girls," that, although not described in detail in this chapter, by this point in the year had been established through several practices, including the differentiation of Queens versus Kings. This local model of gender contributed to the collective male decision to boycott Nikki's title of Math Queen. Interestingly, attempting to offer a counter-discourse about women as inferior to men in mathematics, Ms. Ridley initiated a discourse of "boys versus girls" in the classroom. Boys and girls were expected to compete publicly for success in mathematics. Ms. Ridley's intention was to highlight for both the boys and girls that girls could be successful in mathematics. However, rallying by gender affiliation *against* successful members of the opposite gender was an unintended consequence of "boys versus girls" in the classroom.

After February 15, Nikki's participation patterns changed in the classroom. She volunteered answers less often and occasionally won Math Royalty, but not as often as she had before. When she did win, she continued to mumble, "I rule," and look away from the class. Although Nikki compromised winning Math Royalty on a regular basis, she still managed to maintain a public persona of a successful, smart student in mathematics. It remained a gendered position, in some respects, because of the local model of "boys versus girls" that continued to order interactions in the classroom. However, Nikki's move to forego a consistent identification as Math Queen could be interpreted as a challenge to the local model of gender. Nikki maintained outstanding academic standing, so much so that she was awarded Johnson fifth-grade student of the year, but removed herself from the daily pressure of "boys versus girls" evident in the Math Royalty competition.

Timothy's Negotiation of Competing Models of Mathematics and Personhood

Nikki exemplified the "successful" mathematical person in Ms. Ridley's classroom—quick, accurate, and satisfied with following the given solution path. Students who did not meet these criteria experienced varying degrees of failure in the class. Timothy was quickly cast as one of the slowest students in the class, and, although he was accurate and often satisfied with following a prescribed solution path, his speed meant that he maintained a peripheral position in mathematics across the entire school year in Ms. Ridley's class.

There was reason to believe that Timothy's relative "slowness" was due, at least in part, to a physical disability, which had cognitive ramifications. At birth, and then again at 18 months, a shunt was inserted into Timothy's brain to help monitor the flow of spinal fluid. As a result, Timothy tended to process information slower than his peers and he developed a stutter. Although Timothy qualified for speech services, he did not qualify for special education services at Johnson.[7] Ms. Sanchez, the fifth-grade special education teacher, included him in a small group whom she pulled out of math class for the first 30 minutes of every class period. She argued that he benefited from small group instruction where speed was not of primary importance, and Ms. Ridley agreed. Ms. Sanchez was a young Puerto Rican woman who had completed her undergraduate degree in special education, taught two years in Puerto Rico, and then moved to the U.S. mainland and took a position teaching special education at an urban, neighborhood middle school. She left that school after a few months and began to work at Johnson. She was in her second year at Johnson when I began this study.

From September through January, the pull-out group met with Ms. Sanchez Monday through Wednesdays. I accompanied Timothy on Tuesdays and Wednesdays. However, in January, it was decided that the special education group of students needed to stay in the mainstream classroom for the entire period to ensure they did not miss out on math instruction. Instead of pulling out the group, Ms. Sanchez circulated in Ms. Ridley's classroom to assist her group of students.

Timothy participated in distinct ways in the two classroom settings. He participated in Math Royalty in both settings; however, as I describe below, he experienced the practice quite differently because of the different models of mathematics at play in the different classroom settings.

The Social Construction of Timothy in Relation to Mathematics in Ms. Ridley's Class

Ms. Ridley repeatedly identified Timothy as "slow" in class, in part because he tended to take longer than his peers to start and finish activities. He was often one of the last students to get in line to leave the cafeteria for math class, usually because he was struggling to finish his Morning Work, a sheet of math problems students were expected to complete at breakfast, before class. On days that he did not finish Morning Work, he was sanctioned and lost money from his "paycheck" at the beginning of class for being "unprepared." (Students received a weekly paycheck as part of the behavior management approach. The money earned could be redeemed in the school store for school supplies. Maintaining a certain average was necessary in order to participate in school-wide activities, like field trips.) This sanction was made publicly. Timothy then had to copy the daily objective, his homework, and the Math Royalty problems. He rarely had everything copied by the time Math Royalty started, which meant that he seldom finished Math Royalty by the time Ms. Ridley checked answers. As Timothy told me in late November,

> I feel bad that when I'm, everybody else gets to wear the [Math Royalty] crown but not everybody else does. If everybody got the answers right . . . I'm almost like the only person that's not done copying down the math royalty. Sometimes I can look back and sometimes they is some other people who is not done but I never get to be the math king in Ms. Ridley's class. (*His mother hears him tell me this and says, "Well maybe you'll be king one day. Just keep trying."*) Mom, I can't write that fast! Mom I be stopping to write my daily objective and heading down then I write that first . . . But I don't be having answers, I be the last one to finish. I didn't say "done" and they be going over the answers without me. And I still be doing the work. (INT, 11/26/05)

The pattern of Timothy being left behind continued throughout the lesson. He often did not copy the notes as quickly as others, which meant that, instead of raising his hand to participate in discussion, he continued copying notes that he got from others, or, on occasion, Ms. Ridley gave him her overheads to copy. This meant he started his classwork late, which in turn meant he often did not complete his classwork.

Based on my data, these patterns were established by mid-September, and by early October, Ms. Ridley had established that Timothy was "lower than" and "not as ambitious" as other students:

> Timothy... is special ed and he's obviously a lot lower [than Nikki]. Umm, and stuff does not come as easily to him as Nikki. They're almost like opposite ends of the spectrum academically, which is frustrating. But, umm, not that Timothy can't do the work, it's just that sometimes his disability sometimes can limit what he can do in my class.... He doesn't ask for help... quickly.... I have to, like, coax it out of him. Like, "Are you sure you get this?" "Oh, I'm fine, I'm fine." I'm just like, no you're not. You know what I mean? I know you need my help.... So, but I mean like, it's not like he's like, he can do the work. It's more just like, he's definitely not as ambitious. (INT, 10/04/05)

However, she acknowledged that he was capable of completing the mathematics problems she posed, but believed he did not display participation patterns similar to the higher-achieving students. Across the year, Ms. Ridley characterized him as "lazy" and "coddled by his parents," indicating that the source of his relative slowness was his lack of motivation coupled with "too much support" from his parents:

> I don't even know if the speed is the disability, I feel like in a way it's like this baby thing. Like speed it up man. I don't know if it is a disability. I can visualize him doing homework at night and it taking 3 hours because he's just putzing. I don't think this child has a problem, I think this child has just been allowed to take his good old time on everything and then he comes into an environment like this where it's just not OK. We've had many run ins with his dad complaining about stuff we're doing here. And it's like, you know, if you don't want to follow our rules, take him back to [his neighborhood school]. But you obviously want him here for a reason. So when we come up with something and we have a certain rule that you don't feel good about, our school works, we must be doing something right. I in a way feel like he's been mislabeled and not pushed because of his personality, and the stuttering too. I feel guilty sometimes, I call on him in class and he gets all anxious. But he's getting a little better. (INT, 3/29/06)

The Construction of Timothy and Mathematics in Ms. Sanchez' Pull-Out Sessions

Timothy was not as reserved in Ms. Sanchez' class as he was in Ms. Ridley's classroom. And, notably, he was not positioned as "slow." As it was, "slow" was relative. Even though Ms. Sanchez supported Ms. Ridley's pedagogical strategies in the pullout sessions, in that she reinforced the same procedures that Ms. Ridley emphasized, she did not place an emphasis on speed. And, of the seven students in the pull-out session, Timothy tended to have a better understanding of the material than some of the others, although this was variable.

For the last 10 minutes of every pull-out session, Ms. Sanchez conducted her own version of Math Royalty. She recognized that this group of students could not viably compete in the classroom because speed was not their strength. She also knew that several of them, including Timothy, felt badly that they never won Math Royalty. Ms. Sanchez assigned five or six problems but did not reward speed. Instead, when everyone had finished, she made sure that they each had correct answers. Then, before they left the classroom, she picked one of their names out of a jar to be named Math King or Queen for the day. She usually put a sticker on the King or Queen's forehead, which the students laughed about. The students typically moved the sticker to their shirts or notebooks before returning to Ms. Ridley's classroom. Timothy only won Math Royalty once during my observations. He was incredibly proud, as the following excerpt illustrates.

Ms. Sanchez wrote six Math Royalty problems on the board (see Figure 7.3). The students began to copy the problems onto their individual white boards.

Ms. Sanchez saw that Timothy was the only one who had not finished copying the problems. She finished writing them for him and then told the group they could start. Timothy finished fourth. When everyone finished, Ms. Sanchez went over the answers with the group. She announced, "I'm going to explain these because many of you are making silly mistakes. Timothy, you're the one I think pretty much got it." Ms. Sanchez took his white board from him, looked at it and then returned it. She proceeded to question the students about how to solve each of the problems. At

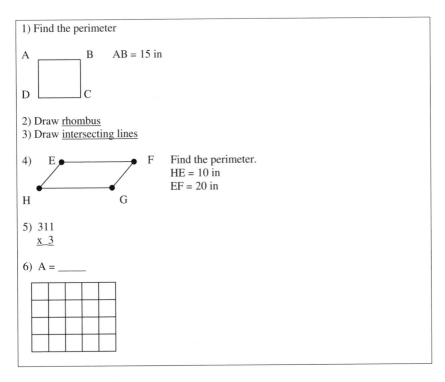

Figure 7.3 Math Royalty with Ms. Sanchez (FN, 12/13/05).

the end of the class, she picked Timothy's name from a jar. "Timothy, you got it. What do you say?" He grinned and yelled, "I RULE!" His peers responded, "YOU RULE!" The students gathered their belongings. On the way back to Ms. Ridley's room, Ms. Sanchez patted Timothy on the back and said, "Good job. You really get this!" Timothy smiled and nodded his head yes.

Ms. Sanchez recognized the difference between how Timothy positioned himself in her class and how he did so in Ms. Ridley's class:

> I think he definitely participates more in the small group than he does in the classroom. He does participate in the classroom sometimes, but not as excitedly as he does in the small group. I think his whole demeanor is different when he's with me than in the classroom. I think his whole stuttering and his whole, "Am I wrong or am I right when I answer questions?" [change when he's with me]. . . . He's not gonna want to participate as much [in Ms. Ridley's classroom]. I mean, he does but he does not act excited [when he's in Ms. Ridley's classroom]. (INT, 1/18/06)

In comparison to how Ms. Ridley described Timothy—in terms of what he lacked—Ms. Sanchez described Timothy's strengths in mathematics, including his neatness, his organization, and his understanding:

> He's very neat. Even though he's slow he's still very organized in his own little way. He has his papers and his work that he turns in, it's always great work that he turns in. I think that he enjoys being here and I think he pretty much understands. . . . I think just the fact that he seems to enjoy being in his classes is a strength for him. Even though he knows he's slow and he knows those things. But he's kind of trying to work with it, so he can be on the same level as his other classmates. . . . He's definitely capable of understanding, but at another speed. So you might have to explain things to him, but he's gonna get it. (INT, 1/18/06)

I asked Ms. Sanchez what she knew of how other teachers characterized Timothy. She explained that they thought he was "slow," but couched this in a critique of the uniform way in which Johnson teachers tended to approach their students:

> They see him as slow. I think that sometimes teachers get so involved in what they're doing that they just don't realize that all of our kids aren't the same. Just because all of our teachers are so involved and hard working themselves it's really hard to kind of, and it's not lowering your standards, but it's kind of having different expectations for the students. And sometimes the comments I hear are he's slow, his parents baby him, that kind of stuff. But it's like, regardless, he's a child. He doesn't necessarily have a learning disability but he does learn at a slower pace than everybody else. This needs to be reinforced and I try to let them know, and I think teachers forget that. (INT, 6/09/06)

Timothy, too, recognized a difference in how he was socially positioned in Ms. Sanchez' class in comparison to Ms. Ridley's. He described several times over the course of the year that he appreciated Ms. Sanchez, especially that she "helped us to ... solve answers" (INT, 7/15/06) in the special education group. He described how he felt comfortable raising his hand in the small group. He did, however, tell me that while he enjoyed the pull-out sessions with Ms. Sanchez, he was happy that in February, they no longer missed Ms. Ridley's class. When I asked him why, he explained: "When I left the classroom, I be coming back and have to copy everything I missed." Timothy was referring to the daily objective, agenda, and homework that they were responsible for copying every day, even when they had a pull-out session.

Mathematical Socialization

Processes of socialization and social identification matter in contexts, like schooling, in which there is knowledge of academic content and personhood at stake (e.g., Heath, 1983; Rymes, 2001; Wortham, 2006). Although mathematics and language differ in important ways, if we assume that social relations are implicated in learning mathematics as they are in learning to speak, read, and write, then it is worthwhile to consider what it might imply to conceptualize mathematical socialization as a two-pronged process, analogous to language socialization: learning to do and use mathematics (*socialization to use mathematics*) and how the doing and using of mathematics is related to who one might become in particular communities (*socialization through the use of mathematics*).

Both Nikki and Timothy were socialized into a construction of mathematics that emphasized speed and accuracy over process and involved completing procedures that were absent of mathematical meaning. They were denied access to challenging and academically purposeful mathematics. This impoverished construction of mathematics, which was facilitated through practices like Math Royalty, was rooted in institutional discourses about Johnson's youth and their previous schools as deficient. A lack of "basic skills" went hand-in-hand with a construction of the youth as academically deficient. Johnson Middle School officials' construction of the youth as deficient was used to justify pedagogy aimed toward a procedural understanding of mathematics.

Nikki and Timothy experienced Math Royalty, and fifth-grade mathematics in general, in different ways. Nikki was "successful" in mathematics, and the public identification as Math Queen helped solidify her identification. However, she deliberately compromised her position as "Math Queen" mid-way through the year because of the social consequences. On the other hand, Math Royalty facilitated the identification of Timothy as "slow" and he was constructed as a peripheral participant in Ms. Ridley's classroom. However, in Ms. Sanchez' classroom, the practice of Math Royalty did not have a negative social effect as it did in Ms. Ridley's classroom. But, if we consider both Nikki and Timothy's experiences beyond the local setting of the classroom, their narratives raise an important question: Through doing mathematics as it was constructed in fifth grade, for what were Nikki and Timothy being socialized?

There is ample evidence that constructing mathematics as a series of procedures is limiting to students—both in relation to more immediate use of mathematics in schooling situations (Hiebert & Lefevre, 1986) and in relation to what mathematicians and professionals who make use of mathematics do (Ball & Bass, 2000). It is not likely that the procedural understanding of mathematics that was given primacy in Ms. Ridley's class would support Nikki, Timothy, and the other 31 students as they moved forward in their academic and professional careers. Somewhat ironically, Johnson Middle school officials framed Johnson as a college preparatory middle school. It is hard to imagine that the type of understanding of mathematics advocated in Ms. Ridley's classroom will serve these students in a college-level mathematics classroom, given that college level-mathematics classes tend to require and further conceptual understandings of mathematics.

It is useful to maintain a finding of language socialization research at the forefront of this discussion—that indeed, socialization is an interactive process. However, this does not mean that individuals have complete freedom in how they position themselves with respect to a classroom. A practice like Math Royalty, as enacted in Ms. Ridley's classroom, perpetuated a narrow construction of mathematics, along with a narrow choice of who students might be positioned as with respect to that practice. In the case of Nikki, she negotiated a limited model of mathematics and personhood. Given the power dynamics of the classroom, Timothy had little room to negotiate how Ms. Ridley positioned him. Math Royalty, as enacted in Ms. Sanchez' classroom, perpetuated that same, narrow construction of mathematics; however, there was more fluidity in terms of whom students might be with respect to the practice. With Ms. Sanchez, Timothy was able to attain success in part because Ms. Sanchez had a wider range of what constituted success in mathematics.

Maintaining a focus on socialization processes inherent in learning mathematics helps teachers, teacher educators, and mathematics education researchers identify and shape both what we intend youth to do mathematically in the immediate and what we intend for youth to do and become, with respect to mathematics in the future. The analysis presented in this chapter highlights the complexity of structuring learning environments for mathematics. Ms. Ridley's classroom, as all classrooms, was a nexus of discourses about youth, about mathematics, and about pedagogy. The local practices were influenced by discourses about poor children of color and mathematics that circulated outside of Johnson Middle School. In order for Ms. Ridley to "do" mathematics teaching differently at Johnson, it is likely that she would have had to interrogate the assumptions that Johnson made about the fifth graders who walked through their doors. In other words, it is likely that focusing only on the pedagogy, without attention to how youth were constructed would have changed little about the teachers' practices. At the same time, it is likely that had Ms. Ridley engaged the students in challenging mathematics aimed at developing conceptual understanding, she might have challenged the prevailing discourses about the youth in Johnson Middle School.

Notes

1 All names of people and places are pseudonyms.
2 "M/St" indicates a male student spoke. "F/St" indicates a female student spoke. Repeated instances of "M/St 1" or "F/St 1" refer to the same student speaking.

3 "F/N" and "INT" refer to fieldnote and interview data, respectively. Only interview data were audio-recorded. The words I attribute to individuals in fieldnotes are based on my memory of the interaction. While I recognize the danger of attributing words to others, I attempted to preserve individuals' speech as best as possible in my fieldnotes. In the case of classroom observations, I took notes as the interactions unfolded.

4 Students who lived in the city district (with their parents'/guardians' signature and permission) had to complete an application in the spring before the academic year they wanted to enroll. Enrollment by lottery meant that the school then randomly selected students from the applicant pool to fill the slots that were open. Once a child in a family was admitted to Johnson Middle School by lottery, her younger siblings were automatically granted admission to the school grades five and above.

5 The school used the categories of African American and Hispanic.

6 "Highly qualified" meant that a teacher (1) was certified by the state; (2) held a Bachelor's degree; (3) completed a content area major; (4) passed a content area test; and (5) completed teacher education coursework.

7 Ms. Sanchez explained to me that, in order to qualify for special education services, Timothy would have had to demonstrate a discrepancy on his performance on a series of tests used for qualifying purposes. He "scored low on all of the tests," thereby disqualifying him from receiving special education instructional services.

References

Anderson, D.D. & Gold, E. (2006). Home to school: Numeracy practices and mathematical identities. *Mathematical Thinking and Learning, 8*(3), 261–286.

Baker, D., Street, B., & Tomlin, A. (2003). Mathematics as social: Understanding relationships between home and school numeracy practices. *For the Learning of Mathematics, 23*(3), 11–15.

Ball, D.L. & Bass, H. (2000). Making believe: The collective construction of public mathematical knowledge in the elementary classroom. In D.C. Phillips (Ed.), *Constructivism in education: Opinions and second opinions on controversial issues* (pp. 193–224). Chicago: The University of Chicago Press.

Boaler, J. (1997). *Experiencing school mathematics: Teaching styles, sex, and setting.* Buckingham, U.K.: Open University Press.

Boaler, J. (1998). Open and closed mathematics: Student experiences and understandings. *Journal for Research in Mathematics Education, 29*(1), 41–62.

Boaler, J. (1999). Participation, knowledge and beliefs: A community perspective on mathematics learning. *Educational Studies in Mathematics, 40,* 259–281.

Boaler, J. (Ed.). (2000). *Multiple perspectives on mathematics teaching and learning.* Westport, CT: Ablex Publishing.

Cobb, P., Stephan, M., McClain, K., & Gravemeijer, K. (2001). Participating in mathematical practices. *The Journal of the Learning Sciences, 10*(1&2), 113–163.

deAbreu, G. (1999). Learning mathematics in and outside school: Two views on situated learning. In J. Bliss, R. Saljo & P. Light (Eds.), *Learning sites: Social and technological resources for learning* (pp. 17–31). Oxford: Elsevier Science.

Dossey, J.A. (1992). The nature of mathematics: Its role and its influence. In D. Grouws (Ed.), *Handbook for research on mathematics teaching and learning* (pp. 39–48). New York: Macmillan.

Gee, J. (1990/1996). *Social linguistics and literacies: Ideology in discourses.* London: Routledge.

Greeno, J.G., & Middle School Mathematics Through Applications Project Group. (1998). The situativity of knowing, learning, and research. *American Psychologist, 53*(1), 5–26.

Heath, S.B. (1983). *Ways with words: Language, life, and work in communities and classrooms.* Cambridge, UK: Cambridge University Press.

Hiebert, J. (2003). What research says about the NCTM Standards. In J. Kilpatrick, W.G. Martin & D. Schifter (Eds.), *A research companion to Principles and Standards for School Mathematics* (pp. 5–23). Reston, VA: National Council of Teachers of Mathematics.

Hiebert, J. & Lefevre, P. (1986). Conceptual and procedural knowledge in mathematics: An introductory analysis. In J. Hiebert (Ed.), *Conceptual and procedural knowledge: The case of mathematics* (pp. 1–27). Hillsdale, NJ: Erlbaum.

Holstein, J.A. & Gubrium, J.F. (Eds.). (2008). *Handbook of constructionist research.* New York: The Guilford Press.

Horn, I.S. (2007). Fast kids, slow kids, lazy kids: Classification of students and conceptions of subject matter in math teachers' conversations. *Journal of the Learning Sciences, 16,* 37–79.

Jackson, K. (2007). *Under construction: Learning mathematics across space and over time. Unpublished Dissertation,* University of Pennsylvania. Philadelphia, PA.

Kieran, C., Forman, E., & Sfard, A. (2001). Learning discourse: Sociocultural approaches to research in mathematics education. *Educational Studies in Mathematics, 46,* 1–12.

Kohlberg, L. (1984). *The psychology of moral development: The nature and validity of moral stages.* San Francisco: Harper & Row.

Lave, J. & Wenger, E. (1991). *Situated learning: Legitimate peripheral participation.* New York: Cambridge University Press.

Lemke, J.L. (2000). Across the scales of time: Artifacts, activities, and meanings in ecosocial systems. *Mind, Culture, and Activity, 7*(4), 273–290.

Martin, D.B. (2000). *Mathematics and success and failure among African-American youth: The roles of sociohistorical context, community forces, school influence, and individual agency.* Mahwah, NJ: Lawrence Erlbaum.

Martin, D.B. (2006a). Mathematics learning and participation as racialized forms of experience: African American parents speak on the struggle for mathematics literacy. *Mathematical Thinking and Learning, 8*(3), 197–229.

Martin, D.B. (2006b). Mathematics learning and participation in the African American context: The co-construction of identity in two intersecting realms of experience. In N. Nasir & P. Cobb (Eds.), *Improving access to mathematics: Diversity and equity in the classrooms* (pp. 146–158). New York: Teachers College Press.

Martin, D.B. (2007). Beyond missionaries or cannibals: Who should teach mathematics to African American children? *The High School Journal, 91*(1), 6–28.

Nasir, N.S. (2002). Identity, goals, and learning: Mathematics in cultural practice. *Mathematical Thinking and Learning, 4*(2 & 3), 213–247.

Packer, M.J. & Goicoecha, J. (2000). Sociocultural and constructivist theories of learning: Ontology, not just epistemology. *Educational Psychologist, 35*(4), 227–241.

Rymes, B. (2001). *Conversational borderlands: Language and identity in an alternative urban high school.* New York: Teachers College Press.

Schieffelin, B.B. & Ochs, E. (1986). Language socialization. *Annual Review of Anthropology, 15,* 163–191.

Stigler, J.W. & Hiebert, J. (1999). *The teaching gap: Best ideas from the world's teachers for improving education in the classroom.* New York: Free Press.

Street, B.V. (Ed.). (1993). *Cross-cultural approaches to literacy.* Cambridge: Cambridge University Press.

Street, B.V., Baker, D., & Tomlin, A. (2005). *Navigating numeracies: Home/School numeracy practices.* Dordrecht: Springer.

Thompson, P.W., & Saldanha, L.A. (2003). Fractions and multiplicative reasoning. In J.

Kilpatrick, W.G. Martin & D. Schifter (Eds.), *A research companion to Principles and Standards for School Mathematics* (pp. 95–113). Reston, VA: National Council of Teachers of Mathematics.

Wortham, S. (2006). *Learning identity: The joint emergence of social identification and academic learning.* New York: Cambridge University Press.

8 Identity at the Crossroads: Understanding the Practices and Forces that Shape African American Success and Struggle in Mathematics

Joi A. Spencer

Three Men Walk into a Mathematics Classroom

Many of the racist jokes that I have been told begin with these five words: *three men walked into a.* While meant by the teller to be a light-hearted jest, these jokes often draw upon deeply held, painful stereotypes. These jokes—and the stereotypes they explicate—are a part of the history, discourse, and fiber of America. They are often as familiar as bedtime nursery rhymes. It is important to note that the running narratives of American life do not stop at the classroom door. Unlike these bad jokes, the messages and discourses about students don't begin with an obvious tagline alerting the hearer to what is to follow. Rather, they seep quietly, almost invisibly, into the practices, dispositions, and policies of schools and classrooms. It is because these messages are so subtle that educators must be on guard and, when detected, must take a vigilant stance against them. Three brief examples may bring greater clarity.

I conduct research at a Southern California middle school. The school's racial population is approximately 60% Latina/o, 35% African American, and 5% Asian and white. On a recent visit to the Advanced sixth-grade math class, I remarked to the teacher that out of the 28 students, there were only three African Americans in the class. She replied that she had not noticed this fact.

Douglass Middle School[1] provides another case of disproportionality. Douglass Middle School is located in Southern California's Local District South East. Opened in 1925, Douglass campus is beyond capacity at 2,348 students. At the time of this study, Douglass was in its fourth year of State Program Improvement. Ninety-nine percent of Douglass's students were classified as Latino and African American. Douglass, like many of the schools in its district, was struggling to meet the needs of its African American students. While only 18% of youngsters at Douglass were African American, 37% of the students placed on the infamous D-track[2] were Black. When I asked counselors about how placement decisions were made for school tracks, I was told that the decisions were made strictly based on achievement test data. Upon investigation, I learned that the newest, most inexperienced teachers were assigned to this track, while teachers with greater seniority shunned the track. Of the two sixth-grade mathematics teachers on this track, one was in her second year of teaching, while the other was in his first.

In a study of students' opportunities to learn mathematics, Oakes, Joseph and Muir, (2003) found that decisions for mathematics course placement were often subjective. In this same study, researchers found that, even when holding grades and test scores constant, Black and Latino students were more likely to be placed in lower tracked math courses, while Asian and white students were more likely to be placed into more rigorous, higher tracked math courses. Some of the arbitrary criteria used for course placement included informal teacher recommendation and parental requests.

These examples demonstrate some of the subtle ways that racial inequity inserts itself into the practices of schools and classrooms. If the teachers, counselors and principals in these examples had been more aware and vigilant against these subtle forces, such practices may never have been instituted.

The type of education that a student receives in mathematics today has the power to alter their life chances. Yet, equity around the type of mathematics education that a student receives remains an elusive goal. Black students are especially vulnerable because they attend a disproportionate number of "at-risk" schools where there are lower percentages of certified teachers and higher percentages of out of field instructors (Oakes, Ormseth, Bell, & Camp 1990; Oakes, Joseph & Muir, 2003). Their situation is further complicated by the complex manner in which race plays itself out in the mathematics classroom.

The purpose of this chapter is two-fold. First, it works to make explicit the notion that I have argued on several occasions: that race and racism play out in complex ways in the in-school mathematics experiences of African American[3] students. I have chosen to address this issue because, despite urgings as well as presentations of evidence from a growing number of authors that racism is a factor that stymies the mathematics education of students, I still witness persistent inequities in schools that I visit throughout the country. Part of this persistence, I believe, comes from our inability as a field to translate these findings into the context of schools and classrooms. Another aspect of this inertia deals with the nature of racism and its manifestation in a twenty-first century, post-Brown context. While many might acknowledge that racial disparities exist, they may be less willing or even unable to articulate how these disparities are connected to, and the results of racism. Stuck in images of firehoses and angry dogs chasing down innocent southern Black children, racism seems far, far away from the current realities confronting African American students. Acknowledging the great victories that have been won against racial injustice in this nation, those of us who devote our work to African American students in the enterprise of mathematics education and in the context of schools cannot help but recognize that a force (possibly more insidious than the former) is in operation.

One of the goals of this chapter, then, is to provide a picture of how the force of racism operates within the context of in-school mathematics education of African American students. I have worked hard to provide examples of the subtle, covert ways that inequity injects itself into schooling situations. In addition to racism, I have worked to show how the experiences of African American children in mathematics are racialized—that is, how their experiences are shaped by their unique historical and social realities and relationships to the dominant culture.

A second purpose for this chapter is to highlight tools that school officials and teachers who are serious about increasing the success of their African American students in mathematics can use. This contribution, I hope, will help practitioners put in place practices that will disrupt some of the forces that stymie too many African American students in mathematics.

Key Constructs in understanding African American Students' Mathematics Success

Racism

> Racism springs not from the hearts of "racists," but from the fact that dominant actors in a racialized social system receive benefits at all levels (political, economic, social, and even psychological), whereas subordinate actors do not. Racial outcomes then are not the product of individual "racists" but of the crystallization of racial domination into a racial structure: a network of racialized practices and relationships that shapes the life chances of various races at all levels. (Bonilla-Silva, Lewis, & Embrick, 2004. p. 558)

Tatum (2007), like Bonilla-Silva, Lewis and Embrick (2004), contrasts the idea of individual bigotry with institutional racism. *Institutional racism*, she writes, "is a system of advantages based on race" (p. 7). There was very little advantage to being African American when it came to mathematics course placement at my high school. The set of institutional and structural arrangements made *being African American* and *being good at mathematics* seem improbable and incongruous, while the opposite was true for being Asian or white.

Racism shapes the lives, relationships, communities, and even the mathematics experiences of students. When interviewing African American community college students, Martin (2000) found that these students told similar stories about their in-school experiences in mathematics. From being told that they were not good in math, to being placed in lower-tracked mathematics courses, the similarities of these students' primary and secondary educational experiences were many. These *racialized forms of experience* (Martin, 2006a), shaped the life-long trajectories of these community college students, as well as those of their children. For some, their early experiences in math had convinced them that they could never excel in the subject.

While deeply consequential, the discrimination experienced in my own high school and by Martin's study participants was rarely overt. Defined by Bonilla-Silva and Lewis, this *new racism* often defies "facile racial readings" (p. 560). This novel arrangement, is characterized by covert racial discourses and practices, as well as an invisibility of the mechanisms that produce inequality along lines of race (Bonilla-Silva et al., 2004). The decision to place all students who had scored below a particular level on their standardized exams, for example, resulted in the over-representation of Black students on D-track. As a result of this decision, greater numbers of African American students were exposed to under-qualified teachers and poor curricular content. Racialized inequality is the result, but the mechanisms that make this inequity so are invisible. We see the result—we know that racism is operating—but we just cannot put our finger on it. It is the covert, even elusive nature of these experiences that makes the work of improving the success of African American students in mathematics so difficult. Institutional racism, racialized forms of experience, and new racism become significant terms as we explore African American student success in mathematics.

Identity

Perry, Steele, and Hilliard (2003) argued that the most important issue concerning African American student achievement is the acquisition of an academic identity. Challenges to these students' adoption of such an identity are many. From historical denial of educational opportunities to current media representations of African Americans, supporting the academic identity development of these children requires an active and conscious effort.

There are major differences in how researchers take up, and make sense of, identity. In more psychological traditions, identity was believed to be a stable feature of individuals. Such a feature was static in nature, remaining more of less throughout the life of the individual (a concise discussion of these issues can be found in Stryker & Burke, 2000). More and more, theorists and researchers in sociocultural traditions have conceived of identity as dynamic and context driven.

Forman (1993) speaks of identity as *who we see ourselves as becoming*. In one example, Forman recalls a young woman interviewee who discusses her decision not to learn how to type. In her discussion, the interviewee describes her belief that typing was assigned to girls that would one day become secretaries (i.e., those who were not academically minded). She goes on to describe that she did not want to be associated or identified in these terms. As a result, she resisted learning how to type. As opposed to passively accepting a definition oneself, individuals actually take an active role in making sense of who they are, and who they want others to understand and perceive them to be.

A second notion of identity is that people in disempowered social positions will often work to define themselves in direct opposition to particular labels or judgements from the larger society. Martin (2000), in his study of successful African American mathematics students, defines this phenomenon as *self-definition by opposition*. A number of successful African American kids highlighted in his study chose to define themselves in ways that defied their schoolmates' or larger societies' label about what it means to be a Black youth.

Mathematics Identity

Mathematics identity is described by Martin (2000, 2006b) as students' beliefs about: (a) their ability to perform in mathematical contexts, (b) the instrumental importance of mathematical knowledge, (c) the constraints and opportunities in mathematical contexts and (d) the resulting motivations and strategies used to obtain mathematical knowledge. Not solely an internal construct, identity here is a negotiation between how we see our selves in relation to mathematics and how others position us in relation to mathematics. As Martin (2006a) writes, ". . . a mathematics identity is expressed in its narrative form as a *negotiated self* (italics added), the results of our own assertions and the sometimes-contested external ascriptions of others" (pp. 206–207). As we work to improve African American success in mathematics, identity becomes an important construct. It allows us to examine mathematics success as not simply the output of individual students, but as a representation of the interplay between internal and external forces upon students.

Achievement

A central concern of this chapter is improving and increasing African American student success in mathematics. However, it is important to draw attention to the use of the term *success* versus *achievement* (Martin, 2007). The decision to use the term success comes from my own dissatisfaction with the use, and subsequent meaning, attached to the term achievement.

Achievement has, as its focus, school grades and performance on tests and examinations. Achievement is used loosely to describe what a student knows. For example, a student who receives straight As is seen as a student who knows a lot about the topics that were covered during her school year. Additionally, achievement is often used to describe what a student is *capable* of knowing. For example, the student who received straight As on her report card is subsequently placed into an advanced mathematics class when she arrives in middle school. This advanced course placement, then, poises the student for admission to college seven years later. The opposite is easy to imagine. A student with low grades is subsequently placed into a remedial mathematics course in middle school and subsequently will not be prepared to attend college seven years later. It is this second use of achievement that poses many problems. Decisions that are highly detrimental to a student's future are made based on past performance. This situation is particularly detrimental to African American students who are routinely placed in lower-tracked mathematics courses.

The term achievement has roots in historical debates of "intelligence." And, while the term intelligence remains unclear, schools make crucial decisions about students based on this term, as demonstrated through student achievement data. As an example, elementary students who perform well on achievement exams are often placed in higher tracked math courses when they reach middle school. The decision about which mathematics course a middle school student is placed in has far-reaching consequences, yet this method of placement is widely used (Oakes et al., 2003).

School achievement is constructed by a multitude of factors. For example, some students, because of the historically poor treatment of their community by schools and other social institutions develop an oppositional stance towards school (Ogbu, 1983). These students often choose *not* to learn. In this sense, their achievement is not as much a measure of what they know or understand, but of their relationship to school as an institution.

Why do certain students demonstrate high achievement in school while others do not? In the case of African American students, there is a great deal of evidence that their in-school mathematics achievement may be uniquely tied to several factors, including (a) institutional racism (Tatum, 2002), (b) the nature of their incorporation into this nation (as involuntary minorities) (Ogbu, 1983), (c) the racialized nature of their in-school experiences (Martin, 2000, 2006a); (d) their history of resistance against unequal educational opportunities (Wollenberg, 1976) and (e) their persistence towards gaining academic knowledge and skill (Siddle-Walker, 1996). Clearly, the reasons why students perform in particular ways in school are complex. We need terms that capture this complexity. Likewise, we need terms that capture the experiences of African American students in a more accurate historical context.

Success is a term altogether different from achievement. Success encompasses school performance, along with the attributes that support school performance, such as academic persistence, resistance to negative forces that often undermine young African American students, academic and mathematics identification, positive racial identity, and the skills and ability to find and maintain academic supports. The term success moves away from the value-laden, deficit-driven notion of achievement (based on a norm outside of African American students experiences) and pushes us to consider this reality from a more accurate standpoint that is more appropriately centered on African American students.

A Study of African American Mathematics Students and Their Teachers

In this section, I present findings from a year-long study of African American students' opportunities to learn mathematics in two central city middle schools: Clovis and Douglass. The data presented here come from student and teacher interviews conducted as part of the study. The focus of the student interviews was on their academic and mathematics identities. Interviews with teachers focused on their understandings about, and dispositions towards, their African American mathematics students. The hope is for teachers to consider these two sets of data—student and teacher interviews—in tandem. What do the student responses reveal about African American student success in mathematics? What direction can they provide us, as we work to improve mathematics success for African American students?

Study Context: Clovis and Douglass Middle Schools

Clovis and Douglass Middle Schools are both located in Local District South East (LDSE)[4]. Located in Southern California, the schools' populations are drawn from a larger Latino and African American working class, working poor, and poor community. LDSE shares many of the woes of schools located in poor communities including high teacher turn-over rates, severe over-crowding, and outdated facilities. Adding to their problems, each of LDSE's middle schools had been placed on California's Program Improvement (PI) Status list. PI-status schools which consistently fail to meet Academic Yearly Progress goals receive increasing levels of intervention from the district and state; ranging from the implementation of student tutoring programs (for schools in first and second year PI status) to total school restructuring including the firing of selected personnel (for schools in their third through fifth year of PI status).

All students seemed to be suffering academically in LDSE. At the time of the study, slightly fewer than 7% of LDSE's middle school students scored proficient or advanced on the California Standardized Test (CST), low academic achievement was experienced disproportionately by African American students. With the exception of one of the LDSE middle schools, fewer than 5% of African American middle school students here scored Proficient or Advanced on the state exam.

Given the paucity of mathematics success amongst African American students at these school sites, I asked, "What opportunity did African American students have to learn mathematics?" Opportunity to learn mathematics was examined from four perspectives: (1) the opportunities that students have to learn mathematics with understanding, (2) the opportunities of African American students to participate in their mathematics classrooms, (3) the explanations that teachers give for both the instruction that they provided and the participation of their African American students and, (4) the mathematics identity of both successful and non-successful African American students. While a great deal of other data were collected to address the study question, for the sake of this chapter, I include only student and teacher interview data.

Student Interviews

Thirty-two sixth-grade students—15 boys and 17 girls—participated in semi-structured interviews in the spring of 2005. I asked each teacher to select at least two successful and two non-successful African American students to be interviewed. The criteria for "successful" and "non-successful" were left to the discretion of individual teachers. Through informal conversations with teachers, and through the interviews with students, I learned that teachers' criteria were based upon students' grades and classroom behavior.

With the exception of one question, successful and non-successful students were asked identical questions. One additional question, "What helps you persist in school and mathematics?" was asked of the successful math students in the sample. Of the 32 students selected, 11 were identified as successful and 21 were identified as non-successful by their teachers. A number of teachers reported to me that they did not have any successful Black students. As a result, more non-successful students were interviewed than successful students (see Table 8.1).

Table 8.1 Student Status

Successful		
	Girls	5
	Boys	6
	Total	11
Unsuccessful		
	Girls	12
	Boys	9
	Total	21

Table 8.2 Student Perception of Math Ability

		Yes	No	Kind of	Undecided
		Are you good in math? (By gender and status)			
Successful					
	Girls	2	0	3	0
	Boys	4	0	2	0
Unsuccessful					
	Girls	0	6	5	1
	Boys	1	7	0	1

Are You Good in Math?

Students were asked whether or not they were good in mathematics. Six students said they were good in mathematics, 13 said they were bad in mathematics, 10 reported that they were "somewhere between good and bad," and three students were undecided. Of the students interviewed, non-successful students were more likely to respond that they were not good students in mathematics. Conversely, only one of the non-successful students reported that he was good in math while six of the successful students reported that they were (see Table 8.2).

The responses of boys and girls varied on this question. Of the 15 boys that were interviewed, five reported that they were good in math, seven reported that they were not good, two reported that they were somewhere in the middle and one was undecided.

Below, I present the interview responses of four students—two labeled as unsuccessful and two as successful. The quotes provide the reader with a more textured look at students in these two categories.

Unsuccessful Math Students

Teachers were asked to identify unsuccessful and successful African American math students from their classes. I did not provide criteria for teachers in their selection. However, on the whole, teachers identified students as unsuccessful based on their classroom grades, rates of homework completion, and classroom behavior. The responses of two students: Mark and Myisha, are presented for this discussion.

Mark

Mark is a 12-year-old student from Douglass. When asked to describe himself to me (not himself as a student), Mark quickly responds that he is smart. In the selection below, Mark is asked to describe himself as a student; that is, provide insight into his academic identity.

JS: Now, describe yourself for me as a student.
M: Well, most of the time, I'm kind of bad in my third [period] and fourth

[period]. In my first and second [period] and fifth [period] and sixth [period], I'm okay, good.

JS: When you say "bad," I need to know more. I don't know what you mean by that.

M: Like talk a lot; I do work but not a lot of work.

Mark's comments reveal that his conception of himself as a student is not necessarily tied to how he sees himself as a young man. More closely, while he describes himself as "smart," he describes himself as a *student* as "kind of bad." As his comments proceed, we realize that he attributes his status as a student to both *behavior* (talk a lot) and *work habits* (I do work but not a lot of work). Interestingly, and probably not coincidentally, these are the same attributes that his teacher has used to classify Mark as "unsuccessful." Not based on his abilities to understand math, or his interest in math activities, Mark sees himself as a student in the same way as his teacher sees him.

Perceptions of Classroom Climate, Teacher and Peer Participation

On an average day, Mark's math class was chaotic. Students were unruly and disrespectful to the teacher. Only in his first full year of teaching, Mark's math teacher often resorted to screaming and, on occasion, cursing to bring his students back in line. Mark offered his commentary on why the students in his class were so disruptive.

JS: You said you're bad sometimes, why is that?

M: Well, I think because the teacher is cussing at the students and the students just cuss back at him: because some students don't like the teacher, like when he cusses at you, you don't like the teacher.

JS: What would have to happen for you to be a good student in that class?

M: I don't know. Oh, the teacher! Like, he's got to discipline the kids because all he really do is send them out.

It is clear that Douglass's strategy of placing the most struggling students with the most novice and unskilled teachers (as was the trend on D-track) was a recipe for disaster. Frustrated by his inability to reach his students and by their seeming disregard for education, the teacher reacted in ways that served to further agitate his students. The agitation and response of the students towards their teacher further fueled the teacher's frustrations. The situation is neither fair for the teacher—he does not have the proper expertise to meet the needs of these students; nor just for the students—they deserve a professional, with the skills necessary for addressing their needs.

Mathematics Identity: Beliefs About Mathematics Ability

It was very difficult to separate out Mark's general academic identity from his mathematics identity. It seemed that his beliefs about himself as a student in general seemed to overlap with his beliefs about himself as a math student.

JS: What would it take for you personally? To become an A student? If I had a magic wand and could make everything perfect, what would you want me to make perfect?

M: My brain.

JS: Why do you say that?

M: I do good in my first and second [periods] but my third and fourth and fifth [periods], like bad, terrible.

Mark did offer some thoughts about his abilities in mathematics specifically. When asked to place himself on a scale between a person who is super in mathematics and one who is not so good, he placed himself on the right side of the center (closer to the person who was not so good in mathematics).

JS: If you were going to describe yourself to me as a math student . . .

M: I don't get like a lot of the stuff. I forget the work. He'll be telling us and I just forget some of the work.

JS: Are you satisfied with your grade [in math]?

M: No.

JS: How do your parents feel about it?

M: My mom, she wants me to do better . . .

Mathematics Identity: Beliefs About the Utility of Mathematics

Mark was asked to discuss whether or not math had utility. In his description, Mark reports that math can be important in getting, "a math job." When pressed to be more specific, Mark discusses work as a cashier.

JS: Do you think that math overall is important?

M: Yes.

JS: Why?

M: Because, say if you're working for a job like, like it's a math job, and if you don't know how to count math, you won't get the job.

JS: What kind of jobs are math jobs?

M: Say you're a cash register [worker], like a cashier or something like that, and if somebody gives you a hundred dollars and they bought them for seventy-five dollars, you won't know and if you didn't do good in that class, you might give them thirty-five dollars back.

Mark's response about the utility of math is significant. First, he does not display, here, an understanding of the many occupations to which mathematics is tied. In his description of a math job as working on a "cash register," he has not invoked mathematics in its twenty-first century context—as a tool of technology, engineering, computers, etc. Not making this connection, he ties himself to a working-class occupation. This vision of mathematics, within the lowest tracked math class, within a struggling school, within a struggling district, within an impoverished community may not be inconsequential.

While Mark's description of the utility of mathematics may be cause for concern, he does express belief in the use of mathematics for his personal benefit. Looking closely at his discussion, Mark describes a scenario where a person does not know the correct change to give his customer. He then ties this lack of knowledge back to not doing "good in class." Math class, then, is seen as a tool for Mark to build his own prosperity and wealth and to not be cheated. Martin and McGee (2009) argue that this notion of "not being cheated" has a historical basis in African American liberation. So, while Mark's invoking this sentiment may seem simple, it has a complex history tied to African American struggle.

Career Goals

In the midst of a great deal of school "failure," Mark chooses a career goal that is far from the world of academics—playing basketball. More textured, though, his comments reveal a struggle. He has not completely given up on the idea of college. Despite what his teachers and grades say, maybe it is a possibility.

JS: If you could look at yourself in the future, what would you be doing?
M: I don't know. Maybe go to college and play basketball.
JS: What do you think you're going to need to do to prepare?
M: I need to do better in my math and science and history.
JS: Why those?
M: Those are the ones that I'm failing.

As he continues his discussion, the tension is revealed again—to get to the goal of college, he must first do better in school. These tensions are not insignificant and demonstrate the struggles of being an African American kid, in an impoverished community, in a struggling school, with an inexcusably poor academic offering. In this situation, Mark takes on a future identity that has been handed to him—a basketball player.

At the end of our interview, Mark asked me a number of questions about the process of getting into college. He seemed very interested in the specifics and asked me about: scholarships, application deadlines, the grades necessary to get into college, the grades needed to stay in college, recruitment, and what it was like living on campus. Near the end of our conversation, Mark told me that his sister was being recruited to a number of colleges. He also spoke fondly of his older brother—a college student in Northern California. Mark's interview, more than any other, seemed to exemplify the struggle of being a student on D-track, surrounded by large numbers of students who have had negative academic and schooling experiences. While he looked up to his older brother for being in college, and to his sister who was presently being recruited to a number of colleges, Mark faced the day-to-day realities and pressures of being a student on Douglass's D-track.

Myisha

Myisha is a 12-year-old student from Clovis. She was very energetic and talkative. Her career goal was to become a doctor so that she could help people.

Academic Identity

When asked to describe herself as a student, Myisha gave a list of courses she enjoyed, "language, history, science, and only sometimes math." Later, she was asked to talk about whether or not she was a good math student:

> Sometimes because in math, it's some difficult stuff that my teacher doesn't teach us, but he's a good teacher. Everybody talks over him; that's why everybody says we need a meaner teacher. When they talk over him I can't hear what he's saying so that he can show me how to do the math.

Mathematics Identity: Beliefs About the Utility of Mathematics

Like all of the interviewed students, I asked Myisha to share whether or not she saw math as an important subject. As she answered this question, she also shared some thoughts on the utility of mathematics:

> It's [math is] more important because when you get older . . . Say you work at the store or something and their change is more than what they had and you give them more money, and you don't know how to count and stuff like that.

When asked to share her future career goals, Myisha stated that she wanted to become a doctor. Like Mark, Myisha not only sees a career goal for math, but sees it as a tool for protecting herself from fraud (getting back the right amount of change in a transaction) and supporting herself (she mentions later on in the interview the importance of knowing how to pay for medical malpractice insurance).

Summary of Non-Successful Students

There are a number of traits that characterize the non-successful. They all saw themselves as either "so-so" or "bad" mathematics students. Being a good math student seemed to be a matter of behavior and not necessarily academic achievement. As evidence of this, students cited their own disruptive behavior (i.e., talking with friends) as evidence of them not being good math students. As such, the majority of these students did not see themselves as good math students.

Asking specifically about mathematics gave students an opportunity to focus more on their actual understanding of subject matter. For example, one student, Shannon (another student identified as unsuccessful), stated her difficulties with equations saying, "I'm not excellent because if you asked me an equation and I wouldn't come up with it like, 'bam.' I'm not that good." Likewise, another student, Akiba, identified her frustrations with fractions.

A third similarity was that many of these students talked about their personal struggles with their behavior. They discussed the difficulty of staying focused on their own class work, pressures from their peers to be disruptive, and the strain of being in classrooms with little order. Their struggles further highlight my own experiences in their classrooms, which I found to be disorganized, unfocused, and highly didactic. Surely, students cannot fully escape the blame for their negative behaviors (i.e., talking out of turn, not participating in class, etc.). However, one wonders if these behaviors are not exacerbated by a preponderance of new and un-experienced teachers, an un-engaging curriculum that is focused on tests, and plac-ing large numbers of students with unsuccessful academic backgrounds in the same classroom as was the case at Douglass.

A fourth similarity was the students' beliefs about the utility of mathematics. The students identified practical and vocational purposes for mathematics. Namely, they agreed that understanding math would help them to count their money, to make accurate purchases, and to give accurate change if they worked on a cash register. When asked about the importance of math, Akiba replied, "Yeah, really important, really important. Because if like when you go places, it's like a lot of numbers that you have to follow and stuff so it's really important to know math . . ."

While most of the students spoke of mathematics as an important subject—even identifying it as more important than other subjects—they did not demonstrate through their actions that they believed in its importance. This sort of lip service to the importance of mathematics makes sense, given that almost none of their career goals were academic in nature. This brings us to a final similarity in the responses of these students—their career goals. Students generally identified career goals that were in the entertainment and sports field. Myisha (who stated that she wanted to be a doctor) and Jefferson (who stated that he would like to be a firefighter or an artist) were exceptions to this.

Successful Math Students

Teachers were asked to identify successful African American students in their classes. I did not provide criteria for the teachers in their selection. On the whole, teachers chose students as successful on the basis of their grades, rates of comple-tion on homework and class-work, and on their in-class behavior. A number of teachers struggled to identify successful African American math students. As such, the ratio of unsuccessful to successful students in the study was nearly 2 to 1.

Daniel

The first successful student highlighted here is Daniel, an 11-year-old student from Clovis. He described himself as someone who is funny, hard-working, and likes sports.

Academic Identity

Like each of the students before him, Daniel was asked to comment on the kind of student that he was. Quite definitively, he replied, "I'm a good student." To this he added:

> I get my work done. Whatever my teacher asks me to do, I do it. Whenever my teacher needs help with something, I volunteer.

Mathematics Identity: Beliefs about Mathematics Ability and the Utility of Mathematics

Daniel was one of a few students who stated that math was his favorite subject. When asked what he liked about math, he replied, "I don't know how but doing math makes me happy." Below, Daniel discusses what he feels to be the utility of math:

> I think math and science are the most important thing you will ever learn because without math, how are you going to be able to get a job? How are you going to be able to take care of people? All right, say you have a kid and he or she needs Pampers and stuff like that; and then you give the store salesman like a twenty or something and they give you less than the amount you're supposed to get back; how would you know that the person that runs the store is not ripping you off? That's why you should just stay in school and learn the things that you need to learn.

Daniel identifies math and science as, "the most important thing you will ever learn." He does not provide a specific career in which he would use math, but does see it as significant. Like both Mark and Myisha, Daniel identifies math as a tool for protecting oneself from getting taken advantage of. In his example of purchasing diapers, knowing math allows him to get the proper change.

Perceptions of Classroom Climate, Teacher and Peer Participation

Daniel was asked to describe a typical day in his math classroom:

> When you walk in Mrs. Pleasant's class, some people act like they're animals, they don't know how to act. Sometimes, Mrs. Pleasant asks them politely to do their work, they don't do it. They just sit there and talk to their friends.

While not enrolled in the D-track course of Mark and Myisha, his mathematics classroom was not free of problems. As our conversation continued, he discussed his ability to maintain his focus—despite the many distractions.

Why do You Persist?

Despite the chaos that often reigned in Daniel's classroom, he managed to stay focused and complete his assignments. Below, he reflects on why he "keeps going" even when his classmates give up:

> Well, what keeps me focused is I have friends in Mrs. Pleasant's class too but I try to go as far away as I can from them so I can get my work done instead of talking to them or them talking to me. I don't want to get in trouble because I know that I want to have good grades so my mother will be proud of me, and I just don't want to get in trouble in Mrs. Pleasant's class.

Career Goals

As we completed our interview, I asked Daniel to tell me what he would like to do in the future. His response was typical to many of the other students that I interviewed:

> I'm planning to play basketball, but if that doesn't work out, I'll probably find myself like a little candy store in the local areas and stuff and sell stuff that the kids want.

Nailah

Nailah is an 11-year-old student at Clovis. During the interview she was very outspoken and confident about her abilities. Her desire was one day to play women's professional basketball. When asked to describe herself, Nailah told me that she loved sports—especially basketball and that she liked to draw and color.

Academic Identity

Like Daniel, Nailah did not hesitate when asked to describe herself as a student. She also admitted that at times she could get out of hand—but she never allowed herself to go too far:

> I'm a good student. I like to be wild sometimes but most of the time, I sit back and do my work. I don't have any problems; when I do have a problem, I go to my counselor.

Mathematics Identity: Beliefs About Mathematics Ability

Choosing math as her favorite subject, Nailah's opinion of math seemed to be shaped by what she saw as its relative ease as well as the challenge that it could sometimes provide:

> Math is going real, real good for me. I get As and Bs in math. I already know how to do the math that we're doing, so it's easy for me. I like everything about math; to tell you the truth, I like everything. It's kind of easy for me to do but at the same time, it's kind of difficult learning something new.

Mathematics Identity: Beliefs About the Utility of Mathematics

Nailah identified mathematics as "more important" than other subjects. When asked about its utility for her, she drew connections to her future career goal—basketball:

> To me, it's (math) more important to me, because if I'm going to be a basketball player, I have to learn how to calculate the math skills. Like the 360 move, you have to add and stuff. You have to do math to do the 360 move.

Why do You Persist?

Like many other students at Clovis, Nailah had to navigate often disorganized class-rooms and disruptive students. Below, Nailah answers my questions about what keeps her focused in the midst of these realities.

JS: I've seen you also in class; you're always participating; you're always at the board. What keeps you focused even when there are people in the class who are not?

N: What keeps me focused is that I want to get good grades on my report card and I also want to show what I learned of the fifth grade, my teacher Mr. B.

JS: So you want him to know that you had a good teacher?

N: Yeah.

Career Goals

Nailah had a goal of playing professional basketball. Here, she also shares what her thoughts about what she'll do if this career goal does not mete out.

N: What I see for myself is being a basketball player and if I'm not going to be a basketball player, what I will be is a teacher—a math teacher. [I plan on playing] professional basketball. I'm planning on being in the LA Sparks.

JS: What happens between now and then?

N: I'm just a kid, and when I grow up, I'm going to already have stuff planned for me and what I'm going to do. If I don't get what I want to get, then I'll probably help my uncles and stuff.

Summary of Successful Students

Students identified as successful by their teachers tended to believe that they were both good students in general and specifically in mathematics. While they expressed that peer pressure existed, they had strategies for how to stand against these pressures. These strategies are not insignificant. The decisions that the successful students in this study made to succeed in the midst of chaotic class-rooms, uninteresting and engaging curriculum, and un-prepared teachers, is remarkable.

Like those identified as unsuccessful, these students pointed to practical uses of mathematics that generally dealt with making purchases at a store. Unlike unsuc-cessful students, they spoke in more specific ways about math's utility. However, they still were unable to identify connections (except the need to count their money) between their career goals and mathematics. Students in this category also chose careers in the sports field. However, unlike those identified as unsuccessful, these students presented back-up career plans such as teaching and real estate. Interestingly, these more traditional career goals took a back seat to student's plans to become involved in sports careers.

Teachers

A total of six teachers participated in reflective video interviews. Using this technique, each teacher interview began with the viewing of a videotaped lesson[5] of their own teaching. For each interview, I chose a 5-minute segment of the teacher's lesson for us to view and discuss. Each of the segments that I chose included interactions among African American students and the teacher. Teachers were asked to provide comments on the video segment and to discuss anything that they noticed. The comments that teachers made on their video segments were then used as a springboard for the remainder of the interview. For each interview, I attempted to understand the particular teacher's thinking about their African American students and the explanations that they gave for the type of participation that they saw among these students.

Subsequently, teacher's conversations moved in unique directions. However, among all of the teachers interviewed, three lines of discourse emerged concerning their Black students: (1) the teachers declared that there was a connection between student knowledge and behavior; (2) socio-economic status shaped students' in-school motivation; and (3) Black culture and community played a role in shaping student participation. Below, I present the responses of two of the math teachers along these three lines of discourse. Mr. Chung is from Clovis Middle School and Mr. Robinson is from Douglass. These interviews were chosen because I believe that they are emblematic of the discourses that exist in many schools. As such, they provide an important reference point for the remainder of this chapter and for future work in work on equity in mathematics education.

Mr. Chung

Mr. Chung was a third-year teacher at the time of this study. An Asian American man in his late 20s or early 30s, Clovis was Mr. Chung's first teaching assignment. Each time I visited Mr. Chung's classroom, I was amazed by what I witnessed. Students in his class were very unruly and disruptive, often running in and out of the classroom and through the school corridors. The class was organized into rows of desks. However, most students moved their individual desks so that they could be closer to fellow classmates or friends. As a result, the room appeared scattered and disheveled. Mr. Chung sometimes began the class by giving a brief (less than 5 minutes) whole-class demonstration of a particular computation. On other days, he simply handed out a practice worksheet to his students as they entered the classroom or wrote a set of computation problems on the board for them to complete. These computation problems were generally multiplication or long-division problems.

As I walked through the classroom on my visits, I often asked students what they were supposed to be doing. To my amazement they often replied, "nothing" or "I don't know." Mr. Chung spent the majority of the class time sitting at his desk and reading a newspaper or drawing during my visits. From time to time a student would come to his desk and request to go to the restroom. There were times when Mr. Chung would get very upset with the students' behavior and stand up and yell at them very sharply. However, most times, the behavior of students was completely ignored. There was rarely any interaction between him and the students during my visits. He rarely spoke to them and they rarely spoke to him.

In our interview, Mr. Chung and I discussed several things, including his reasons for being at Clovis and his views on the struggles of his students. Overall, Mr. Chung did not take up the questions that I asked him about race. Despite the very obvious issues surrounding African American students at Clovis, he consistently adopted a color-blind stance.

African American Students

My interview with Mr. Chung began by asking him to reflect on his African American students. His response demonstrated a reticence to talking about race, which would carry over in the remainder of our talk.

JS: Do you notice anything in particular about African American kids in this particular class?

MC: Nothing really jumps out at me. Nothing really. I don't really focus on that area.

Having spent numerous hours throughout the school year in Mr. Chung's class, I was a bit surprised by his answer to the first question of our interview. On more than one occasion during my observations, African American students had walked out of his class without permission and did not return until the bell was about to ring, had yelled at the teacher, and had refused to do assigned work. Of the students that he had sent out on referral during my observations, all were African American. Despite this striking behavior, Mr. Chung insisted throughout our interview that "Nothing really" jumped out at him concerning the African American students.

Reminiscent of the teachers and administrators at Columbus High School (Pollock, 2001), Mr. Chung's inability to notice the obvious racial patterns in his classroom is not inconsequential. "Reluctant to navigate the question of how race may matter," writes Pollock, "we actively delete race terms from our talk" (p. 9). She continues, "Silence about such patterns, of course, allows them to remain in tact: Racial patterns do not go away simply because they are ignored" (p. 9).

Mr. Chung's inability to see such patterns were active and deliberate. As he stated, "I don't really focus on that area." The issue, then, does exist. He simply made a choice not to focus on it. Who benefits from his choice not to see? Should it be acceptable for a teacher who is employed at a school where 99% of the students come from minoritized groups, to choose not to notice race? Not to be informed about the racialized nature of American society? Not to be astute and active in resisting racism's effects on children of color? Not to prepare his students to notice and fortify themselves against racism? While not noticing may make him comfortable, it sets his students up for great suffering and hardship. Who benefits from his "not seeing"? Certainly, not his students.

Student Knowledge and Behavior

After a brief conversation about his classroom routines, I asked Mr. Chung to discuss his thoughts on why so many of his students seemed to struggle in math class.

He explained to me that most of his students lacked the prior knowledge necessary for his course and as a result they were often confused. This issue of "prior knowledge," he explained, made the difference between students who did their work and those who simply copied down what he wrote on the board or did nothing at all.

JS: What I've noticed . . . is that a lot of the African American kids seem to be disengaged, kind of fooling around, sitting at the back of the room, kind of mouthing off. Is that, again, just what I see when I'm in here or is that something that frequently happens in the classroom?

MC: What I noticed, is that students who are disengaged, I don't really focus on that distinction [race]. I think it's both groups [Latinas/os and Blacks] so I don't really count the number of kids who are African American, who are not. There's always a certain [group] who are disengaged because they have trouble with prior knowledge, the basic skills.

The Role of the Black Community

In addition to the issue of prior knowledge, Mr. Chung stated that the differences in his students often had to do with parental involvement. As evidence, he cited that students whose parents come to "Back to School Night," have fewer behavioral problems, tend to do all of their work and are more engaged in school. This line of reasoning carried over into a discussion of the role of students' socio-economic status.

The Roles of Social Class and the Community in Shaping Motivation

Following up on Mr. Chung's definition of "disengaged" students, I asked him to explain why certain students might have this particular orientation. In his explanation, he connects their disengagement to their class status and their inability to see the benefits of school.

MC: They don't really see how this can help them now and in the future. I think it's mainly social economics, just this area (neighborhood of Clovis). If you see people who have high paying jobs they'll know the importance of school. . . . That may be a reason. A lot of them are not motivated to learn all of this maybe because they don't have, they don't see how it benefits them.

Final Thoughts

As we finished our conversation, I asked Mr. Chung to discuss what he felt his role to be at Clovis Middle School. He replied that his role was to teach the necessary California Content Standards as they had been laid out for him. To my final question, "Why do you choose to stay here?" Mr. Chung replied quite candidly, "Well, because I'm in my last year working toward my credentials, so that's the primary reason."

Mr. Chung exemplifies the passive violence leveled against children of color in central city schools. He rarely yells, follows the state standards, and he does not even notice that his students are Latino and Black. Yet, he does not insist that they grow, strive, achieve, and excel. While he is simply passing through Clovis to earn his teaching credentials, to how many children has he "not taught" mathematics? How many students have "not learned" math from him?

Mr. Robinson

Mr. Robinson was a teacher at Douglass Middle School. A white man in his early to mid 30s, Mr. Robinson was in his second year of teaching. Each day I visited his classroom, he was dressed in a shirt, tie, and slacks. His attire stood out to me because the other male teachers very rarely dressed as formally as he did. Class generally began with a very computational "warm-up." Afterwards, Mr. Robinson would show students the correct procedure for solving these problems.

Mr. Robinson worked hard to run a very disciplined class. However, his students were often resistant to his brand of discipline. On the day of our interview, Mr. Robinson had had a very challenging class, which resulted in the removal of one student from his room. Mr. Robinson's difficulties with this particular student, who happened to be African American, became part of the backdrop for our interview.

In our conversations, he revealed that in the previous year he had had a lot of discipline problems with the students. As a result, he was particularly happy with Douglass's move to a 4-track system, as this had relieved him of so many poorly behaved students.[6] In contrast to Mr. Chung, Mr. Robinson did engage me on questions about his African American students. We begin with a discussion of Douglass's decision to move to a 4-track school system.

JS: One thing that I've noticed in particular is in D-Track, for example, there's almost two-and-a-half times as many African American kids on that track as on the other tracks.

MR: Well, last year I had a lot of what I call D-Track students . . . every student on D-Track is either an ESL or "Language," which means if they're an ESL, they're either just so brand new to the country and to English that they need a couple of years before they just don't care about English. Or they've been here all their lives and they're just so far removed from any academic prowess at all that they're in an ESL class after 6 years. And then the other group is the Black kids who have been here for forever but just don't understand anything about language and, you know, obviously don't read much . . . Perhaps selfishly I'm kind of pleased that I have a group where it's possible to have a meaningful learning experience with those kids . . . But [with D-track students] . . . You have to be just complete dominance over them. And then you can get them to, you know, at least not be running around slapping each other acting crazy.

JS: So, [do] the kids know why they are on D-track?

MR: They know. "I'm on the dumb track, I'm on the asshole track." They know . . . They see it. So that just amplifies the expectation.

Student Knowledge and Behavior

Like Mr. Chung, Mr. Robinson saw a connection between some of his African American students' behavior and their math knowledge. Disengaging from his math class, then, was a cover-up for lacking the necessary knowledge.

The Impact of Social Class on Student Motivation

Mr. Robinson reflected on his own experiences as a student and juxtaposed the motivation of his schoolmates with the motivation of his African American students:

> My experience is different because I went to a school that was public but sort of privileged, and they could have had an orangutan teach the class and those kids would have stayed motivated; they would have known exactly what to do because that's what they had planned for themselves. They could look down the road . . . You can't keep these kids [the type of kids that went to his high school] from succeeding. The kids [at Douglass] are at such a state that they can't even sit through a class. What chance do they have to look down the road and say here's my goals so I can start planning for my future?

The Role of Culture

Mr. Robinson continued by sharing his thoughts about the boisterous behaviors of African American students at Douglass. Douglass's teachers had been admonished to be "culturally relevant" and not to overly punish Black students for their boisterous behavior.

> MR: If I go out there (in the hallway), if I'm listening and I hear a couple of kids slamming each other into the lockers, running full speed through a crowd of people, I don't really have to look through the people to see what's going to happen. It's like we only have 20% Black population, but it's like an 80% chance those are Black kids. It's the self-expectation. "Oh, I'm expected to run around and bounce off something." That's my view.
>
> [Addressing hypothetical Black students] Unfortunately, yes, your culture is being kind of stand out a little bit more because it's more loud, more physical but you know people, the public have spoken; people's safety is most important."

In Mr. Robinson's description, lack of motivation and acting out in school has become a sort of cultural artifact for Blacks. Mr. Robinson offers some solutions for Black students including the need for them to identify as individuals:

> If you have a majority of Blacks it's actually better because . . . you don't feel like everybody is looking at you. You know because physically of all your people the most distinctive look is that of sub-Saharan African people. So—physically

noticeable, often tall people stand out in different ways . . . When you're white you can just say well . . . the community expectation is I'm an individual . . . And I think with the Blacks not so much. You can't just do what you want.

The Role of the Black Community

Mr. Robinson shared his views on what he felt to be a lack of credible African American role models. He cites a number of "fallen" celebrities and discounts several of the alternative role models that I offer.

MR: I had two Black kids in there and they were just sitting there, playing dumb like you wouldn't believe. So, I started thinking about, okay, well, I know you've seen a lot of role models [that have brought] embarrassment, you know. At the top of the world one minute—you don't get any bigger than Michael Jackson. And look where he is now. I'm thinking Mike Tyson; but even if you go back to Mohammad Ali, he had some things that weren't . . . M.C. Hammer and his financial situation. And then I started thinking that this list is not going to stop anytime soon. Don't you [Black students] want to learn from those mistakes?

JS: And then when you think about the positive examples there are so many [and] those are the ones people don't know about. You know like Eric Michael Dyson or . . . Maxine Waters or Toni Morrison . . .

MR: You know I just saw one the other day. Pickett. He went to Notre Dame and played football. He was an athlete student, went to the Oilers . . . broke his leg; now he goes around to all the college campuses and stuff and [tells them], "I'm glad I got my education, I'm glad I graduated from college . . ."

Mr. Chung and Mr. Robinson in Review

The words of Mr. Chung and Mr. Robinson are not inconsequential. They reveal a great deal about how these young teachers understood and read their students' actions. The meaning assigned to these actions (disengaging in class, running in the hallway), then, become the foundation for a powerful set of discourses. These discourses (the students lack prior knowledge, their families do not understand the value of an education, etc.) shape the relationships that the teachers have with their students, the mathematics experiences afforded students, how students see themselves in relation to mathematics, and ultimately will shape the efforts and commitments that students make towards acquiring mathematical knowledge, and mathematically based careers.

On the surface, Mr. Chung and Mr. Robinson take up my questioning concerning African American students in different ways. Mr. Chung states, in a matter-of-fact manner, that he does not see any differences in participation between his two groups of students. Alternatively, Mr. Robinson declares that African American students have a disproportionate number of behavioral issues. Yet, race plays out in very similar ways in their classrooms. In each of their classrooms, the African American children have disengaged from mathematics. For both teachers, the situation for African Americans is virtually intractable. Mr. Chung cites the prior knowledge that they did, or did not, have when they arrived in his classroom as a major cause. As Mr. Chung has no control over the knowledge that students brought to his class, he believes he is powerless in impacting their current status and achievement. Poverty, like prior knowledge, is another reality that the teachers saw themselves as unable to mitigate. More than being poor, the values these children brought to school were blamed for their poor performance and lack of engagement in mathematics. "They could have had an orangutan teach the class," reflects Mr. Robinson on his own schooling situation, "and those kids would have stayed motivated." Here, class has moved beyond a simple description of financial status, to a definition of a set of values. Just as poverty predisposes one to not valuing school, being wealthy is assumed to predispose one to understand its value and importance.

Mr. Robinson makes a case for how African American culture negatively shapes his students' dispositions towards school. By first defining African American culture as "kind of stand out a little bit more . . .," "more loud," and "more physical," Mr. Robinson paints a picture of African American culture that stands in opposition to some normative notion of what is needed for school success. And, even as I offered him several role models who were not from the field of sports, he was not able to move beyond this definition. Drawing further on the lack of connection between Black culture and academic motivation and success, Mr. Robinson suggests that African Americans could benefit from seeing themselves as individuals, the way whites do. Identifying as Black and associating with other African Americans, then, is another suspected cause of Black students' struggles.

Mr. Chung and Mr. Robinson do not shoulder the full blame for their actions against students. Which universities did they attend? Where did they and (in the case of Mr. Chung) are they receiving their training as teachers? Which professors choose not to challenge their views, dispositions, and understandings of race, and racism? Which readings were they given and which were avoided? Certainly, many individuals and institutions have a hand in what happens in Mr. Chung and Mr. Robinson's classrooms.

Translating Research on Race and Mathematics Education to the School and Classroom

There are a number of factors that shape the achievement of African American students in mathematics. Traditional research has examined the impact of teacher content knowledge, teacher pedagogical content knowledge, curriculum, curricular approach, student learning style, and various professional development approaches on African American student achievement. Over the past 7–10 years, the impact of student mathematics identity (Martin, 2000, 2006a, 2006b), out of school mathematics use (Nasir, Hand & Taylor, 2008), parental and community mathematics knowledge (Gonzalez & Moll, 2002; Martin, 2006a), and teaching mathematics with a specific focus towards issues of social justice (Gutstein, 2003; Gau-Bartell, 2006) on African American student achievement in mathematics have been taken up. This work has introduced increased rigor to research centered on improving mathematics success of underserved students. This increased rigor has not resulted from a draw to the novel. Rather, this research has worked to confirm what many already suspected, that issues beyond teaching (including curriculum, teacher content and pedagogical content knowledge, and delivery of instruction), and learning (for example, how do students come to understand fractions) account for the inconsistent success of African American students in mathematics. This research has opened up powerful new directions for inquiry. Yet, for all of its potential and promise, I believe that much of its findings has been lost on schools, classrooms, and teachers. The ability to translate this new work and its wisdom into classrooms is critical for African American mathematics students.

In the final paragraphs of this chapter, I describe concrete ways to incorporate these newest findings into schools and mathematics classrooms.

The Role of Mathematics Identity

In the year-long study, *Balancing the equation: African American students' Opportunity to Learn Mathematics with Understanding* (Spencer, 2006), I talked with 32 middle school students about their mathematics identity. Some of these students expressed that mathematics was important; and many even stated that they wanted to attend college. However, very few saw the role that mathematics would play in helping them attain their goal. Additionally, while students overwhelmingly expressed a desire to go to college, very few of them chose careers that necessitated college attendance. In instances where college attendance was necessary (such as professional sports), those career choices were non-academic in nature.

Numerous students stated that they were not good in mathematics. As evidence, such students offered that they did not know how to do specific mathematical computations such as long division and "equations." The negative mathematics identities of these students, then, were not a result of their inability to think mathematically, but rather of their inability to perform selected mathematical computations as set out by their teachers and mandated by their schools.

Students with negative mathematics identities may be less likely to continue in the study of mathematics. Those who do not perform well on school tasks may disassociate themselves from mathematics—divesting their energies from the endeavor. Eventually, these students will lack the necessary skill to continue their studies. Thus, the cycle of low achievement is completed.[7]

Successful students had a more positive mathematics identity. They spoke of a desire to go to college. Many (particularly girls) wanted academically based professions. Unlike non-successful students, these students choose career goals where college attendance and mathematics achievement were central. Despite the more positive mathematics identity of successful students, there was still reason for concern. Witnessing first-hand the type of mathematics education that even these successful students received, I could not help but wonder if they too had developed a false sense of mathematics identity. Just as the unsuccessful students held inaccurate beliefs about themselves as poor doers of mathematics, the successful students held false notions of their abilities based on the limited experiences afforded them.

More closely, while these students are performing well within the mathematical contexts of their classrooms, what will happen when they encounter mathematics contexts that demand greater levels of rigor and engagement? This dual dilemma emphasizes the importance of providing students with rich, challenging mathematical experiences.

Student Identity

During interviews, students demonstrated identification with popular images of African Americans in the media. The majority of the boys interviewed stated that they would like to become sports stars, while girls stated that they would like to become video dancers and singers (both sets of responses being popular media images of African Americans). These responses are not trivial. In her work on Black working class communities, Pattillo-McCoy (1999), speaks of the unique way in which Black youth are inundated with non-intellectual, non-professional media images. This unique targeting, she writes, "has more serious repercussions for Black youth (p. 166)." Such targeted images place African American students at a greater risk of disengaging from the educational enterprise.

Serious schools must actively counter negative mathematics identities in their African American students. Dialoguing with students about their perceptions of themselves as mathematics students, their career goals, and the importance of mathematics for college and other post-secondary opportunities will provide teachers with important information as they plan future mathematics units and tasks. Allowing students to explore mathematics as a tool for resisting oppression, addressing racism, and impacting their own communities in positive ways should also be central to this work. In *Rethinking Mathematics* (Gutstein & Peterson, 2005), students are presented with a myriad of mathematics problems which challenge them to consider math as a tool for understanding the world and dismantling unequitable social systems such as racial profiling, the unequal distribution of wealth, and environmental racism.

Because so many urban school districts (particularly those who receive Title I funding) are under pressures of school accountability as outlined in the *No Child Left Behind Act*, and state programs that have proceeded from this Act (California Department of Education, 2008), much of their mathematics curriculum remains rote and highly decontextualized. School officials must recognize the impact that this type of curriculum has on students' notions of, and dispositions towards, mathematics. Providing students with alternative visions of mathematics through African American speakers, and clubs like the MESA (Mathematics Engineering, Science Achievement) Program, can provide a powerful counter-narrative for African American students. Such opportunities should be open to all students, not only those with high grades and/or test scores in mathematics.

Parents and the Community

Mr. Robinson, one of the teachers highlighted in this chapter, shared powerful thoughts about the African American parents at his school. It is not only the blatant way in which he expressed these thoughts, but also the manner in which he portrayed these parents' antagonisms as unfounded that is so troubling. When addressing teachers who are frustrated with African American parents, I often point out that many of these parents were themselves victims of negative school experiences. They, too, attended schools that were grossly under-funded, were placed disproportionately into low-tracked classes and experienced first-hand the limited job opportunities provided by their education. In the same manner that I address this issue with the teachers that I work with, schools need to actively facilitate teacher and parent relationships—addressing deficit and racist views.

Hasan's work (2001) with African American parents in a large, low-income district in southern California provides a model for schools. As a part of this work, parents have the opportunity to share their expertise, learn about the mathematics framework of California, question principals, visit classrooms, explore assessment practices, and attend professional development alongside teachers. Parents then design action plans to implement at their particular school sites. Such a project works under the premise that powerlessness fuels indiscriminate rage while empowerment fuels focused effort. Undoubtedly, many other schools can benefit from such efforts to involve—not stereotype and demean—African American parents.

Tracking

Research has repeatedly demonstrated that African American students are assigned disproportionately to low tracked mathematics classes. While Oakes et al. (2003) found disproportionate student placement *even when* math grades and test scores were held constant, many schools justify unequal mathematics track placement by the differential test scores of African American students. Such arrangements are problematic especially given the high correlation between high track mathematics course-taking and college completion.[8]

Programs such as Advancement via Individual Determination (AVID), which provides an additional course and rigorous academic assistance for students who demonstrate potential for college, have been shown to be effective (Hubbard, 1999). Past performance should not serve as a lifetime sentence to low-level mathematics courses. Yet, this is the fate for far too many African American students. Instead of casting aside students who do not have superior grades and/or test scores, AVID provides B, C, and D students with a chance and the means by which to improve.

Instead of allowing disproportionate course placement to go unchecked, schools committed to the liberation of their African American students must actively attend to racial patterns, question why these patterns have emerged, and take the necessary efforts to dismantle them. Countering tracking practices can begin by opening up several routes into higher tracked mathematics courses. Questioning the trend that provides many low tracked and few high tracked math courses at schools that serve African American, Latino, and Native American schools and several high tracked and few low tracked math courses at schools that serve white, Asian, and wealthier students should push principals and math departments to reconsider current arrangements.

Successful African American Mathematics Students

In his study of successful African American students in northern California, Martin (2000) found that these students adopted a stance towards learning that allowed them to navigate school and mathematics learning. This *self-definition by opposition* demonstrated that rather than abandoning their identity as Black Americans, these successful students saw their achievement as a part of who they were and why they made decisions to achieve.

School officials can make use of the expertise of their successful African American math students to the benefit of other students. Schools should fight against the trend to single out these students as exceptions. Statements such as, "you are not like the rest of them (Black students)," and "that student does not see himself as Black, he just sees himself as a student," are harmful because they play on notions that having an African American identity cannot co-exist with being a strong mathematics student (Martin, 2006b). Rather, educators should work to highlight, for non-successful students, just how similar they are to their successful counterparts. Whichever route is chosen, educators should take steps to understand these successful students' experiences.

The Culture of Mathematics Achievement

In many schools and classrooms, "successful math student" is often an identity antithetical to adolescent Black identity. I recall the music that used to be played during our after-school math club in high school. Pink Floyd, REM, and the Beatles were the standard, assumed selections. At a school that was over 90% African American and Latino, the math club was made up of predominately Asian and white students. And while I was personally not familiar with, or accustomed to the music being played, I knew that being successful meant grinning and bearing it. I wonder how many of my peers never even considered joining the math club (or other academic clubs) because they saw it and its participants as "other" than them.

At my high school, what it meant to be "good in math" looked a certain way and sounded a certain way. The pressures to disassociate from other African American students were great. But, it does not have to be this way. One can be good in math and listen to hip-hop. One can be a stellar math student and play basketball or have an Afro or cornrows. These identities do not have to be in opposition of one another but far too many times they are.

There are a number of measures that can be adopted by schools that are serious about supporting African American students. Primarily, faculty and administrators must themselves become familiar with the historic struggle for education by African Americans. Seeing education as a route to freedom, enslaved Africans in this country routinely risked their lives in order to learn to read and write (Belt-Beyan, 2004; Douglass, 1845). This historical knowledge is important because it counters many of the current representations of Blacks as non-academic, and anti-intellectual.

In addition to deepening their own understanding of Blacks' historical efforts, schools must help African American students make these connections. Creating an

African American mathematician speaker series, including assignments in the math classroom where students have to research and write about the works of renowned African Americans in math, is another means of connecting Black students to their intellectual heritage.

Academic success is not antithetical to Black culture. Schools must make it their business to not only celebrate the successes of their Black students on the basketball court, but also in the mathematics classroom, and to invoke these academic accomplishments as living testaments to the commitment of Blacks in America to education and learning.

Teacher Dispositions

Teachers do not walk into classrooms as blank slates. They bring with them a host of notions about, and dispositions towards the students, schools, and communities that they teach in. These dispositions shape the experiences of students. The two teachers highlighted in this chapter saw their African American students' participation in mathematics as static and entrenched. Likewise, it was believed that the students' problematic behaviors and performance in math class emanated from the cultural practices of their parents and communities. With their hands thrown up, failure for their most struggling students became a self-fulfilling prophecy. Lacking a critique of the forces impacting their African American students (such as the gross over-representation of Blacks in non-intellectual roles in the media and the nature of poverty in central cities that have been abandoned by industry), these teachers positioned themselves as enemies against, versus partners with, students, parents, and the community.

Teacher dispositions not only shaped the relationships of students to teachers, but it also shaped the *mathematics content offerings* in classrooms. Teachers in my study with a more positive disposition towards their African American students provided more rigorous mathematical content to their students.

In his study of successful African American mathematics students in difficult high schools, Sheppard (2005) found that, while teachers attributed their students' success to pre-determined factors such as prior knowledge and parental influence (similarly to Mr. Chung and Mr. Robinson), the students attributed their success to personal traits such as tenacity, curiosity, and to their high school teachers' efforts. This difference is noteworthy because, as students saw themselves as malleable, teachers saw them as static.

Tools for examining teacher disposition are essential in increasing African American student success in the classroom (Haberman & Post, 1998). Furthermore, providing teachers with opportunities to examine and reflect on how their dispositions towards students can impact their relationships and effectiveness (Obidah & Teel, 2001) with students is a valuable professional development investment.

Conclusion: Running Against the Wind

The case for African American students is unique. African American students, including those at Clovis and Douglass will have to confront and contend with a master-narrative that defines them in ways that are often in stark contrast to "mathematically astute," "learned," and "academically promising." The classrooms in which they are learning, however, are doing very little to confront, not to mention disrupt, the experiences of these students.

Properties of physics tell us that an object will remain in motion or at rest unless some force interrupts it. Racism, and all of its residue, remains in motion in the institutions and systems in society and in the organization and arrangement of mathematics classrooms across this nation. Racism is an artifact of our past relationships and, unless we interrupt it, things will not change for African American students. We can spend our time fighting other forces such as "lack of motivation," or "lack of prior knowledge," or "bad parenting." But, as time and effort in these battles has proven, we will not get very far in impacting the life chances for African American students. To change our current state will require an exacting, conscientious, deliberate, and opposing force.

Acknowledgements

The author is grateful for the generous support of her research presented in this manuscript by the following: The National Science Foundation under Grant ESI-0119732 to the Diversity in Mathematics Education Center for Learning and Teaching, the Algebra Learning for All Project supported by the Institute for Education Sciences Grant R305M030154, and the Educational Research and Development Centers Program, PR/Award R305B960002, as administered by the Institute of Education Sciences. The author also wishes to thank the community of scholars in the Diversity in Mathematics Education Center for Learning and Teaching at UCLA; University of Wisconsin, Madison; and the University of California, Berkeley for their support.

Notes

1 All school names are pseudonyms.
2 In the 2004–2005 school year Douglass Middle School had switched to a 4-track calendar. Students with the lowest test scores were placed onto the fourth track also called D-track. This created a scenario where the largest percentage of African American students were on this track. Over its first year of implementation, D-track gained a notorious reputation as being the worst track to teach and be a student on.
3 There are several views on what should be the proper names used to describe Black peoples in the United States, the Americas, the larger African diaspora, and Africa. I find these discussions both important and rich. Recognizing both their affordances and constraints, I use the terms African American and Black inter-changeably in this chapter to describe children of African decent living in the United States.
4 A pseudonym.
5 These videotaped lessons were taught as part of a professional development program that each of the math teachers at Douglass and Clovis participated in.
6 In the 2004–2005 school year Douglass Middle School had switched to a 4-track calendar. Students with the lowest test scores were placed onto the fourth track also called D-track. This created a scenario where the largest percentage of African American students were on this track.
7 This same cycle was witnessed in Rist's now famous 1970 study of kindergarten socialization. In this work, Rist argues that students began kindergarten with certain social "markers." These markers led teachers to make decisions about a students' academic ability. As a result,

students were placed at tables and in groups according to their perceived abilities. The cycle of low achievement began to occur when students in the lowest groups were asked fewer questions by the teacher, were asked to participate less, to present their solutions less, and to do fewer tasks for the teacher (i.e., lead the class in the pledge of allegiance or pass our paper), etc. These students were even placed in the classroom in such a way that the board was not directly in front of them. The result was that these students learned less and were perceived by their teachers as knowing less. When the first grade began, teachers were no longer using social markers and perceptions to make decisions about these students. Instead, they had a collection of evidence to convince them of these students' inabilities. Teachers now had the actual "data" in the form of test scores and assessments which "proved" that these students were inferior. In the first grade, students were placed in the very same groups that they were placed in as kindergarteners. These students continued in a cycle of being exposed to less, being questioned less and being presented with less rigorous material.

8 As stated in Adelman, 1999, "Of all pre-college curricula, the highest level of mathematics one studies in secondary school has the strongest continuing influence on bachelor's degree completion. Finishing a course beyond the level of Algebra 2 (for example, trigonometry or pre-calculus) more than doubles the odds that a student who enters post-secondary education will complete a bachelor's degree." Furthermore, his work demonstrates that the impact of rigorous course taking on African American and Latino students is more positive and prounounced than any other pre-college indicator. Additionally, this impact is much greater for African American and Latino students.

References

Adelman, C. (1999). *Answers in the tool box: Academic intensity, attendance patterns and bachelor's degree attainment.* Washington, DC: U.S. Government Printing Office.

Belt-Beyan, P. (2004). *The emergence of African American literacy traditions: Family and community efforts in the nineteenth century.* Westport, CT: Prager.

Bonilla-Silva, E., Lewis, A.E., & Embrick, D. (2004). "'I did not get that job because of a black man . . .' Storylines and Testimonies of Color Blind Racism." *Sociological Forum, 19*(4), 555–581.

California Department of Education (2008). Accountability progress reporting. Retrieved on August 11, 2008 at: http://www.cde.ca.gov/ta/ac/ar/

Douglass, F. (1845). *Narrative of the life of Frederick Douglass.* Boston: Office of the District Court of Massachusetts.

Forman, E. (1993). *Contexts for learning.* New York: Oxford University Press.

Gau Bartell, T. (2006). Striving for excellence in mathematics education: Learning to teach mathematics for social justice. In S. Alatorre, J.L. Cortina, M. Sáiz, & A. Méndez (Eds.), *Proceedings of the twenty-eighth annual meeting of the North American chapter of the international group for the psychology of mathematics education* (Vol. 2, pp. 775–782). Mérida, Mexico: Universidad Pedagógica Nacional.

Gonzalez, N. & Moll, L. (2002). Cruzando el puente: Building bridges to funds of knowledge. *Educational Policy, 16*(4), 623–641.

Gutstein, E. (2003). Teaching and learning mathematics for social justice in an urban, Latino school. *Journal for Research in Mathematics Education, 34*(1), 37–73.

Gutstein, E. & Peterson, B. (Eds.) (2005). *Rethinking Mathematics: Teaching Social Justice by the number.* Milwaukee, WI: Rethinking Schools.

Haberman, M. & Post, L. (1998). Teachers for multicultural schools: The power of selection. *Theory into Practice, 37*(2), 96–104.

Hasan, A. (2001). Lynwood parents investigate technology resources in their community. Retrieved on June 18, 2008 at: http://tcla.gseis.ucla.edu/divide/community/lynwood.html

Hubbard, L. (1999). College aspirations among low-income African American high school students: Gendered strategies for success. *Anthropology and Education Quarterly, 30*(3), 363–383.

Martin, D.B. (2000). *Mathematics success and failure among African-American youth.* Mawhah, NJ: Lawrence Erlbaum.

Martin, D.B. (2006a). Mathematics learning and participation as racialized forms of experience: African American parents speak on the struggle for mathematics literacy. *Mathematical Thinking and Learning, 8*(3), 197–229.

Martin, D.B. (2006b). Mathematics learning and participation in the African American context: The co-construction of identity in two intersecting realms of experience. In N. Nasir & P. Cobb (Eds.), *Diversity, equity, and access to mathematical ideas* (pp. 146–158). New York: Teachers College Press.

Martin, D.B. (2007). Beyond missionaries or cannibals: Who should teach mathematics to African American children? *The High School Journal, 91*(1), 6–28.

Martin, D.B. & McGee, E. (2009). Mathematics literacy for liberation: Reframing mathematics education for African American children. In B. Greer, S. Mukhophadhay, S. Nelson-Barber, & A. Powell (Eds.), *Culturally responsive mathematics education* (pp. 207–238). London: Routledge.

Nasir, N.S., Hand, V., & Taylor, E. (2008). Culture and mathematics in school: Boundaries between "cultural" and "domain" knowledge in the mathematics classroom and beyond. *Review of Research in Education, 32*, 187–240.

Oakes, J., Joseph, R., & Muir, K. (2003). Access and achievement in mathematics and science: Inequalities that endure and change. In J.A. Banks & C.A. Banks, (Eds.), *Handbook of research on multicultural education* (2nd Edition, pp. 69–90). San Francisco: Jossey-Bass.

Oakes, J., Ormseth, T, Bell, R., & Camp, P. (1990). *Multiplying inequalities: The effects of race, social class, and tracking on opportunities to learn mathematics and science* (R-3928-NSF). Santa Monica, CA: RAND.

Obidah, J. & Teel, K. (2001). *Because of the kids: Facing racial and cultural differences in schools.* New York: Teachers College Press.

Ogbu, J. (1983). Minority status and schooling in plural societies. *Comparative Education Review*, 27, 168–90.

Pattillo-McCoy, M. (1999). *Black picket fences.* Chicago: University of Chicago Press.

Perry, T., Steele, C., & Hilliard, A. (2003). *Young gifted and Black: Promoting high achievement among African-American students.* Boston: Beacon Press.

Pollock, M. (2001). How the question we ask most about race in education is the very question we most suppress. *Educational Researcher, 30*(9), 2–12.

Rist, R. (1970). Student social class and teacher expectations: The self-fulfilling prophecy in ghetto schooling. *Harvard Educational Review, 40*(3), 411–51.

Sheppard, P. (2005). *Successful African-American mathematics students in academically unacceptable high schools.* Unpublished doctoral dissertation. Southern University. Baton Rouge, LA.

Siddle-Walker, V. (1996). *Their highest potential.* Chapel Hill: University of North Carolina Press.

Spencer, J. (2006). *Balancing the equation: African American students' opportunities to learn mathematics with understanding in two central city middle schools.* Unpublished doctoral dissertation, University of California, Los Angeles, CA.

Stryker, S. & Burke, J. (2000). The past, present, and future of an identity theory. *Social Psychology Quarterly, 63*(4), 284–297.

Tatum, B. (2007). *Why are all the Black kids sitting together in the cafeteria and other conversations about race.* New York: Basic Books.

Wollenberg, C. (1976). *All deliberate speed: Segregation and exclusion in California schools, 1855–976.* Berkeley: University of California Press.

9 Wrestling with the Legacy of Stereotypes: Being African American in Math Class[1]

Na'ilah Suad Nasir, Grace Atukpawu,
Kathleen O'Connor, Michael Davis,
Sarah Wischnia, and Jessica Tsang

Introduction

In the introduction to this volume, Martin highlights several critical issues with respect to the way African American students are perceived and portrayed in mathematics education research. He argues that a critical focus for research ought to be documenting the *experiences* of African American students in math classes—and that such research should take seriously how African American students experience mathematics participation and learning *as African Americans*. In this chapter, we take up his challenge.

While the bulk of research on mathematics teaching and learning views it as largely a culture-neutral enterprise, mathematics classrooms (as students experience them) are not separate from the broader social worlds of schools, communities, and societies. In the United States, as elsewhere in the world, these social worlds and communities, and the social arrangements by which particular students arrive at them, are deeply informed by issues of race.

What do we mean by race? Race, by definition, invokes historical arrangements of power. While typically used to denote genetically different biological and cultural groups, current science has found that race as a biological concept does not stand up to scientific inquiry (American Anthropological Association, 1998; Omi & Winant, 1994). Nonetheless, race functions as an agreed upon set of categories constructed to create and maintain power relations between groups of people. The American Anthropological Association (1998) writes,

> As they were constructing US society, leaders among European–Americans fabricated the cultural/behavioral characteristics associated with each "race," linking superior traits with Europeans and negative and inferior ones to blacks and Indians. Numerous arbitrary and fictitious beliefs about the different peoples were institutionalized and deeply embedded in American thought. (p. 1)

Thus, race is defined not as distinct biological or genetic groups, but rather as a set of social configurations that support particular patterns of access to power and resources. This quote also makes the point that beliefs about race, and about the negative traits of African Americans and other groups, are deeply embedded in

American thought. We note that race, as a construct, is distinct from the construct of *ethnicity*; though in the real world, the two overlap quite a bit. Ethnicity typically refers to shared cultural practices and lifestyles, highlighting engagement in practices with ethnic group members (Borak et. al., 2004; Wilkenson, 1993). Race usually refers to shared biological or genetic history (though we know that this is a fallacy); people are perceived and responded to based on external features such as hair texture and skin color (Wilkenson, 1993; Panigua, 2004). In this chapter, we use the terms *race* and *racial identity* to highlight the historical issues of power and inequality that frame our individual and group identities.

Psychological and sociological research on racial and ethnic stereotypes has elaborated the beliefs about African Americans that form the content of our culturally shared assumptions about what it means to be African American. There are strong and long-standing cultural stereotypes[2] about African Americans in American society. African Americans are assumed to have low intelligence, to lack an achievement orientation, and to engage in anti-social behavior (Niemann et. al., 1994; Devine & Elliott, 1995; Krueger, 1996; Hudley & Graham, 2001). More recently, contemporary stereotypes of African American (primarily male) youth are tied to media portrayals of African American men as thugs and gangsters (Bailey, 2006; Chan, 2005; Deburg, 2004), and some have highlighted the role of some commercial hip-hop or rap music in perpetuating these images (Rome, 2004).

In the domain of mathematics education, Martin (this volume, 2009) has argued that the research and discourse about African American students confirms a "racial hierarchy of mathematical ability," where African American students are positioned at the bottom. This presumed hierarchy, confirmed by achievement data, is the way that we understand math learning and achievement for African American students. Martin (this volume, 2006b, 2007) has referred to the discourse supporting this hierarchy as a *master-narrative*, by which he means that it is a widely held and socially shared way of thinking and talking about a phenomenon, a framing that does not challenge socially accepted ideas and hierarchies. It is interesting to note that the portrayal of African American students in mathematics as poor performing is aligned with the broader stereotypes about African Americans as unmotivated and unintelligent.

There also exists a master-narrative about the relationship between African American identity and achievement that has been tremendously persistent, even in the face of contradictory evidence. Consider the *acting white* and *oppositional culture* hypotheses (Fordham & Ogbu, 1986; Ogbu, 1987, 1991). These theories argue that students internalize the social and economic realities they face through limited educational and occupational opportunities and come to believe they cannot achieve success through school, and that succeeding in school is for white students. Consequently, in order to succeed, African American students feel that they have to abandon their race and become raceless.

This account has persisted in both scholarly and media accounts of African American students' learning and achievement, despite an ever-accumulating body of evidence to the contrary. Research has suggested that African Americans *are* indeed connected to the dominant achievement ideology (Ainsworth-Darnell & Downey, 1998; O'Connor, 1997) and do not disidentify with doing well in school

(Morgan & Mehta, 2004), or education in general. Further, Ainsworth-Darnell and Downey (1998) used data from a national survey and found that African Americans don't perceive a limited opportunity structure more often than white Americans. Moreover, they reported that among African American students, those with more positive attitudes towards school and higher achievement were seen as popular. These findings help challenge the claim that African Americans hold oppositional identities and that these identities are required for within-group status.

O'Connor (1997) argues that the oppositional identity argument does not account for the variation in how African American students give meaning to, interpret, and respond to the opportunity structures afforded to them. Further, research has illustrated that many African American students succeed academically and possess a Black cultural frame of reference that sustains ties to their communities (Carter, 2005). In mathematics, Walker (2006) found that African American students in a high-minority high school didn't see math achievement as acting white, and that successful students had access to multiple support systems, through which they developed identities as high achievers.

Nor does the *oppositional culture* account hold up to the historical record. Anderson (1988) documents the important role that African Americans accorded to education, post-slavery, and the incredibly strong achievement orientation and focus on learning that were cornerstones of the community, to the extent that people risked their lives to become educated.

In short, the scholarly conversation about race, identity, and school achievement has perpetuated its own master-narrative, in which African American students are portrayed as oppositional to school and unmotivated. The American Anthropological Association (1998) noted that strong stereotypes about race (the master-narrative) are deeply embedded in American thought. In essence, this includes both the African American youth that we study, and the researchers who conduct the studies.

This came into full view in our own research when we held focus groups with African American high school students and asked them simply, "What does it mean to be Black?" Students in these focus groups recounted typical stereotypes about African Americans in answer to this question. They said being Black meant to be a gangster or thug, to listen to rap music, and to do poorly in school, among other stereotypes, thereby reifying the master-narrative. However, the narrative was not preserved whole cloth—students also suggested evidence of a counter-narrative. They said what it meant to be Black was *also* to do well in school, and to understand African American history and culture. Students are clearly, then, managing and negotiating both their long history of experience with the master-narrative about African American students and math achievement and their first-hand or other experiences that may speak to the presence of a counter-narrative.

In this chapter, we consider this master-narrative with respect to the discourse about race that occurs among African American students in high school mathematics classrooms. Tillman (2002) argues that one aspect of a culturally sensitive research approach is to attend to Black self-representation. However, given the pervasiveness of the master-narrative, how does one disentangle the portrayal of African Americans in our society and the self-representation of African American youth? The two are necessarily linked. These are critical issues to consider as we attempt to understand the ways that mathematics teaching and learning are racialized forms of experience (Martin, this volume, 2006a) for African American students; that is, the ways that mathematics teaching and learning are structured by the dominant ideologies and relations of race that exist in larger society. Specifically, in this chapter, we explore how and when issues of race were a part of the classroom discourse of African American students in a diverse high school. As we do so, we consider the master-narrative about race as it enters the mathematics classroom, and the way that it functions in the classroom context.

Non-Dominant Cultural Capital

Key to our analysis is attending to the work that racialized discourse does in math classrooms. One kind of work that discourse does in math classrooms (and other social settings) is the work of signaling cultural capital. Carter (2003) contends that there are two types of capital that many African American students are negotiating: dominant cultural capital and non-dominant cultural capital. Dominant cultural capital stems from Bourdieu's (1977) notion of high status cultural "attributes, codes, and signals;" whereas non-dominant cultural capital consists of tastes of lower status groups articulated through language, music, and interaction style. Carter (2003) argues that African American students exercise and signify both kinds of cultural capital, depending on the context. In one setting, a student may use dominant cultural capital to move up an educational or occupational ladder, while in another context use non-dominant capital to "authentically" position him or herself in his or her peer groups, thus supporting a collective identity. In other words, many students use both forms of capital in different community, family, peer, and school contexts for different goals (Carter, 2003). We would like to suggest that both forms of capital play important instrumental functions. That is, students may rely upon each form of capital to accomplish important goals, with non-dominant cultural capital being used for more nebulous and difficult to define social goals and dominant cultural capital supporting more recognizable forms of achievement. Students can utilize both forms of capital in school contexts.

One cannot explore issues of capital without understanding that capital is always expressed in relation to power. In the case of the dominant cultural capital, the power has to do with access to mainstream resources. In the case of non-dominant cultural capital, the power has to do with access to belonging in a social group and position in that group. In the analyses that follow, students move fluidly between dominant (with respect to mathematics) and non-dominant cultural capital displays as they engage in racialized discourse in math class.

School Context

Washington High School[3] was ethnically diverse, with a student body of over 1500 students that was 38% Hispanic, 23% Black, 20% white, 18% Asian & Pacific Islander, and 1% Native-American. Thirty-one percent of students qualified for free or reduced price lunch, 25% of students were designated as ELL, and 23% of students' parents were college graduates.

African American students at Washington were in the minority relative to Latino students, but shared about an equal proportion of the population as white and Asian American students. With respect to race, Washington was an especially interesting environment. It was a place where students and teachers alike lauded the diversity of the school and were proud of the racial/ethnic mix of the student body. At the same time, race was rarely discussed in the school (other than how great it was to be so diverse), and significant segregation (both academic and social) existed by race in many classes. At the school level, African American students were less often represented in the Advanced Placement track courses, but were over-represented in special education and remedial courses. However, the math department was reform-minded and committed to addressing inequities in achievement. Teachers placed strong focus on conceptual understanding and cooperative learning, and the mathematics department has undergone major reforms in mathematics teaching over the last several years (in line with the NCTM Standards).

In addition to reform math practices, such as encouraging students to share their thinking, working on complex conceptual mathematical problems, and utilizing group work, the math classes at Washington also embraced an approach to instruction called Complex Instruction (Cohen & Lotan, 1997). Complex Instruction involved attending not only to the mathematics students were wrestling with, but also attending explicitly to issues of status and group processes as students solved problems in groups. Complex Instruction also supported teachers in developing a sophisticated conceptualization for the wide variety of ways different students might contribute to the classroom learning endeavor. For instance, in addition to simply giving right answers, students might ask good questions, or facilitate discussions.

In general, teachers felt that the reform-oriented teaching was serving students well, and department and district-level analyses of achievement, as well as university-conducted assessments confirmed that overall, students were learning more mathematics than students at comparison high schools. However, teachers shared a narrative (informed by an examination of D and F rates) that African American students were not being as well served with respect to their mathematics learning. We want to make clear that this chapter is in no way about the merits or pitfalls of reform teaching for African American students. Rather, our focus is on how issues of race surfaced in the high school mathematics classrooms that we studied. Our purpose in this section is to simply describe the classrooms and schools where our research took place.

The Data

The data that we draw on in this paper were collected over a year of intense observation in several mathematics classes, ranging from first year Algebra classes to Calculus. The larger two-year study involved multiple methods, including observations of mathematics classrooms, student interviews, and a survey. Classroom observations took place over the course of one school year (or two

14-week semesters), in two to three classes per semester. For most of this time, classes were observed at least twice per week, and were often observed by more than one member of our team. This process resulted in at least 52 days of observation for each of six classes. Observations were recorded in the form of fieldnotes, which were sketched during the observation, then elaborated later on word processor.

Fieldnotes were analyzed beginning with a process of open coding (Miles & Huberman, 1994; Emerson et. al., 1995) whereby each member of our five-member team read all fieldnotes in their entirety and recorded potential themes and recurring ideas and events in the notes. Once each team member had read all of the notes, and had open coded at least half of them, we met and discussed possible themes and codes. One theme that was prominent in this initial discussion was the racial talk in the classroom among African American students. We then coded the full corpus of notes to identify all moments of racialized talk (and later we expanded this to include racialized behavior, and moments where race was implicit, but perhaps not explicit). We coded both the form of this racialized talk, to capture the range of ways that racialized talk and behaviors occurred in the mathematics classroom, and the functions that such talk seemed to serve (from the perspective of the speaker) in the moments of classroom interaction.

We draw on these data in this paper, and we share specific moments of racialized classroom talk and interaction to explore several interrelated issues around racial stereotypes and the management of fear of failing among African American students. In this way, we highlight the ways that being African American came to bear on participation and engagement in the high school math classrooms we studied.

Social Talk Among African American Students in Math Class

The initial question that framed our analysis for this chapter was quite straightforward. We wanted to know when African American students talked about race in math class, what were they saying? However, our analytical lens quickly broadened when we realized that the dynamics of race in the math classrooms we studied were much more complex than simply talk *about* race. We decided to focus not just on racial talk, but racialized discourse and participation, which we defined as moments when students explicitly or implicitly used speech registers or language that referenced race or when race seemed salient in their interactions with one another. This included talk explicitly about race, using exclusively African American Vernacular English (AAVE), referencing Black popular culture or cultural practices, and singing or rapping African American music. It also included more ambiguous moments when race seemed to be "on the table" or "in the air."

Before we share our analyses, we want to emphasize that we are focusing on regular, but relatively infrequent, moments in the classrooms that we studied. Most moments in the lives of these classrooms were not explicitly racialized. During most classroom interactions, African American students (as a group) were indistinguishable from other students. On a given day, most students in these classrooms were writing down problems, answering questions, posing questions, working together to solve problems. Students frequently volunteered to go to the board to solve a problem and raised their hand to ask or answer a question. By and large, students were vocal and visible in class—expressing opinions, commenting on classroom comings and goings, and sharing with one another about their successes and challenges. Student interactions with teachers were largely positive—students joked with teachers, pushed their limits occasionally, and asked for help when they needed it.

Some of the moments that we recount don't fit with that norm of participation for African American (as well as other) students, so in some ways, this chapter is about relatively infrequent moments in classroom life. However, we think they are critical to examine, as they are moments where master-narratives about race are invoked, and about the purposes such invoking may serve for students.

Invoking Stereotypes

In this section, we offer examples of the ways that talk about race in the classroom often confirmed racial stereotypes. While the stereotypes themselves are not at all novel, it is striking to see these stereotypes being played out in student talk, especially in a school where the accepted discourse about race was limited to focusing on the positive attributes of racial diversity. In the first interaction that we share, an African American female student, Catherine, makes several references about race (including racial stereotypes) to her predominantly African American table group.

Vignette 1: Racial Stereotypes in Math Class: "Y'all Too Black!"

During a group activity where students were solving geometry problems together, an African American female, Catherine, asked her African American male peer, "Why you eatin' that snickers bar like a slave? . . . you know how slaves used to have to eat out of their hands and stuff." Other African American students laughed. Subsequently, Catherine needed help with the math, so she (on behalf of the group) solicited help from the (substitute) teacher. The teacher encouraged the group to discuss the math problem amongst themselves. However, the group chatted socially. A few moments later, the teacher reprimanded the group for not working and they accused her of not helping when they asked for help. The students then re-engaged in a discussion about math. Shortly after, Catherine began to sing, and when her peer asked why she was singing, she responded "Because I'm Black." A few moments later she chastised her classmates using similar language, "Ya'll too Black . . . [you're] uncivilized."

Vignette Analysis

This example illustrates that racial stereotypes were alive and well in this high school mathematics classroom, and that they found voice among African American students. It is particularly interesting that Catherine made references to race three times in this exchange—the first was about slavery (likening the eating habits of her classmate to that of a slave), and the second was that she offered her own "Blackness" as an explanation for why she sang in class. The third was that she argued that some of the other African American students were "too Black," and thus "uncivilized."

These characterizations of "Blackness" and what it means to be African American are informed by our societally shared definitions, and often outright racist notions of what constitutes "Black" behavior (i.e., being uncivilized is equivalent to being "too Black"). In other words, students seemed to have taken up (at least to some degree) stereotypical notions about African Americans. We suggest that the invocation of these themes is a sign that students were struggling with their meaning and relevance.

Next, we present a longer discussion, one that unfolds over the course of almost a whole class period, which is not explicitly racialized until the very end. The derogatory comment about Africans with which the conversation culminates provides further evidence of the salience of racial stereotypes for students. We also find it noteworthy that such a comment occurs by a successful African American student on a day when a set of assignments for the semester have been returned, on which students did not perform as well as they would have liked. In other words, there may be connections between racialized talk and student concerns about their academic performance.

Vignette 2: "Africans Look Like Monkeys": Racialized Talk and Fear of Stigma

It was the last day of regular class before finals at the end of the first semester. The class began as students were asked to fill out a "student skills" evaluation—their sense of how well they had mastered various skills in Algebra. One group consisted of four girls: Beverly and Sierra, both African American female students who cared a lot about math, but had experienced some challenges in the class; Lucille, an Asian American female student; and Grace, a white female student. After the student skills evaluation, students were to put together their individual portfolios that consisted of their assignments, tests, projects, and quizzes for the semester. There was a lot of talk and socializing as they worked. Sierra said, "This is too much. I'm claustrophobic." Beverly responded: "This isn't claustrophobic." Sierra: "I know, claustrophobic means tight places. But there is just too much papers all over the place. I feel like I'm getting nervous." She placed her hands over her face.

As the students worked with a pile of papers already on their desks, the teacher began to pass out more tests and papers. Beverly asked, "Oooooo, can I pass them out?" The teacher responded, "No Beverly, these tests are private. Some people may not want you to see their grade." Beverly said, "I know. That's why I wanted to pass them back." She snickered. As the papers were being passed back, students looked at their tests, exclaimed and laughed over bad grades. Beverly said to the teacher, "Can I redo this?" The teacher responded, "That was old Beverly. You didn't do the graph on it." Beverly said, "Oh, I don't like to graph. Haha, I got a 73/200 on this." She continued to laugh. Grace comments that she can't show the portfolio to her mom, for fear of being "beat."

Once all of the papers were passed back, the teacher asked the students to work on a problem, which she identified as difficult. While working, the following conversation took place in the group.

Beverly:	"This is hard. I hate these problems."
Sierra:	"Me too. It makes my head hurt. I hate thinking."
Beverly:	"Haha . . . you hate thinking?"
Sierra:	"I hate thinking about math."
Beverly:	"Oh! My head hurts too." (She describes how her headache goes all the way up her pony tail.)
	Grace begins a discussion about one of the problems: "Let's use 5."
Sierra:	"No, Let's use 10. Wait no, nothing with zeros."
Lucille:	"I got it figured out!"
Beverly:	"No, don't tell them!" She intensely works on the problem then says, "Okay, I got it, now you can tell them. I really didn't care. I just didn't want you to say it out loud so that I can hear. I wanted to do it by myself."

A few moments later, Sierra asked the African American teaching assistant (who was a high school student who had previously done well in Algebra), "What is the KKK?" She responded, "It's white people who hate Black people." The student then asked, "What does it mean?" The TA answered "It means Ku Klux Klan." Lucille commented that even she knew what it meant. Jokingly, the teaching assistant responded (referring to Sierra), "Well, she's not really Black. She got some Indian in her." Sierra corrected her, "No, Haitian." Moments later Beverly interjected, "You know how Black people can tell if someone is African?" Sierra responded, "Cause they're hecka hecka black." The girls began to giggle. Then, the TA commented, "Not only that, but all Africans look like monkeys." More laughter ensued from the group.

Vignette Analysis

A complex set of social and cultural processes took place over the course of these interactions. First, Sierra expressed how being in the classroom with all of her prior work spread about made her feel claustrophobic. Later, she confirmed this anxiety by describing a headache that she gets when she is thinking about math, and Beverly reported a similar reaction. They get back papers where they have not done well (Beverly announces that she got 73 out of 200 on a test). She laughs, but it is clear that she cared a great deal about her performance in math, and that she was concerned. Despite these physical and visceral reactions to math class (which may be more likely a fear of failing math), the girls persisted when asked to solve a difficult problem. Beverly even insisted on not being told the answer and on figuring it out for herself. Even in the midst of their conversation about their poor performance and frustration, they continued to engage in the mathematics.

The conversation that ended the segment revealed that underneath these concerns about failure and performance, race is salient. The exchange about the Ku Klux Klan and Africans, on one hand, seems a bit random in the midst of the talk about solving math problems and math performance. However, we argue that it may illustrate the ways in which fear of being inferior *by virtue of being African American* may undergird the responses of African American students in the math classroom. The references to Africans looking like monkeys or being "hecka hecka black" draw on long-held derogatory images in our culture about Africans and African Americans. It may be that bringing these stereotypes and derogatory images to light, but attributing them to Africans (and not African Americans) serves to distance the African American students and the TA from these images, even as they fear confirming them with their poor performance in math.

This series of exchanges seems to suggest that students may have been managing their own fear of failure, and perhaps worrying that others would think they are not smart by virtue of their race. In this case, students distance themselves from Africans, perhaps with the goal of distancing themselves from stereotypes about African descendent people in this country.

Wrestling with Stereotype Threat: Managing the Fear of Failure

In the last section, we highlighted the ways in which African American students gave voice to stereotypical and derogatory statements about African Americans, highlighting the continued salience of such stereotypes in the daily experience of high school students. In the second vignette, the data suggested that there may be a connection between the racialized stereotypical discourse and students' fear of failing, perhaps in a kind of *stereotype threat* related reaction.

In referencing stereotype threat, we refer to the work of Claude Steele and colleagues, who have found evidence that the mere psychological threat of confirming negative stereotypes about one's race can suppress performance on academic tasks (Steele, 1997). Although this body of research has primarily found effects in domain identified individuals being tested at the edge of their abilities, we suspect that a related process plays out *in situ* for a larger population. We use the term loosely here to highlight, in general, the ways that the fear of being stereotyped by virtue of race may be related to classroom performance and interactions. In this section, we consider this potential intertwining of fear of being racially stereotyped academically and engagement and participation in math class (including the racialized positioning of oneself).

Kelvin was an African American male student who shifted from high levels of engagement to high levels of disengagement. He was often unsure of himself with respect to understanding the math, but was not afraid to ask questions or try out solutions. He got frustrated easily, and could disengage due to his not being sure of his ability to be a mathematical thinker. Kelvin was struggling with issues of identity and achievement. He was uncertain about his future with academics and was experiencing anxiety over potential failure. In response to these feelings, he tried on, and explored, different types of African American identities and stances toward school to help position himself with his classmates in ways that offered him more security.

Below, we share two vignettes involving Kelvin. In the first, Kelvin clearly positions himself as academically oriented and he participates fully in the mathematics work of the classroom. In the second, Kelvin receives negative feedback about his performance in math and both questions his ability in math and engages in racialized discourse to distract himself from his fear of failing.

Vignette 3: "Thank You, My Fellow Classmates": Kelvin Day 1

On this day in early December, Kelvin and Joel (both African American male students) came into the class running. Joel tried to sit down and Kelvin pulled the chair out from under him. Joel fell on the floor. They begin class by discussing the prior night's homework. The teacher asks the class to decide which problem or section they need help with. Kelvin moved to another table (he was seated with Ishmael) to check his homework because Ishmael didn't have his homework. He sat down at another group and said to a classmate "Wassup pimp." Joel, from another table, asked Kelvin why he left his group and he said, "cause Ishmael ain't got no homework." Kelvin announced to the group, "Ok, I don't get how to do any of these." The group talked about the homework problems, with various group members offering explanations to Kelvin. When finished, Kelvin said, "Thank you, my fellow classmates."

Later, as the students were working in groups on a "challenge" problem, Kelvin and Ishmael began to sing a rap song. The teacher went over to them and offered to help. She left for a second and Kelvin continued to work while Ishmael got up and started to walk around. Kelvin continued to work, complaining that he had "done everything on the poster." He pointed to something small that Ishmael did and said that is "all he's done in the last 30 minutes." About 10 minutes later, Kelvin said to Ishmael, "You just gotta draw a square right there." Ishmael replied, "I don't know how." Kelvin sighed heavily, "Oh my god, fine, I'll do it!"

Two days later, students were sharing their posters with one another by hanging them on the wall and doing a gallery walk. Kelvin went to another group and said that he wished his poster looked like theirs. He explained that he did the whole poster and Ishmael didn't do anything.

The teacher started to roll a die to decide who would present their poster first. However, both Kelvin and Ishmael volunteered. Kelvin and Ishmael had side conversation to decide who would present what parts. Kelvin was frustrated because Ishmael seemed to feel uncomfortable presenting the questions. Kelvin asked, "You want me to do all of them?! . . ."

Vignette Analysis

In this first series of interactions, after his initial playful entry into the classroom space, Kelvin was highly involved in the problem-solving and the making of the poster that were happening in the classroom. At the same time, Kelvin was off task occasionally. In the opening section of the vignette, Kelvin was eager to get assistance on homework problems he was not able to complete. He sought out students who would be able to help him because his group mate was unprepared. Kelvin partnered with the male student with the highest math status in the class. He was open about his mathematical uncertainty and stayed engaged with the group's explanations. As he took his leave from the group, he expressed gratitude to his classmates with an unusually formal and polite "thank you my fellow classmates." This phrase suggests a playful hyper-studiousness.

Throughout the series of interactions, Kelvin was highly involved in seeking out the resources that he needed to complete the mathematical work. In the assignment, Kelvin was able to pick up the slack for a less prepared student in his group. He did the lion's share of the work on the poster for his two-student team, and took responsibility for the presentation of the work. At the same time, he felt bad when he perceived that his poster was lacking in comparison to the others and he wanted his classmates to know that he did all the work. We saw these responses as signs of Kelvin's commitment to doing high quality work and fear of being seen as an incompetent person.

However, on another day (occurring in late October), illustrated in Vignette 4, Kelvin is much less involved in the mathematical work of the classroom, he expresses worries about his ability in math, and engages in racialized discourse as a form of coping.

Vignette 4: "I Hate This Class": Kelvin Day 2

On this day, the teacher passed back quizzes. When she handed back Kelvin's quiz, he said, "I don't want that" (he received a D). Marcus (also an African American male) said that he got an A+. Kelvin yelled across the room, "yea, right!" Joel (African American male) said that he didn't finish the quiz. Marcus actually got a C. Throughout the period, Kelvin is (uncharacteristically) loud, anxious, hyper, and disruptive (as evidenced by his loud outbursts, running around through the class, talking while the teacher is talking). As the teacher gives instructions, Kelvin says, "I hate this class! It is so confusing. Everything used to be so easy."

Several moments later, Kelvin was having a loud conversation with another African American student. He sang a song about the "dope man." Kelvin said "that nigga is in the army, that nigga is old and fat. Man your mom goes through boyfriends like nothing."

Vignette Analysis

In the previous vignette, we came to know Kelvin as a diligent student who cared about his performance in math class. In this vignette, Kelvin got back work that indicated that he was doing poorly in the class. He responded initially by complaining about the difficulty of mathematics, then later in the class period engaged in racialized discourse, including rapping and singing, and repeatedly using the word, "nigga." One interpretation of this series of events might be that the two events (the worry about grades and the racialized discourse) were unrelated. We suggest that (like in Vignette 2), the occurence of the racialized behaviors and talk may very well be tied to the prior experience of fearing doing poorly in mathematics.

Formal evaluations were times of high anxiety for Kelvin. In this vignette, he was aware that he hadn't done well on this test and made it public that he wanted to avoid learning about his score. Another African American male student attempted to mislead Kelvin about his score, claiming he got an A+. Kelvin readily dismissed the student's claim. As seen above, these students were clearly invested in achievement and being seen as smart. It is when this portrayal of self became difficult to establish that Kelvin had trouble focusing on his work and tended to rely upon expressing non-dominant cultural capital, which bordered on reifying stereotypical portrayals of African Americans (e.g., references to a promiscuous mother; a song about drug dealing). In these instances, Kelvin uses much more AAVE than he normally did in class and was more likely to bring up subjects generally considered inappropriate for side conversations during math class.

It is important to note that Kelvin's proclaimed dislike of mathematics was likely related to his lack of confidence in his ability to be successful. What is more striking is how clearly he articulates the trajectory of his declining confidence and enjoyment in the class. It was when Kelvin was feeling disgruntled with the course and his ability to be successful that he opened discussions about the sexual lives of others or rap songs about drug dealers. However, we must emphasize that bringing up these topics for conversation did not lead to Kelvin's complete disengagement in the class. Some days, students like Kelvin experienced several shifts in and out of engagement. In the end, Kelvin did pass the course and move to the next level mathematics class. What appeared to have been off-task distraction may have actually been instrumental in helping Kelvin achieve his success by allowing him to defuse his fears and anxiety. Vocalizing his fears and temporarily disengaging may have allowed Kelvin to achieve an equilibrium that supported taking up math tasks again.

Functions of Racialized Talk in Math for African American Students

The racialized talk served specific and important functions for African American students in the classrooms that we studied. In this section, we argue that the racialized talk among African American students in math classes served at least three functions. First, racialized talk was used for play and social connection in order to introduce levity into a situation through integrating humor via language or behavior. Second, racialized talk served an image-making function by allowing students to display their cultural verve. This non-dominant cultural capital allowed students to "authentically" position themselves in their peer groups to support a collective identity (Carter, 2005). Finally, racialized talk seemed to be used in part to manage the fear of failing or the potential stigma of not being smart in math. In our observations, this particular function seemed to operate most in response to evaluation or perceived failure in the context.

To some degree, we saw all of these functions operating in the prior vignettes. For instance, Catherine, in the first vignette, seemed to use the racialized talk as a source of play and social connection to other African American students, even as she gave voice to prominent stereotypes about African Americans. Kelvin, in Vignette 4, turns to racialized talk to position himself as socially competent (as he feared being mathematically incompetent). For him, the racialized talk served both the second and third functions.

We'd like to share one final moment of interaction in an Algebra classroom where there was a greater amount of racialized discourse than in some other classes to illustrate the multiple functions that racialized discourse seemed to serve in the math classrooms that we studied. In this vignette, a group that is predominantly composed of African American students engaged in racialized talk as they moved in and out of working on the mathematics problems that the teacher has assigned.

Vignette 5: "It's Tookie, not Tiki": Multiple Functions of Racialized Talk

The teacher instructed the class to work on a group warm-up problem. In one group of four (three African American and one Latino) students, the teacher decided to help them get started and then walked away. Joel (African American male) asked the teacher if she was married. He then stopped himself and said, "I'm off-task. Way off." Catherine (African American female) chimes in to say, jokingly "He said way off." Kelvin responded, "Like you fell off, like off a thirty thousand foot cliff." Richard (Latino) replied, "... and somehow survived." Kelvin then comments, "he said somehow survived." Moments later, Joel started to sing. Kelvin asks, "Why you always singing about cheeks. You about to be the next Michael Jackson." Joel responded, "The next Tiki Williams." Kelvin corrects him and says, "It's Tookie, not Tiki, Tookie Williams." Catherine commented that he "fried like some chicken." Lastly, Kelvin responded, "he could kill you with his hands." After this exchange, one of the students began to sing the national Black anthem. As they talked and sang they move in and out of doing their math assignment.

Vignette Analysis

In this example, we see that one of the primary purposes the students' off-task behavior seemed to serve was play and social connection. However, image-making and managing the fear of stigma or failure was also illustrated in this classroom moment. Importantly, this example shows that these functions were not mutually exclusive; rather the talk most often served multiple functions simultaneously.

The off-task behavior in this example can be characterized by social play. A student acknowledged that he was off-task by asking the teacher a personal question. The students lighten the moment through humor and make jokes concerning how far from working on math they really are. Then Kelvin recognizes the potential consequences of such off-task behavior through offering an analogy of falling off a cliff.

As a way to further connect with each other, the students engaged in singing and a discussion about key entertainment and political figures in the African American community. This social talk connected students to one another by supporting a sense of belonging and a sense of community among the African American students. This dialogue also allowed students to display their cultural knowledge and serves as an image-making opportunity. Through this interaction, the students position themselves as capable group members within the broader African American community. This display of shared knowledge operates as non-dominant cultural capital as it reveals levels of social competence within the cultural community. Specifically, the students referenced two high profile people in the African American community—Michael Jackson, a well-known entertainer, and Tookie Williams, an ex-gang member who turned his life around in prison and encouraged young people not to join gangs, but who was executed in prison.

Lastly, in this example, it could be that the connections students maintained with one another through social talk during the math task helped offset the potential frustration and alienation of struggling with problem-solving and with receiving negative feedback. This seemed particularly true for some students, for instance,

Kelvin, who often talked explicitly about how he worried about failing, and often withdrew or was uncooperative when evaluation was salient. His comments about "hating the class" because it's "so confusing" indicates that he may already frame mathematics courses as something he struggles to successfully complete. However, through talk he could manage his fear of failing by re-channeling his energy instead of avoiding the task altogether. Even though he makes a reference to the potentially serious ramifications of off-task behavior, he still engages in racialized talk with the group to emphasize a cultural, rather than academic connection. The support of shared cultural connections and the temporary reprieve from the pressures of performance that engaging in this way provides can be a resource for re-engaging.

Concluding Remarks

We have made the point in this chapter that racial stereotypes are alive and well in high school math classes, and that racialized talk and behavior on the part of African American students in math class may serve multiple functions for students. This research highlights the complexity of this racialized discourse, and problematizes perspectives that social talk is simply a distraction which pulls students away from classwork. Although this might be true to some degree, we suggest that there are some instances where it is the social talk that *allows* them to engage in the mathematics—even during moments of self-doubt or difficulty. Racialized talk often encourages students to connect with one another, show areas of strength and competency in domains valued by their cultural community, and allows students to regulate feelings of anxiety related to failure.

One might ask whether our findings at Washington High are "generalizable" to other school populations. In other words, were the patterns that we saw with respect to racialized talk and behavior at Washington representative of those in other schools in other districts? Were these patterns specific to "reform" math classrooms? We believe that the highly social nature of these reform classes do make aspects of race and identity more readily observable, although we suspect that they are as powerful in other mathematics contexts.

To some degree, all the classroom cultures are constituted by readily available cultural notions of identity and ability. That is, the outside world intrudes upon the classroom. For African American students in math classrooms, these intrusions take the form of classic stereotypes and assumptions about mathematical ability. The best teachers attempt to offer an alternative to the standard view of race and achievement in math when creating their classroom cultures. They seek to challenge and subvert dominant cultural ideas and offer alternative (counternarratives) ways of thinking about the self and math that can support achievement.

How teachers end up responding to students' "off-task" and racialized talk and interactions is of critical importance for supporting the students in engaging the mathematics. We hope that the student voices that we have highlighted in this chapter make clear the importance of teachers understanding students' need for social connection during the learning of difficult content. In our view, optimally teachers can find ways to make it work within the classroom structures. There is unlikely to be one method of responding to racialized talk that could work for all teachers. In highlighting the complexity of this talk, and the work it accomplishes, we hope to caution against simplistic readings of kids' behaviors that lead to their being dismissed as unconcerned with their own futures and unmotivated. We aim to help teachers and teacher educators become aware of the complexity of students' experiences, become more able to understand their students, and hopefully develop responses to students that will be most effective for the students' learning.

We also hope that our work will highlight the important ways that simply participating in everyday events in high school mathematics classrooms can be a form of racialized experience, even in a school where it was taboo to talk explicitly about race. Students are wrestling daily with the legacy of strong and pervasive stereotypes about African American students, and there is often little support for students in making sense of these negative stereotypes. We saw in this chapter that, even in a school that works hard to recognize multiple intellectual contributions to classroom life, and where math teachers care deeply about "equity," the master-narrative about race, and the baggage that goes along with being African American in this country, is a force to be reckoned with for students.

Notes

1 We would like to thank the Spencer Foundation, as a grant to the first author made this research possible. We would also like to thank the LIFE Center, funded by the National Science Foundation through the Science of Learning Center program, for their generous support of this research. All opinions and errors are solely ours, and do not reflect the funding institutions.
2 Stereotypes can be defined as "mental representations of the characteristics of a particular social or cultural group that are shared among members of society" (from Stangor & Schelter, 1996, cited in Hudley & Graham, 2002).
3 All names of schools and individuals are pseudonyms to protect the identities of the teachers and students.

References

Ainsworth-Darnell, J.W. & Downey, D.B. (1998). Assessing the oppositional culture explanation for racial/ethnic differences in school performance. *American Sociological Review*, 63, 536–553.
American Anthropological Association (1998). Statement on "Race." Online at www.aaanet.org/stmts/racepp.htm. Downloaded June 29, 2008.
Anderson, J. (1988). *The education of Blacks in the South, 1860–1935.* Chapel Hill: University of North Carolina Press.
Bailey, A. (2006). Year in the life on an African American male in advertising: A content analysis. *Journal of Advertising*, 35(1), 83–104.
Boaler, J. & Staples, M. (2005). Transforming students' lives through an equitable mathematics approach: The case of Railside School. *Teachers College Record.*
Borak, J., Fiellin, M., & Chemerynski, S. (2004). Who is Hispanic? Implications for epidemiologic research in the United States. *Epidemiology & Society*, 15(2), 240–244.
Bourdieu, P. (1977). *Outline of a theory of practice.* Cambridge: Cambridge University Press.
Carter, P. (2003). "Black" cultural capital, status positioning, and schooling conflicts for low-income African American youth. *Social Problems*, 50(1), 136–155.

Carter, P. (2005). *Keepin' it real: School success beyond Black and White.* Oxford: Oxford University Press.

Chan, D. (2005) Playing with race: The ethics of racialized representations in E-games. *International Review of Information Ethics.*

Cohen, E. & Lotan, R. (1997). *Working for equity in heterogeneous classrooms: Sociological theory in practice.* New York: Teachers College Press.

Deburg, W.L. (2004). *Hoodlums: Black villains and social bandits in American life.* Chicago, IL: University of Chicago Press.

Devine, P. & Elliott, A. (1995). Are racial stereotypes really fading? The Princeton trilogy revisited. *Personality and Social Psychology Bulletin, 21*(11), 1139–1150.

Emerson, R., Fretz, R., & Shaw, L. (1995). *Writing ethnographic fieldnotes.* Chicago, IL: University of Chicago Press.

Fordham, S. & Ogbu, J. (1986). Black students' school success: Coping with the burden of acting White. *Urban Review, 18*(3), 176–206.

Hudley, C. & Graham, S. (2001). Stereotypes of achievement striving among early adolescents. *Social Psychology of Education, 5,* 201–224.

Krueger, J. (1996). Personal beliefs and cultural stereotypes about racial characteristics. *Journal of Personality and Social Psychology, 71,* 536–548.

Martin, D.B. (2006a). Mathematics learning and participation as racialized forms of experience: African American parents speak on the struggle for mathematics literacy. *Mathematical Thinking and Learning, 8*(3), 197–229.

Martin, D.B. (2006b). Mathematics learning and participation in the African American context: The co-construction of identity in two intersecting realms of experience. In N. Nasir & P. Cobb (Eds.), *Diversity, equity, and access to mathematical ideas* (pp. 146–158). New York: Teachers College Press.

Martin, D.B. (2007). Beyond missionaries or cannibals: Who should teach mathematics to African American children? *The High School Journal, 91*(1), 6–28.

Martin, D.B. (2009). *Researching race in mathematics education.* Teachers College Record, *111*(2), 295–338.

Miles, M. & Huberman, A. (1994). *Qualitative data analysis: An expanded sourcebook.* Thousand Oaks, CA: Sage.

Moody, V. (2004). Sociocultural orientations and the mathematical success of African American students. *The Journal of Educational Research, 97*(3), 135–146.

Morgan, S.L. & Mehta, J.D. (2004). Beyond the laboratory: Evaluating the survey evidence for the disidentification explanation of black-white differences in achievement. *Sociology of Education, 77*(1), 82–101.

Murrell, P. (1994). In search of responsive teaching for African American males: An investigation of middle school mathematics curriculum. *Journal of Negro Education, 63*(4), 556–569.

Niemann, Y., Jennings, L., Rozelle, R., Baxter, J., & Sullivan, E. (1994). Use of free responses and cluster analysis to determine stereotypes of eight groups. *Personality and Social Psychology Bulletin, 20,* 379–390.

O'Connor, C. (1997). Dispositions toward (collective) struggle and educational resilience in the inner city: A case analysis of six African American high school students. *American Educational Research Journal, 34,* 593–629.

Ogbu, J. (1987) Variability in minority school performance: A problem in search of an explanation. *Anthropology and Education Quarterly, 18*(4), 312–334.

Ogbu, J. (1991). Minority coping responses and school experience. *Journal of Psychohistory, 18*(4), 433–456.

Omi, M. & Winant, H. (1994). *Racial formation in the United States: From the 1960s to the 1990s* (2nd ed.). New York: Routledge.

Panigua, F. (2005). *Assessing and treating culturally diverse clients.* Thousand Oaks, CA: Sage.

Rome, D. (2004). *Black Demons: The media's depiction of the African American male criminal stereotype.* New York: Greenwood Press.

Stangor, C. & Schaller, M. (1996). Stereotypes as individual and collective representations. In C.N. Macrae, C. Stangor, & M. Hewstone (Eds.), *Stereotypes and Stereotyping.* (pp. 3–40) New York: Guilford.

Steele, C. (1997). A threat in the air: How stereotypes shape the intellectual identities and performance. *American Psychologist, 52*(6), 613–629.

Stinson, D. (2006). African American male adolescents, schooling (and mathematics): Deficiency, rejection, and achievement. *Review of Educational Research, 76*(4), 477–506.

Tillman, L. (2002). Culturally sensitive research approaches: An African-American perspective. *Educational Researcher, 31*(9), 3–12.

Walker, E.N. (2006). Urban high school students' academic communities and their effects on mathematics success. *American Educational Research Journal, 43*(1), 43–73.

10 Opportunities to Learn Geometry: Listening to the Voices of Three African American High School Students

Marilyn E. Strutchens and S. Kathy Westbrook

Introduction

In this chapter we explore how Josh, Keisha, and Tony, three tenth-grade African American students, fared in a geometry course in a southeastern United States high school.[1] Our goal is to illuminate the mathematics teaching the students encountered, the decisions that the students made related to their success or failure in the class, the students' family influences on their performance, and how other school and community factors contributed to their performance in the course. We use Critical Race Theory (CRT) and an opportunity-to-learn framework as lenses through which we examine their experiences and outcomes in the course.

Theoretical Underpinnings

Prior to 1995, many scholars studying African American student schooling outcomes borrowed theories that were used in gender studies and other areas as the underpinnings for their research perspectives. For example, Strutchens (1993) used critical education theory as a lens to examine the societal and cultural factors affecting sixth-grade African American students' performance in a mathematics class. Critical education theory, as defined by Weiler (1988), rests upon a critical view of the society, asserting that society is both exploitive and oppressive, but is also capable of being transformed in meaningful ways. *Reproduction* and *production* are key considerations in critical education theory. Reproduction theory is "concerned with the process through which existing social structures maintain and reproduce themselves" (Weiler, 1988, p. 6). Production theory is "concerned with the ways in which both individuals and classes assert their own experience and contest or resist the ideological and material forces imposed upon them in a variety of settings" (Weiler, 1988, p. 11). Although critical education theory had merit in studies of African American students, it does not focus on the impact of race and racism, which are crucial considerations in understanding much of what African American students experience in some schools and classrooms.

In 1995, Gloria Ladson-Billings and William Tate introduced CRT to education. Critical race theory evolved from critical legal studies, a movement that challenged the traditional legal scholarship focusing on doctrine and policy analysis in favor of law which focuses on individuals in social and cultural contexts (Ladson-Billings,

2003; Ladson-Billings & Tate, 1995). Unmasking and exposing racism in its various instantiations, highlighting the voices of oppressed groups (storytelling), critiquing liberalism, and documenting that whites have been the main beneficiaries of civil rights legislation are hallmarks of CRT (Ladson-Billings, 1999). Moreover, "CRT posits that racism is endemic in society and in education, and that racism has become so deeply engrained in society's and schooling's consciousness that it is often invisible" (Bartlett & Brayboy, 2005, p. 366). Due to its tenets, CRT has become widely used in educational studies of groups that struggle against racial oppression (Dixson & Rousseau, 2005). Solórzano and Yosso (2002) provided a definition of CRT within the context of education:

> Critical race theory in education is a framework or set of basic insights, perspectives, methods, and pedagogy that seeks to identify, analyze, and transform those structural and cultural aspects of education that maintain subordinate and dominant racial positions in and out of the classroom. (p. 25)

Counter-story methodology has been used by many educational scholars who employ CRT (Dixson & Rousseau, 2005). Solórzano and Yosso (2002) defined "the counter-story as a method of telling the stories of those people whose experiences are not often told" (p. 32). Below are other characteristics of counter-stories identified by Solórzano and Yosso (2002, p. 32):

1   The counter-story is a tool for exposing, analyzing, and challenging the majoritarian stories of racial privilege.
2   Counter-stories can shatter complacency, challenge the dominant discourse on race, and further the struggle for racial reform.
3   Counter-stories need not be created only as a direct response to majoritarian stories.

In this chapter, we use counter-stories to discuss the experiences that Josh, Keisha, and Tony had in their geometry class. In doing so, we offer a biographical, experiential, and first-hand account analysis of the students' mathematical experiences in relation to their school as well as the larger socio-historical context.

Opportunity-to-Learn Framework

We believe that the opportunity-to-learn framework, as discussed by Tate (1995, 2005), is an appropriate lens to use alongside CRT in examining whether the three students received equitable instruction that would provide them with a variety of options for future coursework and careers. Tate (2005) presented three opportunity-to-learn (OTC) variables that should be taken into consideration when determining whether or not students are provided sufficient access to learn mathematics curriculum expected for their grade level and age:

1   Content exposure and coverage variables measure the amount of time students spend on a topic (time-on-task) and the depth of instruction provided. These

variables also measure whether or not students cover critical subject matter for a specific grade or discipline.

2   Content emphasis variables affect the selection of topics within the implemented curriculum and the selection of students for basic skills instruction or for higher-order skills instruction.

3   Quality of instructional delivery variables reveals how classroom pedagogical strategies affect students' academic achievement. (p.15)

Tate (1995) suggested that opportunity-to-learn models that have equity as an intent should begin with the recommendations of the *Professional Teaching Standards for Mathematics* (National Council of Teachers of Mathematics (NCTM), 1991) which call for teachers to (a) build on strengths from students' linguistic, ethnic, racial, gender, and socioeconomic backgrounds; (b) help students to become aware of the role of mathematics in society and culture; (c) expose students to the contributions of various cultures to the advancement of mathematics; (d) show students how mathematics relates to other subjects; and (e) provide students with opportunities to apply mathematics to authentic contexts. In addition, research related to how people learn has led educators and researchers to believe that, in order for teachers to help students reach their full academic potential, teachers must be aware of the students' needs, both academic and cultural, and they should integrate assessment with teaching, so that they are constantly aware of students' progress and whether or not what is being taught is understood (Bransford, Brown, & Cocking, 1999).

Background Information

Josh's, Keisha's, and Tony's stories are a part of a larger study conducted by Westbrook (2005), where she sought to explore the voices of six African American students regarding factors that affected their mathematical experiences in a geometry course. Their stories included the students' suggestions for addressing issues that were barriers to their success in the course. Barriers related to the students' achievement included the teachers' pedagogical strategies, the course curriculum, students' extra-curricular activities, and/or the students' parental involvement.

Multiple–single individual case studies were conducted through extensive student interviews, classroom observations, and parent and teacher interviews. The six students were considered as individual case studies. Even though the students, teachers, and parents were interviewed with the same initial set of questions, the result can be described as multi-single units. Data collection consisted of student, teacher, and parent interviews, classroom observations, archival records from students' school records, and students' classwork and homework. Families' socioeconomic level, students' gender, and students' prior success in mathematics class were considered so that the participants differed in these categories. Further, student interview questions were designed so that Westbrook (2005) could discern whether or not the students felt that the education offered to them in mathematics was sufficient and equitable. Parent and teacher interview protocols replicated the questions asked in the student interviews so that triangulation of data sources as well as different types of data could occur. Research questions included:

1   How do African American students in this study view their mathematics experiences currently and in the past?

2   Do the African American students in this study consider mathematics important to learn? Do they see a relationship between mathematics knowledge and future job opportunities or education? Do they view mathematics as an empowering tool?

3   Are parents, guardians, community, and peers influential sources for the African American students in this study in achievement and specifically mathematics achievement?

4   How do the African American students in this study interact with their mathematics teacher? Do the students perceive their teacher as encouraging, and knowledgeable? Is there a relationship of mutual respect and admiration between the student and the teacher?

We organize our discussion of the students' experiences by first providing demographic information about the larger social context including their town, community, and school. Next, we describe the course in which the students were enrolled and highlight the intended course curriculum compared to what the students actually covered. Then, we discuss the teacher and her role in shaping students' experiences. We then present snapshots of each student's story as we interpreted and gave meaning to it. We end the chapter by discussing the broader implications of our analysis.

The Setting

The study took place in a small city in a southeastern state. The city is located near a beautiful man-made lake sporting several marinas and resorts, and was the former home of a huge athletic apparel and textile corporation. Since the large athletic apparel corporation moved more than 20 years ago, the economy of the city has steadily declined. According to the 2000 census, there were 15,000 people residing in the city (U.S. Census Bureau, 2003). The racial make-up of the city was 70.56% white, 28.37% African American, and 1.52% from other races (U.S. Census Bureau, 2003). The median income for a household in the city was $29,309, compared to the United States median of $43,564 (U. S. Census Bureau, 2003).

The city's schools, grade K-12, are accredited through the Southern Association of Colleges and Schools and were ranked third in the state on a recent "report card" on state schools. During the time of the study, a superintendent who had a strong presence in the schools and a good working rapport with teachers led the school system. He encouraged his mathematics teachers to participate in a systemic initiative to improve their mathematics teaching and attended several of the professional development events with his teachers to show his support.

The local high school had a population of 983 students during the time the study was conducted. Thirty-five percent of the students were eligible for free or reduced price meals, compared to 51.6% of the state. About 38% of the students were African American and 62% were white. At the time of the study, 77.5% of the secondary teachers were highly qualified (Alabama State Department of Education, 2004).

The Course

Here we provide a description of the geometry course that the students should have experienced, based on the Alabama Course of Study, in order to refer back to later as we talk about the students' stories and whether or not they had the opportunity to learn the mathematics that was intended for them to learn based on state standards. According to the Alabama Course of Study (2003) the geometry course on which the students were enrolled should have engaged students in problematic situations in which they formed conjectures, determined the validity of these conjectures, and defended their conclusions to classmates (Alabama Course of Study, 2003). Moreover, the state document asserted that an emphasis should be placed on the power of deductive reasoning, both formally and informally in a variety of formats. The Alabama Course of Study also encouraged the use of dynamic geometry software in the classroom to support classroom instruction. This statement aligns with the authors of the Alabama Course of Study claim that the "2002–2003 Mathematics Course of Study Committee extensively used the *Principles and Standards for School Mathematics* (National Council of Teachers of Mathematics, 2000)" as a guide to create the document. The authors of the state document wrote:

> The recommendations of the *Principles and Standards for School Mathematics* (PSSM) from the National Council of Teachers of Mathematics (NCTM) are incorporated into the conceptual framework, position statements, and content standards of this course of study. The content in each grade level and course is organized using the five PSSM content standards. These five content standards that serve as strands in this document are Number and Operations, Algebra, Geometry, Measurement, and Data Analysis and Probability. The PSSM process standards of Problem-Solving, Reasoning and Proof, Communication, Connections, and Representation should be integrated into instruction as outlined in PSSM. (p. 1)

Thus, according to the Alabama document, the course should have emphasized use of calculators and computers, encouraged teachers to pose problems that might be solved by students using a variety of strategies, and facilitated students working in small heterogeneous groups (Senk & Thompson, 2003). Some of the content objectives listed in the Alabama Course of Study are listed below:

1 Justify theorems related to pairs of angles, including angles formed by parallel and perpendicular lines, vertical angles, adjacent angles, complementary angles, and supplementary angles.

2 Verify the relationships among different classes of polygons by using their properties.

3 Verifying the formulas for the measures of interior and exterior angles of polygons inductively and deductively.

4 Solve real-life and mathematical problems using properties and theorems related to circles, quadrilaterals, and other geometric shapes.

The verbs used in the objectives indicated that the students should be highly active in their learning of geometry.

The Teacher

Mrs. Smith is a 12-year veteran, white high school mathematics teacher. She has lived all of her life in the same region of the state and has spent all of her career in the city where the study took place. Mrs. Smith majored in mathematics for her undergraduate studies and completed a Master's in Applied Mathematics from a nearby state university. Although she has taught geometry from another text, Mrs. Smith stated that this was only her second year teaching geometry from the textbook adopted by the school system in 2003. This text took a very traditional approach to the subject. The school system had chosen to supplement the textbook with units from a reform curriculum but Mrs. Smith had not chosen to use the units in her class. During the summer prior to the study, Mrs. Smith participated in a 2-week professional development program that focused on using best practices from the research in mathematics education and the NCTM Standards documents (1989, 1991, 1995, 2000). The program was also designed to help teachers to become familiar with the pedagogy and instructional materials related to the reform-based units that were adopted by the school system.

Mrs. Smith's classroom had been recently renovated. It was clean and well organized. The walls of her classroom were covered with inspirational posters such as "Strive to do your best" and "You can be successful." Along one wall were all of the geometry terms covered in class. As the chapters from the geometry book were covered and new terms were introduced, Mrs. Smith printed the geometry vocabulary on brightly colored paper and pasted them onto the geometry wall of terms. The classroom was meticulously organized with all of the transparencies, worksheets, homework checks, tests, and assignments placed where Mrs. Smith could readily place her hands on them. Students had access to two bookshelves in the back of the classroom where Mrs. Smith kept a classroom set of textbooks and workbooks, so that the students did not have to bring their own mathematics book to class.

When asked to describe herself as a teacher, Mrs. Smith stated that the most important thing for her is to break down mathematics so that her students can understand the material. Mrs. Smith described a college mathematics professor who lectured so that no one in the class could understand. Mrs. Smith was determined to do just the opposite and make mathematics easy for her students.

A Typical Day in Mrs. Smith's Geometry Class

When the bell rang, students went to their assigned seats. Mrs. Smith put prepared transparencies with answers to the even problems from the homework of the previous night on the overhead projector. She set a timer for 10 minutes and allowed the students to ask questions on those problems that they did not understand. Mrs. Smith explained that the timer helped keep her on track so that there was time for her to cover the new material. If a student had a question at the end of the 10 minutes, Mrs. Smith reset the timer for a few more minutes. During the time of this study, very few students asked questions about homework.

At the end of the question period, Mrs. Smith passed out a half sheet of paper with a homework quiz on it. The questions on the short quiz were similar to the homework that the students had been assigned to do the previous evening. After the quiz, Mrs. Smith passed out a double-sided sheet of main ideas for the next section or two of the book. This paper was to be used as a guide for the students to take notes and organize the lecture and book material. During the first observation, which took place the second week of the semester, most of the students appeared to be taking notes on this paper. On subsequent visits, fewer and fewer students were taking notes as Mrs. Smith lectured, but most of the students were quiet and mannerly.

Other than when the students were taking a quiz or a test, Mrs. Smith lectured for most of the 90-minute block. A student occasionally asked a question or volunteered an answer when a question was presented to the class. Mrs. Smith called upon students who volunteered and only rarely called on a student who did not volunteer. When this occurred, it was frequently to correct or interrupt a student's behavior.

There were no deviations from the routine described except on two occasions: (1) near the end of the second observation with less than 10 minutes remaining in the class period, Mrs. Smith directed groups of four students whose desks were the closest together to work on a problem or two and to compare their solutions; and (2) at another time, after Mrs. Smith changed the seating arrangement, students had different groups with which to work. The group work on these two occasions lasted no more than 5–10 minutes, and the groups did not share with the class the results of their group work.

The pedagogy demonstrated by Mrs. Smith aligned with the typical pedagogy faced by African American students: often directive, controlling, and debilitating (Chunn, 1988; Haberman, 1992). This is in contrast to the kind of mathematics teaching advocated for in the NCTM *Standards*, with its emphasis on active learning, deep understanding of concepts, and the development of problem-solving and reasoning skills (NCTM, 1989, 1991, 1995, 2000). Her teaching was also at odds with the instructional practices described in the Alabama Course of Study (2003) for the geometry course.

Student Participants

The African American students who participated in the case studies were chosen based on their performance in class, socioeconomic status, and the teacher's recommendation.

Josh: Hidden Rules

Josh did what was necessary to maintain consistently good grades; even he admitted that he could have done better. To keep from being bored in school and to keep the homework load light, he did his homework as the teacher was lecturing. Josh was an only child of college-educated parents. Josh's father, a retired engineer, died unexpectedly during his ninth-grade year. Being close to his mother, Josh did not want to disappoint her, but he was not sure that he wanted to be an engineer like his father.

There did not seem to be a question of whether or not Josh would attend college. Josh's mother was well aware of what classes Josh needed to take in order to get admitted to, and be successful in, college. But Josh's mother was not successful in convincing the school which mathematics courses Josh should take when he was in the eighth grade. Josh and his mother believed that Josh should have been placed in algebra in the eighth grade instead of pre-algebra. Josh's mother made several visits to his school in an attempt to get this placement changed, but was not successful. Josh's seventh-grade mathematics teacher did not recommend him for algebra, and her veto seemed to carry more weight with the school than Josh's mother. Through teacher interviews, Wells and Oakes (1996) learned that teachers in their study equated race with intellectual potential and made recommendations aligned with their beliefs. Additionally, it was found that parents with political and social power were the ones who could navigate the system for their children and insist that their children receive something extra from the school (Wells & Oakes, 1996). Brantlinger (2001) maintained that the white-middle class controls the educational system where decisions are made which reinforce the status quo benefiting only their children.

Josh had the potential to make excellent grades in mathematics, although he usually did the work that he thought was necessary to make a *good* grade in geometry. While admitting that he did not study for tests and did not pay attention in class, Josh did not see a conflict because he understood the material. Josh made a B for his final average because he received a D on his final exam. In a telephone conversation with Josh and his mother, after school had ended, Josh stated that he did not understand how the final exam average was calculated, as there was not a particular test given in his class which was called a final exam. Josh was correct. The final exam for his geometry class consisted of an accumulation of quizzes given throughout the semester and accounted for a total of 20% of his final grade. This process of accumulating quizzes to produce a final exam average was a departmental decision made by the mathematics teachers at Josh's school. Josh's unawareness of the accumulation of quizzes given throughout the semester serving as the final exam was related to his not paying attention in class.

Josh's teacher was aware that Josh was not paying attention to her in class, and that he was often working on sections of homework other than the section they were supposed to be working on at the time. Since Josh made fairly good grades, Josh's lack of attention did not disturb his teacher. Josh's teacher believed that all the students understood how they earned their grades since it was a departmental decision. Josh believed that he could learn mathematics on his own and did not need the teacher to explain the material, as he could read the book himself and had no problem following the examples to do his assignments.

Josh's opportunity to learn was hindered by Mrs. Smith's pedagogy. Since Josh was capable of reading the text and understanding it for himself, he needed the teacher to challenge him in ways that would help him to reach his full mathematics potential (NCTM, 1989, 1991, 2000). He needed his teacher to use the dynamic geometry software described in Alabama's Course of Study for Mathematics so that he could make conjectures and test them out. He needed worthwhile tasks that were authentic and that helped him to see the connections of mathematics to the real world (Tate, 1995; NCTM, 1989, 1991, 2000). He needed Mrs. Smith to be culturally and cognitively responsive to his needs (Tate, 1995, 2005).

Keisha: Is Anyone Listening To Me?

The most vocal of the students in this study, Keisha, was not shy in expressing her opinions and telling others what she thought about school, her teachers, and learning mathematics. Even though Keisha's eighth-grade mathematics percentile score on the Stanford Achievement Test-version 10 (SAT-10), a normed-referenced test, was 56 percentile, she had done well (As and Bs) in previous mathematics classes. Keisha was placed in pre-algebra in the eighth grade, and Algebra A in her ninth grade year. If Keisha had proceeded on this track, she would have taken Algebra B in tenth grade, Geometry A in eleventh and Geometry B in twelfth, effectively giving her 2 years of mathematics instead of 4. During her ninth-grade year, Keisha was fortunate to have an algebra teacher who recognized Keisha's talent for hard work and determination. This teacher encouraged Keisha to take a second math course the same year so that she could proceed to advanced algebra/trigonometry class by the end of twelfth grade. When asked about how to help other students be more successful, Keisha stated "at the middle school make them (all students) take algebra and pre-algebra in the seventh grade."

A year after the original study, Keisha stated that she was the only African American girl in her group of friends to move on to Algebra II in the eleventh grade. In this particular school, the higher the level of mathematics, the fewer African American students, compared to white students, were in the class.

Keisha was the type of student who was easy to teach because she was determined to do well to ensure her success in college. Keisha knew that she could be successful, but did not see herself as the best math student, "I ain't gonna say I'm the best math student, but I know I'm not the worst." It was evident that Keisha wanted to be successful, not only from what she said, but by her actions. Keisha studied, did her homework, asked questions, and sought help when she needed it. Because of Keisha's determination, she was an "easy" student to teach.

Although Keisha, Josh, and Tony were in the same geometry class for tenth grade, their reactions to geometry and attentiveness to the teacher differed greatly. Keisha relied on the teacher to explain geometry to her, as she did not think she could understand the book without someone to translate the material for her. The teacher began the class period with a prepared overhead of the solutions to all the homework problems displayed. A 10-minute timer was set, and students had the opportunity to ask questions about the problems they missed or did not understand. Keisha was one of a handful of students who always had a question about homework for the teacher. Josh never asked questions and, as stated later, by midsemester, Tony no longer asked questions.

After the 10-minute question session ended, the students took a two to four question quiz covering the homework. Keisha's response to this testing procedure was the following: "The homework quiz . . . is a good thing, but if you don't get it (the first time), then there goes your grade." Keisha preferred the way a previous teacher did. "Do like Mrs. XXX and give a grade if you try it (homework), and then learn how to do it . . . go over it slowly."

Mrs. Smith attended a professional development institute centered on NCTM's Standards (1989, 1991, 1995, 2000) reform-based mathematics teaching during the summer prior to the year Keisha was in her class. This professional development was 2 full weeks and emphasized the value of cooperative group work with appropriate tasks. Occasionally during the school term in the geometry class, groups were assigned problems from the book. Some of the students talked to their group members while others, like Josh, continued to work alone as they sat in groups. The positive benefit of cooperative group work did not seem to be realized in the class for Keisha nor for Josh or Tony. (Tony could not contribute to his group as he did not know anything about what they were required to do.) Keisha recognized that it was helpful to her to talk to others about the problems they were assigned. Keisha expressed that she would like to be able to work with her friends. Keisha also knew that two of her friends in the class were very good in mathematics and could say things in a different way from her teacher, as she stated her friends could "break it down differently."

Keisha said she liked some of the mathematics classes she had taken, but none of her friends liked math, probably because her friends did not understand math. The reasons most commonly given by Keisha and her friends for studying mathematics was to progress to the next level, to get accepted into college, and possibly to use mathematics in a career. Keisha liked algebra and believed that she might need it in her career. We note that a challenging and relevant curriculum has been linked to mathematics achievement for students (Gutiérrez, 2000; Lee & Smith, 1993, 1995a, 1995b; Lee, Smith, & Croninger, 1997; Schoenfeld, 2002). Further, the degree of understanding that a student has is directly related to the number of connections the student can make with her own knowledge and personal experiences (Heibert & Carpenter, 1992). However, by the end of her geometry semester, Keisha was convinced that she did not need geometry, as it was not relevant to her chosen field of study. Keisha's conclusion was based on the instruction that she had received, which was disconnected from authentic real-world problems and from the lives of the students. In our view, Keisha's opportunity-to-learn mathematics, as advocated by NCTM (1989, 1991, 1995, 2000) and Tate (1995 2005), was not realized.

Keisha was on the flag/dance team during football season and on the girls' basketball team for the remainder of the school year. While not one of the school's star athletes, Keisha enjoyed the activities and stayed busy outside of class. Keisha recognized the difficulty of staying abreast of her academic work with the time spent out of the classroom and away from her studies.

> I did miss a lot of school, but I don't think it had nothing to do with it, because I made up all my work. But I do know one thing, I'm telling the counselors,

next time I have math, I don't want it during basketball season. Cuz like at the first of the beginning of the season I have football, but that's like every Friday, and then I go back. But I don't want math during basketball season.

While there are some students who do not need to be present in class to be successful, there are many more who suffer from missing class and attempting to teach themselves. It is interesting to note here that Keisha told her counselor not to enroll her in mathematics during football season.

Keisha's family was supportive, and her mother was actually in school during the time of the study. Keisha's mother was enrolled at the local community college taking classes to get a nursing degree. Keisha spoke often of her mother's and of her grandmother's support and encouragement for Keisha to get a college degree, even though her grandmother had not been to college herself. Keisha stated, "I do the best I can, cuz I just expect it out of me for myself." Not all students have support from family, as Keisha put it, "Cuz, their parents don't care or either they don't want to be nothing in life . . . They don't care . . . If your mama don't care what you do why should you?" Keisha wanted to be successful in school, to graduate, and to attend and be successful in college. Perry (2003) stated that African Americans have a strong and powerful academic tradition of freedom for literacy, and literacy for freedom, racial uplift, citizenship, and leadership. Keisha and her family displayed this determination to attain education for advancing their opportunities.

Again Keisha was a motivated student who knew what she needed. Moreover, Mrs. Smith did not meet her needs. She did not help Keisha to make connections between the mathematics that she was learning and her career goals, nor did she provide a learning environment that inspired Keisha to want to learn more.

Tony: Missed Opportunities

Tony was a good student with standardized test scores indicating that he was capable of doing exceptional work. Tony scored at the 86-percentile level in mathematics on the Stanford Achievement Test-version 10 (SAT-10) in the eighth grade and he passed the mathematics portion of the State High School Graduation Exam in tenth grade. Tony enjoyed mathematics and wanted to take college preparatory classes so that he could attend and succeed in college. From kindergarten through ninth grade, Tony made above average grades in all subjects. In tenth grade, Tony was placed in geometry. His placement in geometry could have led to his taking Algebra II in eleventh grade and then pre-calculus with trigonometry in twelfth grade. Tony was on track to complete high school and be academically prepared to succeed in college.

In addition to having above average grades all through his school career, Tony had an above average number of absences. During his first year in public school, according to his school records, Tony was absent for 46 days. This pattern of absences continued every year. Acknowledging that he was not in class every day, Tony stated that he missed school frequently, either sick with allergies or injured from playing sports. Tony was an athlete and, during a single school year, he might be a member of the football, basketball, and baseball teams. When the teams had games out of town, Tony missed school.

Even though the school system had a policy of limiting the number of yearly absences allowed for a student to be eligible to be promoted to the next grade level, there were exceptions as to what constituted an absence. When a parent checked a student out of school at noon, the student was not counted absent. Or, if the student was attending a school function or played on one of the sports teams, the time missed from school was not counted as being absent. Tony played on at least one sports team and sometimes on three every year from middle through high school.

Tony had several siblings, and it appeared that Tony's parents required Tony to help with the other children. Tony's mother often came to the school to check Tony out to go home shortly after lunch, which according to the school was not an official absence. Whereas the verbal evidence from Tony's parents indicated strong support for Perry's (2003) argument that African Americans have a strong and powerful academic tradition, the actions of Tony's parents showed that they either did not know how to support Tony in academic endeavors or did not choose to make sure that he did not miss important learning opportunities. Although he was one of the school's star athletes, we wonder who was looking out for Tony's interests and making sure that he was getting the *academic* training he would need to be successful?

Geometry class was in the afternoon, and missing class meant Tony did not have the opportunity to understand the assignments nor what material was covered in class. At the beginning of the semester, Tony asked questions about the homework, and his questions indicated he understood much of the material but, as the semester progressed, his behavior changed. Tony asked fewer questions; and near the end of the term, he was often off-task with his head down or working on something other than geometry. As the course progressed, Tony fell further and further behind. Tony did not seek help or ask questions in class, but he did acknowledge that he could have done the work and kept up with class if he had been in school more.

Tony's teacher recognized that Tony was missing many classes, but did not know why he was out of class other than for the sports games and practices. Tony's teacher had nearly 90 students and did not seek an answer as to why he missed school so often. Tony finished the term with a D in geometry, which meant he was recommended to a transitional class instead of Algebra II. Tony could not take Algebra II until his final year in high school.

Through the lens of critical race theory, Singer (2005) explored the impact of racism on college athletes and concluded that African American student-athletes are exploited for their athletic prowess to the detriment of other areas of development and training such as academic pursuits. The situation for Tony was similar. As an athlete who appeared to be talented and useful to the team and school, he was not supported academically. Singer (2005) referred to this as an academic exploitation, where the victims are more often African American than white. At Tony's school, the majority of the football team was African American and the majority of the calculus class was white.

Conclusion

We presented Josh's, Keisha's, and Tony's stories. While the reasons for their success and failure varied, there were some common themes among the students. The geometry course in which the three students were enrolled was teacher-centered: student discourse was rarely heard, investigations, inquiries, or justifications were not present, and connections were not made to the students' everyday lives. Rethinking Schools (2000) provided eight principles for reforming school, and one of them stated that the "curriculum must be geared toward learning for life and the needs of a multicultural democracy." (p. 2). The principle contained several tenets:

1 Curriculum must be based on respect for students, their innate curiosity, and their capacity to learn. It should be hopeful, joyful, kind, visionary, so students are made to feel significant and cared about—by the teacher and by each other.
2 A curriculum geared toward life is rooted in children's needs and experiences. It expects students to pose critical questions and to "talk back" to the world.
3 A democratic curriculum must be rooted in social justice, and be explicitly multicultural and anti-racist. Teachers must admit they don't "know it all" and have much to learn from their students and their students' families.
4 At the same time, the curriculum must be academically rigorous and teachers must set high expectations for all children. A democratic curriculum not only equips children to change the world but also to maneuver in the one that exists. (p. 2)

Although the State Course of Study was NCTM Standards-based (1989, 1991, 1995, 2000), Mrs. Smith chose to use the traditional textbook from cover to cover and did not integrate her students' culture nor recognize the world in which they live. Mrs. Smith did not investigate why students were not succeeding in her class, why they had numerous absences, or how she could better help the students to understand the concepts. Even though she had participated in a 2-week summer institute focusing on standards-based, reform-oriented mathematics teaching, the teacher had not adopted the strategies as her own. Of the three students, Keisha was the only student who complained about her teaching style; Josh taught himself, and Tony did not see a way to succeed.

The most successful students in this study, Josh and Keisha had parents who had attended college or were attending college. Furthermore, while all of the parents verbally supported their children in school and encouraged them to do their best, the evidence supported Useem's (1992) finding that the higher educated parents were more knowledgeable about their child's mathematics placement. Josh and Keisha experienced problems accessing algebra at the eighth-grade level. This is alarming, based on the findings of Horn, Nunez, and Bobbitt (2000) that indicated, if students took algebra in the eighth grade, they were more likely to complete advanced courses in high school regardless of parents' level of education. Another finding reported by Horn, Nunez, and Bobbitt (2000) was that students who completed mathematics beyond Algebra II substantially increased their chances of enrolling in a 4-year college. Tony's opportunity to enroll in a 4-year college may have decreased when he received a "D" in geometry and had to be placed in algebraic connections.

Both Tony's and Keisha's performance in the geometry class could have been affected by sports; but Keisha became aware of how much time participating in sports took away from her studies and asked the counselor not to place her in a mathematics class during basketball season. On the other hand, Tony played sports year-round and missed geometry too many times to understand what was going on in the class. He ended up getting a "D" in the class. Neither Tony, the school's personnel, nor Tony's parents curtailed his participation when his performance dropped in his class. Critical race theory is also helpful in understanding Tony's academic and sports conflict. He was providing a service to the school, but the school personnel did not insure that he was getting the education that he needed.

The students did not state that they were experiencing racist practices. However, there appeared to be a pattern of counseling African American students into pre-algebra in the eighth grade, which lessened their chances of taking all of the upper-level mathematics courses offered at the school. Also, the teacher did not teach the intended curriculum which further impacted the students' opportunity to learn.

Notes

1 All names are pseudonyms.

References

Alabama State Department of Education (2003). *Alabama Course of Study: Mathematics* Montgomey, AL: author.

Alabama State Department of Education (2004). *Accountability.* Retrieved July 15, 2005, from http://www.alsde.edu/Accountability/Accountability.asp

Au, W., Bigelow, B., Burant, T., Christensen, L., Salas, K.D., Levine, D., Miller, L., Peterson, B., Swope, K., Tenorio, R., & Walters, S. (2000). A vision of school reform. *Rethinking School, 14*(4). Retrieved June 20, 2008, from http://www.rethinkingschools.org/archive/14_04/vis144.shtml.

Bartlett, L. & Brayboy, B.M. J. (2005). Race and schooling: Theories and ethnographies. *The Urban Review, 37*(5), 361–374.

Bransford, J.D., Brown, A.L., & Cocking, R.R. (Eds.). (1999). *How people learn: Brain, mind, experience, and school.* Washington, DC: National Academy Press.

Brantlinger, E. (2001). Poverty, class, and disability: A historical, social, and political perspective. *Focus on Exceptional Children, 33*(7), 1–19.

Chunn, E.W. (1988). "Sorting Black students for success and failure: The inequality of ability grouping and tracking." *Urban League Review 11*(1–2), 93–106.

Dixson, A.D. & Rousseau, C.K. (2005). And we are still not saved: Critical race theory in education ten years later. *Race, Ethnicity, and Education, 8*(1), 7–27.

Gutiérrez, R. (2000). Advancing African-American, urban youth in mathematics: Unpacking the success of one math department. *American Journal of Education, 109*, 63–111.

Haberman, M. (1992). The pedagogy of poverty vs. good teaching. *Education Digest, 58*(1), 16–20.

Heibert, J. & Carpenter, T.P. (1992). Learning and teaching with understanding. In D.A.

Grouws (Ed.), *Handbook of research on mathematics teaching and learning* (pp. 65–97). New York: Macmillan.

Horn, L., Nunez, A.M., & Bobbitt, L. (2000). Mapping the road to college: First-generation students' math track, planning strategies, and context of support, NCES 200–153. Washington, DC: U.S. Department of Education & National Center for Educational Statistics.

Ladson-Billings, G. (1999). Just what is critical race theory and what's it doing in a nice field like education? In L. Parker, Deyhle, D., & Villenas, S. (Ed.), *Race is . . . race isn't; Critical race theory and qualitative studies in education* (pp. 7–30). Boulder, CO: Westview Press.

Ladson-Billings, G. (2003). Racialized discourses and ethnic epistemologies. In N.K. Denzin & Y.S. Lincoln (Eds.), *The landscape of qualitative research* (2nd ed. pp. 398–432). Thousand Oaks, CA: SAGE Publications.

Ladson-Billings, G. & Tate, W.F., IV. (1995). Toward a critical race theory of education. *Teachers College Record, 97*(1), 47–68

Lee, V.E. & Smith, J.B. (1993). Effects of school restructuring on achievement and engagement of middle-grade students. *Sociology of Education, 66*(3), 164–187.

Lee, V.E. & Smith, J.B. (1995). Effects of high school restructuring and size on early gains in achievement and engagement. *Sociology of Education, 68*(4), 241–270.

Lee, V.E., Smith, J.B., & Croninger, R. (1997). How high school organization influences the equitable distribution of learning in mathematics and science. *Sociology of Education, 70*(2), 128–150.

National Council of Teachers of Mathematics (NCTM). (1989). *Curriculum and evaluation standards for school mathematics*. Reston, VA: Author.

National Council of Teachers of Mathematics (NCTM). (1991). *Professional standards for teaching mathematics*. Reston, VA: Author.

National Council of Teachers of Mathematics (NCTM). (1995). *Assessment standards for school mathematics*. Reston, VA: Author.

National Council of Teachers of Mathematics. (2000). *Principles and standards for school mathematics*. Reston, VA: Author.

Perry, T. (2003). Up from the parched earth: Toward a theory of African-American achievement. In T. Perry, C. Steele & A.G. Hilliard III (Eds.), *Young, gifted, and black* (pp. 1–108). Boston: Beacon Press.

Schoenfeld, A.H. (2002). Making mathematics work for all children: Issues of standards, testing, and equity. *Educational Researcher, 31*(1), 13–25.

Senk, S. & Thompson, D. (Eds.). (2003). *Standards-oriented school mathematics curricula: What does research say about student outcomes?* Mahwah, NJ: Lawrence Erlbaum Associates, Inc.

Singer, J.N. (2005). Understanding racism through the eyes of African American male student-athletes. *Race Ethnicity and Education, 8*(4), 365–386.

Solórzano, D. & Yosso, T. (2002). Critical race methodology: counter-storytelling as an analytical framework. *Qualitative Inquiry, 8*(1), 23–44.

Strutchens, M.E. (1993). A*n exploratory study of the societal and ethnic factors affecting sixth grade African American students' performance in mathematics class*. Unpublished doctoral dissertation, University of Georgia. Athens, GA.

Tate, W.F. (1995). School mathematics and African American students: Thinking seriously about Opportunity to Learn standards. *Educational Administration Quarterly, 31*(3), 424–448.

Tate, W.F. (2005). Ethics, engineering and the challenge of racial reform in education. *Race, Ethnicity and Education, 8*(1), 121–127.

Useem, E. (1992). Middle schools and mathematics groups: Parent's involvement in children's placement. *Sociology of Education, 65*(4), 263–279.

U.S. Census Bureau. (2003). *American community survey: 2003 ranking tables.* Retrieved May 15, 2005, from http://www.census.gov/acs/www/Products/Rankings/index.htm

Wells, A.S. & Oakes, J. (1996). Potential pitfalls of systemic reform: Early lessons from research on detracking. *Sociology of Education* (Extra Issue), 135–143.

Weiler, K. (1988). *Women teaching for change: Gender, class and power. Critical studies in education.* New York: Bergin & Garvey.

Westbrook, S.K. (2005). *An exploratory study of the factors associated with the mathematics achievement of six tenth grade African American students.* Unpublished doctoral dissertation, Auburn University. Auburn, AL.

11 Negotiating Sociocultural Discourses: The Counter-Storytelling of Academically and Mathematically Successful African American Male Students[1]

David W. Stinson

Introduction

In the past decade or so, there has been a growing number of scholars who have extended the focus of mathematics education research into the sociocultural and sociohistorical arenas to more fully understand the mathematics schooling *experiences* of students (see, e.g., Atweh, Forgasz, & Nebres, 2001; Boaler, 2000; Burton, 2003; Martin, 2007; Nasir & Cobb, 2007; Powell & Frankenstein, 1997; Secada, Fennema, & Adajian, 1995; Walshaw, 2004). Lerman (2000) coined this extension the "*social turn* in mathematics education research" (p. 23). Yet, in making the social turn, he cautioned that the greatest challenge for mathematics education researchers will be to "develop accounts that bring together agency, individual trajectories (Apple, 1991), and the cultural, historical, and social origins of the ways people think, behave, reason, and understand the world" (p. 36).

The study reported in this chapter, derived from my dissertation (Stinson, 2004), is a broad examination of mathematics achievement that brings together agency and the sociocultural and sociohistorical ways that people think, behave, reason, and understand the world by examining the construction (but not determination) of four academically and mathematically successful African American[2] male students. In particular, the study examines the influence of sociocultural and sociohistorical discourses on the agency of four African American men in their early 20s who had demonstrated achievement and persistence in school mathematics (K-12). The term *discourses* includes language and institutions, as well as complex signs and practices that order and sustain sociocultural and sociohistorical constructed forms of social existence: forms that work to either confirm or deny the life histories and experiences of the people who use them (Leistyna, Woodrum, & Sherblom, 1996). In short, capital "D" *Discourses* are innumerable and "are always language plus other 'stuff'" (Gee, 1999, p. 17; see also Foucault 1969/1972)[3]. In the context of the study, *agency* is broadly defined as the participants' ability to accommodate, reconfigure, or resist the available sociocultural discourses that surround male African Americans. In other words, agency extends beyond their mathematical agency (see Gutstein, 2006, 2007 for a discussion on students' mathematical agency). Moreover, the intended meaning of the term *negotiate* is its more robust definition: "to deal with (some matter or affair that requires the ability for its successful handling)" (i.e., to accommodate); "to arrange for, or bring about, through conference, discussion, and compromise" (i.e., to reconfigure); or "to successfully travel along or over" (i.e., to navigate, or in this context to resist) (*Merriam-Webster's Collegiate Dictionary*, 1999). Or said more directly, there are three ways to negotiate: by "sucking it up," by compromising, or by refusing to yield.

Although the study began as an exploration of the participants' achievement and persistence in school mathematics, it quickly expanded beyond their experiences with mathematics and into an exploration of *how* particular sociocultural discourses affected their agency as they negotiated those discourses in their pursuit of mathematics success, and academic success in general. In other words, the participants' achievement and persistence in school mathematics were just two components in their larger efforts toward academic success. Therefore, while the study began with a zoomed-in analytical lens on the participants' experiences with mathematics, I promptly refocused the lens, as suggested by Lerman (2001), zooming out so that I might address the practices and meanings (i.e., methods of negotiation) within which my African American male participants became school-mathematical actors (Lerman, 2001).[4]

This study grew out of my 5-year experience as a White mathematics teacher in a Black high school. This experience afforded me the opportunity to be exposed to many African American male (and female) students who excelled in school mathematics. Through this exposure, I became puzzled by the scarcity of education literature, and societal discourses in general, that focused on African American students who achieve and persist in mathematics, concomitant with the abundance of literature (and discourses) that has focused on African American students who appear to reject mathematics, and schooling in general. In other words, where were the success stories of African American students? In particular, where were the success stories of African American male students? It just didn't add up (Ladson-Billings, 1997).

Given that at the core of male African Americans' experiences in school and society is persistence and triumph (Polite & Davis, 1999), my desire to understand how my African American male students, in particular, might have incorporated a positive *mathematics identity* (Martin, 2000) within their larger efforts toward success led to a broader examination of their schooling experiences. Through this broad examination, I wanted to determine how my African American male students defined success and to what sociocultural factors they attributed their success. Specifically, seeing that they were achieving in ways that were counter to the literature and prevailing societal discourses, I wanted to understand how sociocultural discourses about African American males shaped their perceptions of themselves as mathematics learners and as African American students, and how they negotiated such discourses.

Exposing Complexities

Martin (2000), in his study examining mathematics success and failure among African American youth, developed a multilevel framework for analyzing *mathematics socialization* and *mathematics identity* among African American students. Martin's study included an analysis of sociohistorical context, community and school forces, and individual agency. His analysis of sociohistorical context included an examination of the social and historical policies and practices of racism and discrimination (i.e., White supremacy) that prevent "African-Americans from becoming equal participants in mathematics and other areas of society" (p. 29). His analysis of community and school forces included an examination of how African American students' beliefs about mathematics and about African Americans as learners of mathematics are influenced by the beliefs and expectations held by community members and school personnel. And his analysis of individual agency included an examination of mathematically successful African American students as they responded to community and school forces.

After his initial analysis of 35 mathematically successful seventh-, eighth-, and ninth-grade African American students, Martin (2000) claimed, "Students are capable of recognizing and responding to . . . [community and school] forces in ways that help them resist the negative forces and to take advantage of the positive forces that they encounter" (p. 185). He suggested that a further analysis of mathematically successful African American students could provide insight into how students negotiated community and school forces and "how these forces can serve as barriers or springboards to success" (p. 125). Taking note of Martin's suggestion, I argue that a study that aims at exposing the complexities of how successful African American male students resist, oppose, or even reconfigure negative sociocultural forces as they embrace those forces that are positive requires a "somewhat eclectic" (Sfard, 2003, p. 354) theoretical approach.

The eclectic theoretical framework of the study reported in this chapter draws on tenets from poststructural theory (see, e.g., St. Pierre, 2000), critical race theory (CRT; see, e.g., Tate, 1997), and critical (postmodern) theory (see, e.g., Kincheloe & McLaren, 1994, 2000). While borrowing tenets from these theoretical frameworks, I do not intend to suggest that these frameworks share the same philosophical foundations; I understand that the ontological, epistemological, and ethical considerations of these frameworks are different (Paul & Marfo, 2001). For the purpose of this study, however, I followed Sfard's (2003) suggestion and viewed these differences as complementary and/or incommensurable.

In short, I characterize the eclectic theoretical framework employed in this study as a critical postmodern[5] framework, which places concepts from critical theory, such as empowerment, class struggle, asymmetrical relations of power, praxis, and so forth, under critique, while providing postmodern theory a foundation that precludes it from being perceived as nihilistic or inactive (Kincheloe & McLaren, 1994). Or, as Lather (1991, 2007) suggested, postmodern theory helps us to "get smart" about the limits and possibilities of critical theory. I next provide a synopsis of each of the theoretical frameworks, stating explicitly what each framework contributed to the study; more specific details of theoretical concepts borrowed from the frameworks are discussed, in turn, as I present the study's findings.

Poststructural Theory

Poststructural theory adopts an anti- or post-epistemological standpoint, and is fiercely anti-foundationalist and anti-realist (Peters & Burbules, 2004). In part, poststructural theory provides theoretical critiques and language that redefines terms, such as *person* and *agency*, among many others (St. Pierre, 2000). For instance, the poststructural critique redefines the person as a discursively consti-tuted subject (cf. Foucault, 1969/1972), rather than as an individual. The term *indi-vidual* implies that there is an "independent and rational being who is predisposed to be motivated toward social agency and emancipation—what Descartes believed to be the existence of a unified self" (Leistyna, Woodrum, & Sherblom, 1996, p. 341). Poststructural theory rejects this notion of an essential, unified self who is always present, because it minimizes the force of sociocultural discourses on the person. Effectively, the subject of poststructural theory is subjugated—but not determined—by the sociocultural discourses that constitute the person (Butler, 1990/1999).

Although it might appear that the discursively constituted subject lacks the abil-ity to act, the subject of poststructural theory does possess agency, albeit a re-theo-rized agency (St. Pierre, 2000). This re-theorized agency of the subject produces at once a restricting effect on the production of knowledge and actions, and an enabling effect on the production of different (and at times subversive) kinds of knowledge and actions (Butler, 1990/1999). Agency, therefore, within the post-structural frame, is "up for grabs, continually reconfigured and renamed as is the subject itself . . . [and] seems to lie in the subject's ability to decode and recode its identity within discursive formations and cultural practices" (St. Pierre, 2000, p. 504). In short, this redefining of agency enables a different logic "in which struc-ture and agency are not either-or but both-and and, simultaneously, neither-nor" (Lather, 1991, p. 154).

The redefining of the subject and agency was a significant theoretical shift bor-rowed from poststructural theory throughout the study. By using this shift, I began with the acknowledgement of research participants—characterized as discursive subjects, not as individuals—who negotiated (consciously or not) sociocultural discourses regarding male African Americans.

Critical Race Theory

CRT begins with the notion that racism is "normal, not aberrant, in American soci-ety," resulting in its appearing both normal and natural to people in U.S. culture (Delgado, cited in Ladson-Billings, 1998, p. 11). Theoretically, CRT provides a dif-ferent theoretical analysis of how the discourses of race and racism operate within U.S. social structures, an analysis that keeps race in the foreground. Moreover, because CRT borrows theories and methodologies from liberalism, law and society, feminism, Marxism, and poststructuralism (Tate, 1997), it acts as a bridge in this study between the often dichotomized theories of poststructural theory and critical theory (cf. Hill, McLaren, Cole, & Rikowski, 2002).

CRT asserts that race is a permanent and endemic component of U.S. society and culture (Ladson-Billings, 1998). Bell (1992) wrote: "Black people will never gain full equality in this country. . . . This is a hard-to-accept fact that all history verifies. We must acknowledge it, not as a sign of submission, but as an act of ultimate defi-ance" (p. 12). Equally as important, CRT allows and finds value in the storytelling of the individual experience. Specifically, CRT values "counterstories," stories of "raced" people whose experiences are often not told; stories that expose, analyze, and challenge the majoritarian stories of racial privilege (Solórzano & Yosso, 2002). CRT also maintains a critique on liberalism and argues for radical solutions, and claims that Whites have been the primary beneficiaries of civil rights legislation (Ladson-Billings, 1998). There are no common or agreed-on doctrines or methodologies of CRT; however, CRT scholars are united in two common goals: to understand the construction and perpetuation of the privileged White ideology of the United States and to radically disrupt the bond between law and racial power (Ladson-Billings, 1998).

The analytical process of foregrounding race as a permanent and endemic component of U.S. society and culture, borrowed from CRT, amends the ethical obligation of examining the numerous negative consequences of slavery, segregation, racism, and discrimination (i.e., White supremacy) on the schooling experiences of the study's African American participants. The study was not about the continued real consequences of such injustices on the schooling experiences of African American students (cf. Kozol, 1992), but about how my participants, as revealed through their counterstories of success, demonstrated that they could accommodate, reconfigure, or resist such injustices as an act of ultimate defiance in their pursuit of success.

Critical Theory

Critical theory, in the most general sense, maintains sociopolitical critiques on social practices and ideology that mask systematically distorted accounts of reality that attempt to conceal and legitimate asymmetrical power relations (Bottomore, 1991). Included in these critiques is an examination of how social interests, conflicts, and contradictions are expressed in thought and produced and reproduced in systems of domination (Bottomore, 1991).

Freire (1970/2000b), a contemporary critical theorist, popularized the concept of *conscientização* (critical consciousness)—"learning to perceive social, political, and economic contradictions, and to take action against the oppressive elements of reality" (p. 35)—which provides a methodology for this study. The goal of Freirian research is to blur the distinctions between research, learning, and action by providing the researcher and the participants opportunities to collectively engage in the struggle toward social justice (Lather, 1986, 1991). This methodology encourages reciprocity, turning participants into coresearchers while providing the means for researcher's and participants' *self*-empowerment (Lather, 1986, 1991).

Building from a foundation of critical theory, the study began as a "joint search" (Freire, 1969/2000a, p. 45) between me (the researcher) and the participants as we attempted to trouble the discourse of the "achievement gap"[6] problem between Black students and their White counterparts by telling the "other side of the story." This attempt aimed to self-empower me and the participants with deeper understandings of their successes in hopes of motivating *conscientização*. I was engaged in this joint search because I have an allegiance to equity and social justice in U.S. public schools, specifically in the mathematics classroom.

Researching *With*

Because I recognized the study's participants as self-empowered, discursively constituted subjects who negotiated the consequences of White supremacy in their pursuit of success, the study began, methodologically, with the goal of doing research *with* rather than *on* the study's participants. Participative inquiry, which recognizes both researcher and participants as active subjects, aligned with this goal and the eclectic theoretical framework. This form of inquiry emphasizes the systematic testing of theory in live-action contexts, resulting in changed lived experiences for all those engaged in the inquiry; the fundamental importance of experiential knowing, acknowledging that people can learn to be, and learn from being, self-reflexive about their world and their lived experiences; and an extended epistemology, suggesting that experiential knowing arises through engagement with others (Reason, 1994).

Participant selection for the study was conducted through a purposive sampling (Silverman, 2000) of five African American men between 20 and 25 years of age. The criteria for sampling included having attended Keeling High School[7] (a pseudonym, as are all proper names throughout) from their ninth to twelfth grade, having completed at least one mathematics course with me (I taught at Keeling High through the 1995–1996 to 1999–2000 academic years), and having demonstrated achievement and persistence in high school mathematics.[8] I invited 16 of my past African American male students (out of approximately 90 who were eligible) by electronic and U.S. postal mail to participate in the study. Six of the 16 students contacted responded to my inquiry, five agreed to participate, and four completed the study: Ethan, Keegan, Nathaniel, and Spencer. At the time of the study, these four young men were either completing their undergraduate degree or in graduate school. Professionally, they were a teacher, and future preacher, doctor, and lawyer, respectively. (See Stinson, 2004, chapter 5 for a detailed description.)

Data collection included a combination of written artifacts and interviews. Each participant completed a demographic and schooling survey instrument,[9] wrote a brief autobiography and mathematics autobiography,[10] and completed four interviews. The first interview was an individual face-to-face, semistructured, traditional question-and-answer interview (Hollway & Jefferson, 2000) in which I attempted to obtain descriptions of the lived worlds of the participants with respect to their interpretations of the meaning of their schooling and mathematics experiences (Kvale, 1996). The fourth interview was also a face-to-face interview but used a narrative approach, asking the participants to summarize their schooling and mathematics experiences, which required me to be a good listener and the interviewees (i.e., the participants) to be storytellers rather than respondents (Hollway & Jefferson, 2000). The second and third interviews, like the first, were semistructured but conducted over the telephone. Prior to each of these interviews, the participants were asked to read, reflect on, and respond to three manuscripts (six manuscripts total[11]) that discussed specific theoretical perspectives regarding African American children's schooling experiences.

In making decisions about which theoretical perspectives to have the participants read, I attempted to expose them to literature that discussed the prevailing theoretical perspectives that, I believe, were present in their schooling experiences. The purpose of engaging the participants in reading the historical and current literature was not to have them confirm or disconfirm the applicability or usefulness of the various theoretical perspectives presented but to provide language for them to express their (and their friends') schooling and life experiences. In other words, it provided the participants and me with a common vocabulary for our conversations throughout the study. For instance, rather than me trying to interpret from the participants' interview responses whether they engaged in "cool pose" behaviors, the participants were able to explicitly speak about what they believed were cool pose behaviors and whether they had engaged in such behaviors. For all intents and purposes, the engagement with the literature acted as a catalyst, motivating deeper reflections about their schooling experiences. Developing deeper reflections and understandings of how one functions or operates within a sociocultural and sociohistorical context, by participants and researcher alike, is an important component of participative inquiry. In short, engaging the participants in the literature provided opportunities for the participants to tell their counterstories in response to these prevailing (and, I might add, often limiting) theoretical perspectives.

Weaving Theory

The following discussion is a focused critical postmodern theoretical analysis of the participants' data; it is not a presentation of their data. I do, however, provide some extracted direct quotations—representing "power in reserve" (Geertz, cited in Freeman, deMarrais, Preissle, Roulston, & St. Pierre, 2007, p. 28)—from the participants' data throughout the discussion to support the analysis. In other words, the extracted quotations are an attempt to represent a collective consciousness of the participants. In making such a data presentation decision, I do not intend to suggest that the participants spoke from a single monolithic "voice"—they were never monolithic—but to suggest that, for the current purposes of this study, the extracted quotations provided support to the theoretical analysis.

Counter-Storytelling of Success

The different voices of the participants were readily observed as they told their counter-stories of success. When explicitly asked, "How do you define societal success?" the participants' general responses were as helping others by effecting positive change (Ethan); as affecting people's lives by being a just testament (Keegan); as achieving what one desires by excelling past one's goals (Nathaniel); or simply, as living a happy life by caring for loved ones (Spencer). But no matter how the participants conceptualized success, implicitly or explicitly stated throughout their conversations was the undisputed need for education, whether it was to pass knowledge on or to ensure that one could financially care for loved ones. The valuing of or need for education, specifically formal education, was a common theme found throughout the participants' counter-storytelling as they discussed success.

Many external and internal sociocultural factors identified by the participants contributed to their valuing of education, which ultimately resulted in their success. The factors identified were extreme, ranging from the external force of God to the internal force of self-motivation, with the force of fear—fear of disappointing family and community members—somewhere in-between. When asked to describe what factors, events, organizations, or individuals led them to be successful in academics, and mathematics, there were four clear factors that resonated in the conversations of all four participants: (a) observing or knowing family or community members who had benefited from a formal education by achieving financial and societal success; (b) experiencing encouraging and forceful family and community members who made the expectations of academic and mathematics success explicit; (c) encountering caring and committed teachers and school personnel who established high academic expectations for students in general and developed relationships with students that reached beyond the school and academics; and (d) associating with high-achieving peer-group members who had similar goals and interests. These four factors have been previously reported as influential in the schooling success of minority students (see, e.g., Berry, 2005; Hébert & Reis, 1999; Martin, 2000; Moody, 2000; O'Connor, 1997; Walker, 2006).

Observing or knowing family or community members who had benefited from a formal education was instrumental to the participants' valuing of education. The life experiences of these individuals from their inner circle of family and community members provided the participants with proof that there was a "pay-off" to education and with determination that they too could succeed. Knowing and seeing other African Americans who had succeeded provided the participants with tangible evidence of the value of working toward academic success. Spencer, for example, mentioned how his mother completing her undergraduate degree had improved the family's financial situation. Nathaniel said, "I got a sense [from my parents] that learning was something important, it was something that . . . put food on our plate, and eventually led us to moving up in social standing."

Not only did these individuals from their inner circle provide the participants with tangible evidence of the value of a sound education, but they also made the expectations of success explicit. These explicit expectations of success loudly reverberated through each participant's counter-story. The participants were constantly surrounded by family and community members who were not "too shy to remind" (Keegan) them about the expectations of academic success, and success in general.

Expectations of success were established not only by family and community members, but also by teachers and school personnel. Within the context of schools, there was no other single factor identified throughout the participants' conversations that matched the impact[12] on success of the positive encounters with caring and committed educators who established high academic expectations and developed student relationships that went beyond the school and academics (see Ladson-Billings, 1994, for a discussion of caring and committed teachers and African American students). These educators were credited with giving "me that motivation to achieve" (Keegan) and "90% of my educational development" (Spencer), and compelling "them to want to learn" (Ethan) and "engaging [them] in other things . . . where you develop a trust" (Keegan).

Likewise, in the context of schools, associating with high-achieving peer-group members who had similar goals and interests provided the participants with interactive, academically supportive peer groups that positively impacted their success. The participants noted, "When I was in honors courses there were other [African Americans] who were interested in [academics]" (Keegan), and "when it came to academic success . . . at Keeling High we were pretty much competitive . . . [not] necessarily competitive against mainstream; we were competitive against each other" (Ethan). This academically competitive, high-achieving peer group provided daily, interactive reminders that being an academically successful student and an African American student were not contradictory identities.

Negotiating the "White Male Math Myth" Discourse

In their larger efforts for academic success, the participants had incorporated a positive mathematics identity (Martin, 2000), in effect, negotiating the "White male math myth" discourse. The participants' beliefs about their mathematics abilities, however, were as different as the participants themselves. For instance, they defined their mathematics abilities as something very natural, "like eating or talking" (Ethan); or as learning "ways of maneuvering through mathematics" (Keegan); or as "something I had to work at . . . I got better at it because I kept working at it" (Nathaniel; Spencer echoed this sentiment). The participants all held strong beliefs about the instrumental importance of mathematics, perceiving "mathematics as something that was very important and necessary for success" (Keegan). And either implicitly or explicitly, each participant remarked that mathematics was "the backbone of a lot of things" (Nathaniel), claiming that knowledge in mathematics helped one to "know a little more about what somebody else is saying" (Nathaniel).

The participants believed that their opportunities to learn mathematics were unbounded, given that they perceived the learning of mathematics "as the same whether you are Black, White, Asian, young or old . . . [something that] everyone can learn . . . because of its very nature" (Spencer).[13] Furthermore, because each of the participants perceived mathematics as "very important and necessary for success" (Keegan), they were motivated to "work harder because the [advanced] classes were harder" (Nathaniel), leading them to achieve advanced mathematics knowledge. How each participant acquired such an "uncharacteristic" mathematics identity (i.e., discussions about African American male students who embrace mathematics are rarely, if ever, located in sociocultural discourses or the research literature)—successfully negotiating the "White male math myth"—I argue is to be found in part in how he understood sociocultural discourses of U.S. society in general and how he negotiated the specific discourses that surround male African Americans.

Negotiating Sociocultural Discourses

Throughout the participants' counter-stories of success, it became apparent that the participants were keenly aware of the sociocultural discourses present in U.S. society and how they operated, and that most operated inequitably. Collectively, although the participants did not use the vocabulary of poststructural theory, CRT, or critical theory, they were clearly speaking the language of these theories as they provided their perspectives on the discourses of U.S. society and throughout their conversations in general. In the following discussion, I weave together various concepts from these three theoretical frameworks. The aim of the discussion is to illustrate how I used theory as a way to honor the data (St. Pierre, 1997). By using an eclectic array of concepts from these three frameworks side by side, the participants' counter-stories are analyzed not as stories of how they "overcame" unjust sociocultural discourses, but as stories of how successful African American male students accommodate, resist, or even reconfigure negative sociocultural discourses as they embrace those discourses that are positive.

Discourse of the Male African American

As noted previously, the study began, theoretically, with African American male students characterized as discursive subjects who negotiated (consciously or not) sociocultural discourses regarding male African Americans. This theoretical shift, borrowed from poststructural theory, characterizes the person not as an individual whose life experiences have formed the basis of her or his knowledge and actions, but rather as a discursive formation who can explain her or his experiences only through the discourses that are made available to her or him (Scott, 1992). Thus, it becomes the available discourses that form the basis of the subject's knowledge and actions rather than the life experiences in and of themselves.

Foucault (1969/1972) claimed that discourses are "practices that systematically form the objects of which they speak" (p. 49); consequently, "one remains within the dimension of discourse" (p. 76). He, however, and most important, joined power and knowledge through discourse, identifying discourse both as an "effect of power" and as providing "a point of resistance" (Foucault, 1976/1990, p. 101). This poststructural redefining of discourse allows for the understanding of "how knowledge, truth, and subjects are produced in language and cultural practice as well as how they might be reconfigured" (St. Pierre, 2000, p. 486).

The understanding that the image of the male African American had been constructed through discursive formations and cultural practices was evident in the striking similarities in the participants' conversations as they spoke about the *constructed* African American male adolescent. The image that was painted, in part, by all four participants was the jewelry-donned, baggy clothes, player "thug" who projected a nonchalant attitude toward school and academics. The discourse of the thug was so prominent that Keegan noted that even he had fallen prey to it when mentoring "troubling" young Black boys: "I'm even guilty of it . . . when [Black boys] are not performing as well, if they are acting bad and not really doing well in school . . . you say, 'Oh Lord, this going to be a thug . . . I can't help them.'"

Discourse of White and Black

Ethan's comment that "society has decided that we want White behaviors and Black behaviors" exemplifies the participants' understanding that cultural markers such as White and Black behaviors, or the thug, were mere constructions, preserved and perpetuated by institutions, such as the media. Understanding that what many take as "real" is only a construction, allows a discursively constituted subject the ability to decode and recode her or his identity. In fact, Keegan argued, "Stereotypes uplift me. When someone says, 'I'm not as smart as another culture' or 'I'm not as bright,'

I laugh that in their face . . . they are not talking about me." Butler (1990/1999) identified the subject's ability to decode and recode its identity in a rebellious manner (or not) as "subversive repetition" (p. 32). Subversive repetition, a concept borrowed from poststructural theory, conveys that even though the subject is subjected to repeating oneself through the available discourses, the discourses themselves are open to intervention and resignification. For instance, Keegan noted, "To be successful in society you don't have to get rid of your Blackness, but you can be successful by doing this, doing *a*, doing *b*, doing *c*." Although the participants subverted the negative discursive formation of the African American male, their collective counter-storytelling illustrates that the discourse had a negative impact on their pursuits of success, in that it was a discursive formation that required continuous negotiation.

Ethan's comment about "White and Black behaviors" also exemplifies the participants' understanding of sociocultural and sociohistorical binaries and how these binaries act to "name" marginalized subjects, a concept borrowed from critical theory. A marginalized subject can be identified as any person on the right side of binaries such as White–Black (or non-White), male–female, rich–poor, educated–non-educated, and so on. There is nothing "real" about these binary features, no biological or "scientific" explanation for which side of these binaries came to be privileged. But then again, these are very real features, in that they are culturally and historically situated and constructed features located within societal discourses that assist in dividing and differentiating subjects, often leading to unjust social practices.[14] Clearly subjects live at intersections of these binaries; therefore, which binary feature is most significant to a person at any given moment depends on the context in which the person is located.

Poststructural theory provides a means for de-constructing these binary oppositions through Derrida's (1974/1997) deconstruction of language and cultural practices. The deconstruction of binaries identifies the first term, that is, the "privileged" term, as being dependent on its identity by the exclusion of the other term, demonstrating that, in reality, primacy belongs to the second term, that is, the subordinate term (Sarup, 1993). The first move in deconstruction, then, is to overthrow the privileged term with the other term, displacing this term—now the first term—by putting it under erasure,[15] revealing what was always already present (Spivak, 1974/1997). Keegan demonstrated an understanding of deconstruction, stating, "I could be Black and successful . . . just because I am wearing a suit, or I don't have an earring in my ear, or . . . a tattoo, does not mean that I am trying to appear White." Keegan's comment is an acknowledgement that the world has been constructed through language and cultural practices; consequently, it can be deconstructed and reconstructed again and again (St. Pierre, 2000).

Earlier, when I stated that different binary features lead to injustices, I did not intend to suggest that the injustices that different marginalized subjects experience are equivalent; I understand that they are different. There is, however, a commonality in these binary identity labels, in that marginalized racial, ethnic, and cultural groups are often oppressed within sociocultural discourses that have been designed and maintained by people who recognize only "one universal subject of history—the white, Anglo, heterosexual male of bourgeois privilege" (McLaren, cited in

Torres, 1998, p. 178). The maintenance of this universally acclaimed subject results in hegemony, a concept borrowed from critical theory.

Hegemony is the manner in which imposed ideology warrants the reproduction of social and institutional practices and discourses that enable dominant groups to not only maintain their positions of power and privilege but also have consensual support from the "Others" (Leistyna et al., 1996). For instance, Ethan's statement exemplifies hegemonic discourses: "You must instill into your child, or to yourself, the values of the middle-class, upper-class White values, because that is the only way you are going to survive." Keegan, on the other hand, equated adhering to hegemonic discourses as playing a game: "Sometimes, I believe to be successful you have to play the game. I don't want to call it a game, but you have to know what you are doing."

The participants' understanding of how to work within and against hegemonic discourses illustrates a "double-consciousness"[16] (Du Bois, 1903/1989, p. 3), a concept I position within CRT. As Nathaniel said, "Being a Black male . . . going into a store with your book bag, your sort of want to ease people's fears, . . . so . . . you may say, 'Can I put my bag over here?'" Double-consciousness allows those that have been marginalized to see and understand positions of inclusion and exclusion—margins and mainstreams—and applies not only to African Americans but also to any people who are constructed outside of the dominant discourses (Ladson-Billings, 2000).

Critical theorists, in general, contend that an examination of hegemonic systems of domination brings about an awakening of consciousness and awareness of social injustices, motivating self-empowerment and social transformation (see, e.g., Freire, 1970/2000b). Spencer demonstrated his self-empowerment as he spoke about being in a classroom where he is one of a few (if not the only) African American male students: "I make sure that I raise my hand to answer the questions early . . . I try to prove my worth, show that I belong." Actions such as Spencer's were plentiful throughout the participants' counter-storytelling, illustrating that the participants were continuously working within, and against, the discursive image of the male African American. Coupled with their self-empowerment was a sense of social transformation, a belief that social change is possible by working within and against hegemonic discourses. Ethan argued, "We must make somebody uncomfortable at the top; we must not only make them uncomfortable, but we must educate them on why things must change."

The participants' desire to change current sociocultural discourses, such as the injustices of racism, however, never stood as an obstacle to their success. In other words, they understood the permanency of racial injustices, not as a sign of submission, but as an act of ultimate defiance. Nathaniel claimed that the dismantling of affirmative action would limit opportunities for African Americans, making it "a little bit harder for African Americans to do what their parents did . . . say a generation ago." Similarly, Ethan practically shrugged off racial injustices:

> So what can I say, it was tougher because a lot of the options and opportunities, facilities and things that Caucasians have, we don't have . . . but . . . as an African American male you have got to do what you need to do.

The participants' collective counter-storytelling around self-empowerment and social transformation, however, required a retheorizing of power in general. Poststructural theory provides such a retheorizing. Power in a poststructural frame is not an object that can be shared, deployed, or taken away, but is a dynamic and productive event that exists in *relations* (Foucault, 1976/1990). Foucault (1976/1990) claimed that power relations are dependent on a "multiplicity of points of resistance," arguing that "there is no single locus of great Refusal, no soul of revolt, source of all rebellions, or pure law of the revolutionary. . . . Instead there is a plurality of resistances, each of them a special case" (pp. 95–96). In other words, in a Foucauldian conceptualization of power, revolution—or refusal—can be achieved not only by the united actions of working men from all countries (Marx & Engels, 1848/1978), but also, and more important, by the solitary actions of the discursively constituted subject—even the solitary action of raising one's hand early on.

Discourses of Deficiency and Rejection

Not only did the participants negotiate the hegemonic discursively constituted image of the African American male adolescent but also various theoretical perspectives that I positioned in one of two categories: the discourse of deficiency or the discourse of rejection. (For a detailed discussion of these discourses, see Stinson, 2006.)

Discourse of Deficiency

The discourse of deficiency focuses on the perceived deficient cultural, schooling, and life experiences of Black children. Ogbu (1978a, see also Ogbu, 2003) provided a historical summary and critique of theoretical perspectives that attempted to explain the lower academic achievement of Black students, and specifically the Black–White achievement gap. I located these theories in the discourse of deficiency: The *cultural deprivation theory* claims that Black children come from home and neighborhood environments that are somehow culturally disadvantaged; the *culture conflict theory* claims that Black communities fail to equip Black children with the White, middle-class skills necessary for school success and that schools fail to fully utilize the unique experiences of Black children; the *institutional deficiency theory* claims that the very institution of school is organized to favor middle- and upper-class, non-minority children; the *educational equality theory* claims that the schooling opportunities and experiences for Black children are not equal; and the *heredity theory* claims that Black children have inferior genetic endowments for intellectual work.

The participants most often reconfigured the discourse of deficiency, arguing that these theories related to the socioeconomic status of the student or to a different era. Specifically, both the cultural deprivation theory and culture conflict theory were most often reconfigured as relating to the socioeconomic status of the student, not to the race or ethnicity of the student: "Because Keeling [High School] was made up of vast socioeconomic status . . . a lot of the mainstream cultural aspects were still there" (Ethan). Even when the cultural deprivation theory was acknowledged as being applicable, or was accommodated, a caveat was offered so as not to overplay the theory, or an argument was provided stating that the deprivation (or conflict) could be overcome: "I believe that [being in] a strong school environment . . . that some of those [cultural] things could be overcome" (Spencer). The institutional deficiency theory and educational equality theory were most often reconfigured as meaningful only in a different era: "With the state of our schools [today], we are definitely improving in the types of educational access that is available to people" (Spencer).

When accommodated, these theories were accompanied by an argument that one could succeed in spite of the deficiency or inequities through personal drive: "One of my best friends went to one of the worst public schools . . . but she had a personal drive about herself. She ended up going to Princeton . . . and now she is in graduate school at Stanford" (Keegan). And the heredity theory was clearly resisted as participants either provided anecdotes that refuted the theory or declarations of contempt for the theory: "I think that it is still sad that we are dealing with those . . . thoughts . . . that African Americans are inferior genetically, which I think is just stupid" (Keegan).

Discourse of Rejection

The discourse of rejection broadly focuses on the systematic rejection[17] of school and academics by African American students or on the systematic rejection of culture-specific "Black behaviors" by African American students. Both forms of rejection are argued to be coping strategies employed by African Americans in managing the negative effects of racism and discrimination. In particular, the participants responded to readings regarding five prevailing theories—three theories that explore the rejection of schooling and academics: Majors and Billson's *cool pose theory* (Majors et al., 1994; see also Majors & Billson, 1993), Steele's (1997) *stereotype threat theory* (see also Steele 1999, 2003), and Ogbu's (1992) *cultural-ecological theory* (see also Ogbu, 2003)—and two theories that explore the rejection of Black behaviors: Fordham's (1988) *raceless persona theory* (see also Fordham, 1996) and Fordham and Ogbu's (1986) *burden of "acting White" theory.*

Majors and Billson's (1993) cool pose theory suggests that some Black males develop ritualized forms of masculinity that allow them to cope and survive in an environment of oppression and racism. Specifically, cool pose "entails behaviors, scripts, physical posturing, impression management, and carefully crafted performances that deliver a single, critical message: pride, strength, and control" (p. 4); it is often manifested in culturally specific demeanors, gestures, stances, walks, handshakes, and so on, and through culturally specific clothing, hair, and other "fashion" styles. These ritualized forms are often perceived as being in opposition to school success. The discourse of cool pose was reconfigured by the participants as they developed strategies that allowed engagement in cool pose behaviors in social settings while limiting the negative impact on their school and academic success:

Once I came into the classroom, I would sort of shed those cool pose behaviors and adopt a more traditional educational behavior . . . those things [I did in the hallways] weren't necessarily brought into the classroom . . . they were two different environments. (Spencer)

Steele's (1997) stereotype threat theory centers on how societal stereotypes about specific groups "can influence the intellectual functioning and identity development of individual group members" (p. 613). The theory claims that African American students participate in "disidentification" (p. 614) with schooling because of the threat of confirming the negative stereotype regarding the intellectual capabilities of African Americans. This discourse was reconfigured by some participants and accommodated by others. Those who reconfigured the discourse argued that it acted as "propulsion" or "motivation" to achieve (Ethan) to prove the stereotype wrong. Those who accommodated the discourse developed strategies that demonstrated that they "deserved to be there," that they did "belong" (Spencer).

Ogbu's (1992) cultural–ecological theory asserts that the American racially stratified caste system contributes to the academic underachievement of specific "racial" minorities in U.S. schools. One key component of this theory is the notion of "cultural inversion" (p. 8), which is the rejection of certain forms of behaviors, events, symbols, and meanings by involuntary minorities (i.e., minorities who were brought to the United States against their will or who had been conquered or colonized) because they are characterized as White. This characterization results in involuntary minorities' adopting cultural behaviors, events, and so forth that are often in opposition to the dominant White culture. Another key component is "acting White" (p. 10), which is when involuntary minority students must choose between adopting "appropriate" attitudes and behaviors that are consistent with school rules and standard practices that are perceived and interpreted by minority students as typical of White students and adopting attitudes and behaviors that the minority students consider appropriate for their racial or ethnic group but that are not necessarily conducive to school success.

In general, the participants most often resisted the discourse of cultural inversion, arguing that it "didn't necessarily apply" (Ethan) or "never . . . was very real in . . . life" (Keegan). And when the discourse was accommodated, like the discourse of cool pose, the cultural inversion behaviors were effectively managed by relegating them to the hallways and other out-of-classroom venues so as to limit the negative impact on school and academic success. The discourse of acting White was resisted, as it was argued that the term *nerd* could be applied to all races, "to the Black community, to the White community, to Asians, whatever" (Nathaniel). The discourse was accommodated, however, as the concept of acting White was often applied to other "White" things, such as White dress, White English, White music, and so forth, an accommodation also noted by Bergin and Cooks (2002; see also Horvat & O'Connor, 2006).

Fordham's (1988) raceless persona theory contends that African American students who achieve school and academic success are often conflicted, feeling the need to reject their racial and cultural identity in the process of achieving school and academic success. Fordham set forth her theory by borrowing the anthropological concept *fictive kinship*, defined as "a kinship-like connection between and among persons in a society, not related by blood or marriage, who have maintained essential reciprocal social or economic relationships" (p. 56). She suggested that fictive kinship within the African American community is a learned cultural symbol that denotes a Black collective identity, resulting in community terms such as "brother," "sister," and "blood."

Similar to Ogbu's (1992) cultural–ecological theory, Fordham (1988) claimed that members of the Black collective identity develop cultural norms that are often oppositional to the norms of White America. This discourse was most often resisted, with one noted exception, Keegan's, as the participants troubled a Black collective void of success, given that the participants had parents, family and community members, and teachers who explicitly made the concept of success colorless: "My ignorance [that success was perceived as having a color] allowed me to not necessarily take on a raceless person, but to keep my ethnicity, to not necessarily feel educational success was a color" (Ethan). In contrast, Keegan accommodated the discourse, noting that in his earlier schooling, he experienced a raceless persona: "I felt raceless, felt like success was sometimes being outside the race I guess, not being Black enough." The racelessness experienced by Keegan, however, began to fade after he was placed in the honors program in middle school, which resulted in being surrounded by other African American students who had similar interests.

Fordham and Ogbu's (1986) burden of acting White theory is a coupling and extension of Fordham's *fictive kinship* and Ogbu's *acting White*. This theory attempts to explain how African American students who are high-achievers or perform satisfactorily, although well below their potential (i.e., underachievers), in schools manage the burden of acting White. Given that the participants did not perceive academic success as White, for the most part, they resisted this discourse: "Because I was surrounded by so many African Americans who actually wanted to achieve, the burden of acting White was not necessarily there . . . none of us saw success as Black or White, we saw it as being successful period" (Ethan). Nevertheless, a burden of acting uncool was present in the participants' experiences, in effect reconfiguring the discourse: "Because you are making certain types of grades [peers] may try to belittle you. But I guess to be accepted in any group, you have to show them otherwise, that hey, 'I am smart, but . . . I am still cool'" (Nathaniel).

Refuting Horatio Alger, Jr.

Evidently, the participants waded through a plethora of sociocultural discourses—discourses that had attempted to *construct* them as African American male adolescents. Although at times the counter-storytelling of success from each of the participants was similar, the stories were never monolithic—not across participants, and not even within participants. Taken as a whole, however, throughout their counterstories, the participants recounted how they accommodated, reconfigured, or resisted (some of) the specific discourses that surround male African Americans. Applying an eclectic array of theoretical concepts side by side to the participants' counterstories, I believe, illustrates the complexities of *how* particular sociocultural discourses affected their agency as they negotiated those discourses in their pursuit of success.

This eclectic array, I argue, frees the participants' counterstories from being essentialized to the often simply told Horatio Alger, Jr., story of success—"Oh, look how these young Black men overcame society's racial injustices and became successful, pulling themselves up by their own bootstraps"—to stories that more respectfully and accurately explain how these young men achieved success. In short, present throughout each participant's counterstory was recognition of race as a permanent and endemic component of U.S. society—not as a sign of submission, but as an act of ultimate defiance—and recognition of himself as a discursive formation who could, and did—as a *self*-empowered subject—accommodate, reconfigure, or resist hegemonic sociocultural discourses as a means to subversively repeat his constituted "raced" self.

Returning to Mathematics

Given that this study began contextually located in the mathematics classroom, I close the chapter with what I believe is the key implication of this study for mathematics education researchers and teacher educators, and mathematics teachers in general. Since 1989 the National Council of Teachers (NCTM) has called for mathematics for all (NCTM, 1989). This call has led to the proliferation of *Mathematics for All* rhetoric (Martin, 2003). Although sounding rather honorable, absent within much of this rhetoric is a critical examination of the sociocultural and sociohistorical inequities faced by Black students (and other historically marginalized students), both inside and outside of the mathematics classroom (Martin, 2003). Therefore, some of the difficult questions that must be asked by those who take seriously the NCTM's call are: How does racism (sexism, classism, etc.) affect the mathematics experiences of students? How much of the assessment system in mathematics (and pedagogical practices in general) is driven by (unconscious or not) race bias? Can changing the racist practices in the mathematics classroom eliminate (or at least alleviate) the effects of racism on students? (Weissglass, 2002).

To arrive at plausible—and nonessentializing—answers to these questions (and others), those engaged in mathematics education research must explore the wider social and political picture of mathematics teaching and learning (Gates & Vistro-Yu, 2003). Through such an examination, mathematics education researchers and teacher educators, and mathematics teachers in general, I believe, will develop a deeper understanding of how students and teachers, classrooms and schools—and the discipline of mathematics itself—are (and always have been) embedded in, and affected by, a multiplicity of hegemonic sociocultural and sociohistorical discourses.

Notes

1 This chapter has been revised from an earlier, longer version that appeared in *American Educational Research Journal, 45*(4), 975–1010.

2 The terms *African American* and *Black* are used interchangeably throughout this chapter to describe a person of African descent who claims the "cultural identity" of the United States.

3 Throughout the chapter, when the term *discourses* is used, I am referring to Gee's (1999) capital-D *Discourses*, although, for reading ease, I do not capitalize the term. Furthermore, for reading ease, when using the term *sociocultural discourses*, the intended meaning is sociocultural and sociohistorical discourses, acknowledging that discourses of any particular society or culture are, in fact, contextually and historically constructed within sociocultural and sociohistorical milieus.

4 As noted, the participants' successes in mathematics was just one component of their overall efforts toward success; therefore, for reading ease, when using the term *success*, I am referring to academic and mathematics success or schooling success in general.

5 Often the words *postmodernism* and *poststructuralism* are used interchangeably in the literature, but there are acknowledged differences in the terms (for a brief discussion see Peters & Burbules, 2004). Within the context of Kincheloe and McLaren's (1994) essay, they intended the term *postmodern theory* to be an "umbrella term" for postmodernism and poststructuralism.

6 See Hilliard (2003) for a critical discussion of how the "gap" is erroneously framed, and how it might be reframed.

7 Keeling High was an "urban high school located in a suburban community" (according to a description found on the school's web site), 10 miles from a large city in the South; it was situated in a 95% African American community where the mean home value was $220,000. Keeling High had approximately 1,300 students, with 99% of the students being identified by race or ethnicity as Black by the school system. Although the student population was homogenous racially, it was very diverse socioeconomically, ranging from the working poor to the middle upper class (44% of the students were eligible to receive free or reduced-price lunches). The school provided an embedded mathematics and science magnet program (25% of the students were enrolled in the program) for Newberry County, a large (over 70,000 students) and well-funded school system (i.e., school facilities were modern and well maintained).

8 The descriptor "demonstrated achievement and persistence in high school mathematics" was met if a participant achieved one or more of the following criteria his junior or senior year of high school: (a) completed an Advanced Placement calculus or statistics course with a grade of C (70%) or better; (b) completed a joint-enrollment calculus or statistics course with a grade of C (70%) or better; or (c) scored in the 4th quartile (top 25 %) of the mathematics portion of the Scholastic Achievement Test.

9 The survey instrument was adapted from Taylor-Griffin (2000) and asked each participant to answer typical questions regarding his primary, secondary, and college schooling years (e.g., schools attended, grade point average achieved, courses completed, honors awarded, test scores earned) and his family demographics (e.g., persons in household, parents' or guardians' education, household income).

10 The biographies were adapted from Moody (1997) and asked each participant to write a brief autobiographical story of his life, highlighting significant events as he progressed through his schooling years. Specifically, it asked each participant to discuss (but not limit himself to) whether he believed that his experiences were unique to being a male African American, any extracurricular activities that he was involved in (either through school or other civic and community organizations) that he believed contributed to his academic success, any significant person(s) that contributed to his current status in life, and specific learning experiences with his teachers (and college professors). The mathematics autobiography was similarly fashioned but focused specifically on each participant's experiences with mathematics.

11 The six manuscripts were: Ogbu's (1978b) book chapter, "Black-White Differences in School Performance: A Critique of Current Explanations"; Majors, Tyler, Peden, and Hall's (1994) book chapter, "Cool Pose: A Symbolic Mechanism for Masculine Role Enactment and Coping by Black Males"; Steele's (1997) essay, "A Threat in the Air:

How Stereotypes Shape Intellectual Identity and Performance"; Ogbu's (1992) essay, "Understanding Cultural Diversity and Learning"; Fordham's (1988) essay, "Racelessness as a Factor in Black Students' School Success: Pragmatic Strategy or Pyrrhic Victory?"; and Fordham and Ogbu's (1986) essay, "Black Students' School Success: Coping with the "Burden of 'Acting White'" (for a review of these theoretical perspectives see Stinson, 2006).

12 Participants were asked to indicate which factors they mentioned had the most influence or impact, and it is their own determination of relative influence of factors that is meant here.

13 Either directly or indirectly, each participant perceived mathematics as being somewhat "culturally free" (e.g., "the same whether you are Black, White, Asian, young or old"). How the participants developed such a perspective was not explored per se. I inferred from their conversations, however, that, although each participant expanded the utility of mathematics beyond mere school mathematics, the four participants also viewed success in school mathematics as just one component in their larger efforts toward success. For instance, Ethan's statement "I was always . . . willing to learn . . . what I needed to do to achieve, and if the core curriculum [which included mathematics] was what they needed me to do it," typifies the participants' positioning of success in mathematics within their overall efforts toward success. In short, each participant, like Martin's (2000) mathematically successful African American students, incorporated a positive mathematics identity within his overall academic success.

14 The Executive Board of the American Anthropological Association in 1998 adopted the organization's official statement on race that disputed the concept of race as any biological human taxonomy. The board, however, securely positioned race as an influential and powerful social and political construct that "distorts our ideas about human differences and group behaviors, [stating that] . . . scientists today find that reliance on such folk beliefs about human differences in research has led to countless errors" (American Anthropological Association, 1998, ¶ 9). They concluded their statement, asserting,

> The "racial" worldview was invented to assign some groups to perpetual low status, while others were permitted access to privilege, power, and wealth. The tragedy in the United States has been that the policies and practices stemming from this worldview succeeded and all too well in constructing unequal populations among Europeans, Native Americans, and peoples of African descent. Given what we know about the capacity of normal humans to achieve and function within any culture, we conclude that present-day inequalities between so-called "racial" groups are not consequences of their biological inheritance but products of historical and contemporary social, economic, educational, and political circumstances. (¶12)

Butler (1990/1999) offered a similar argument regarding the construct of gender; likewise, Foucault (1976/1990) offered an argument regarding the construct of sexuality.

15 Spivak (1974/1997) explained Derrida's (1974/1997) *sous rapture* (under erasure) as learning "to use and erase our language at the same time" (p. xviii). In other words, *under erasure* is a strategy of using the only available language, while not subscribing to its premises, or operating according to the vocabulary of the very thing that it defines (Spivak, 1974/1997).

16 Du Bois (1903/1989) introduced the concept *double-consciousness* in the following passage:

> The Negro is a sort of seventh son, born with a veil, and gifted with second-sight in this American world,—a world which yields him no true self-consciousness, but only lets him see himself through the revelation of the other world. It is a peculiar sensation, this double-consciousness, this sense of always looking at one's self through the eyes of others, of measuring one's soul by the tape of a world that looks on in amused contempt and pity. One ever feels his twoness,—an American, a

Negro: two souls, two thoughts, two unreconciled strivings; two warring ideals in one dark body, whose dogged strength alone keeps it from being torn asunder. (p. 3)

17 The term *rejection* is used here to differentiate it from the critical theory concept *resistance*. In this context, *rejection* is referring to an act of refusing or discarding, most often followed by negative consequences, whereas *resistance* is understood as a legitimate and often positive response to domination, assisting individuals or groups to resist the negative forces of oppression as part of a larger political struggle that works toward social justice (Leistyna et al., 1996).

References

American Anthropological Association (1998). American Anthropological Association statement on "race." Retrieved May 30, 2002, from http://www.aaanet.org/stmts/ racepp.htm

Atweh, B., Forgasz, H., & Nebres, B. (Eds.). (2001). *Sociocultural research on mathematics education: An international perspective*. Mahwah, NJ: Lawrence Erlbaum.

Bell, D.A. (1992). *Faces at the bottom of the well: The permanence of racism*. New York: Basic Books.

Bergin, D.A. & Cooks, H.C. (2002). High school students of color talk about accusations of "acting White." *Urban Review, 34*(2), 113–134.

Berry, R.Q., III. (2005). Voices of success: Descriptive portraits of two successful African American male middle school mathematics students. *Journal of African American Studies, 8*(4), 46–62.

Boaler, J. (Ed.). (2000). Multiple perspectives on mathematics teaching and learning. Westport, CT: Ablex.

Bottomore, T.B. (Ed.). (1991). *A dictionary of Marxist thought* (2nd ed.). Malden, MA: Blackwell.

Burton, L. (Ed.). (2003). *Which way social justice in mathematics education?* Westport, CT: Praeger.

Butler, J. (1999). *Gender trouble: Feminism and the subversion of identity*. New York: Routledge. (Original work published 1990.)

Derrida, J. (1997). *Of grammatology* (G.C. Spivak, Trans., Corrected ed.). Baltimore, MD: Johns Hopkins University Press. (Original work published 1974.)

Du Bois, W.E.B. (1989). *The souls of Black folk* (Bantam classic ed.). New York: Bantam Books. (Original work published 1903.)

Fordham, S. (1988). Racelessness as a factor in Black students' school success: Pragmatic strategy or Pyrrhic victory? *Harvard Educational Review, 58*(1), 54–84.

Fordham, S. (1996). *Blacked out: Dilemmas of race, identity, and success at Capital High*. Chicago: University of Chicago Press.

Fordham, S. & Ogbu, J.U. (1986). Black students' school success: Coping with the "burden of 'acting White.'" *The Urban Review, 18*(3), 176–206.

Foucault, M. (1972). *The archaeology of knowledge* (A.M. Sheridan Smith, Trans.). New York: Pantheon Books. (Original work published 1969.)

Foucault, M. (1990). *The history of sexuality. Volume I: An introduction* (R. Hurley, Trans.). New York: Vintage Books. (Original work published 1976.)

Freeman, M., deMarrais, K., Preissle, J., Roulston, K., & St. Pierre, E.A. (2007). Standards of evidence in qualitative research: An incitement to discourse. *Educational Researcher, 36*(1), 25–32.

Freire, P. (2000a). *Education for critical consciousness* (Continuum ed.). New York: Continuum. (Original work published 1969.)

Freire, P. (2000b). *Pedagogy of the oppressed* (M.B. Ramos, Trans., 30th anniversary ed.). New York: Continuum. (Original work published 1970.)

Gates, P. & Vistro-Yu, C.P. (2003). Is mathematics for all? In A.J. Bishop, M.A. Clements, C. Keitel, J. Kilpatrick, & F.K.S. Leung (Eds.), *Second international handbook of mathematics education* (Vol. 1, pp. 31–73). Dordrecht, NLD: Kluwer Academic.

Gee, J.P. (1999). *An introduction to discourse analysis: Theory and method.* New York: Routledge.

Gutstein, E. (2006). *Reading and writing the world with mathematics.* New York: Routledge.

Gutstein, E. (2007). "And that's just how it starts": Teaching mathematics and developing student agency. *Teachers College Record, 109*(2), 420–448.

Hébert, T.P. & Reis, S.M. (1999). Culturally diverse high-achieving students in an urban high school. *Urban Education, 34*(4), 428–457.

Hill, D., McLaren, P., Cole, M., & Rikowski, G. (Eds.). (2002). *Marxism against postmodernism in educational theory.* Lanham, MD: Lexington Books.

Hilliard, A.G., III. (2003). No mystery: Closing the achievement gap between Africans and excellence. In T. Perry, C. Steele, & A.G. Hilliard, III (Eds.), *Young, gifted, and black: Promoting high achievement among African-American students* (pp. 131–165). Boston: Beacon Press.

Hollway, W. & Jefferson, T. (2000). *Doing qualitative research differently: Free association, narrative and the interview method.* Thousand Oaks, CA: Sage.

Horvat, E.M. & O'Connor, C. (Eds.). (2006). *Beyond acting White: Reframing the debate on Black student achievement.* Lanham, MD: Rowman & Littlefield.

Kincheloe, J.L. & McLaren, P. (1994). Rethinking critical theory and qualitative research. In N.K. Denzin & Y.S. Lincoln (Eds.), *Handbook of qualitative research* (pp. 139–157). Thousand Oaks, CA: Sage.

Kincheloe, J.L. & McLaren, P. (2000). Rethinking critical theory and qualitative research. In N.K. Denzin & Y.S. Lincoln (Eds.), *Handbook of qualitative research* (2nd ed., pp. 279–314). Thousand Oaks, CA: Sage.

Kozol, J. (1992). *Savage inequalities: Children in America's schools.* New York: Harper Perennial.

Kvale, S. (1996). *Interviews: An introduction to qualitative research interviewing.* Thousand Oaks, CA: Sage.

Ladson-Billings, G. (1994). *The dreamkeepers: Successful teachers of African American children.* San Francisco: Jossey-Bass.

Ladson-Billings, G. (1997). It doesn't add up: African American students' mathematics achievement. *Journal for Research in Mathematics Education, 28*(6), 697–708.

Ladson-Billings, G. (1998). Just what is critical race theory and what's it doing in a nice field like education? *International Journal of Qualitative Studies in Education, 11*(1), 7–24.

Ladson-Billings, G. (2000). Racialized discourses and ethnic epistemologies. In N.K. Denzin & Y.S. Lincoln (Eds.), *Handbook of qualitative research* (2nd ed., pp. 257–277). Thousand Oaks, CA: Sage.

Lather, P.A. (1986). Issues of validity in openly ideological research: Between a rock and a soft place. *Interchange, 17*(4), 63–84.

Lather, P.A. (1991). *Getting smart: Feminist research and pedagogy with/in the postmodern.* New York: Routledge.

Lather, P.A. (2007). *Getting lost: Feminist efforts toward a double(d) science.* Albany: State University of New York Press.

Leistyna, P., Woodrum, A., & Sherblom, S.A. (Eds.). (1996). *Breaking free: The transformative power of critical pedagogy.* Cambridge, MA: Harvard Educational Review.

Lerman, S. (2000). The social turn in mathematics education research. In J. Boaler (Ed.),

Multiple perspectives on mathematics teaching and learning (pp. 19–44). Westport, CT: Ablex.

Lerman, S. (2001). Cultural, discursive psychology: A sociocultural approach to studying the teaching and learning of mathematics. *Educational Studies in Mathematics, 46*, 87–113.

Majors, R. & Billson, J.M. (1993). *Cool pose: The dilemmas of Black manhood in America.* New York: Lexington Books.

Majors, R., Tyler, R., Peden, B., & Hall, R. (1994). Cool pose: A symbolic mechanism for masculine role enactment and coping by Black males. In R. Majors & J.U. Gordon (Eds.), *The American Black male: His present status and his future* (pp. 245–259). Chicago: Nelson-Hall.

Martin, D.B. (2000). *Mathematics success and failure among African-American youth: The roles of sociohistorical context, community forces, school influence, and individual agency.* Mahwah, NJ: Lawrence Erlbaum.

Martin, D.B. (2003). Hidden assumptions and unanswered questions in *Mathematics for All* rhetoric. *The Mathematics Educator, 13*(2), 7–21.

Martin, D.B. (2007). Beyond missionaries or cannibals: Who should teach mathematics to African American children? *The High School Journal, 91*(1), 6–28.

Marx, K. & Engels, F. (1978). Manifesto of the communist party. In R.C. Tucker (Ed.), *The Marx-Engels reader* (2nd ed., pp. 469–500). New York: Norton. (Original work published 1848.)

Merriam-Webster's collegiate dictionary (10th ed.). (1999). Springfield, MA: Merriam-Webster.

Moody, V.R. (1997). *Giving voice to African Americans who have been successful with school mathematics.* Unpublished doctoral dissertation, University of Georgia, Athens.

Moody, V.R. (2000). African American students' success with school mathematics. In M.E. Strutchens, M.L. Johnson, & W.F. Tate (Eds.), *Changing the faces of mathematics: Perspectives on African Americans* (pp. 51–60). Reston, VA: National Council of Teachers of Mathematics.

Nasir, N.S. & Cobb, P. (Eds.). (2007). *Improving access to mathematics: Diversity and equity in the classroom.* New York: Teachers College Press.

National Council of Teachers of Mathematics (NCTM). (1989). *Curriculum and evaluation standards for school mathematics.* Reston, VA: National Council of Teachers of Mathematics.

O'Connor, C. (1997). Dispositions toward (collective) struggle and educational resilience in the inner city: A case analysis of six African-American high school students. *American Educational Research Journal, 34*(4), 593–629.

Ogbu, J.U. (1978a). *Minority education and caste: The American system in cross-cultural perspective.* New York: Academic Press.

Ogbu, J.U. (1978b). Black–White differences in school performance: A critique of current explanations, *Minority education and caste: The American system in cross-cultural perspective* (pp. 43–65). New York: Academic Press.

Ogbu, J.U. (1992). Understanding cultural diversity and learning. *Education Researcher, 21*(8), 5–14.

Ogbu, J.U. (2003). *Black American students in an affluent suburb: A study of academic disengagement.* Mahwah, NJ: Lawrence Erlbaum.

Paul, J.L. & Marfo, K. (2001). Preparation of educational researchers in philosophical foundations of inquiry. *Review of Educational Research, 71*(4), 525–547.

Peters, M. & Burbules, N.C. (2004). *Poststructuralism and educational research.* Lanham, MD: Rowman & Littlefield.

Polite, V.C. & Davis, J.E. (1999). Introduction. In V.C. Polite & J.E. Davis (Eds.), *African American males in school and society: Practices and policies for effective education* (pp. 1–7). New York: Teachers College Press.

Powell, A.B. & Frankenstein, M. (Eds.). (1997). *Ethnomathematics: Challenging Eurocentrism in mathematics education*. Albany: State University of New York Press.

Reason, P. (1994). Three approaches to participative inquiry. In N.K. Denzin & Y.S. Lincoln (Eds.), *Handbook of qualitative research* (pp. 324–339). Thousand Oaks, CA: Sage.

Sarup, M. (1993). *An introductory guide to post-structuralism and postmodernism* (2nd ed.). Athens, GA: University of Georgia Press.

Scott, J.W. (1992). "Experience." In J. Butler & J.W. Scott (Eds.), *Feminists theorize the political* (pp. 22–40). New York: Routledge.

Secada, W.G., Fennema, E., & Adajian, L.B. (1995). *New directions for equity in mathematics education*. Cambridge, UK: Cambridge University Press.

Sfard, A. (2003). Balancing the unbalanceable: The NCTM Standards in light of theories of learning mathematics. In J. Kilpatrick, G. Martin, & D. Schifter (Eds.), *A research companion for NCTM Standards* (pp. 353–392). Reston, VA: National Council for Teachers of Mathematics.

Silverman, D. (2000). *Doing qualitative research: A practical handbook*. Thousand Oaks, CA: Sage.

Solórzano, D.G. & Yosso, T., J. (2002). Critical race methodology: Counter-storytelling as an analytical framework for education research. *Qualitative Inquiry, 8*(1), 23–44.

Spivak, G.C. (1997). Translator's preface. In J. Derrida, *Of grammatology* (G.C. Spivak, Trans., Corrected ed., pp. ix–lxxxvii). Baltimore: Johns Hopkins University Press. (Original work published 1974.)

St. Pierre, E.A. (1997). Circling the text: Nomadic writing practices. *Qualitative Inquiry, 3*(4), 403–417.

St. Pierre, E.A. (2000). Poststructural feminism in education: An overview. *International Journal of Qualitative Studies in Education, 13*(5), 467–515.

Steele, C.M. (1997). A threat in the air: How stereotypes shape intellectual identity and performance. *American Psychologist, 52*(6), 613–629.

Steele, C.M. (1999, August). Thin ice: "Stereotype threat" and Black college students. *The Atlantic Monthly*, 44–54.

Steele, C.M. (2003). Stereotype threat and African-American student achievement. In T. Perry, C. Steele, & A.G. Hilliard, III (Eds.), *Young, gifted, and black: Promoting high achievement among African-American students* (pp. 109–130). Boston: Beacon Press.

Stinson, D.W. (2004). African American male students and achievement in school mathematics: A critical postmodern analysis of agency. *Dissertations Abstracts International, 66*(12). (UMI No. 3194548)

Stinson, D.W. (2006). African American male adolescents, schooling (and mathematics): Deficiency, rejection, and achievement. *Review of Educational Research, 76*(4), 477–506.

Stinson, D.W. (2008). Negotiating sociocultural discourses: The counter-storytelling of academically (and mathematically) successful African American male students. *American Educational Research Journal, 45*(4), 975–1010.

Tate, W.F. (1997). Critical race theory and education: History, theory, and implications. In M. Apple (Ed.), *Review of research in education* (Vol. 22, pp. 195–247). Washington, DC: American Educational Research Association.

Taylor-Griffin, S. (2000). *Successful African-American men: From childhood to adulthood*. New York: Kluwer Academic.

Torres, C.A. (1998). Multiculturalism, *Democracy, education, and multiculturalism: Dilemmas of citizenship in a global world* (pp. 175–222). Lanham, MD: Rowman & Littlefield.

Walker, E.N. (2006). Urban high school students' academic communities and their effects on mathematics success. *American Educational Research Journal, 43*(1), 43–73.

Walshaw, M. (Ed.). (2004). *Mathematics education within the postmodern.* Greenwich, CT: Information Age.

Weissglass, J. (2002). Inequity in mathematics education: Questions for educators. *The Mathematics Educator, 12*(2), 34–39.

12 "Come Home, Then": Two Eighth-Grade Black Female Students' Reflections on Their Mathematics Experiences

Yolanda A. Johnson

Introduction

The title of this chapter is in reference to a powerful personal experience that occurred during the pursuit of my doctoral degree. Discouraged, fed up with school, and wanting to return home, I expressed all of these emotions to my father over the phone. I was just looking for sympathy, but was shocked by his nonchalant reply, "come home, then." I continued to recall the conversation with my father in the ensuing months and the idea to "come home, then" took on several forms which provoked guiding thoughts for me. First of all, *come home, then* is a longing for a safety net, which is a place of comfort. This place is one of love and acceptance, which people tend to miss when away for school-related or work-related endeavors. My father understood me, which he articulated in our conversation. By telling me to come home, he was actually causing the opposite to occur. He knew that was not the option that I was going to take, but by verbalizing the act, he brought out my personal conflict which I had to confront instead of continuing to ignore. He knew that his words would have a reverse effect on me because he knew that even though I wanted to come home to a more comfortable place, I did not want to give up; I was just expressing myself out of frustration. I believe my father was igniting in me the idea, "don't *talk* about it, *be* about it." I either needed to *be* about school or about coming home, but talking about either was not getting me anywhere. Secondly, *come home, then* represents a common ground between Black females. By sharing the bonds of race and gender, the female students profiled in this chapter and I also share common experiences that create an atmosphere of understanding that goes beyond words. We know these shared experiences through firsthand perspectives. Experiences are unique for each individual. However, there are commonalities that we share and can reflect upon. Finally, *come home, then* represents an invitation for readers to explore and understand the mathematics experiences of two African American eighth-grade females.

This chapter is divided into three sections. The first section presents the theoretical framework for understanding the mathematics experiences of African American female students through Black feminist thought and critical social theory. The second section presents results from a research study[1] that explored the past and present experiences of two eighth-grade African American female students. The goals of the study were to explore the following: their beliefs about the nature of mathematics, their beliefs about their mathematics abilities, and their beliefs about their futures in mathematics. The final section of this chapter consists of a discussion of themes that emerged through this research. This discussion continues by connecting the participants' experiences to the theoretical underpinnings of Black feminist thought. I conclude with a discussion of how the results can be used in future conversations in the mathematics education community on how we can contribute to the success of African American female students.

Theoretical Framework

The research described in this chapter is rooted in Black feminism, a critical social theory that merges gender and race and that helps explain the unique experiences of the two African American girls profiled. In the narrative presented below, I will briefly describe critical social theory and Black feminism and how my study is framed within the latter. For the purpose of this work, I deliberately focus on Black and white cultures. The rationale for this focus is the role that the dominant, white culture played in the development of Black feminism and the experiences of the two girls whom I discuss in this study.

Critical Social Theory

Kincheloe & McLaren (2000) presented a reconceptualized critical theory that "is intensely concerned with the need to understand the various and complex ways that power operates to dominate and shape consciousness" (p. 283). This consciousness is also developed through Black feminism, which adds gender to the double consciousness discussed by Du Bois (1903/1990) in *The Souls of Black Folk*. Du Bois stated that the "American Negro" lives in a world which "yields him no true self-consciousness" or a "sense of always looking at one's self through the eyes of others," otherwise known as double-consciousness (p. 8). This double-consciousness is felt through possessing "two souls, two thoughts, two unreconciled strivings" (p. 8). In addition, Black American women also have to deal with reconciling gender, thereby creating a multiple consciousness (King, 1989). King averred that racism, sexism, and classism have a multiplicative relationship, in that Black women face simultaneous oppression, as opposed to racism being added to sexism which is added to classism. Thinking of our oppression in this additive way makes it seem that one is worse than the other; or if someone deals with one of these -isms, then steps towards a solution have been made. Instead, Black women have racism, multiplied by sexism, multiplied by classism, and all three are interdependent and connected in a way that is difficult to separate. However, this marginalized position can also serve as a powerful one, allowing one to view positions of inclusion and exclusion to formulate specific epistemological stances (Ladson-Billings, 2000). In this way, Black women's social positions give them the power to formulate an epistemology grounded in Black feminism. Critical social theory takes into account considerations of how social institutions function to produce and reproduce race, class, and gender dynamics as well as how they "interact to construct a social system" (p. 281). In order to talk about the lives of African

American girls at the nexus of race and gender, I draw insights from the theory of Black feminism.

Black Feminism

Patricia Hill Collins (1990b) suggests that "Black feminist thought consists of specialized knowledge created by African-American women which clarifies a standpoint of, and for, Black women. In other words, Black feminist thought encompasses theoretical interpretations of Black women's reality by those who live it" (para. 10). In general, the ideas of Black feminists are referred to as Black feminist thought (Collins, 1990a), employing an Afrocentric feminist epistemology. On the journey to finding voice, Black women intellectuals are faced with deciding between Eurocentric masculine epistemology, representing the interests of the elite white male, and Afrocentric feminist epistemology, which addresses the concerns of the Afrocentric feminist. Collins (1990a) noted that "[e]pistemological choices about who[m] to trust, what to believe, and why something is true are not benign academic issues. Instead, these concerns tap the fundamental question of which versions of truth will prevail and shape thought and action" (pp. 202–203). This critical view of the truth reinforces how Black feminism is a critical social theory.

There are four dimensions of the Afrocentric feminist epistemology, namely, concrete experience as a criterion of meaning, the use of dialogue in assessing knowledge claims, the ethic of caring, and the ethic of personal accountability (Collins, 1990a, pp. 208–219). First, using experience as a criterion of meaning, Collins pointed out that there are two types of knowing—knowledge and wisdom—that are divided by experience. Second, in her discussion on the use of dialogue in assessing knowledge claims, Collins stressed connectedness as vital in the knowledge validation process. People become empowered through a connection to a community. Dialogue is the conduit for this connection. In the third dimension, the ethic of caring, Collins suggested, "that personal expressiveness, emotions, and empathy are central to the knowledge validation process" (p. 215). Giving the impression of advocacy is a way of displaying that one possesses this ethic of caring. Finally, Collins discussed the ethic of personal accountability, where every idea has an owner whose identity matters. In other words, the individual is just as important as his ideas.

An Afrocentric feminist epistemology is referred to as such because all members of the African Diaspora share common experiences. Race, class, and gender oppression generate similarities in the epistemologies of subordinate groups. Black women have a both/and conceptual orientation (Collins, 1990a) in that we are both *Black* and *female*, not able to choose one or the other marginalized group. Thus the Afrocentric feminist epistemology takes aspects of the natural experiences of having African descent coupled with a feminist standpoint to create the Afrocentric feminist epistemology. All of the dimensions contribute to the knowledge validation process, or how one comes to know and how it is valued.

To be feminist "in any authentic sense of the term is to want for all people, female and male, liberation from sexist role patterns, domination, and oppression" (hooks, 1981, p. 195). Liberation, or freedom, is "the indispensable condition for the quest for human completion" (Freire, 2000, p. 47). Thus, this liberation is universal and something that must be acquired, not given.

Black feminism grew out of the Civil Rights, Black Power, and Feminist movements of the 1960s and 1970s. The Civil Rights and Black Power movements addressed issues of minorities, in general, and Black people in particular, but did not specifically address issues of gender oppression. The Feminist movement addressed gender oppression, but for middle class white females who wanted to enter the work force, like their male counterparts. These were not the issues that Black women had. Since their issues were not addressed, some Black women currently have no desire to take ownership of the term feminism when referring to their cause, which shows a connection to the white-dominated Feminist movement.

I used Black feminist thought and an Afrocentric feminist epistemology in this research because it resonates with how Black feminism arose. Equity studies of Black students tend to focus on Black males and those on gender tend to focus on white females, leaving the Black female out. Similarly, in the feminist movement, the first and second waves had, as their center, issues relevant to the white middle class female. In the Black Power movement, those in the forefront were the Black males. Ideally, gender and racial equity benefit the Black female. However, when Black females are placed in the background and not the forefront and their unique issues are not addressed, this benefit is not guaranteed, thus making obvious the need to focus specifically on the Black female.

I argue that, by sharing the experiences of two Black female students, the mathematics education community can begin to address a missing part of the conversation on race and gender in relation to mathematics teaching and learning. Within the last 20 years, the mathematics education community has published a plethora of literature aimed at helping teachers understand the strengths and needs of students from culturally diverse backgrounds (e.g., Jacobs, Becker, & Gilmer, 2001; Martin, 2000; National Council of Teachers of Mathematics, 2000; Secada, 2000; Secada, Fennema, & Adajian, 1995; Strutchens, Johnson, & Tate, 2000; Trentacosta & Kenney, 1997; Fisher, 2000; U.S. Department of Education. National Center for Education Statistics, 2001). Many of these mathematics education studies tend to compare the mathematics experiences of Black and white students, Black males and Black females, or Black females and white females through a narrow examination of academic achievement. Very few studies focus specifically on Black females and their achievement or experiences in mathematics (Kusimo, 1997; Kusimo, Carter, & Keyes, 1999; Moody, 2000, 2001). In particular, these mathematics education reform efforts have addressed gender or racial equity issues, but rarely both. Consequently, our understanding of the mathematics experiences of students from culturally diverse backgrounds has been limited to conversations about race *or* gender.

Although past studies have added to mathematics education research, this current study has a focus specifically on mathematics education and African American females, which is rarely done (Moody, 2000, 2001). This study will add to the body of research on Black females and aid teachers and researchers in their collaborative efforts to improve mathematics education experiences for all students. After uncovering and interpreting what the girls experienced to get to where they were, I articulate the understandings that I gained in order to reach the goal of adding another component to improving instruction and informing teachers of the need to give attention to students' backgrounds. Through looking back on past experiences and taking into account present ones, we created a story to help us move forward.

Context and Objectives

In my study, I was interested in the experiences that shape the academic achievement of these two eighth-grade African American female students in one middle school mathematics class. I also wanted to explore their strengths and identify how those strengths could be used towards mathematics achievement. Finally, I was interested in their expectations and the perceptions that they had of themselves in relation to their mathematics ability and the usefulness of mathematics for their futures.

In order to best capture the experiences of the female students profiled, I chose to use critical ethnography, which is the methodology that is suggested for critical research. This methodology includes catalytic validity which points to the degree to which research moves those it studies to understand the world and the way it is shaped in order for them to transform it (Kincheloe & McLaren, 2000). The qualitative research design utilized in this study was the intrinsic case study (Stake, 2000), with characteristics of an embedded single case study (Yin, 2003) in order to gain a better understanding of a particular case.

The participants in this study were Bianca and Lakesia,[2] students from one mathematics classroom at a Midwestern junior high school, which I have named Perfecto Junior High School. My first exposure to Perfecto Junior High School was through a school club for the Black students. A colleague was a teacher at the school and asked me if I could help him with the female students at his school. These students had been feeling as if they were singled out by the teachers in the building. Whenever they were in the hallways, they were reprimanded or pulled aside by the teachers because they were too loud (Fordham, 1993, 1997) or had violated the dress code in some way. Also, at school dances, they were singled out because of the way they danced. These girls also approached my colleague in frustration because the Black boys at the school were romantically interested in the white girls, causing the Black girls to doubt their beauty and self-worth. In response to these concerns, my colleague started the "Heritage Club.[3]" This club, which met after school, was described in the school's clubs and activities brochure as "a comfortable environment [to] discuss issues that impact minority students. Meetings are held once each month."

Students at Perfecto were divided into teams. Mrs. Hill was the math teacher on the Futurist Eighth-grade Team. She had a total of six Black female students in four classes. I asked all Black female students to participate in the study. Their participation was based on their parents' willingness to allow their daughters to engage in individual and group interviews and to allow me to observe the mathematics class for the second quarter of the school year. Two girls' mothers from sixth-hour granted permission, which led me to focus on that class, and particularly on Bianca and Lakesia, whom I discuss in detail. During the second quarter of the school year, I observed Bianca and Lakesia in their mathematics classroom and conducted individual and combined interviews with them as well as two individual interviews with their teacher and one with each of their mothers. As I reviewed the participants' interview transcripts, I realized that the girls might be able to tell me more about their past experiences in mathematics, which led me to conduct a third individual interview at the beginning of the fourth quarter of the same school year. After reviewing fieldnotes from classroom observations and field trips, as well as interview transcripts, I coded the data for emergent themes.

The Heritage Club sponsor created a place to come home for the students. However, he felt the female students may be more comfortable discussing certain issues with an adult female. I participated in discussions with these students, listening to their concerns and serving as a facilitator to ensure that everyone had an opportunity to say what was on their mind. I also accompanied the students on field trips and community service projects. These snapshots of the students' lives only provided a thumbnail image of their school experiences. I was more interested in their classrooms, especially mathematics, to gain a broader perspective of the students.

Classroom Context

Mrs. Hill's sixth-hour Pre-Algebra class had 29 students enrolled. There were three Black females, two Black males, one Asian Indian female, twelve white females, and eleven white males. The students were seated at tables, with three to four students at each table. Bianca sat at a table at the front and Lakesia sat at the table behind Bianca's. Since the students were seated at tables, cooperative groups and hands-on work were convenient. This cooperative work took on the form of students comparing answers from the homework or working together on a worksheet. Also, when Mrs. Hill introduced the students to the graphing calculator, she allowed them to explore certain functions of the calculator based on her verbal prompts.

Each class session, Mrs. Hill placed a copy of notes at the first table, for the students to pick up before they went to their seats. She used them as an organizational tool for her students, which she believed was especially helpful for her learning disabled (LD) students. The notes paper had the day's date, warm-up problems, an outline of the notes for the day, and the homework assignment pre-printed to maximize the 50-minute class time.

Based on the 21 observations I made, her lessons progressed in the manner described by her outlined notes. Variations to this occurred when she scheduled a quiz. Instead of introducing something new, Mrs. Hill would review and then give the students their quiz. She scheduled quizzes on three of the days I observed. On two of those days, Mrs. Hill reviewed homework immediately prior to the quiz and one day there was a substitute so the entire class was set aside for the quiz. During three of the class periods I observed, the students were organizing their portfolios. They also had two projects during this quarter. One was in conjunction with their science class where the students worked in groups and had to build a catapult. They worked on the catapults during two of the classes I observed. Their other project was the Redesigning project, where the students had to analyze any store-bought product's package (i.e., tissue, cereal, detergent) and redesign it. The new product's ratio of surface area to volume had to be smaller. This project had them involved during four of the classes I observed. As a review for their semester final, Mrs. Hill made up a game for the students to play during the last two classes I observed.

Lakesia and Bianca Coming Home

The idea behind Black feminist thought is that Black females have a unique standpoint based on the common experience of being Black *and* female in a white male-dominated society. We do not have the option of choosing to be Black or female. We are simultaneously members of two marginalized groups making our unique experiences similar, which is why I was originally asked to join the Heritage Club at Perfecto Junior High. The Black male teacher sponsors recognized the *both/and* (Collins, 1990a) conceptual orientation (*both* Black *and* female) of the female students in the club and knew they could only address some of the girls' concerns, since they were not able to identify with the girls' femaleness.

Lakesia: "Doing Math From the Top of My Head Makes Me Feel Smart."

Lakesia was a quiet, attentive student who took pride in her high grades, which she maintained in mathematics despite her dislike for the subject. In mathematics, she preferred strict teachers like her seventh-grade mathematics teacher who "was strict, but I liked the way she was strict. She just wanted her work done" (Interview, 12/06/02). When I asked her about how she approached her work in her mathematics classes, she said that it takes her a long time and "it gives me a headache. And my sister, she just loves math because she wants to be an accountant when she grows up, like her dad. So, I'll ask her and she . . . I don't like when she teaches me because I'll ask her a question and she'll be like, 'It's not explainable, just do it', and I don't [get] what she [says]. So she'll just be thinking in her head. I'll need a calculator" (Interview, 11/15/02). When I asked her more about why the homework gives her a headache, she said she understood while in class, but when she worked on her own, she would forget. She tried to do her homework without looking at her teacher's class notes.

L: . . . 'cause I'll want to remember it like on top of my head so like next year it will be easy to me, but I can't. I have to look at my notes.

YJ: . . . Why do you feel like you have to do it from the top of your head when you're doing problems for the first time?

L: I don't know. I just like to feel smart.

YJ: So, being able to do it off the top of your head makes you feel smart?

L: Yeah, it makes me feel smart, I guess.

Lakesia wanted to learn concepts quickly so she could perform procedures from the top of her head, like she felt her sister did. What also helped her learn the concepts was having several examples, which her seventh-grade math teacher did. But, when she did not understand in her Pre-Algebra class, she did not ask her teacher for help or for more examples. However, her performance in Pre-Algebra led Mrs. Hill to believe Lakesia had a strong background in mathematics. Since she did not come to Mrs. Hill for help and still performed well on her homework, tests, and quizzes, she saw Lakesia as a good, capable math student. Not only was Lakesia surprised that Mrs. Hill thought so favorably of her academic ability, in general she thought her quietness led teachers to believe that she was a poor student. Janae, her mother, knew that Lakesia struggled in mathematics. However, they were both glad that Lakesia could make As and Bs in mathematics as opposed to the grades she made when they lived in a larger urban city. Lakesia said that the subject was easier then, but she still made bad grades. When asked to explain the change, she stated ". . . maybe because of the teachers [at Perfecto] and the environment . . . I didn't get good grades [in the city] because of the environment . . . It's just Black [people]. It would be like down here except . . . it's like a couple of white people down there and down there . . . all the people are Black . . . it's different . . . I mean, I didn't get bad, bad grades. I just got Bs and Cs instead of As and Bs compared to down here. It wasn't that bad, I just didn't like it" (Interview, 12/06/02). At the time of the interview, she was still dealing with some after effects of the transition from the other school in the sixth grade, even though her academic performance was better.

> We call our math "Dumb Math." We call their math "honors." Not necessarily that we're dumb, but it's just that [the Algebra students are] more advanced than us, that's why they're called advanced math, because they got an A in sixth grade and then in seventh grade they were in advanced math and then they came to eighth grade and they went to advanced math. I'm not dumb, I just got a B in sixth grade and that was because I came in the school year late. And [my teacher] didn't explain stuff to me, so I got a B. (Interview, 12/06/02)

Lakesia was aware of labels students have based on mathematics classes, especially when comparing Algebra to non-Algebra students. This placement in a lower class did not discourage her and she wanted to continue taking more math classes because she liked the challenge of mathematics.

Bianca: "I Want Someone Who's Got My back."

Bianca had a younger brother who was in the seventh grade at Perfecto, as well as two older sisters and an older brother. Bianca tended to bully other students. She may have felt that her actions were in jest; however, she was more aggressive than playful. Her mother, Charlotte, expressed that she wished Bianca had better control of her temper.

Bianca was an independent worker, even though she earned low grades. She took pride in being able to do her work on her own, as opposed to asking the teacher or peers for help. She believed her teacher would not understand her if she asked her to show her how to do something from class. She felt Mrs. Hill would "probably think [she was] disrespecting her." Even though I did not ask the girls to compare Black and white teachers, Bianca continued to bring up her second-grade teacher whenever I asked about elementary experiences. Second grade and fifth grade were the only years she remembered. Her second-grade teacher was the only Black teacher she'd had in elementary school and her eighth-grade Social Studies teacher was also Black. She said, "I can tell them how I'm feeling and they'll understand, and they won't just be like 'well, why do you feel that way?' just questioning me. They'll understand why I feel that way" (Interview, 12/06/02). She also felt that Black teachers pushed her "and they would try until they couldn't [any] more, to help us," which made her feel like "somebody got my back." When I asked her to recollect past school experiences, she brought up her second-grade teacher (who was Black) and her fifth-grade teacher who wasn't. Neither of the memories were of mathematics, but they gave me insight on what she appreciated in classes. Her second-grade teacher made up songs and dances for the students to learn different concepts. Her fifth-grade teacher had the students go outside to re-enact the Civil War at the end of the unit that included the war.

This ethics of caring dimension of Afrocentric feminist epistemology showed through Bianca's need for teachers to push her and she felt Black teachers afforded this type of agency more readily than non-Black teachers, even though I did not ask her to make such a comparison. The formation of these caring and compassionate relationships the girls valued are what Ladson-Billings (1997) viewed as important for improving the mathematical performance of Black students.

In the context of this study, *come home, then* takes on the meaning of a place of acceptance that fosters an understanding of the Black female participants. I used an Afrocentric feminist epistemology to analyze the data and to develop the themes presented below. Of the four dimensions mentioned earlier, lived experience as a criterion of meaning and ethics of caring appear in this study. The girls' experiences shaped their perceptions of their strengths, abilities in mathematics and usefulness of the subject. Their experiences and resulting perceptions were a vital part of addressing the objectives of the study from their perspective. Also, the value that they placed on nurturing and advocacy relate to the ethics of caring that Collins (1990a) presented. I have organized this section according to three emergent themes: Shaping Mathematics Identity, Connecting Personal Strengths to Mathematics, and Future in Mathematics.

Shaping Mathematics Identity

This theme includes the participants' general attitude about mathematics and their perceptions of their mathematics ability which included the perceptions of the participants, their mothers and their teacher. I was interested in what they currently thought of mathematics and what they thought about their achievement.

A main contributor to a student's experience in a classroom is the teacher, which is why I will briefly discuss the teacher in this section. Bianca mentioned that she did not feel that Mrs. Hill "had [her] back," or was an advocate for her. This feeling is not necessarily because Mrs. Hill was not Black. If students sense that the teacher

possesses an ethic of caring (Collins, 1990a), they will establish a mutually empa-
thetic relationship with the teacher and will be more comfortable in the teacher's
class. If they have a personal relationship with the teacher, the positive influence
affects their academic performance in a positive manner, which is many times the
feeling in a Black teacher's class for Black students (Walker & McCoy, 1997).
However, the authors of the *Principles and Standards for School Mathematics*
(NCTM, 2000) state that middle school students "are drawn toward mathematics if
they find both challenge and support in the mathematics classroom" (p. 210),
which can come from a teacher of any racial background.

Lakesia took pride in her grades and said she felt smart when she could do mathematics in her head, especially if she were doing something she had recently been
taught. She did not use her gender as an explanation for her performance in or attitude toward math, even though she thought boys were better at math "for some reason." Bianca did not believe boys were better at mathematics, but she did have
doubts about her ability, claiming that the subject was hard. Mrs. Hill tried to help
by giving Bianca adapted quizzes and notes that the LD students used.

Lakesia expected to do her best in mathematics and she believed she was capable
of taking advanced mathematics courses when she entered high school. Bianca's
self-confidence led her to state during one of the earlier interviews that she could
take advanced mathematics in high school. By the end of the fall semester, she
doubted her abilities and opted not to take any courses beyond Geometry. Overall,
their perception of their ability in mathematics was based on how well they were
doing in Pre-Algebra at the time of this study, as opposed to past experiences in
mathematics, in general.

This thread was the closest to addressing the research question, regarding the
girls' beliefs about their peers' expectations. Neither girl spoke of their peers very
often. Lakesia stated that she shared her grades with her peers who expected her to
do well. Bianca mentioned she did not want to repeat the eighth grade and appear
"dumb" to her peers. Both outlooks were the extent of the influence of peers from
the girls' perspectives. The image they portrayed was important to them. Lakesia
had an interest in maintaining a positive academic image, while Bianca was concerned with preventing aspects of a negative academic image to define her.

Connecting Personal Strengths to Mathematics

When I think of strengths in relation to Black women, the image of the matriarch,
strong Black woman comes to mind. This is a trait that many young Black girls
notice in their mothers and want to emulate (Collins, 1990a; Joseph, 1986). This
idea is illustrated through self-reliance, an independence that manifested itself in
the participants in this study. The theme emphasized what they viewed as their personal strengths and how to apply them to mathematics. Their past experiences and
influential people in their lives led them to have an understanding of their
strengths. Bianca helped me to see how much people influence her when I asked her
to name her strengths. She misunderstood the question and started listing friends,
family, church and saying that they really inspired and encouraged her. She went on
to say,

[my auntie and uncle] talk to me . . . if I do something wrong, they'll just sit down and talk to me and say, you know you did wrong. They won't even ask me to repent, they'll say, that's up to you what you want to do. They'll just talk to me about [it]; they won't have to get upset or nothin'. I think they inspire, too. (Interview 4/21/03)

When I re-worded the question and asked again, she said, "Oh, what am I good at? Singing, writing poems, writing stories . . ." That response confirmed some things she said in later interviews. Even though she was a weaker student, she started understanding Pre-Algebra better when she was able to explain her strategies to her friends. She didn't always understand the way the teacher presented the information but, when she found a strategy that worked and explained it to her friends, she was able to retain the information better. Since she felt her strength was in writing poems and stories, she was more of a verbal person. Having the opportunity to verbalize mathematics in her own way allowed a chance for the subject to start making sense.

I had hoped that Bianca and Lakesia could apply their strengths to mathematics, but they did not see the connections that I saw. Lakesia felt like her strengths were that she "did right" in school.

Like, instead of thinking about what everybody else think . . . be a leader, not a follower . . . People ask me for advice and they say I'm a good advice person . . . Everybody will be like, 'go to Lakesia, she'll tell you the right thing.' Sometimes it don't be hard to tell them. Most of the time it will be like my past experiences, so I'll know what to do. . . . (Interview 4/2/03)

In addition to giving good advice, she saw her quiet nature as a strength.

And they say I'm quiet but I just don't like to be loud a lot 'cause, I don't know, I just don't like to be loud and rude. Just runnin' around being silly. It's time to be in school, not time to be doing crazy stuff. I mean, you can have fun sometimes, but don't do it all day. (Interview, 4/2/03)

Though all of the information in this section is directly related to strengths, underlying throughout are experiences which contributed to the development or identification of the strengths. Bianca mentioned people first when I asked about her strengths. Both girls had an influential Black female in their lives who affected the way they learned. For Lakesia, it was her older sister who was a good mathematics student that helped her with her homework when she struggled. Lakesia tried to approach mathematics in the same manner as she thought her sister did. Working problems quickly or not using notes made Lakesia "feel smart" like her sister. For Bianca, her second-grade teacher was influential to her. This teacher taught with songs and dances that Bianca would mention during our discussions. Bianca was a student who thought school should be fun, and also liked to sing and dance. Thus, being taught in this way made her feel that she was learning and having fun at the same time.

Lakesia and Bianca had strengths that they named, but could not see how those characteristics could help them with mathematics. Lakesia studied people. "I sit quietly in the kitchen with no distractions while my mother cooks so I can learn" (Interview, 11/15/02). Lakesia's listening and attentiveness transferred over into her mathematics class and helped her learn and memorize procedures, even if she wasn't directly involved in experiencing it, like with her mom in the kitchen. Bianca's communication skills helped her talk through solutions and explain them to her peers.

Bianca's strengths that she noted were writing and singing. She was a student who needed to learn in ways that would keep her attention and interest. Most notable to her were songs and dramatizations in past classes and having fun. Granted, school cannot always be fun by a child's definition, but if it is interesting and engaging, more than likely a child will learn. Black students, in particular, learn holistically, relationally, and intuitively through direct contact with teachers and peers (Malloy, 1997).

Future in Mathematics

The girls' past and present experiences provided a basis for them to determine their outlook on mathematics. These experiences also led to the identification of their strengths. Finally, these concrete experiences led to the formation of their ideas about the usefulness of mathematics for their future and their projected ability in the subject. This theme includes the usefulness of mathematics as viewed by the participant, the mother and the teacher, as well as the participants' future goals, including the desire to attend college and the future mathematics courses required for that endeavor.

Neither girl had a career goal directly related to mathematics, but Lakesia's was in the sciences. She aspired to become a pediatrician, but her mother wanted her to become a teacher because she was more of a "people person." Bianca had so many aspirations that she was almost unrealistic. She wanted to do things that she saw on television. Her interest in becoming a singer, an actress, and even a lawyer were from what she saw on television. She wanted to major in Psychology because a lawyer on television had taken a Psychology class and he inspired her because she "liked the way he [handled] stuff" in his court scenes. Bianca also had some exposure to college because of her mother's part-time job in the cafeteria at a local private university. After school, she would go there to wait for her mother to get off work, giving her access to a college campus and its students for more information.

Since Lakesia aspired to become a pediatrician, she expressed the need for doing well in mathematics, yet she did not know why. She knew she would take advanced mathematics courses in high school because she felt she had the ability. Bianca, on the other hand, doubted her ability and did not want to take any courses beyond Geometry. She felt math was hard and did not want to try. This lack of effort was, perhaps, a combination of a lack of confidence and motivation. However, based on what I could gather about Bianca, her motivation was more of an issue than confidence. By the spring semester, she was slightly more confident and motivated to work in all of her classes, including mathematics, to prevent repeating the eighth grade.

Lakesia's ability to relate to people and communicate is one that could make her a good teacher, the career that her mother wished for her to pursue. She, however, wanted to become a pediatrician and figured that she would need to know mathematics in order to do that.

Bianca could not decide on her future goal, wanting to become an entertainer, lawyer, politician, and a business owner. She had a lot of dreams but did not seem to make the connection between now and the future.

Implications for Future Research

The reason I decided to focus on students in the eighth grade, enrolled in Pre-Algebra was because I wanted to gain insight on perceptions of mathematics prior to the transition into the gatekeeper course, Algebra. I also thought that since the students were close to elementary school at the time of the study, they would be able to reflect on their experiences due to their freshness. Had the goal of the research been to develop an intervention program for Black female students, this would have been a good target audience. However, since that was not goal of this study, I did not have the results that I expected where they could talk freely about their K-6 education and some of middle school. This was possibly due to the fact that they were too close to the experience and did not have enough time to reflect objectively and look back on their K-6 education, nor the opportunity yet to look back upon their entire K-12 education to be experienced. Perhaps, if a follow-up study is done once these young ladies are in college or have completed college, they will be able to provide a clearly broader picture and perspective of their mathematics experiences as a whole and supply more connections between their strengths and mathematics ability, as well as the usefulness of the subject for themselves in general. If the study is repeated with more participants, there may be more of a contrast in the findings and possibly the recollection of more experiences could be provoked in the group discussions. Finally, in part of Bianca's interview, she discussed teachers to whom she could relate, giving characteristics of teachers she liked. Even though she was focusing on teachers she liked, there is a noteworthy implication. A student will perform for a teacher who they think respects them, someone with whom they can relate, and someone with whom they feel a connection. Sometimes that connection is because of the subject, because of the ethnicity or gender of the teacher, or because of the teacher's personality. Whatever it is, teachers need to realize that making a connection with students speaks volumes.

Concluding Thoughts

A person can have a house without having a home. A house is the actual building where someone lives, whereas a home elicits a feeling. People often speak of home in a reminiscent fashion once they have moved away from the place where they were raised and with which they are familiar. When winter holidays approach, families anticipate gathering at home with close family and friends to reflect on the past year and project what is to come in future years. In this study, my participants were in a position to reflect on past school experiences in mathematics and project what the future holds for them in this regard. Though they were not able to take full advantage of this position, the journey has commenced for them and hopefully a foundation has been laid that will give them the same comfort that most people feel in knowing they can always come home.

Notes

1 The research reported in this chapter is part of a dissertation study conducted at Illinois State University under the direction of Dr. Norma Presmeg.
2 Both pseudonyms.
3 A pseudonym.

References

Collins, P.H. (1990a). *Black feminist thought: Knowledge, consciousness, and the politics of empowerment.* London: Harper Collins Academic.

Collins, P.H. (1990b). "Defining Black Feminist Thought." The Feminist eZine. Retrieved May 23, 2008 from http://www.feministezine.com/feminist/modern/Defining-Black-Feminist-Thought.html.

Du Bois, W.E.B. (1990). *The souls of Black folk.* New York: Literary Classics of the United States, Inc. (Original work published 1903.)

Fisher, T.A. (2000). Predictors of academic achievement among African American adolescents. In S.T. Gregory (Ed.), *The academic achievement of minority students: Perspectives, Practices, and Prescriptions* (pp. 307–334). Lanham, MD: University Press of America, Inc.

Fordham, S. (1993). "Those loud black girls": (Black) women, silence, and gender "passing" in the academy. *Anthropology and Education Quarterly, 24*(1), 3–32.

Freire, P. (2000). *Pedagogy of the oppressed* (M. B. Ramos, Trans. 30th Anniversary ed.). New York: Continuum.

hooks, b. (1981). *Ain't I a woman: Black women and feminism.* Boston: South End Press.

Jacobs, J.E., Becker, J.R., & Gilmer, G.F. (Eds.). (2001). *Changing the faces of mathematics: Perspectives on gender.* Reston, VA: National Council of Teachers of Mathematics.

Joseph, G.I. (1986). Black mothers and daughters: Their roles and functions in American society. In G. I. Joseph & J. Lewis (Eds.), *Common differences: Conflicts in black and white feminists perspectives* (pp. 75–126).

Kincheloe, J.L., & McLaren, P. (2000). Rethinking critical theory and qualitative research. In N.K. Denzin & Y.S. Lincoln (Eds.), *Handbook of qualitative research* (2nd ed., pp. 279–313). Thousand Oaks, CA: Sage Publications, Inc.

King, D.K. (1989). Multiple jeopardy, multiple consciousness: The context of a Black feminist ideology. In M. Wyer (Ed.), *Feminist theory in practice and process* (pp. 75–105). Chicago: The University of Chicago Press.

Kusimo, P.S. (1997). *Sleeping Beauty redefined: African American girls in transition.* Charleston WV: Appalachia Educational Lab. (ERIC Document Reproduction Service No. ED407207)

Kusimo, P.S., Carter, C.S., & Keyes, M.C. (1999). *I'd like to go to Harvard but I don't know where it is: Bridging the gap between reality and dreams for adolescent African American girls.* Paper presented at the Annual Meeting of the American Educational Research Association, Montreal, Quebec, Canada.

Ladson-Billings, G. (1997). It doesn't add up: African American students' mathematics achievement. *Journal for Research in Mathematics Education, 28*(6), 697–708.

Ladson-Billings, G. (2000). Racialized discourses and ethnic epistemologies. In N. K. Denzin & Y.S. Lincoln (Eds.), *Handbook of qualitative research* (2nd ed., pp. 257–277). Thousand Oaks, CA: Sage Publications, Inc.

Malloy, C.E. (1997). Including African American students in the mathematics community. In M.J. Kenney (Ed.), *Multicultural and gender equity in the mathematics classroom: The gift of diversity* (pp. 23–33). Reston, NJ: National Council of Teachers of Mathematics.

Martin, D.B. (2000). *Mathematics success and failure among African-American youth: The roles of sociohistorical context, community forces, school influence, and individual agency.* Mahwah, NJ: Lawrence Erlbaum Associates, Publishers.

Moody, V.R. (2000). African American students' success with school mathematics. In W.G. Secada, M.E. Strutchens, M.L. Johnson, & W.F. Tate (Eds.), *Changing the faces of mathematics: Perspectives on African Americans* (pp. 51–60). Reston, VA: National Council of Teachers of Mathematics.

Moody, V.R. (2001). The social constructs of the mathematical experiences of African-American students. In B. Atweh, H. Forgasz, & B. Nebres (Eds.), *Sociocultural research on mathematics education: An international perspective* (pp. 255–276). Mahwah, NJ: Lawrence Erlbaum Associates, Publishers.

National Council of Teachers of Mathematics (NCTM). (2000). *Principles and standards for school mathematics.* Reston, VA: Author.

Secada, W.G. (Ed.). (2000). *Changing the faces of mathematics: Perspectives on multiculturalism and gender equity.* Reston, VA: National Council of Teachers of Mathematics.

Secada, W.G., Fennema, E., & Adajian, L.B. (Eds.). (1995). *New directions for equity in mathematics education.* New York: Cambridge University Press.

Stake, R.E. (2000). Case studies. In N.K. Denzin & Y.S. Lincoln (Eds.), *Handbook of qualitative research* (2nd ed., pp. 435–454). Thousand Oaks, CA: Sage Publications, Inc.

Strutchens, M.E., Johnson, M.L., & Tate, W.F. (Eds.). (2000). *Changing the faces of mathematics: Perspectives on African Americans.* Reston, VA: National Council of Teachers of Mathematics.

Trentacosta, J. & Kenney, M.J. (Eds.). (1997). *Multicultural and gender equity in the mathematics classroom: The gift of diversity* (1997 Yearbook). Reston, VA: National Council of Teachers of Mathematics.

U.S. Department of Education. National Center for Education Statistics. (2001). *Educational achievement and Black–White inequality* (NCES 2001–061). Washington, DC: Author.

Walker, E.N. & McCoy, L.P. (1997). Students' voices: African Americans and mathematics. In M.J. Kenney (Ed.), *Multicultural and gender equity in the mathematics classroom: The gift of diversity* (pp. 71–80). Reston, VA: NCTM.

Yin, R.K. (2003). *Case study research: Design and methods* (3rd ed.). Thousand Oaks: Sage Publications.

13 "Still Not Saved": The Power of Mathematics to Liberate the Oppressed

Jacqueline Leonard

Introduction

"The harvest is past, the summer is ended, and we are still not saved."

The words of Jeremiah 8:20 can be used to describe the plight of African Americans in the United States. Specifically, the failure of the educational and legal systems to provide Black children with a quality education perpetuates the pedagogy of poverty (Bell, 1987; Haberman, 1991; Knapp, 1995). In 2002, 32.3% of all Black children lived in poverty (Proctor & Dalaker, 2003). While this figure is down from 44% in 1993, the jobless rate for Black youth between the ages of 16 and 19 hit a historic high of 78.3% in July of 2003 (Children's Defense Fund, 2003). Thus, roughly a third of Black children were poor, and more than three-quarters of Black youth were unemployed in 2003.

However, it was the storm that devastated the Gulf Coast on August 29, 2005 that caused the world to take notice of the stark difference between poor African Americans and the rest of U.S. society (Irvine, 2007). Attention has been brought to the inadequacies of the educational and health systems that serve these U.S. citizens (Irvine, 2007; Leonard, 2007). Before Hurricane Katrina, the state of health, education, and economic affairs for African American citizens was worse than it was before *Brown vs. Board* (Bell, 1987, 2004). Post-Katrina, the mortality rate in New Orleans surged to an alarming level as the death rate reached 14.3 per 1000 (Sternberg, 2007). Teachers recruited to New Orleans through the Teach for America Program ended up working in predominantly white private schools instead of the Black public school system in New Orleans Parish because of large salary gaps (Darling-Hammond, 2007). While the Central Business District has rebounded and the overall unemployment rate in New Orleans has declined, Blacks continue to experience high unemployment rates, which was 20% higher than the national average in 2006 (Holzer & Lerman, 2006). Thus, Jeremiah 8:20 may be interpreted as: *Another year is past, the summer is ended, and high mortality, mis-education, and unemployment are still the order of the day*. A call for action has been made, especially to African American educators, scholars, and researchers to improve educational conditions for poor Black students in New Orleans and elsewhere (Ladson-Billings, 2006; Martin, 2007). However, individual responses to the call are hampered by the challenges of a hegemonic system of education that continues to privilege and benefit white students (Blanchett, 2006; Martin, 2007; Martin, this volume).

Perspectives and Purpose

Numerous studies have been conducted on the underachievement of African American students in education (Campbell, 1995; Entwisle & Alexander, 1992; Stiff & Harvey, 1988; Tate, 1997). Simultaneously, numerous theories have emerged to explain this underachievement. Some theories suggest that African Americans cannot learn because they are less intelligent (Herrnstein & Murray, 1994). However, these theories provide no real evidence that Black students differ from other social groups in their capacity to learn (Martin, 2000). Other theories, such as the theory of social capital, suggest that Black students are not achieving because of cultural deficits (Coleman, 1987). However, this theory does not explain why some African American students fail to achieve in predominantly White settings (Bell, 1987; Morris, 2004; Ogbu, 2003) or how African American culture can be used to enhance student achievement (Delpit, 1995; Ladson-Billings, 1994; Leonard, 2008). Furthermore, theories that suggest African American students are underachieving simply because they come from low-socioeconomic backgrounds (Bonds, 1981) fail to explain the strength, resilience, and social agency that cause some Black students to achieve in spite of socioeconomic status (Martin, 2000; Morris, 2004; Ogbu, 2003).

Yet, underachievement does not imply inability. Research studies that unwittingly legitimize standardized testing as the sole means of demonstrating mathematical knowledge are shortsighted and inaccurate. Tests are cultural products and every student brings his/her conceptual frame to a testing situation that varies with the cultural and linguistic background he/she possesses (Solano-Flores & Trumbell, 2003). This is especially true of low socioeconomic students who tend to apply their emotional and personal perspectives to standardized test items and project their own concerns and experiences onto the way they solve problems (Solano-Flores & Trumbell, 2003; Tate, 1995). Thus, standardized test items often function to disadvantage students of color.

As a doctoral student at the University of Maryland, I found that studies on the underachievement of Black students in mathematics were replete in literature (Entwisle & Alexander, 1992; Stiff & Harvey, 1988; Tate, 1997). However, the focus on achievement gaps, now called gap-gazing (Gutiérrez, 2008), alarmed me because it did not resonate with my own experiences as a mathematics student, or with my experiences as a mathematics teacher in poor urban schools. These studies not only caused me to reflect on my own mathematics education and opportunity to learn (OTL), but the mathematics education and OTL of the African American students I had taught as well. These experiences provided me with the impetus to engage in research that would value African American students' ways of learning and understanding mathematics and compelled me to report these students' mathematical successes (Leonard, 2004; Leonard, Davis, & Sidler, 2005; Leonard & Guha, 2002). Like Ford (1993), I found that socioeconomic status (SES) alone does not predict the academic performance of Black students. Family and students' beliefs and values are also highly correlated with academic achievement. Shaping those beliefs and values in specific ways to enhance African American students' opportunity to learn and to achieve in mathematics education is the focus of this paper.

The purpose of this theoretical chapter is to address African American students' learning in mathematics using the constructs of *mathematics identity* and *mathematics socialization* (Martin, 2000). "*Identity* is most often defined as an amalgamation of self-concept, self-understanding, and evaluating oneself in relation to others" (Nasir, 2005, p. 217). "Mathematics socialization describes the processes and experiences by which individual and collective mathematics identities are shaped by sociohistorical, community, school, and intrapersonal contexts" (Martin, 2000, p. 19). Development of a positive mathematics identity (Leonard, 2008; Martin, 2000; Nasir, 2005; Nosek et al., 2002) is crucial to sustaining interest in mathematics as a subject domain and to understanding its importance in maintaining an equitable and just society. Mathematical knowledge and expertise is empowering and life altering, especially for those who are marginalized and oppressed. From negotiating a fair price for a new automobile at the dealership to obtaining an impartial and representative jury of one's peers for a civil action, knowledge and application of mathematics, specifically in the area of data and statistics, are needed to ensure fair and equitable practices in all aspects of social, cultural, and political life.

An example of mathematics identity and socialization can be found in the life of Bessie Coleman, the first American woman to obtain an international pilot's license in 1921 (Grimes, 2002). Bessie was born into a family of sharecroppers in Waxahachie, Texas. However, as a young child, she quickly learned how the family's livelihood depended upon its ability to negotiate a fair price for commodities such as cotton. In June 1904, the price of cotton at the Cotton Exchange was 11.6 cents a pound. Cotton was sold in bales, which were about 1,400 pounds. It was not uncommon for sharecroppers to get cheated out of their money when they took their cotton to the gin. According to Borden and Kroeger (2001), as a child, Bessie not only calculated the correct amount she should receive for the family's cotton based on the price, but she was shrewd enough to put her foot on the scale to tilt the balance in her family's favor.

Mathematics education in the United States is a racialized and gendered experience (Campbell, 1995; Kitchen, 2007; Leonard, 2008). When it comes to the mathematics education of Black children, the scales remain unbalanced. We are in need of human *feet* to tip the scales in favor of poor, invisible, and marginalized children like those in New Orleans and other rural and urban cities in the US. The headlines that depicted New Orleans as third world America in 2005 are still relevant today. The US receives a failing grade on human rights when it comes to addressing disparate treatment of Blacks in education, housing, health, and the criminal justice system (ACLU, 2007). The Lower North Ward in New Orleans could have been renovated with far less than the $566 billion spent to date on the war in Iraq (National Priorities Project, 2008). Neglecting the health, education, and welfare of African Americans in the US, while challenging the human rights record of other nations, contributes to a negative perception of the US around the globe and places a strain on foreign policy. If the US wants to be taken seriously in the world as a global leader and as a role model for democracy, then it must live up to its creeds and make fundamental changes in educational, political, and social policies (Gutstein, 2006).

Ideologies of Empowerment and Liberation

I use the theme of community and schools to personify the struggles of the Black community and how mathematics can be used to enhance African American children's mathematics literacy, identity, and socialization and to promote social justice. I begin by describing the ideologies that ground the ideas of empowerment and liberation that I present in this chapter. After describing each of these ideologies in relation to mathematics cognition among African American students, I use the titles of Negro spirituals and gospels to describe the historical past and present state of African Americans' mathematics education.

Spirituals were often inspired by the Scriptures and have no known author. These songs, which originated in the Black Church, exemplify the Black experience in America, often Africanize the Black Christian experience, and tell stories of oppression, hope, and liberation in song (Lincoln & Mamiya, 1990). The titles of the spirituals used in this chapter are as follows: *I Been in de Storm so Long; I Couldn't Hear Nobody Pray;* and *Children, Go Where I Send Thee.* I use the spiritual entitled *I Been in de Storm so Long* to describe the long struggle for racial justice and equality in American schools beginning with *Plessy vs. Ferguson* and ending with *Brown vs. Board. I Couldn't Hear Nobody Pray* describes the slow wheels of justice after the ruling of *Brown vs. Board* and how this decision impacted my education in the St. Louis Public School system and, by implication the education of other Black children in America. Clara Ward's (1951) gospel, *How I Got Over,* is used to explain how I used mathematics to attain access to higher education and accomplish my life's goals. I also use the spiritual, *Children, Go Where I Send Thee,* as a metaphor to describe my teaching experiences in urban communities. Finally, I use Keith Pringle's (1991) gospel, *When All God's Children Get Together,* to make recommendations and draw conclusions that can be implemented in the present and future.

The ideologies that support the framework of this paper are Critical Race Theory (Dixson & Rousseau, 2005; Ladson-Billings, 1998), Liberation Theology (Cone, 1990), and Pedagogy of the Oppressed (Freire, 2006). Critical Race Theory challenges the colorblind approach of a traditional liberal civil rights stance and can be traced to the works of Derrick Bell and Alan Freeman in the mid-1970s (Delgado, 1995). Critical Race Theory holds the premise that racism is normative in the United States because its roots emerge from and were supported by the Constitution, which denied the humanity of slaves in favor of White property owners (Bell, 1987; Ladson-Billings, 1998). There are systemic and institutional forces at work that continue to oppress persons of color "in society in general and education in particular" (Dixson & Rousseau, 2005, p. 8). Race has become a metaphorical way of "referring to and disguising forces, events, classes, and expressions of social decay and economic division" (Morrison, 1992, p. 63). In critical race discourses, persons of color speak from a different frame of reference and have a different voice from the dominant culture, which deserves to be heard and understood (Delgado, 1995). Lynn (1999) summarized some of the purposes of Critical Race Theory and identified the explanatory power it holds:

1   Recognizes the centrality of race and intransigence of racism in contemporary American society.
2   Rejects East–West European Modernist claims of neutrality, objectivity, rationality, and universality.
3   Historicizes its analysis by relying heavily on the experiential knowledge of people of color (p. 608).

Critical Race Theory is an important framework when it comes to mathematics identity and socialization because it provides a different lens to examine the mathematics education of Black children. Rather than focusing on underachievement or test scores, Critical Race Theory gives credence to the voices of African American students and how they view their mathematics education. Specifically, I use my own voice to discuss my identity, socialization, and achievement in mathematics. However, Critical Race Theory is not sufficient to describe my experience because it is also rooted in the liberation theology of Black Methodist preachers in my life. These men and women instilled a sense of faith and belief that God is active on the part of the those who are oppressed and marginalized in society. As a result of this belief, I use my faith and knowledge of mathematics to advocate for my rights, the rights of my progeny, and the rights of children to receive a high quality education. Thus, a framework that examines spirituality and social justice is also needed.

Liberation theology emerged in the 1970s from the work of Latin American Catholics who believed it was not enough to be concerned about the poor (Dorr, 1984; Prahlad, 2005). Rather, they advocated for enabling the poor "to experience their God, the God who is on their side to protect them against oppression" (Dorr, 1984, p. 16). Oppression is the lack of educational and economic opportunity. Liberation is the act, or means, by which access to higher education, higher paying jobs, and entrepreneurship, is acquired. Salvation in this sense is the realization of educational opportunity and affluence.

Liberation theologians claimed that God is actively engaged in behavior that topples oppressive structures and emancipates the oppressed (Dorr, 1984). Particular texts, such as Exodus, function to show God as the liberator of slaves and marginalized people in response to poverty, injustice, and oppression. However, this theological view is not without controversy. Like the work of Paulo Freire (2006), liberation theology argues in favor of political action that may result in revolution. "It is absolutely necessary that the oppressed participate in the revolutionary process with an increasingly critical awareness of their roles as Subjects of the transformation" (Freire, 2006, p. 127). Thus, it should be no surprise that the ideology of liberation theology resonated with Black theologians in the 1960s.

Black theology grew out of the Black power movement of the 1960s as theologians like James Cone sought to understand the violent acts perpetrated by the status quo against Black leaders and protesters. Black theology is unique in its message, activism, music, and spiritual expression. Cone (1990) linked Black theology to liberation theology by relating it to the antebellum religion of Black slaves (Prahlad, 2005).

Black theology is a theology of black liberation. It seeks to plumb the black condition in the light of God's revelation in Jesus Christ, so that the black community can see that the gospel is commensurate with the achievement of black humanity. (Wilmore & Cone, 1980, p. 102)

Moreover, just as Moses was the figure who freed the Hebrew slaves from their oppression in Egypt, Black liberation theologians view Jesus as the liberator of Blacks from chattel slavery and racial injustice. This theme permeates many of the spirituals that emerged during the antebellum period (Lincoln & Mamiya, 1990).

The spirit of the Lord is upon me, because he has anointed me to preach good news to the poor. He has sent me to proclaim release to the captives and the recovery of sight to the blind, to let the oppressed go free. (Luke 4: 18–19)

Thus, Black liberation theology offers a framework that not only deals with oppression, but empowers those who are oppressed by lifting up their humanity as a God-given attribute. Black liberation theology calls for more humane treatment of Blacks in America, in general, including Black children in the U.S. educational system.

While the Black Church, just as the Black community, is diverse with various subcultures and is not monolithic, it has been in the forefront of social and political change (Robinson, 2008). Nevertheless, some believe most Black churches are not political and are primarily concerned with "salvation" (Robinson, 2008). This view does not reflect my Black Church experience where voter registration is common, public schools are adopted, and community development corporations (CDCs) started. Furthermore, such views underestimate the power of the Black Church to use its collective voice to overturn the tables of oppression as Jesus overturned the tables of the moneychangers in the temple (John 2: 14–16). Rev. Dr. Martin Luther King quoting Amos 5: 24 said "Let justice roll down like waters, and righteousness like an ever-flowing stream."

However, when Black ministers become too vocal, they often become marginalized and viewed as unpatriotic. For example, nearly everyone knows Rev. Jeremiah Wright and his association with Senator Barack Obama. I, too, am familiar with Rev. Wright, having met him in the 1990s when I was a seminary student at Southern Methodist University. Rev. Jeremiah Wright and Rev. Vashti McKenzie (first female bishop of the African Methodist Episcopal Church) were invited by the Black seminarians to SMU because they are icons in the Black Church.

Later after moving to Philadelphia, I heard Rev. Wright preach at his father's church there. When I visited relatives in Chicago, I also heard Rev. Wright preach at his former church, Trinity. What I heard was not inflammatory but powerful and inspirational liberation theology. Wright's style of preaching was not very different from sermons I had heard at politically active St. Luke "Community" United Methodist Church in Dallas, Texas, where I met Mickey Leland and Barbara Jordan when they visited St. Luke in the 1990s. In addition to attending services at Trinity,

I was invited by church staff to tour the facility. I learned they had an education wing where volunteers offered GED classes and computer training. Such ministries are proactive ways to encourage people to tap their God-given potential and put their energies and skills to work to improve their economic condition.

Sadly, Rev. Wright was the center of controversy simply because of his association with Senator Obama. The news media sensationalized Rev. Wright based on a short sound bite from one of the sermons he delivered prior to retirement (Robinson, 2008). While I will not repeat the controversial statement here, it does not take a great deal of thought to realize it was taken out of context. The American public does not know what was said before or after the statement as Wright himself stated in a news conference at the National Press Club (NPC) on April 28, 2008. However, *inflammatory* comments made at the NPC regarding the U.S. response to September 11, 2001 and the HIV/AIDS epidemic in the Black community led many television and radio hosts and newspaper reporters to condemn Rev. Wright, and some went so far as to demonize him. While Wright's accusation that the government introduced HIV/AIDS as a form of racial genocide may seem preposterous, it is not unfounded given the Tuskegee experiment. For the sake of medical research, Black men infected with Syphilis were not treated when there was a known cure (Thomas & Quinn, 1991). Like the prophet Jeremiah, Rev. Jeremiah Wright felt compelled to tell a nation "we are still not saved." Nevertheless, rather than address this and other atrocities and injustices that have outraged the Black community over the years, political opponents used the opinions of Rev. Wright to diminish Senator Obama's presidential campaign (Baugh, 2008).

More recently, the Republican campaign and Republican Vice-Presidential candidate, Sarah Palin, have tried to portray Senator Obama as anti-American because of his association with Professor William Ayers. Professor Ayers was part of a radical political group called the Weather Underground, which bombed government buildings to protest the Vietnam War (McEwan, 2008). Palin has characterized Ayers as a terrorist. Guilt by association implies that Obama is a terrorist, too (McEwan, 2008). Thus, the Republicans attempted to derail Obama's road to the White House by using his former associations with Wright and Ayers to paint him as an individual who is unpatriotic and dangerous. But millions of Americans turned the page on race and negative campaign tactics to elect Barack Obama as the first African American president of the United States on November 4, 2008.

Obama and his campaign strategists did the math by increasing the number of registered voters by hundreds of thousands, many of whom had never voted in any general election. Moreover, Obama energized young, diverse, and marginalized voters with a Populist message of hope to change the political landscape in this country. My 27-year-old daughter, a doctoral student in Urban Education, pulled me off the sidelines when she volunteered to work for the Obama campaign. I found myself canvassing neighborhoods, making hundreds of phone calls, giving senior citizens rides to the polls during both the primary and the general election, and, yes, even making small contributions on the Internet. Dr. Martin Luther King, Jr. believed the poor and disenfranchised could change their circumstances with the power of their collective vote. Dr. King's dream of an America that measures a person by the content of his or her character instead of the color of his or her skin was realized on Election Day 2008. The question remains whether we will seize the moment and write new mathematical equations to level the playing field and balance the scales of economic power and wealth on behalf of the oppressed.

Freire's *Pedagogy of the Oppressed* (2006) echoes Black liberation theology's focus on the struggle for humanity. Freire's experiences of class prejudice in Brazil shaped his philosophy and work, which Apple (2003) suggests led to a realization that oppression was "color-coded" and gendered (p. 108). Freire (2006) stated the following on oppression:

> The pedagogy of the oppressed is an instrument for their critical discovery that both they and their oppressors are manifestations of dehumanization . . . As the oppressors dehumanize others and violate their rights, they themselves also become dehumanized. As the oppressed, fighting to be human, take away the oppressors' power to dominate and suppress, they restore to the oppressors the humanity they had lost in the exercise of oppression. (pp. 48–58)

Freire's statement implies that the lives of the oppressed and the oppressor are inextricably linked. The oppressed cannot be liberated unless they advocate for their humanity, and the oppressor cannot be liberated from his/her oppressive acts until he/she repents of these acts. Hence the spiritual nature of reconciliation such as that promoted after the dismantling of apartheid in South Africa must take place in this country. Rather than repentance and reconciliation after passage of *Brown vs. Board* in 1954 and Civil Rights legislation in 1964, new forms of oppression and resistance emerged to deny full citizenship and adequate schooling for African American students in the form of white flight, busing, and privatization of schools (Leonard, 2008; Leonard, Taylor, Sanford-De Shields, and Spearman, 2004). Yet, "Blacks need neither segregated schools nor mixed schools. What they need is education" (Du Bois as cited in Bell, 1987, p. 120). "It is important that we begin to implement new teaching strategies, begin new discourses, and create paradigms and models of educational research that are not only inclusive of culturally sensitive approaches for African Americans but also have the potential to significantly change their lives and their communities in emanicipatory ways" (Tillman, 2002, p. 9).

Historical Background

I Been in de Storm so Long

The inadequate mathematics education of African American children is pervasive and complex, having roots in "share cropper" and "separate but unequal" schools for Black children (Du Bois, 1995, Moses & Cobb, 2001). In order to frame this experience, it is necessary to look at the historical record on education for Black children in this country. First, I must point out that the founding fathers used mathematics when they applied the 3/5ths rule to count slaves in the U.S. Census. This action not only dehumanized Black people, but denied their *wholeness*. While there were some who disagreed, the prevailing thought during colonial times was that only white men were whole and rational beings capable of making decisions about a nation that was ironically founded on principles of religious freedom, liberty, and justice.

Prior to the debates that were held in Philadelphia in the mid-to-late 1780s to frame a constitution for the United States, a religious conference was held in Baltimore on Christmas Eve in 1784 and lasted for 10 days (Heitzenrater, 1995; Norwood, 1974). Under the direction of John Wesley, founding father of Methodism in England, Thomas Coke and Francis Asbury led the proceedings. At the conclusion of this conference, Coke and Asbury ordained each other as the first bishops of a newly formed Methodist Episcopal Church in America. Three Black men attended the Christmas Conference: Harry Hoosier, Absalom Jones, and Richard Allen. These men were Methodist preachers and had full participation in the Christmas Conference. Hoosier, also known as "Black Harry" was "the most famous Black preacher" at the time (Norwood, 1974, p. 168). Although he could not write, he had a powerful gift of preaching and often traveled with Coke and Asbury. Because of John Wesley's stance against slavery and his acceptance of Black ministers, "a large percentage of Negro members and ministers" belonged to the early Methodist church (Norwood, 1974, p. 168). In contrast to religious practices today, 11 o'clock on Sunday morning in the 1780s was not the most segregated hour in America in the Methodist Episcopal Church. In God's house, Blacks not only had souls, they were *whole* beings.

However, the laudable values and beliefs of the early Methodist Church were short lived. While John Wesley abhorred slavery and was an active abolitionist, some Methodist clergy members in the South owned slaves (Norwood, 1974). The church's stance on slavery was noted at the Conference of 1780, which was also held in Baltimore.

> Does this conference acknowledge that slavery is contrary to the laws of God, man, and nature, and hurtful to society, contrary to the dictates of conscience and pure religion, and doing that which we would not others should do to us and ours?—Do we pass our disapprobation on all our friends who keep slaves, and advise freedom? (Norwood, 1974, p. 93)

The issue of slave ownership divided the Methodist Episcopal Church and southern Methodists left the Church in 1830 and would not reunite until 100 years later (Norwood, 1974). Prior to this event, ill-treatment of Blacks at St. George's Church in Philadelphia led to the formation of the two historic Black churches in this city. The oldest Black Methodist congregation, Mother African Zoar, began in 1794 (Norwood, 1974). The second church, Bethel African Methodist Episcopal Church (AME) was dedicated as a worship space by Bishop Asbury in 1794 and founded in 1796 (Norwood, 1974). Richard Allen became the first AME bishop. Allen was not only a pastor, but he was a leader in the Free African Society, which was formed to improve conditions for Blacks and advocated for the abolition of slavery (Harding, 1981; Norwood, 1974). Thus, the Black Methodist Church began its work for social justice on behalf of Black people.

Methodist churches were places of learning as well. As early as 1790, Sunday schools for poor children included religious education as well as the three Rs: reading, writing, and arithmetic (Norwood, 1974). Moreover, the United Methodist Church was supportive of my research by providing grant dollars to run Saturday science and mathematics clubs in urban churches in Philadelphia (Leonard, 2002). Thus, it is not unprecedented for the Black Church to draw from this heritage and to help develop African American children's mathematics identity and socialization.

Since the ruling of *Plessy vs. Ferguson* in 1896, which called for separate but equal education, Blacks have received a less than adequate education in the United States (Leonard, 2008). Because education is a state function, federal legislation did little to ensure the ruling was carried out. Even after the ruling of *Brown vs. Board* in 1954, the American legal system failed to remedy separate but unequal education for African American children (Bell, 1987; Dixson & Rousseau, 2005; Ladson-Billings, 2006). Instead, two kinds of public education systems emerged in America: one for predominantly white middle-class students and one for poor working-class students of color. In schools concentrated with poor Black and Latino/a students, the kind of mathematics education they receive is often limited to basic skills and computation (Gutstein, 2006; Leonard, 2008; Martin, 2003; Stiff & Harvey, 1988). Gutstein (2006) believes that those who support this view have a limited understanding of mathematics literacy, which he calls *functional* literacy. Functional literacy focuses on the "competencies needed to function appropriately within a given society" (Gutstein, 2006, p. 5). Instead, Gutstein (2006) suggests a focus on *critical literacy*, which examines "relationships between ideas, looks for underlying explanations of phenomena, and questions whose interests are served and who benefits" (p. 5). Ladson-Billings's (2006) use of critical literacy focuses attention on the unpaid educational debt owed to African American and other children of color by the nation's failure to embrace *Plessy vs. Ferguson* and *Brown vs. Board*. While the government passed legislation to promote equity in our nation's schools, it could not pass legislation to change people's hearts. As Carter G. Woodson stated (1998) decades earlier:

> Instead of teaching . . . Negro children less [mathematics], they should be taught much more of it than the white children, for the latter attended a grade school consolidated by free transportation when Negroes go to one-room rented hovels to be taught without equipment and by incompetent teachers educated scarcely beyond the eighth grade. (p. 4)

More than 50 years after *Brown v. Board*, the majority of African American children still attend racially and economically segregated schools (Bell, 2004). Public schools remain highly segregated along racial and social class lines because the neighborhoods that feed students to the local school remain highly segregated (Ogbu, 2003). To illustrate the impact of segregation in public schools, I highlight demographic differences between two communities in Delaware County, Pennsylvania. Chester, a small town of less than 40,000, is 75.8% Black and suffers from declining factories and population and the loss of nearly all of its middle class (Staples, 2002).

According to the U.S. Census Bureau (2000), 9.7% of residents were unemployed, and the median household income in Chester was $25,429. While more than 69% of adults 25 or older are high school graduates, only 8.3% hold a Bachelor's degree. According to the greatschools website, enrollment figures for Chester High School revealed the student population of 1679 was 93% African American, 5% Hispanic, and 1% white in 2007. The recently hired school superintendent, Dr. Gregory Thornton, has implemented a number of new strategies, including a credit recovery program to lower the 12.7% dropout rate, which was one of the highest in the Commonwealth of Pennsylvania (Seixas, 2007).

In contrast, nearby Wallingford is a suburban community of less that 12,000 that is 94% white (U.S. Census Bureau, 2000). More than 92% of adults 25 or older are high school graduates, and more than 50% have a Bachelor's degree. The unemployment rate was 2.2%, and the median household income was $68,750 in 2000. Strath Haven High School, which is located in Wallingford, is less than three miles away from Chester High School. School district data show 1,288 students were enrolled at Strath Haven in 2007 (86% white, 9% Black, 4% Asian, and 1% Hispanic), and the dropout rate was zero in 2005–2006 (Seixas, 2007). According to the greatschools website (2008), 25 advanced placement courses were offered at Strath Haven, while no advanced placement courses were listed for Chester High School.

Clearly, these stark demographic data have an impact on each community's view of itself and perceptions others have of the students, the schools they attend, and the communities they come from. As long as such disparities exist, social stratification along racial lines will remain unchanged. "So long as there are ghetto neighborhoods and ghetto hospitals and ghetto schools, . . . there will be ghetto desperation, ghetto violence, and ghetto fear because a ghetto is itself an evil and unnatural construction" (Kozol, 1995, p. 162). The storm of separate but unequal education has not passed but has lasted far too long.

Along with Gutstein (2006), I contend that critical mathematics literacy is needed to challenge unjust practices and to advocate for high quality mathematics education for Black children. Mathematics can be used to read, that is interpreting, and write, which is critiquing, the world (Gutstein, 2006). For example, data show that only 12% of all underrepresented minorities (URMs) combined received Bachelor's degrees in science, technology, engineering, and mathematics (STEM) fields in 2002 (NSB, 2002). However, jobs in STEM fields like computer science and mathematics are expected to grow more than 37% and 10%, respectively, by 2016 (Bureau of Labor Statistics, U.S. Department of Labor, 2008). URMs should be represented in the STEM workforce to the same degree as they are in the general population. Blacks make up roughly 12.3% of the general population, and Hispanics and Native Americans make up roughly 12.5% and 0.9%, respectively (National Science Foundation, 2007). Ideally, 28% of all students graduating with Bachelor's degrees in STEM should be URMs.

However, opportunities that promote a diverse workforce are often the result of *interest convergence*, which is promoting Blacks' interests simply to satisfy the dominant group's needs (Bell, 2004; Dixson & Rousseau, 2005; Martin, this volume). The largest job growth continues to be in the service industry where low-skilled workers continue to receive low wages that perpetuate poverty (Gutstein, 2006). What is being done to ensure that Black students are prepared in mathematics, which is prerequisite to STEM careers and entrepreneurial opportunities?

I share my own story of a post *Brown* public school experience to illuminate the complex issues of race, socioeconomic status, and academic achievement in mathematics. According to Martin (this volume), narratives about African Americans' mathematical experiences *as African Americans* should be placed alongside traditional forms of knowledge production to rely on culturally sensitive research methods rather than the comparative racial paradigm. Thus a critical analysis from a personal perspective is presented to explain the far-reaching effects of *de facto* segregation and poverty on my life and on the lives of the Black children I taught in urban schools.

An Analysis of Mathematics Education for Black Children

I Couldn't Hear Nobody Pray

When the Supreme Court ruled in *Brown v. Board* (1954) that school segregation was unconstitutional, southern school districts published gaps in the test scores of Black and White students to justify their opposition to desegregation (Ogbu, 2003). Evidently, the news must not have reached the Midwest because my mother was a junior in high school in Mississippi when *Brown vs. Board* was decided, but when I began my education at Pierre Laclede School on the north side of St. Louis, Missouri, in 1962, the schools in St. Louis were still segregated 8 years post *Brown*.

At the time, my neighborhood was clean and neat. The streets were lined with two-story homes that were owned primarily by Black working-class families. Interspersed among these homes were four family flats where some families rented a five-room apartment. My family of six—mother, grandmother, two brothers, sister and I—lived in one of these flats. Our home was 2.5 blocks from the school, which was centrally located in the community. Whites, who were often absentee landlords, owned many of the apartment buildings, which were often in a state of disrepair. For example, I recall loose plaster and paint chips falling from the walls in our apartment. Yet, these poor and crowded living conditions did not hinder my learning of mathematics and did not deter me and my siblings from achieving despite such obstacles (Martin, 2000; Ogbu, 2003).

Early School Mathematics Experiences

I attended Laclede from kindergarten to eighth grade (1963–1971). Student attendance was high and mobility was low. The teaching staff was also very stable. One of the male teachers at the school went to the same Methodist church that I attended, and several teachers lived in the neighborhood. There were high expectations established by teachers and parents. It was totally unacceptable to misbehave in school. When teachers called parents, there was an almost immediate response. The parents supported the teachers—period. Like the school described by Morris (2004),

Laclede was a flagship school. Incentives for academic excellence included free tickets to Cardinals baseball games. It was a very big deal when I received two free tickets to a game, since the Cardinals won the World Series in 1967. While Laclede was segregated, like the two schools Morris (2004) described in his study, it provided the cultural capital and social agency that I and so many other African American students needed (Delpit, 1995; Morris, 2004).

Morris (2004) conducted a 3-year study of two African American schools, one of which was located in St. Louis, Missouri. Fairmont Elementary School (pseudonym) maintained a strong relationship with African American families in a working-class neighborhood in North St. Louis. The shiny hardwood floors and meticulously clean school environment Morris (2004) described at Fairmont was indicative of the St. Louis Public Schools. The image brought back memories of hardwood floors at Laclede, which were so well polished that you could see your reflection in them. While parents had the opportunity to participate in a desegregation plan, most of the parents chose to keep their children at Fairmont because they were highly satisfied with the education their children received there. Parents and teachers worked "interdependently to meet children's social and educational needs" (Morris, 2004, p. 87). In addition to positive parent–teacher relationships, the students' culture and interaction styles were valued in the classroom. As a result of teachers' use of cultural and social capital (Dance, 2002), the children at Fairmont experienced academic success, just as my siblings and I did at Laclede.

I have few memories of learning and doing mathematics at Laclede. However, it was in Mrs. Battle's (pseudonym) eighth-grade class that I realized my talent in mathematics. I was especially good at solving fraction problems. I also remember that I enjoyed helping my female friends add and subtract fractions with unlike denominators. Ms. Battle often let us work together on mathematics problems out of the textbook. She spent more time teaching mathematics than any of the other teachers I had had previously. I believe it was her understanding of the consequences for us as eighth graders that motivated her to focus on mathematics more than any other school subject. Like the teacher in Rousseau and Powell's study (2005), the ramifications of high stakes tests influenced Ms. Battle's curriculum and instruction long before the NCTM *Standards* were published. Unless we scored well on the district's assessments in mathematics, we were subject to being tracked into low-level classes in high school.

In addition to a heavy dose of mathematics, I recall a great deal of fervor over a school bond issue. Even though the teachers and students rallied for passage of the bond, it failed. As a result, the music and art programs were severely cut at our school. Since we could not have both music and art, as we had had in the past, the school administration decided that my eighth-grade class would have art and Mr. Peters' (pseudonym) seventh- and eighth-grade split would have music. I was very dismayed about this decision. I sang in the choir at the church I attended on Sunday. For a few weeks, I went along with the change. However, I began to brood whenever I heard music emanate from Mr. Peters' classroom. Then one day, I had a chance to do something about it. Eighth graders were often called upon to read announcements or recite the Pledge of Allegiance during an assembly, and it was my turn. I fulfilled my obligation by reading the required piece. Then, with my heart pounding so hard in my chest that I could barely breathe, I said in a loud voice, "Why can't we have music and art?" There was dead silence for a moment as the entire student body sat stunned. I was a quiet, shy, and studious girl who never broke the rules. Then, all of a sudden, the students started to cheer in support of my statement. To my surprise, it was decided within a matter of days that we could choose to have either music or art. I was excused to sit in Mr. Peters' class whenever the music teacher came in. This experience not only made my year, but it also empowered me. I learned early in life how to read and write the world (Gutstein, 2006), that is, advocate for justice and fairness.

In the spring of each year, students were given the Iowa Test of Basic Skills (ITBS). In St. Louis, like other cities in the Midwest, the ITBS was a high-stakes test that determined whether students were promoted to high school, which high school they would attend, and what courses they would take (Gutstein, 2006). At the end of my eighth-grade year, I learned that I had scored 12.1 in mathematics on the ITBS test, which was the highest score on school record at that time. While my overall score on the ITBS was 11.0, mathematics was my highest score. Not only did I do well on the ITBS, but other students did, too. A few of my classmates left Laclede to attend parochial or private college prep schools. While I attended a public high school in St. Louis, I was enrolled in Honors English and algebra.

High School Mathematics Experience

I began my high school journey in 1971 at Soldan High School. However, the stable neighborhood where I lived had become a dilapidated ghetto within 10 short years. The ghetto was not a healthy place to be. I was determined that I would be "somebody" and get out of the ghetto. The theme of wanting to be *somebody* is prevalent in the literature on successful African American students and challenges racial stereotypes (Ford, 1993; Martin, 2000). I believe the theme emanates from the Civil Rights movement and the protest songs of the sixties. I was *young, gifted and Black,* and believed I could become anything I wanted to be.

When I began my freshman year of high of school, I agreed to participate in a vocational education program because my mother did not want me to graduate without a job. The program required busing me to South St. Louis, which was predominantly white. For the first time in my life, I attended school with whites. However, these students were the minority at the vocational education school, which was predominantly African American. My mother encouraged me to participate in this program because the literature stated students would be prepared for careers in accounting and data processing. Participation in the program required me to take core courses like English, science, and social studies at my home high school. However, I took mathematics, accounting, data processing, and typing at the vocational high school. My mother and I believed this program had many benefits and would increase my chances of employment when I graduated.

After 2 years of high school, I had a 3.8 GPA, including all As in Algebra. I knew Algebra was a tough subject. I often stayed up late at night working on one problem until I got it right. I liked making good grades and was intrinsically motivated by my personal goals and aspirations. Yet, I did not realize that selecting a vocational education track was not preparing me for college. Unsure about my career choices, I learned during my junior year that a college recruiter from the University of Missouri in Columbia was visiting my high school. Several of my friends and I attended the session, which was conducted by an African American male. He went through the list of college entry requirements: 4 years of English, 3 years of mathematics, 3 years of science, 3 years of history, sociology, or psychology, and 2 years of foreign language. My eyes welled up because, even though I had the GPA, I did not have the coursework. I was on track to fulfill the English, science, and social studies prerequisites. However, I had only taken one mathematics course and had no foreign language course on my transcript. What was I going to do with 3 years of keypunch and typing classes if I could not go to college? Pressures to enter the workforce pushed talented and capable college prep students like me into a vocational education track. Thus, *interest convergence* creates a negative impact on society when capable students are sidetracked from achieving higher education to satisfy workforce needs.

For the second time in my life as a minor, I made a bold decision. Without the approval of my mother, I went to the high school counselor and dropped out of the vocational education program and enrolled in college prep courses for my senior year. According to my senior year report card (which I still have), I enrolled in British literature, advanced composition and literature, trigonometry, physics, Spanish, and physical education (which was required for high school graduation). I decide to capitalize on English by taking the advanced composition course. I believed that 5 years of English might compensate for only 2 years of mathematics. At the end of the year, I had a GPA of 3.667. Document analysis of my SAT scores revealed I took the test twice, once in November and again 3 months later in February. My total score rose 120 points during this period. Exposure to the testing format and additional mathematics and English instruction throughout the year were contributing factors to my success on the test. Despite 5 years of English and only 2 years of mathematics, I scored higher in mathematics on the SAT. My SAT score in mathematics, compared with all college bound students, was in the 57% percentile. I was elated when I was accepted to three colleges: St. Louis University, University of Illinois at Chicago, and Boston University. Moreover, I received a full scholarship to attend St. Louis University and Boston University. I decided to attend BU.

College Mathematics Experiences

My initiation to Boston was not a positive one in the fall of 1975. Although the nation's Bicentennial was approaching, Boston was going through a series of racial conflicts around school busing to desegregate the public schools. The city was a foreign and unwelcome place to me. It was as a freshman at Boston University that I came to the stark realization that I had been deceived. Because of segregation in my neighborhood, church, and school system, I held the naïve belief that most people in America were Black. For the first time in my life, I saw myself as a minority. Because of the busing issue, Boston University decided to desegregate the dorms. I was assigned a Jewish roommate who was a well-to-do student from Brookline. She majored in music, and we got along well. However, it was unnerving to hear a white male shout, "*I got a Jap for a roommate!*" the day I moved into the Brownstones on Bay State Road. Needless to say, many students, including me, changed roommates before the semester was over. My second roommate was an African American female from Bronx, New York.

Because I loved science and wanted to help others, I chose to major in Physical Therapy. I had done the research and learned Physical Therapy was a hot career. I was relieved that there was not a single mathematics course in my program. While I liked mathematics, I was afraid that it would be too hard at the college level since I did not have Calculus in high school. Prior to the start of classes, I was required to take a placement test for my chemistry course. Allied health majors would be placed in either a regular or accelerated chemistry course. Being a bit uneasy about the difficulty of college chemistry, I prayed that I would test into the regular chemistry course. Needless to say, nobody heard my prayer. I tested into the accelerated class. The only other African American student in the cohort placed into the regular class. While we were friends, we did not have the same texts and could not really study together. Although I had managed to graduate 17th in my high school class of more than 500 students, nothing had prepared me for my freshman year at a predominantly white institution. The experience of walking into an all-white chemistry class where I was the only student of color was intimidating. Yet, having been motivated during freshman orientation by speakers like Arthur Ashe and advocates like Floyd Flake, my first year of college was a success. I managed to earn a C in accelerated chemistry and had a C+ average at the end of my freshman year.

During the summer following my freshman year of college, I had a difficult time finding a job. If I told potential employers that I wanted a full-time permanent job, I would have been hired. Some of my friends lied about being college students and got summer jobs right away. Because of my religious convictions, I refused to lie but continued to look for work almost every day. Boston University expected me to earn $900 from summer employment and reduced my financial aid package accordingly. I remember receiving a promising lead by the Missouri Job Corp program to work as a math clerk at a well-known St. Louis brokerage firm. When I arrived, the receptionist told me I needed to take a mathematics test. I was not deterred. I took the test and passed it with flying colors. When she saw that I did not miss any of the items on the test, she was taken off-guard and simply told me that the job had been filled. It was my first experience with racism. I did not see any person of color in the entire firm. I believed I was not hired for this job simply because of my race.

Because of this experience, I can empathize with students, parents, and community members who wonder why they should struggle to learn mathematics. What good is knowing mathematics if you are not going to get to use it (Martin, this volume)? What good is going to college if you are not going to get hired for what you studied to do? Despite daily inquiries and hitting the pavement to complete job applications, I was not hired that summer. While the financial aid office gave me additional loan money to cover the $900 shortfall, I went back to college disillusioned about my future. Working a part-time job at night to make ends meet and going to school in the day, *I couldn't hear nobody pray.* I became frustrated and overwhelmed. Before the semester was over, I took a leave of absence and dropped out of college during my sophomore year.

How I Got Over

Two years later, I transferred to St. Louis University where I received a great deal of academic support from my advisor and emotional support from my family. I was married and had a very supportive spouse. I decided my major would be education because of the positive experiences I had working in the Sunday school at my church. Certification requirements dictated that I needed to take two courses in mathematics. My advisor told me that I could take a course called *Mathematics and Man*, which was a non-content course. Instead, I chose to take *College Algebra/Trig.* I felt well prepared and believed I would be successful. For the second course, I decided to take *Survey of Calculus.* I was pleased to have female instructors for both of these courses. I earned a B in the algebra/trig course and an A in the survey of calculus course, which I absolutely loved. Because of these positive experiences, I decided to focus on an interdisciplinary major in mathematics and science (I already had a number of science courses after having been a Physical Therapy major) within the teacher education program. Because of conflicts with the course schedule, I took two additional mathematics courses at an Historically Black College (HBCU) nearby. I enrolled in *Calculus I* and *Basic Programming;* I also earned As in these two courses. It was not only the Jesuit tradition but also the female teachers I had, particularly in mathematics at St. Louis University and the HBCU that solidified my mathematics identity. Doing well in mathematics gave me a tremendous boost in self-confidence. In 1981, I was the first in my immediate family to earn a Bachelor's degree.

I believed I had finally *gotten over,* that is overcome the struggle, to attain a college education. However, my struggle for higher educational attainment was hardly over. A dilemma arose when I began matriculating as a doctoral student at the University of Maryland at College Park. Although I had a 3.2 GPA from St. Louis University, better than a 3.0 GPA from graduate programs in Texas, and quantitative and analytic GRE scores in the 53rd and 67th percentiles, respectively, I was told after I arrived that I was given special admission status. It was explained to me that I needed to earn a 3.5 GPA during the first 12 semester hours to prove that I could do doctoral work. Dissatisfied with the situation, I wrote a letter of appeal to the Graduate School and made the following argument: "If students whom the College deemed to be more capable than I were held to a lower standard of maintaining a 3.0 GPA, why was the bar raised for me if I was truly a weaker student?" In other words, the scales were tipped against me. I had to earn a higher GPA in order to obtain the same status that was afforded to other students. Such a decision was unjust and unfair and placed me under unnecessary stress. The Graduate School agreed with my argument, and the 3.5 GPA stipulation was dropped. Again, I had advocated for myself and won. This time I used mathematics and logic to frame my argument. Contrary to the opinion of those who did not believe I belonged at the University of Maryland, I completed my courses and dissertation in 3.5 years, when it normally takes students about 5 to 7 years to complete the program. Once again, I used mathematics to read and write my world (Gutstein, 2006). In other words, I critiqued department policy and called for change that was actually implemented. In 1997, I graduated from Maryland with a Ph.D. in mathematics education.

Children, Go Where I Send Thee

In the Methodist Church, the notion of itinerancy is common knowledge. While God calls, the bishop sends. Pastors in consultation with the bishop and congregation are appointed to a church one year at a time. Depending on the needs of the district and the church, if things go well, the pastor is often reappointed until it is time to move on. This notion of being sent describes my early teaching career.

In September 1981, I began my teaching career as a middle school science teacher in University City, Missouri. Because of economic conditions in 1983, the district closed one school and laid off a high percentage of teachers, including me. While I found another position at a fledgling religious school, it was for less pay. I struggled with career choices but decided to relocate to Dallas, Texas, in 1984. In Texas, there was plenty of room to grow, and teaching jobs were abundant.

After passing the district's writing and mathematics tests, I was asked to teach Chapter 1 Kindergarten in a working-class community for the Dallas Independent School District (DISD). I had 18 students who had little to no pre-school experience. The children came to school not knowing their letters, numbers, or sounds. I made it my personal responsibility to expose these children to literacy and mathematics through sight, sound, and touch. When students became proficient, I negotiated with other kindergarten teachers in regular and advanced kindergarten classes to become the children's teachers. Because of the transient nature of the school, children were always coming and going. Thus, African American and Hispanic children who came to me with very low reading and mathematics skills were able to drop the Chapter 1 label and move ahead before they went to first grade. In my mind, this was the way the system was supposed to work. Students should not be given a 12-year sentence in remedial education simply because they started off behind. Teachers should work diligently to help them catch up and then move them along the continuum accordingly.

While working at this school, I was exposed to the Project SEED program (Phillips & Ebrahimi, 1993). Project SEED is a specialized mathematics program designed for disadvantaged students. In this program, upper elementary students learned how to solve a number of abstract problems involving the addition and subtraction of exponents and logarithms. I visited a class and was amazed at what Black fourth-grade students were doing in Project SEED classes. Not only could they solve complex problems, they could explain why they solved them the way they did. At that moment, my goal was to become a Project SEED specialist. I completed a secondary mathematics certification program and did just that. From 1986 to 1988, I traveled from class to class across the city, teaching children to think and articulate their thinking about abstract mathematics concepts.

During this time, the DISD was placed under a court-ordered desegregation plan. The District's answer to desegregation was busing Black children in predominantly West and South Dallas to predominantly white schools in North Dallas. In addition to this, funding was provided for diverse students to attend schools that would be transformed into magnet schools. When parents of Black and white students challenged the busing plan, schools in South and West Dallas were renovated to create learning centers. The best teachers were recruited to work in the learning centers, which had state-of-the-art computer labs, Project SEED instruction, and after-school programs. If these schools met yearly academic goals, teachers would receive bonus pay. I applied for and was hired in the fall of 1988 as a mathematics teacher in one of the learning centers in South Dallas. Simultaneously, I went back to school to earn a Master of Arts in Teaching Mathematics at the University of Texas at Dallas.

Around the same time, *Edgewood vs. Kirby* (1989) made its way through the court system. This lawsuit was filed against the Texas Education Agency because of disparate state funding resulting in property rich districts receiving more per pupil expenditures than property poor school districts (Kozol, 1991). The plaintiffs claimed that their child was not receiving an adequate education because of disparate school funding. While the final ruling in *Edgewood vs. Kirby* found the Texas method for funding schools unconstitutional, the wheels of justice were so slow the child of the plaintiffs had graduated from high school before the issue was resolved. The use of property taxes to support schools results in further inequities when incentives such as 10-year tax abatements are used to lure middle- and upper-class residents back to urban cities like St. Louis and Philadelphia. Such policies place an unfair burden on the poor, whose taxes continue to rise, while the wealthy pay nothing to support urban schools for an entire decade.

While I believe policy changes in school funding laws are absolutely necessary, teachers cannot wait for changes to occur at the macro level. If change was going to occur in my classroom, I believed it had to start with me. Teachers are political beings with the power to change the classroom and school environment (Gutstein, 2006; Ladson-Billings, 1994; Martin, 2007; Rousseau & Powell, 2005). In order to improve the quality of mathematics education in my classroom, I applied for, and received, a $500 mini-grant from the Junior League of Dallas. The grant provided me with materials needed for my African American students to learn mathematics using real-world contexts. According to the *Dallas Morning News*:

> Geometry and math will be the lessons in South Dallas' Dunbar Learning Center's innovative project. The students will build a model city. Teacher Jacqueline Brown [married name] said she will teach fourth graders about "plane figures, symmetry, angles, perimeter, and area" while they construct 30 miniature buildings. (Macias, 1992)

I had no idea what impact the project would have on my fourth-grade students and my own pedagogy. This project, which was called *The City* (Leonard, 2004), changed the way I taught mathematics forever and changed my beliefs about Black children's interest and motivation in mathematics. It was not simply a mathematics unit, *The City* project allowed students to read and write their own world using mathematics (Gutstein, 2006). While some of the buildings were depictions of the students' own shotgun houses (a building where the front door is parallel to the back door such that a bullet could go straight through the house), the students decided which businesses, organizations, and facilities needed to be in the community they created (Leonard, 2004).

My students literally ran from science to mathematics class, asking me, "Are we going to work on our projects today?" If I said yes, the students literally jumped up and down with excitement. We used foam board, Popsicle sticks, mini-hot glue guns, wallpaper, and tempera paint to build and construct artifacts using a scale of 1 inch = 1 foot. Children were so excited they went home and told their families. Within a week, one student's grandmother came to my classroom and asked if she could work alongside her grandchild on the project. I consented. Not long after that, another student's older brother came into my classroom asking if he could help his younger brother with his project. One of the Project SEED specialists at the school saw the activity in my classroom and volunteered his time to work with students. A teacher colleague in the school came into my classroom during her planning period to help children with their projects. All of sudden, my classroom project became a community project as parents and caregivers, teachers, and specialists worked alongside Black children as they learned mathematics in an authentic and meaningful way. Learning mathematics did not have to be an isolating experience. It was a community experience that helped students to develop mathematics identity and mathematics socialization.

Research suggests that African American students and females prefer to learn in collaborative groups (Boykin & Toms, 1985; Campbell, 1995). African American children are more likely to develop mathematics identity when their learning styles and interests are taken into consideration in the mathematics classroom (Ladson-Billings, 2004; Leonard, 2008). The African American children in my classroom were artistic and loved color. They used their artistic talent to design and paint their building projects however they wanted. They were in control instead of being controlled. They were planners, decision-makers, and make-believe architects performing mathematical operations in context. Every student was on task, and every student was learning. The positive attitudes of the community and the support of school administrators, teachers, and staff helped to socialize these students to believe that mathematics had purpose and meaning, and they could do mathematics and be successful at it.

Most importantly, I would never be the same. I, too, had found my own voice and pedagogical style. Rather than being afraid to deviate from the textbook for fear of declining mathematics scores, I was convinced that African American children would retain the information better if the mathematics was anchored to an unforgettable experience or context. Without drilling my students and focusing solely on textbook mathematics, my students performed well above established goals for the academic year. In a few short years, students at Dunbar Learning Center moved in rank from one of the lowest performing to one of the top performing elementary schools in the DISD in mathematics and science. In fact, two students in my fourth-grade class had a perfect score on the Texas mathematics assessment. After teaching mathematics for 3 years, I discovered the power of learning mathematics within a community of learners.

Parents can reinforce mathematics identity and socialization in a number of ways as well. Mathematics is everywhere—in the kitchen, in the garden, in a car, on a bus, or in a subway train (Leonard & Guha, 2002). Everyone, regardless of race, ethnicity, or gender does mathematics on a regular basis. From deciding what time to get up in the morning in order to be ready for school or work to how much money can be spent on lunch per day given a certain allowance, mathematics is in all aspects of our lives. Furthermore, mathematical knowledge leads to better choices and decision-making. For example, a community-based group known as ACORN tries to raise public awareness about predatory mortgage lending. These lenders take advantage of working-class people, who may not understand such concepts as balloon payments and adjustable rate mortgages. However, knowledge of simple interest rates and amortization may help prevent potential homebuyers from getting ripped off. If the average loan in a specific city is 6%, why should a lender charge 10% or more? While interest rates vary depending on a person's credit score, exorbitant interest rates increase the chances of foreclosure. Adjustable rate mortgages may be good when interest rates are low, but when interest rates (as well as property taxes and homeowner's insurance) rise, so do the mortgage payments. In general, the higher the interest rate or Annual Percentage Rate (APR) the more the consumer pays and the more profit the company makes. Doing mathematics allows consumers to judge what is, and what is not, of value to them. Clearly, the ability to do mathematics has a profound impact on one's quality of life.

The premise of Freire's (2006) *Pedagogy of the Oppressed* is that the oppressed must liberate themselves. One non-violent way for this to happen is to use mathematics to expose and redress inequities and injustices and to acquire the knowledge needed to access economic power. In order for liberation to occur, collaboration between African American leaders and African American citizens is essential. Historically, there is a precedent for such communication to occur in the Black Church (Harding, 1981). Through the Black Church, the African American community can promote the development of mathematics identity and mathematics socialization. Clergy can help African Americans to develop identity by "mathematizing" sermons.

For example, in Matthew 18: 12, Jesus explains that God is like a shepherd who has 100 sheep. If one is lost, the shepherd leaves the 99 and searches for the one until it is found. This story can be used to underscore God's concern for the poor and disenfranchised. Moreover, numeracy can be developed as powers of 10 are explored. What if there were 1,000 or 10,000 sheep? The percentage of sheep lost and found could be presented in a variety of scenarios that will result in 100% of the sheep being accounted for. Sermons could also include surveys for members to rate themselves on a continuum. This idea is not original but was used by Rev. Kevin Kosh as he preached a sermon about spirituality at Union Memorial United Methodist Church in St. Louis on June 11, 2007. Pens came flying out as members of the congregation circled a number from 1 to 10 on each of 10 items discussed and then totaled their score at the end of the sermon. My spirituality score was 79%, indicating that I still had some growing to do. Not only was this activity engaging, but also it exercised mental mathematics and reasoning skills, while deepening my commitment to spirituality.

Conclusion and Recommendation

When All God's Children Get Together

The shortcoming of *Brown v. Board* was its inability to provide the majority of African Americans with educational and economic opportunity (Bell, 1987, 2004). Quality education for all Black students was derailed as debates about how to achieve desegregation resulted in the forced busing of Black children from their neighborhoods, the massive firing of Black teachers and administrators, and the loss of flagship institutions that were beacons of excellence in Black communities (Cooper, 2002; Tillman, 2004). The African American community has yet to recover from these unintended but negative consequences of *Brown* (Tillman, 2004). Given the reality that segregation is not going away, those who educate poor children without adequate school funding and resources continue to make bricks without straw (Exodus 5: 7).

If society at large and policymakers adhere to the call for equity and social justice on moral and ethical grounds, then the spirit of *Brown v. Board* will be realized. When high academic achievement translates into real economic opportunity, African American children will have more incentive to achieve and persist in their education because economic parity has become a reality. This is not to say that learning for learning's sake does not have intrinsic value. It does. Mathematics literacy leads to higher education and greater economic access, which leads to "salvation" that transcends Blacks from objectification to human beings in need of the same inalienable rights that the framers of the Constitution sought for themselves. Yet, it is love, not fear of the other that will break down the barriers of racial injustice in our society. "There is no fear in love, but perfect love casts out fear" (I John 4: 18). For Freire (2006), love is not a feeling of euphoria; it is a call to action:

> Because love is an act of courage, not of fear, love is commitment to others. No matter where the oppressed are found, the act of love is commitment to their cause—the cause of liberation. (Freire, 2006, p. 89)

In the words of Rev. Dr. Martin Luther King:

> "Hatred paralyzes life; love releases it. Hatred confuses life; love harmonizes it; Hatred darkens life; love illuminates it."

I believe those who have been wounded by hatred and racism can be made whole with love. Christians, regardless of race, ethnicity, and gender are called to love one another. Jesus said in Luke 10: 27, "You shall love . . . your neighbor as yourself." However, how one defines a neighbor dictates how one enacts this commandment to love (Tate, 2003). Where is the love for Black and other oppressed people of color in a nation that calls others to adopt democracy? The prophet Amos condemns those who "sell the righteous for silver and the needy for a pair of shoes—they that trample the head of the poor into the dust of the earth, and turn aside the way of the afflicted" (Amos 2: 6b–7). Love requires that Blacks are included at the table instead of simply being discussed at the table (Martin, this volume). Critical Race Theory and Black Liberation Theology provide a space for Black scholars and theologians to critique the existing social order (Ladson-Billings, 1994). *Pedagogy of the Oppressed* (Freire, 2006) provides a vehicle to transform it. Mathematics is a tool that can be used to critique and measure progress.

"Mathematical power can serve critical literacy and emancipation" (Gutstein, 2006, p. 7). Critical mathematics literacy enables the oppressed to use mathematics to accomplish their own ends and purposes. Mathematical power gave me the authority to voice objections to unfair practices and call into question actions that disenfranchised me while privileging others. After six generations of share-croppers, I was able to break the cycle of poverty and become a role model for my two younger siblings, who earned Bachelor's degrees, and my two daughters, who have Master's degrees. Critical mathematics literacy can be used to critique existing hierarchies and social structures that create barriers and limit Black children's opportunity to learn. I believe it was my positive mathematics identity and social-ization, faith in God, self-determination, and support of significant others that allowed me to realize my dreams and experience success in higher education. Communities, schools, and churches must work together to instill hope and con-tinue to work for social change on behalf of poor children in this nation. Such com-munity efforts, which have been documented in the literature (Morris, 2004), illustrate the strength and resilience of African Americans and help to dismantle negative stereotypes.

> Just as the biblical Nazareth was considered hopeless and yet from this place emerged the one that Moses and the prophets had written about, who knows what might arise from a careful study of contemporary urban and predomi-nantly African American schools and communities that manifest agency? We just might find that the solutions resides within the "souls" of Black people – rather than elsewhere. (Morris, 2004, p. 105)

When all God's children get together to help Black children develop mathematics identity and socialization to actualize Woodson's (1998) vision of mathematics education that he called for decades ago, when mathematics is used to bring atten-tion to, and overturn, oppressive and inhumane practices that block equal access to higher education and economic empowerment for African Americans and others who continue to experience racial discrimination, then we can claim we have been to the water, we have been baptized, and we are saved.

Acknowledgements

The author acknowledges Victoria R. Cloud and Cara M. Moore for editing this paper, which was presented in Washington, DC, September 26, 2004 at The Frederick D. Patterson Institute Conference: Still Not Equal.

References

American Civil Liberties Union (ACLU). (2007). *Race and ethnicity in America: Turning a blind eye to Justice.* New York: ACLU.

Apple, M.W. (2003). Freire and the politics of race in education. *International Journal of Leadership in Education, 6*(2), 107–118.

Baugh, J. (1–7 May 2008). Obama and the "bitter" pill. *St. Louis American,* A4.

Bell, D. (1987). *And we are still not saved: The elusive quest for racial justice.* New York: Basic Books.

Bell, D. (2004) *Silent covenants: Brown vs. Board of Education and the unfulfilled hopes for racial reform.* New York: Oxford University Press.

Blanchett, W. (2006). Disproportionate representation of African American students in special education: Acknowledging the role of white privilege and racism, *Educational Researcher, 35*(6), 24–28.

Bonds, C.C. (1981). Social economic status and educational achievement: A review article. *Anthropology and Education Quarterly, 12*(4), 227–257.

Borden, L. & Kroeger, M.K. (2001). *Fly High! The story of Bessie Coleman.* New York: Margaret K. McElderry Books.

Boykin, A.W. & Toms, F.D. (1985). Black child socialization: A conceptual framework. In H. McAdoo & J. McAdoo (Eds.), *Black children: Social, educational, and parental environments* (pp. 33–51). Beverly Hills, CA: Sage.

Brown v. Board of Education of Topeka, 347, U.S. 483 (1954).

Bureau of Labor Statistics, U.S. Department of Labor, *Occupational Outlook Handbook, 2008–09 Edition,* Computer Scientists and Database Administrators. Retrieved on March 13, 2008 from http://www.bls.gov/oco/ocos042.htm.

Campbell, P.F. (1995). Redefining the "girl problem in mathematics." In W.G. Secada, E. Fennema, & L.B. Adajian (Eds.), *New directions for equity in mathematics education* (pp. 225–241). New York: Cambridge University Press.

Children's Defense Fund. (2003). June jobless rate among America's teens highest in 55 years. Retrieved August 23, 2004, from http://www.cdfny.org/News/PressReleases/71003TeenJoblessnessNY.pdf

Coleman, J. (1987). Families and schools. *Educational Researcher, 16*(6), 32–38.

Cone, J.H. (1990). *A black theology of liberation* (20th anniversary ed.). Maryknoll, NY: Orbis. (Original work published 1970)

Cooper, P. (2002). Does race matter: A comparison of effective black and white teachers of African American students. In J. J. Irvine (Ed.), *In search of wholeness: African American teachers and their specific classroom practices,* (pp. 47–63). New York: Palgrave.

Dance, L.J. (2002). *Tough fronts: The impact of street culture on schooling.* New York: Routledge.

Darling-Hammond, L. (2007). Countering aggressive neglect: Creating a transformative educational agenda in the wake of Katrina (Foreword). In S.P. Robinson & M.C. Brown, II. (Eds.), *The children Hurricane Katrina left behind: Schooling context, professional preparation, and community politics* (pp. xi–xx). New York: Peter Lang.

Delgado, R. (1995). (Ed.). *Critical race theory: The cutting edge.* Philadelphia: Temple University Press.

Delpit, L. (1995). *Other people's children: Cultural conflict in the classroom.* New York: The New Press.

Dixson, A.D. & Rousseau, C.K. (2005). And we are still not saved: Critical race theory in education ten years later. *Race Ethnicity and Education, 8*(1), 7–27.

Dorr, D. (1984). *Spirituality and justice.* Maryknoll, NY: Orbis Books.

Du Bois, W.E.B. (1995). *The souls of black folk.* New York: New American Library. (Original work published 1903)

Edgewood Independent School District v. Kirby, 777 S.W.2d. 391, 394 (Tex. 1989).

Entwisle, D.R. & Alexander, K.L. (1992). Summer setback: Race, poverty, school composition, and mathematics achievement in the first two years of school, *American Sociological Review, 57,* 72–84.

Ford, D.Y. (1993). Black students' achievement orientation as a function of perceived family orientation and demographic variables. *Journal of Negro Education, 62*(1), 47–66.

Freire, P. (2006). *Pedagogy of the oppressed* (30th Anniversary ed.). New York: Continuum.

greatschools. (2008). Retrieved on June 2, 2008 from <http://www. greatschools.net/ moderl/browse_school/pa/2892/.>

Grimes, N. (2002). *Talkin' about Bessie: The story of aviator Elizabeth Coleman.* New York: Scholastic.

Gutiérrez, R. (2008). A "gap-gazing" fetish in mathematics education? Problematizing research on the achievement gap. *Journal for Research in Mathematics Education, 39*(4), 357–364.

Gutstein, E. (2006). *Reading and writing the world with mathematics: Toward a pedagogy for social justice.* New York & London: Routledge.

Haberman, M. (1991). The pedagogy of poverty versus good teaching. *Phi Delta Kappan, 73,* 290–294.

Harding, V. (1981). *There is a river: The Black struggle for freedom in America.* Orlando, Florida: Harcourt Brace.

Heitzenrater, R.P. (1995). *Wesley and the people called Methodists.* Nashville: Abingdon Press.

Herrnstein, R.J. & Murray, C. (1994). *The bell curve: Intelligence and class structure in American life.* New York: Free Press.

Holzer, H. & Lerman, R.I. (2006). Employment issues and challenges in Post-Katrina New Orleans. Retrieved on June 2, 2008 from <http://www.urban.org/publications/ 900921.html>

Irvine, J.J. (2007). What Hurricane Katrina uncovered about schooling in America. In S.P. Robinson & M.C. Brown, II. (Eds.), *The children Hurricane Katrina left behind: Schooling context, professional preparation, and community politics* (pp. 21–28). New York: Peter Lang.

Kitchen, R. (2007). An overview of schooling in high-poverty communities. In R. Kitchen, J. Depree, S., Celedón-Pattichis, S., & J. Brinkerhoff, J (Eds.), *Mathematics education at highly effective schools that serve the poor: Strategies for change* (pp. 1–19). Mahwah, NJ: Lawrence.

Knapp, M. (1995). *Teaching for meaning in high-poverty classrooms.* New York: Teachers College Press.

Kozol, J. (1991). *Savage inequalities: Children in America's schools.* New York: HarperCollins.

Kozol, J. (1995). *Amazing Grace: The lives of children and the conscience of a nation.* New York: Crown.

Ladson-Billings, G. (1994). *The dreamkeepers: Successful teachers of African American children.* San Francisco: Jossey-Bass.

Ladson-Billings, G. (1998). Just what is critical race theory and what's it doing in a *nice* field like education? *Qualitative Studies in Education, 11*(1), 7–24.

Ladson-Billings, G. (2006). From the achievement gap to the education debt: Understanding achievement in U.S. schools. *Educational Researcher, 35*(7), 3–12.

Leonard, J. (2002). Let's go fly a kite. *Science and Children, 40*(2), 20–24.

Leonard, J. (2004). A tale of two cities: Integrating language arts, mathematics, and social studies. *Middle School Journal, 35*(3), 35–40.

Leonard, J. (2007). Hurricane Katrina: Catastrophe of opportunity? In S.P. Robinson & M.C. Brown, II. (Eds.), *The children Hurricane Katrina left behind: Schooling context, professional preparation, and community politics* (pp. 29–39). New York: Peter Lang.

Leonard, J. (2008). *Culturally specific pedagogy in the mathematics classroom: Strategies for teachers of diverse students.* New York: Routledge.

Leonard, J. & Guha, S. (2002). Creating cultural relevance in teaching and learning mathematics. *Teaching Children Mathematics, 9*(3), 114–118.

Leonard, J., Davis, J.E., & Sidler, J.L. (2005). Cultural relevance and computer-assisted instruction. *Journal of Research on Technology in Education, 37*(3), 263–284.

Leonard, J., Taylor, K.L., Sanford-De Shields, J., & Spearman, P. (2004). Professional development schools revisited: Reform, authentic partnerships and new visions. *Urban Education, 39*(5), 561–583.

Lincoln, C.E. & Mamiya, L.H. (1990). *The Black Church in the African-American experience.* Durham & London: Duke University Press.

Lynn, M. (1999). Toward a critical race pedagogy. *Urban Education, 33*(5), 606–626.

Macias, A. (1992, December 29). Inside education: Edible projects give students a state of science. *Dallas Morning News*, education extra, np.

Martin, D.B. (2000). *Mathematics success and failure among African American youth: The roles of sociohistorical context, community forces, school influence, and individual agency.* Mahwah, NJ: Lawrence Erlbaum.

Martin, D.B. (2003). Hidden assumptions and unaddressed questions in *Mathematics for All* rhetoric. *The Mathematics Educator, 13*(2), 7–21.

Martin, D.B. (2007). Beyond missionaries or cannibals: Who should teach mathematics to African American children. *The High School Journal, 91*(1), 6–28.

McEwan, M. (2008). *Palin's selective terrorism definition.* Retrieved on October 29, 2008 from http://www.guardian.co.uk/commentisfree/cifamerica/2008/oct/29/sarah-palin-abortion-terrorism-ayers

Morris, J.E. (2004). Can anything good come from Nazareth? Race, class, and African American schooling and community in the urban south and midwest. *American Educational Research Journal, 41*(1), 69–112.

Morrison, T. (1992). *Playing in the dark: Whiteness and the literacy imagination.* Cambridge, MA: Harvard University Press.

Moses, R.P. & Cobb, Jr., C.E. (2001). *Radical equations: Math literacy and civil rights.* Boston: Beacon Press.

Nasir, N.S. (2005). Individual cognitive structuring and the sociocultural context: Strategy shifts in the game of dominoes. *Journal of the Learning Sciences, 14*(1), 5–34.

National Priorities Project. (2008). *Cost of the Iraq War.* Retrieved on October 29, 2008 from http://www.nationalpriorities.org/costofwar_home

National Science Board (NSB) (2002). *Science and engineering indicators—2002.* (Report No. NSB-02-1). Arlington, VA: Author.

National Science Foundation (2007). *Women, minorities, and persons with disabilities in science and engineering.* Arlington, VA: U.S. Government Printing Office. Retrieved on April 3, 2008 from http://www.nsf.gov/statistics/wmpd/

New Oxford Annotated Bible. (1991). New Revised Standard Version. New York: Oxford University Press.

Norwood, F.A. (1974). *The story of American Methodism.* Nashville: Abingdon Press.

Nosek, B.A. & Banaji, M.R., & Greenwald, A.G. (2002). Math = me, me = female, therefore math $\neq$ me. *Journal of Personality and Social Psychology, 83*(1), 44–59.

Ogbu, J.U. (2003). *Black American students in an affluent suburb: A study of academic disengagement.* Mahwah, NJ: Lawrence Erlbaum.

Phillips, S. & Ebrahimi, H. (1993). Equation for success: Project SEED. In NCTM (ed.), *Reaching all students with mathematics* (pp. 59–74). Reston, VA: The Council.

Plessy v. Ferguson, 163 U.S. 537 (1896).

Prahlad, A. (2005). *The African American experience: Liberation theology.* Retrieved June 26, 2007 from http://aae.greenwood.com/doc.aspx?i=0&type=all#textml

Pringle, K. (1991). *When all God's children get together.* New York: Savoy Records.

Proctor, B.D. & Dalaker, J. (2003). Poverty in the United States: 2002. *U.S. Census Bureau Report.* Retrieved August 20, 2004 from http://www.census.gov/prod/2003pubs/p6-222.pdf

Robinson, E. (2008, May 1–7). This is how we pick a president. *St. Louis American,* A4.

Rousseau, C.K. & Powell, A. (2005). Understanding the significance of context: A framework to examine equity and reform in secondary mathematics. *The High School Journal, 88*(4), 19–31.

Seixas, C. (2007, October 11). Grant awarded for arts education in Chester. *The Phoenix.* Retrieved on May 3, 2008 from http://www.swarthmorephoenix.com/2007/10/11/news/grant-awarded-for-arts-education-in-chester.

Solano-Flores, G. & Trumbull, E. (2003, March). Examining language in context: The need for new research and practice paradigms in the testing of English-language learners. *Educational Researcher, 32*(2), 3–13.

Staples, B. (2002, March 4). Editorial observer; fighting the culture of poverty in a worst-case school. *The New York Times.* Retrieved on March 20, 2008 from <http://query.nytimes.com>

Sternberg, S. (2007, June 22–24). New Orleans deaths up 47%: Post-Katrina surge as city's lost doctors. *USA Today,* A1.

Stiff, L. & Harvey, W.B. (1988). On the education of black children in mathematics. *Journal of Black Studies, 19*(2), 190–203.

Tate, W.F. (1995). Returning to the root: A culturally relevant approach to mathematics pedagogy. *Theory Into Practice, 34*(3), 166–173.

Tate, W.F. (1997). Race–Ethnicity, SES, gender, and language deficiency trends in mathematics achievement: An update. *Journal for Research in Mathematics Education, 28*(6), 652–679.

Tate, W.F. (2003). The "race" to theorize education: Who is my neighbor? *International Journal of Qualitative Studies in Education, 16*(1), 121–126.

Thomas, S.B. & Quinn, S.C. (1991). The Tuskegee Syphilis study, 1932 to 1972: Implications for HIV education and aids risk education programs in the black community. *American Journal of Public Health, 81*(11), 1498–1505.

Tillman, L.C. (2002). Culturally sensitive research approaches: An African-American perspective. *Educational Researcher, 31*(9), 3–12.

Tillman, L.C. (2004). (Un)intended consequences?: The impact of the *Brown v. Board of Education* decision on the employment status of black educators. *Education and Urban Society, 36*(3), 280–303.

U.S. Census Bureau (2000). Zip Code statistics. Retrieved on May 3, 2008 from http://factfinder.census.gov/home/saff/main.html?_lang=en.

Ward, C. (1951). *How I Got Over.* Philadelphia: Clara Ward.

Wilmore, G.S. & Cone, J.H. (1980). *Black Theology* (2nd ed.). Maryknoll, NY: Orbis Books.

Wilson, W.J. (1987). *The truly disadvantaged: The innercity, the underclass, and public policy.* Chicago: University of Chicago Press.

Woodson, C.G. (1933/1998). The mis-education of the Negro. Trenton, New Jersey: African World Press. (Original work first published 1933)

Section IV

Collaboration and Reform

14 University/K-12 Partnerships: A Collaborative Approach to School Reform

Martin L. Johnson and
Stephanie Timmons Brown

Introduction

Institutions of higher education should be encouraged to enter into partnership with schools to provide information and guidance to schools on the skills and knowledge graduates need in order to enter and successfully complete postsecondary education, and schools should provide information and guidance to institutions of higher education on the skills, knowledge and preservice training teachers need, and the types of professional development educators need in order to meet the purposes of this Act (Goals 2000: Educate America Act, 1994).

Colleges and Universities have long histories of partnering with K-12 schools (Clarken, 1999; Edwards, Abel, Easton, Herbster, & Sparapani, 1996; Florez, 2002; Hutchinson, Lovell, Nordan, & Cleere, 1994). The nature of the partnerships, referred to in the literature as *school–university partnerships*, differ according to the mission and vision of the different colleges or universities and the vision of the leadership of the K-12 institution. The literature describes three main types of partnerships—laboratories for pre-service teachers, professional development for in-service teachers, and comprehensive direct services for students and parents. As seen below, each type of partnership has a distinct purpose and has potential of impacting academic achievement of African American students.

Laboratories for Pre-Service

Most higher education institutions that have a college or school of education or an education program that prepares teachers develop "partnerships," "agreements," and other "arrangements" with K-12 schools to provide laboratories in which pre-service teachers develop their "on-the-job" teaching skills. Such arrangements also provide a service to existing teachers by providing professional development and exposure to new research findings, experimental curricula, teaching methodologies, and assessment techniques. Most "partnership schools" are purposefully chosen, based on the goals of the teacher education program. If a goal of the program were one of preparing teachers to teach in highly diverse schools, we would expect to see participating schools that reflect a high degree of racial and ethnic diversity.

Professional Development for In-Service Teachers

Through professional development collaborations between universities and schools, in-service teachers enroll in quality learning opportunities such as courses, workshops, and seminars. In the wake of *No Child Left Behind* requirements and state standards, the last 8 years have created increasing numbers of professional development activities as standards require teachers to complete additional courses focused on content-based subjects such as mathematics, science, and reading. For many superintendents, principals, and other educators, the purpose of professional development is to give teachers the tools they need to help *all* students master challenging material. The underlying assumption is that a more knowledgeable (content-specific) teacher will be a more effective teacher for *all* students. Therefore, instead of tailoring professional development opportunities for teachers based on the population of students they serve, it seems as if courses and workshops are offered with a generic population of students in mind. In fact, it is a challenge to find examples of professional development offerings in mathematics that are co-constructed with the school partner and are specifically designed to meet the needs of African American students. Through federal grant programs such as National Professional Development and Improving Teacher Quality—programs designed to serve "at-risk" or "disadvantaged" populations—universities can access resources to provide courses that are both content-focused and culturally relevant. Despite the opportunity to create unique professional development opportunities, it is still common practice for universities to rely on canned course offerings with little consideration for the students who will be impacted.

Direct Services to Parents and Students

The third type of university–school partnership focuses on a myriad of services directly offered to students, parents, and teachers. Through these partnerships, services such as academic enrichment, college tours, financial aid and college application assistance, curriculum enhancement, and parent-focused activities are provided. Students may participate in after-school and Saturday tutoring in mathematics and reading, as well as other enrichment activities on college campuses. Parents may be offered workshops on how to become more involved at their child's school or how to help their child with math homework, through such activities as Family Math Night sessions. Teachers sometimes work with University faculty and pre-service teachers to develop STEM-related curriculum units that complement their district's curriculum and raises student interest in math and science.

So, why do colleges and universities participate in direct-service type of partnerships? Ascher and Schwartz (1989) suggest that "schools and colleges recognize that they are dealing with related parts of a common problem: helping disadvantaged students get the education they need to join an increasingly sophisticated labor force. . . . and believe that collaboration can help them solve problems of mutual concern." (p. 2). Universities and schools often unite under the honorable intentions (as described by Ascher & Schwartz, 1989) of preparing disadvantaged students for college, but in the midst of university budget cuts these intentions are easier to implement and are more readily supported at the college-level when federal dollars are available. Over 40 years ago, out of the Economic Opportunity Act of 1964, the first TRIO program—Upward Bound—was created. TRIO programs are educational outreach programs designed to motivate and support students from disadvantaged backgrounds, particularly those students who are the first-generation to attend college. This program and the two subsequent programs (Talent Search and Student Support Services) provide federal grants to colleges and universities, so that higher education institutions may direct outreach services to students and their families.

While each of these partnership types can potentially be employed, as Danny Martin (this book) describes in Chapter 1, as a liberatory resistance approach, university–school partnerships reviewed in the literature (Edwards et al., 1996; Harkavy, 2005; Erickson & Christman, 1996; Powers & DeWaters, 2004; Waddle & Conway, 2005) suggest that these partnerships are rarely designed with a mission and focus on academic achievement of African American students. Instead, most school–university partnerships focus on university processes of training pre-service students as part of traditional teacher preparation programs and/or professional development offerings narrowly focused on content. The direct-services type of partnership also has the potential to be liberatory in design, particularly since federal programs such as TRIO were originally legislated with the disadvantaged student in mind. In the 1960s, disadvantaged was synonymous with Black or African American students. Today, "disadvantaged" has a much broader definition, making programs like TRIO's impact dependent upon who implements the program and who the implementers determine needs the services.

University and School Partnership—A Balancing Act

Developing partnerships between universities and K-12 institutions require serious and deliberate planning. Borthwick, Stirling, Nauman, & Cook (2003) have provided a list of advantages and disadvantages to establishing such partnerships as perceived by K-12 institutions. Among the perceived advantages by the K-12 institution is the opportunity for professional development based on research. For teachers who need re-certification courses, they view professional development opportunities as means to meet these requirements. For schools that act as laboratories for pre-service teachers, the Holmes Group Report (1995) suggests that student teachers benefit from more exposure to diverse populations of students. This experience has the potential of promoting all teachers' understanding of various cultures and how to make curriculum more relevant for students. Cultural relevancy, however, must be a conscious goal and concern of the teacher education program if this outcome is to be realized. According to Henderson-Sparks, Paredes, and Gousalez (2002), the pre-service laboratories also benefit students. Students gain from the increased attention from caring adults and from the different teaching styles of teachers in training. When partnerships offer direct services to parents and students, parents note that university-based activities positively impact their students' interests in, and aspirations to, college, an interest that they say was minimal before participating in some college-based programs.

Leading among the disadvantages is the resistance of teachers to add more to their already busy schedules by working with intending teachers, enrolling in special courses, or traveling to sites outside of school. In general, there is also teacher resistance to taking on additional school responsibilities. Pressured by the standards of NCLB, teachers fear that their students will earn poor test scores, which may negatively impact their performance appraisals. A negative appraisal could result in being viewed as less than competent and then transferred to another school. To avoid such a scenario, teachers may simply work harder at effectively employing their current teaching style in hopes of maintaining or improving student academic performance rather than taking on additional responsibilities (Borthwick et al., 2003). Add to this concern the documented low expectations many teachers have of strong African American student achievement, and some of the challenges to developing partnerships that go beyond the status quo of commonly found professional development are easily seen.

The above notwithstanding, numerous school–university partnerships are, and can be, effectively created if they are guided by either fundamental elements, a partnership typology, and/or philosophical principles. According to Carroll, LaPointe and Tyler (2001), school–university partnerships usually have four essential elements:

1   Educator preparation that places emphasis on preparing college students for the education profession;
2   Professional development that seeks to provide opportunities for teachers to strengthen pedagogical knowledge, attitudes, and skills;
3   Curriculum development that seeks to improve the education and school experience of all students; and
4   Research that promotes educational renewal at both the school and the university.

The extent to which partnerships that display these "essential" components address teaching and learning of African American children relates directly to the philosophy of the persons involved in the choosing and implementing of the teacher education program. For instance, new partnerships could seek school placements in which intending teachers interact and work with teachers who have knowledge of different cultures and can develop and implement instruction that consider student cultures within their methods of instruction. Professional development in participating schools should help existing teachers select curricula that are culturally relevant and meaningful to students. Schools selected with the criterion of improving teachers' skills with African American students should also be a fertile ground for research related to issues that affect African American students directly. Overall, the "essential" elements mentioned by Carroll, LaPointe, & Tyler (2001) could also guide the development of partnerships when the schools are urban and the students are African American.

There is no one structure for all school–university partnerships. Callahan and Martin (2007) have developed a typology of school–university partnerships. In their research they report that partnerships differ around very critical dimensions: the leadership structure of the partnership; the way information is shared within the partnership; the nature of participation within the partnership; the nature of decision making; and the nature of change patterns within the partnership. Each of these dimensions affects the development, operation, and sustainability of any school–university partnership, regardless of the K-12 students the partnership serves. Partnerships may also involve multiple partners including research universities, businesses, community groups, community colleges, and K-12 schools. Regardless, the above dimensions apply if the partnership is to be more than an agreement to work together.

Griffiths (2000) argues that there is a set of "philosophical principles" that theoretically guide the development and programming of any collaboration (while her work focuses on collaborations within and across institutions, it certainly applies to school–university partnerships). According to Griffiths, the reasons for collaboration fall into one of three categories; epistemological, ethico-political, and pragmatic (p. 384).

Epistemological perspectives can be found in arguments that claim collaboration leads to better knowledge about both institutions and the clients they both serve; faculty and students. Epistemological perspectives are often evoked when issues of diversity, including race, ethnicity, and gender, are proposed in connection to achievement. Few partnerships can be found in the research that explicitly states the improvement of student achievement by race, ethnicity, or gender, as the major reason for its existence. However, accreditation agencies such as NCATE argue that diversity and evidence that new teachers can teach diverse students effectively are necessary conditions for the accreditation of teacher education programs. Colleges and schools cooperate with each other to satisfy the NCATE diversity standard, at least in name, but few programs collect good data to relate levels of diversity and student achievement or to document how teachers are prepared to actually be effective in classrooms of African American students (or any other minority group).

Ethico-political perspectives suggest that knowledge is not neutral with respect to ethics and politics, but that ethics and politics influence educational outcomes. Researchers who ascribe to this perspective believe that the values of equality, democracy, and social justice are part of the values they use when establishing the partnership and such a perspective should guide partnership activities, including how the research is conducted as well as how outcomes are evaluated. Such partnerships often spiral out of university departments or programs that see how research, curriculum development, and teacher preparation that address social issues and issues of equity are of prime importance to improving the academic achievement of African American students, and can increase the probability of impacting achievement through bringing the two institutions together in a partnership. Participatory Action Research (PAR) (Hittleman & Simon, 2002) in which all partners participate and see the value of participating in the research and teacher preparation and professional development is an example of this approach to collaboration. The value of goal setting and goal commitment cannot be understated in this approach to developing collaborations with schools that serve large numbers of African American students; often urban schools.

The pragmatic perspective to collaboration is an attempt to use appropriate research knowledge to address K-12 issues schools consider important *at that time*. According to Griffiths (2000), if the partners are clear as to why the collaboration was established, that is, on which of the previous perspectives it was established, there is a logical next step that determines how that collaboration should be conducted. This perspective suggests that such partnerships may already be in place with an agenda, but that agenda will be over time to address new issues as they arise. Often, colleges and universities solicit a list of issues from K-12 and organize a response. While this approach insures that current K-12 issues are addressed in real time, it is questionable if such arrangements result in systemic change—the type of change often needed to impact achievement of African American students. While each perspective could be the guiding philosophy for a partnership, most school–university partnerships are begun from a purely pragmatic approach. Griffiths' work, however, provides a good framework from which to discuss and evaluate school–university partnerships that directly impact African American students.

Successful Collaborative Efforts

It has been reported that school–university partnerships judged to be successful involve a variety of K-12 and K-16 institutions. The literature provides some examples of successful collaborations among universities and K-12 schools (Edwards et al.,1996; Harkavy, 2005; Erickson & Christman, 1996), but provides significantly fewer examples of partnerships that specifically focus on mathematics instruction and its impact on African American students. Powers and DeWaters (2004) describe a partnership between Clarkson University and four schools in Northern New York State. Clarkson University developed 3- to 10-week long project-based science and technology units for middle school students to increase aptitude in mathematics. This partnership and its units were developed with the idea of bringing relevancy and connectivity to the coursework. For this study, however, the units were developed to create connectivity for female students, not necessarily minority students,

The partnership between Southeast Missouri State University and a rural elementary school is a university and local school focused on mathematics achievement (Waddle & Conway, 2005). Similar to other university partnership, this one provided mathematics methods professional development to in-service teachers. From 1994–2002, university faculty planned and provided research-based professional development courses to this school to determine its impact on teacher instructional practices, delivery of staff development, and student achievement. According to Waddle and Conway, teachers' attitudes moved from teacher-centered to a more student-centered attitude. Results also indicated a substantial increase in teacher collaboration about curriculum development and an increase in student math scores during and immediately following the program. This program like others, however, did not specifically focus on the academic achievement of African American students.

Unlike the previous two examples of collaborative efforts, the following partnership focuses on African American students and offers a more comprehensive collection of services. Talent Quest (Carroll et al., 2001) describes a major school reform effort between Johns Hopkins University, Howard University, and K-12 schools in major urban areas. The purpose of Talent Quest is to work with communities, school leaders, parents, and university leaders to co-construct a partnership that will help to "transform" urban schools through professional development and direct services. Developed by Howard University's staff in 1999, Talent Quest provides sufficient experience for the researchers to reflect on this project and to develop school reform models, evaluate and refine programs, and disseminate results. Carroll et al. offer these recommendations for others seeking to develop school reform collaborations of this type:

1   Additional time may be needed to develop, implement, and evaluate school reform among all stakeholders.
2   Stakeholder status, power, and responsibilities must be co-constructed and clearly communicated.
3   Each stakeholder must understand, appreciate, and help to facilitate each stockholder's different talents.
4   Partnership participants must realize that most schools operate in reactive rather than in proactive mode. Competing agendas such as insufficient time, faculty turnover, inadequate funding and resources, and changing priorities, often leave schools in a continuing crisis.

The above section provides evidence that school–university partnerships, having goals that go beyond the preparation of new teachers, do exist. Most of the above partnerships address the larger needs of school reform and renewal. The Maryland Institute for Minority Achievement and Urban Education (MIMAUE), described later in this chapter, began with goals of changing school academics and climate.

Role of Research I Universities

Research I universities have as their major mission the creation of new knowledge through research and then finding ways to apply the research findings to problems of society. While the mission of most Research I universities is, in part, to use their research to better humans and the environment, many also include, as part of their charge, the improvement of K-12 education. Research universities take pride in helping define the most intractable problems in society and through the creative abilities of its faculties, propose ways of addressing these issues. It is our contention that research universities are well suited to impact K-12 education and the major issues of African American student achievement because the research of interest in most colleges of education covers the many areas needed to operate an effective K-12 school system; curriculum, teaching and learning, leadership and administration, assessment and evaluation. It would then be expected that any partnership between a college of education at a Research I university and K-12 school(s) would have research as one of its major goals. For K-12 schools that serve African American students, that research should focus on issues that help to improve the effectiveness of the school serving African American and other minority students.

It would be important, therefore, to review all research agenda to purposefully include research on social and educational issues that directly apply to and impact African American students and families. Faculty at the university should collaborate with the schools to jointly design research, gather data, study and inform practice, and serve as a resource partner to the school(s). Research findings should reveal issues and problems that occur in a school's teaching and learning environment that may support or hinder African American (or other minorities) student achievement. We highly recommend that school officials *and* researchers collaborate and jointly participate in the writing of research reports to ensure that the results highlight the strengths of African American students and not only the weaknesses. It would be expected that university faculty would be interested to learn more about school leaders' day-to-day school issues and ultimately study these issues. In other words, *research should inform practice and practice should inform research.*

McLaughlin and Black-Hawkins (2007) suggest that while the above discussion may represent good belief statements, in actuality the usefulness of educational research to practitioners and policy-makers is small. They argue that reform must take place at the whole school level and not just at the teacher level. They describe relationships between universities and schools not as partnerships but as "complementary" relationships; that is, the agendas of both parties stay intact and operationalize a parallel agenda. The degree of mutual engagement in each other's agenda is limited. Their research raises the question of how well two different institutions can work together for the mutual benefit of both or if the two institutions need to agree on a common agenda for the partnership to be effective. It cannot be denied that the reward system for faculty at research universities gives most weight to research, and often the research a faculty person wishes to do does not conform to the issues schools deem to be most important at that time or cannot be accommodated for a variety of good educational reasons. Certainly, the need for a common agenda before the partnership begins is critically important. The point of view articulated by McLaughlin and Black-Hawkins raises the excellent question of "who" can promote and implement a research position focusing on African American educational issues and even how well the research reported throughout this volume can be applied to schooling issues involving African American students *unless* there is shared agreement of its usefulness by both the universities and the schools.

Another area of concern that has been raised is the impact of school–university partnerships on academic achievement of students in K-12 schools. While the research usually addresses this issue for *all* students, it has major importance for African American students. One of the major reasons for establishing many professional development and direct services partnerships is to improve academic achievement, often in core subjects such as reading and mathematics. Lenski et al. (2001) studied the relationship between school–university partnerships and students' learning. Their initial efforts were to determine a research methodology that would allow them to tease out the impact of the partnership within the complexity of the school environment. Using a group of researchers from Research I and Research II universities as experts, Lenski et al. sought consensus on a methodology that would allow them to study the academic impact of the partnership. The authors report that, while all research participants agreed that finding links between school partnerships and K-12 student learning achievement is important, studying this relationship can prove to be very difficult. The researchers did conclude that qualitative methods would give more insight into the impact of the partnership; they also cautioned that, given the many variables operating in a school learning environment, drawing conclusions about the impact of the partnership is almost impossible.

New and creative methods are needed to carefully tease out the academic influences of school–university partnerships on student achievement. This is one of the many areas where the university usually has expertise. The findings of Lenski et al. not withstanding, partnerships with schools that educate African American students must be able to determine the impact of the collaboration to ensure the continuation of the partnership. The necessary team of university and K-12 researchers must be assembled for such a task. The scarcity of resources, time constraints and, most of all, the future success of students depends on finding the most effective and efficient ways of teaching and stimulating higher levels of achievement of African American children.

Research I universities participate in the highest level of basic and applied research found in the world. Because of this high level of research and the development of new and exciting knowledge, they are also well suited to take the lead in addressing the nation's efforts at increasing the participation of underrepresented groups in science, technology, engineering, and mathematics (STEM) education fields. National efforts by the National Science Foundation (NSF) and the United States Department of Education through many of their large-scale programs (e.g., the Urban Systemic Initiatives Program, Urban Systemic Program, Math and Science Partnership Program) have supported a growth of university/K-12 partnerships through federal policy and federal funding. Through the aforementioned NSF and USDE programs, these agencies have identified university/college partnerships as a strategic element to training teachers, conducting research, and engaging students in the mathematics and science fields. Many of these programs fail to adequately address specific issues underlying the achievement difficulties found in urban schools and with African American students. Most programs still operate with the "mathematics for all" philosophy and "good mathematics for all students is good mathematics for African American students" philosophy. This approach to professional development does not allow for professional preparation that addresses specific needs of African American students and teachers of African American students. The relationship of mathematics and culture is not yet seen as important to the learning of mathematics, although many researchers have already shown how the two are related.

A common component of university-led STEM research projects includes providing and studying student enrichment activities that are used as motivators or "hooks" to draw young minds into the STEM areas. Many programs allow for middle and high school students to visit university laboratories and experience new and fascinating science at first hand. Another component of these research projects requests university faculty to serve as coaches for teachers and visit classrooms to share their expert knowledge. Many programs that report success in recruiting underrepresented groups into science careers link their success to some program or scientific endeavor in which students actively participate.

Furthermore, many pre-service teacher education programs include a research component as part of the preparatory courses for teachers. The intent is for new teachers leaving the university to be prepared to use their science knowledge as well as their knowledge about how students learn science in their classrooms. New degree programs and major modifications to existing teacher education programs have also resulted from national efforts to improve STEM education for underrepresented youth. However, it is still difficult to find evidence that programs at the national level have had major impact on the nation's ability to improve the numbers of students from underrepresented groups who are involved in STEM majors or careers. Yet all programs state as goals the inclusion and improved achievement of African American students, but few present data to show actual improvement of African American students.

It is clear, however, that research universities who partner with K-12 schools on STEM efforts have the *opportunity* to develop new science and mathematics courses for teachers and other students, recruit a new group of students to science and mathematics education, and possibly bring new and exciting research information into K-12 schools. It would seem that a school–university partnership could be developed at Research I universities for the purpose of improving STEM education for students at the university and students in K-12 settings. *It seems further possible that Research I universities can have a major impact on the mathematics and science achievement of African American students if it accepts this challenge as part of its mission.* In the next section we will discuss one such undertaking by a Research I university.

Maryland Institute for Minority Achievement and Urban Education

The Maryland Institute for Minority Achievement and Urban Education (MIMAUE, The Institute) was established in spring 2001 as a result of concerns within the College of Education at the University of Maryland, College Park and the State of Maryland regarding the achievement levels of Maryland's K-12 minority students with special concern for African American students. A group of state educational administrators, K-12 leaders, college leaders, politicians, and lay persons convened to discuss how a Research I college of education could partner with K-12 institutions to address leadership, curriculum, teaching, and learning issues reported as critical in improving African American student achievement. The first activity of the group was to host a national conference (Achievement—A Shared Imperative) (www.education.umd.edu/MIMAUE) to bring state and local attention to the issues of African American student achievement. This activity revealed the depth of the achievement issue and the possible role the university could accept through partnering with K-12 schools. As a result of this activity, it was decided that the College had a moral imperative to help address K-12 achievement issues. Consequently, the Dean of the College and the Chief Executive Officer (CEO) of a local school system decided to focus early efforts on improving reading and mathematics scores at one high school, one middle school and two elementary schools, all part of a partial feeder pattern in one of the five administrative regions of the system. Every school in this project was a majority minority school with approximately 85% of all students being African American. Monthly meetings were established and led by the Dean of the College and the CEO of the school system. Administrators and faculty from the College, deputy superintendents and other leaders from the school system also participated. Through a Participatory Action Research (PAR) model (see Hittleman & Simon, 2002, for more detail on PAR) the cultures of the two organizations, relative strengths, and offerings from each institution, and issues from the schools were discussed along with possible actions that would be needed to address the issues. Most commonly discussed topics focused on school leadership needs, professional development needs of teachers, inspirational needs of students, and the need for university faculty to use school sites and school issues for research purposes. An early decision was to develop the partnership as a long-term relationship, one in which every activity taking place with teachers or students would be mutually agreed upon by both the schools and the university.

As the partnership progressed, the need for resources became prominent. Together, the school and university leadership developed a 5-year plan intended to improve student achievement in mathematics and reading at the partnership schools. This plan involved leadership retreats and seminars for administrators to focus on issues of goal setting, school reform models, and issues within a school such as assigning teachers to specific classes. Professional development for teachers was planned with helping non-certified teachers become more proficient in teaching mathematics and English as major goals. Safety-net activities such as in-school and out-of-school tutoring, recruiting University students to assist with science projects in middle and high school, and extra incentives for high achievement were all part of the comprehensive plan. Local businesses and corporations were excited about this plan and supported this partnership effort to a level of more than a half-million dollars. The university also contributed by allowing every teacher in the partnership schools to enroll in six graduate credit hours of coursework with tuition waived. As of May 2008, more than 175 teachers have taken advantage of this offer to take courses that counted toward initial certification or re-certification.

Since its beginning in 2001, the Institute has partnered with the schools to implement the following:

- *Leadership retreats:* These retreats are geared towards building leadership capacity. Administrators and teacher leaders are brought together off-site to participate in training sessions and workshops run by university faculty, county staff, and external consultants. Participants use the training to develop school-wide plans that address their specific student and teacher needs and operational goals for the improvement of their schools both academically and for the improvement of school climate.
- *Professional development:* The Institute offers a variety of professional development courses. During the Institute's early years, we focused on offering reading and mathematics methodology courses for elementary, middle, and high school teachers. Because nearly all of the teachers who participated in these courses taught "majority–minority" classrooms, we assumed teachers were

sensitive and responsive to their students' cultures. As some of the initial offerings ended, we realized that teachers needed to learn more about their students' culture and how to develop teaching strategies and materials to allow the student's culture to be recognized. These early offerings led the Institute faculty to modify professional courses in a way that would cultivate cultural proficiency in teachers and incite culturally relevant and content-focused teaching strategies. Our culturally relevant professional development now enables educators to create an instructionally powerful and rich learning environment, particularly for African American students.

- *Student-to-student activities:* For the past 3 years, University of Maryland honors' students have taught and mentored high school students about topics ranging from "what is a liberal education" to "what does it take to be admitted to a 4-year college." With more than 36,000 students enrolled at University of Maryland, the Institute regards university students as an invaluable resource from which to recruit college students to work with high school students. High school students are sometimes more receptive to the advice, mentoring, and instruction of a person close to their age. Not only did high school students relate well to college students, participating African American and Latino high school students noted that interacting with college students, particularly minority college students made them believe that college was possible for them.

- *Family Math nights:* This annual family event consists of various booths focusing on activities to increase student abilities in math. Activities reinforced number logic, predictions, geometric concepts, number sense, statistics, and measurement. Families have the opportunity to participate with interactive sessions such as computerized Jeopardy. Parents learn with activities that may be incorporated with daily routines. Approximately 150 families representing pre-kindergarten through sixth-grade attended this event last academic year.

- *Elementary School Based African American Male Mentoring Program:* This program was adapted based on training modules defined and described in "Empowering Young Black Males—III: A Systematic Modular Training Program for Black Male Children and Adolescents"(Lee, 2003). Lee's training program "offers specific strategies for empowering young African American males to help them achieve optimal educational and social success" (2003, p. ix). A critical part of the program is empowering the adults who support and work with these students, thus the program's focus is on community mentors, parents, and school staff. The modules consist of: one-on-one weekly mentoring sessions, monthly group sessions with all mentors and mentees, parent empowerment workshops, and teacher/school counselor professional development.

- *Academic Climate Program:* This activity is an academic achievement recognition program that celebrates the academic success of students who earn a GPA of 3.0 or higher. The program creator describes the process as "paying attention to kids that pay attention." The result empowers students to take control of their own academic destiny and emphasizes high academic achievement. The number of students who have earned a GPA of 3.0 has increased from 18.5% to

23.1% from fall 2006 to fall 2007. The school's administrators and teachers are encouraged by the increased camaraderie and student-to-student support that has fostered as a result of the Institute-sponsored programs. Based on results from the program, more students have achieved this goal than in previous years. School personnel note that a larger number of students exemplify a contagious spirit that has impacted the academic climate of the entire school.

- *University Colloquia:* Beginning in fall 2002, the Institute has sponsored a four-session, semester-long colloquia on a topic related to academic achievement of minority youth. Topics range from *Violence in the Schools* to *Helping African American Students in Mathematics and Science.* Experts from various educational areas serve as consultants and discussants. The colloquia are open to all teachers, administrators, and others in the educational community. A complete list of colloquia topics and description of sessions can be found at ww.education.umd.edu/MIMAUE.

- *Research Project About Latino Parents:* At the request of the school administration the Institute conducted a major research study to investigate the attitudes of Latino parents towards their child's school. Through surveys, the study also assessed Latino parents' level of participation at their child's school—factors that impact their level of participation. Survey results indicated that communication and transportation barriers were among the key issues that hindered parents' involvement in schools. Although information was sent home in Spanish, the study revealed that most parents could not read or write in their native languages beyond the elementary level and thus could not read information sent home. As a result of this study, schools in the Administrative Region added parent liaisons and other staff in an attempt to be more inviting and encouraging to Latino parents.

The MIMAUE partnership began with all three "principles" suggested by Griffiths (2000). Epistemologically, there was the understanding that the university needed to be involved with the K-12 schools as partners. Geographically located in the midst of a majority-African American school district, partners decided to serve our surrounding districts where we believed we could make the greatest impact. From the pragmatic perspective, the reality of everyday life in schools helped the partnership focus on what real steps it could take to have an impact on teaching and learning. Clearly, as the partnership matured, it moved from an epistemological perspective to a more pragmatic perspective. Currently, almost all efforts are aimed toward the pragmatic goals of improving student performance on state mandated tests.

The Maryland Institute for Minority Achievement and Urban Education is an example of a partnership formed between a Research I university and K-12 school system with the intent of providing both professional development for teachers and administrators and providing other direct services. The Institute continues to develop partnerships with K-12 schools in the State of Maryland and each new partnership brings a new set of concerns, challenges, and expectations.

Valadez and Snyder (2006) give a list of components that should guide the development of any school–university partnership. Our experience suggests that these are the issues that must be addressed if a partnership is to be "successful" and sustainable. We discuss each of these components in reference to the partnership between MIMAUE and the urban school systems in which we currently work. It is our experience that all of these components are of great importance and must receive adequate attention, especially when seeking to develop partnerships with urban schools and critical when the partnership is focusing on improvement of academic performance of African American students.

Mutually Agreed Upon Goals

The goals of the university and those of K-12 institutions are different. Finding mutual goals that can support a long-term partnership is difficult and, in some cases, may not be possible. The leaders of this school university partnership met for at least 6 months before going forward with any project. A major issue centered on what impact the university would have on school leadership, school curriculum, and instructional methodologies and if the result would be consistent with district and school requirements and mandates. This was expected in a district under pressure already to improve achievement. The introduction of possibly new assessment indicators into the school was also a concern. As one major compromise, the partnership decided to use whatever measures the schools were required to collect as measures of our success.

Commitment to the Goals of the Partnership

The persons "around the table" are most important in establishing the partnership and determining the level of commitment. Frequent changes of university and/or school leadership place extra tension on school–university partnerships. As persons around the table change, so may the partners' perceptions or interpretations of the goals. A change in the school, district, or university leadership can potentially impact how goals are interpreted and how much importance should be placed on the partnership's identified goals. Changes in leadership at the school level impacted our partnership in critical ways, most noticeably when principals were transferred or new regional directors were named who were not involved in the original group. The efforts to expand the number of schools within the partnership were curtailed with every change of leadership. For our partnership, we have learned to be as explicit as possible about the goals for the partnership. This requires partners to agree on who will be included in the target population based on criteria such as, but not limited to, race, level of academic achievement, geographic area focus (which may equate to focus on a particular racial group), and student grade level.

Appreciating and Bridging Cultural Differences

Universities are interested in school change and studying that change through systematic research. Schools are interested in improving curriculum and teaching methodologies to increase student learning often measured through a standardized test. These differences have to be realized and appreciated if the partnership is to make any progress. While it is important to know the concerns and focus of the partnering agent, it is equally important to understand the organizational culture of each partner as well. Private industry is often compared to a school environment; yet anyone who has interacted with both entities is sure to recognize the differences in the way each organization operates. The same is true when comparing how universities and schools operate. Each partner needs to understand the other's operational issues; such as the length of time it takes to process a contract at a university and when is the appropriate time of the year to ask high school teachers to complete a survey. Each organization's capacity to respond quickly and effectively is inherently linked to the organizational culture of that particular entity. For our partnership, we have recruited faculty and staff who have worked either in, or closely with, both the school and university environments. These individuals serve as effective liaisons between the university and schools, understanding the needs and concerns of both entities. Also, our staff consider the realistic time frame in which issues may be appropriately addressed. Even as they navigate the institutional cultures, they carefully consider how the time frame in which decisions are made impact on the African American students and their families that we serve.

Communication

A common approach is to establish monthly meetings, but good partnerships need more means of communication than monthly meetings to be effective. Correspondence by electronic means including message boards and online chats can help with discussions and decision-making between meetings. Effective implementation of a partnership may require building relationships and strong lines of communication with district personnel who typically do not directly participate with partnership activities, but who are critical to program implementation. For example, if the partnership includes a parent involvement component, a partnership member may need to communicate with the district's director of parent involvement to gain a better understanding of how to align the partnership's goals with those of the district. For our partnership, we have given significant effort to this last point about communication—getting to know key school district personnel for each reform activity. The creation of the partnership may have started with your school or College's of Education dean but, once the work begins, it is vitally important to keep the school district employees informed about the partnership and its activities. This allows for cooperative planning and supportive implementation. This can be done even at a Research I university as long as university faculty and staff are willing to initiate and maintain working relationships with district staff.

Shared Power

Both partners must see that the programs are co-constructed and decisions are made in an atmosphere of trust, each party trusting that the other is working towards improving conditions for students, teachers, and parents. Obviously, the different partners have different strengths and capabilities, yet both must be a part of the decision-making process. This means that persons with comparable authority must be a part of the decision-making team, for instance, a Dean and a CEO. This buy-in at the executive level is important to the decision about with whom the partnership will work and what target population it will serve. In one of the districts with which we work, this is almost a non-issue since almost all the schools in the surrounding district are majority African American. In other districts, however, it is important to receive the support from the Dean and the district CEO to direct efforts towards African American students.

Sufficient Resources

Partnerships often bring new and different resource challenges to the participants. Businesses and other interested community corporations and leaders have great interest in schools that develop young people to be productive citizens. Consequently, if presented with a positive and optimistic plan, they will usually help with both human and financial resources. Since schools are public entities supported by public funds, businesses and community corporations are often more inclined to supply resources to other non-profit entities that will provide supplemental services to school. These resources may allow the awarded entity to focus on a certain geographic area, race, gender, or other criterion as stipulated by the granting company or agency. For a partnership like ours, this allows the university to focus on issues or populations that the partnership has deemed most critical. So, for example, based on disaggregated data, there is currently a focus on improving academic achievement for African American males. We have identified companies that are interested in supporting academic enrichment activities focused on this population. Because school districts often define their goals as academic achievement for *all*, they are often not the recipients of funding with such an explicit focus. Clearly, the CEO of the school system should know what is being promised, what is being collected, and how it is being disbursed.

Planning for Sustainability

What happens when a new CEO or Dean comes with a different vision? The extent to which you can adjust to the new direction and show that your partnership is still useful to both entities will determine, for the most part, if it is to be sustained. These partnerships, unlike the ones involved with teacher training, are usually less permanent and will end when the goal is accomplished or when the resource burden becomes too great for either partner to justify the continuation of the partnership.

Ongoing Evaluation

Evaluating the impact of the partnership on student learning is a major goal of the MIMAUE partnership. As stated earlier, this is a very difficult goal to implement. Earlier partnership efforts were developed to collect anecdotal evidence from teachers and students and standardized test data. Our research methodologies were not sufficient to tease out the impact of the many partnership activities on student achievement, although teachers and administrators reported evidence of increased student achievement. Current projects are designed with more powerful research methods and are approved by the Institutional Research Board (IRB) at both the university and the school system.

Conclusion

In conclusion, the research reported in this chapter indicated that school–university partnerships have potential for reforming many aspects of current educational practice with African American students. Those reforms must take place through the shared agreement of different institutions. The great promise is that, as a result of strong, effective partnerships, schools will be reformed and students liberated to perform at higher and higher levels in mathematics and all other subjects. It is not clear if a partnership focusing on African American student achievement would have been possible in a district in which African American students represented a small minority. Our partnership initially impacted only four to eight schools in a system that has over 100 schools. (The Institute has since expanded and in fact works with other surrounding school districts.) Even with this small number, it was evident that partnerships between research universities and K-12 schools rely heavily on who has the social capital to invest in developing the relationship, the nature of the goals selected to guide the partnership, who has the resources, who decides on how the resources are used, and how the partnership is evaluated. Without clear determinants of the above, the institutions will remain on separate tracks and researchers will continue to do research and theorize and schools will continue to base new practice on their knowledge of what worked from existing practice. Teachers will continue to be prepared in the same way and they will continue to teach in the same way. This is a losing proposition for African American students. Our desire is for research findings to inform and improve practice, and for practice to inform the type of research needed to improve achievement for African American students. We believe that effective partnerships hold the promise for this to happen.

References

Ascher, C. & Schwartz, W. (1989). School–College alliances: Benefits for low-income minorities. ERIC Document Reproduction Service No. ED 308 277.

Borthwick, A.C., Stirling, T., Nauman, A.D., & Cook, D.L. (2003). Achieving successful school–university collaboration. *Urban Education*, 38(3), 330–371.

Callahan, J.L. & Martin, D. (2007). The spectrum of school–university partnerships: A typology of organizational learning systems. *Teaching and Teacher Education*, 23, 136–145.

Carroll, G., LaPointe, V., & Tyler, K. (2001). Co-construction: A facilitator for school reform in school, community and university partnerships. *The Journal of Negro Education*, 70(1/2), 38–58.

Clarken, R. (1999). University/School Collaboration: A Case Study. Paper presented at the 51st Annual Meeting of the American Association of Colleges for Teacher Education, Washington, DC.

Edwards, P., Abel, F.J., Easton, S.E., Herbster, D., & Sparapani, E.F. (1996). Disadvantaged Rural Students: Five Models of School–University Collaboration. Paper presented at the 76th Annual Meeting of the Association of Teacher Educators, St. Louis, MO.

Erickson, F. & Christman, J.B. (1996). Taking stock/making change: Stories of collaboration in local school reform. *Theory into Practice, 35*(3), 149–157.

Florez, V.E. (2002). School/university partnerships: An agenda that works. *Teacher Education and Practice, 15*(1&2), 74–87.

Goals 2000: Educate America Act (1994). Title III: State and Local Educational Systemic Improvement, Section 301, finding 12. United States Congress. H.R.1804.

Griffiths, M. (2000). Collaboration and partnership in question: knowledge, politics, and practice. *Journal of Educational Policy, 15*(4), 383–395.

Harkavy, I. (2005). University-assisted community school program of West Philadelphia: Democratic partnerships that make a difference. *New Directions for Youth Development, 107*, 35–43.

Henderson-Sparks, J., Paredes, L., & Gonzalez. (2002). Student Teacher Preparation: A Collaborative Model to Assist At-Risk Students. *Preventing School Failure, 46*(2), 80.

Hittleman, D.R. & Simon, A. J. (2002). *Interpreting educational research: An introduction for consumers of research.* Upper Saddle River, NJ: Merrill Prentice Hall.

Hutchison, R.N., Lovell, N.B., Nordan, R.W., & Cleere, R. (1994, November). School- university partnerships: A status report. Paper presented at the Annual Meeting of the Mid-South Educational Research Association, Nashville, TN.

Lee, C. (2003). Empowering young Black males, III: A systematic modular training program for Black male children and adolescents. Greensboro, NC: Caps Press.

Lenski, S.D., Grisham, D.L., Brink, B., Mahurt, S., Jampole, E., Cohen, S., et al. (2001). Researching the relationship between school–university partnerships and students' learning. *Journal of Reading Education, 26*(3), 23–28.

McLaughlin, C. & Black-Hawkins, K. (2007). School-university partnerships for educational research—distinctions, dilemmas and challenges. *The Curriculum Journal, 18*(3), 327–341.

Powers, S. & DeWaters, J. (2004, October). Creating project-based learning experiences for university/K-12 partnerships. Paper presented at the meeting of the ASEE/IEEE Frontiers in Education Conference, Savannah, GA. Retrieved September 24, 2008 from http://ieeexplore.ieee.org/iel5/9652/30543/01408627.pdf?isnumber=30543&prod=STD&arnumber=1408627&arnumber=1408627&arSt=+F3D&ared=+18-23+Vol.+2&arAuthor=Powers%2C+S.E.%3B+de+Waters%2C+J.

Thorkildsen, R. & Scott Stein, M.R. (1996). Fundamental characteristics of successful university–school partnerships. *The School Community Journal, 6*(2), 79–92.

Valadez, J.R. & Snyder, J. (2006). Social, cultural, and political influences on the development of an educational partnership. *Journal of Latinos and Education, 5*(1), 29–47.

Waddle, J. & Conway, K. (2005). School reform through a school/university partnership. *Current Issues in Education* [On-line], 8(8). Available: http://cie.ed.asu.edu/volume8/number8.

Contributors

Grace Atukpawu is a graduate student in the School of Education at Stanford University.

Dr. Robert Q. Berry III is an Assistant Professor in mathematics education in the Curry School of Education at the University of Virginia. His scholarly interest focuses on equity issues in mathematics education and the work of elementary mathematics specialists. Recent publications include, *The Stories of African American Middle School Boys who are Successful With School Mathematics* (published in the *Journal for Research in Mathematics Education*) and *Co-teaching: A Collaborative Instructional between an Elementary Mathematics Specialist and a Classroom Teacher.*

Dr. Daniel Chazan is an Associate Professor and Director of the Center for Mathematics Education at the University of Maryland. He is a co-PI on *Thought Experiments in Mathematics Education* (ThEMaT) with Patricio Herbst of the University of Michigan and co-PI of the Mid-Atlantic Center for Mathematics Teaching and Learning, leading the Urban Case Studies project. In 2000, he published *Beyond Formulas in Mathematics and Teaching: Dynamics of the High School Algebra Classroom* (Teachers College Press) and, in 2007, *Embracing Reason: Egalitarian Ideals and High School Mathematics Teaching* (Taylor & Francis).

Dr. Lawrence M. Clark is an Assistant Professor in the Center for Mathematics Education at the University of Maryland. Prior to his appointment at the University of Maryland, Dr. Clark served as the National Director of Mathematics for Project GRAD USA, a national school reform initiative in several urban school districts. His research interests focus primarily on examining and exploring influences on secondary teachers' mathematics instructional practices, particularly in schools with a history of low achievement in mathematics. He is the co-author of *Where is the Mathematics: Examining Teachers Mathematical Learning Opportunities in Practice-based Professional Learning Tasks* (Journal of Mathematics Teacher Education).

Michael Davis is a researcher at the Lawrence Hall of Science at the University of California, Berkeley.

Dr. Kara J. Jackson is a postdoctoral research fellow in mathematics education at Vanderbilt University. Her research interests lie at the intersection of foundations of education and mathematics education, and her work focuses on processes of mathematics learning, socialization, and identity development across contexts, including school and home, and how to support teachers to provide access to equitable learning opportunities in mathematics for all students.

Dr. Martin L. Johnson is a Professor Emeritus in the Department of Curriculum and Instruction, University of Maryland College Park. His specialty areas are Mathematics Education and Urban and Minority Education. He was a Founding Director of the Maryland Institute for Minority Achievement and Urban Education (MIMAUE). He is also co-editor of *Changing the Faces of Mathematics: Perspectives on African Americans* (National Council of Teachers of Mathematics).

Dr. Whitney Johnson is a Lecturer in the Center for Mathematics Education at the University of Maryland. She served as Project Director for the *Case Studies of Urban Algebra I Teachers Project* and is Principal Investigator for a research project titled *Teaching Black Students Data Analysis in a High Stakes Context*. In this project Dr. Johnson is exploring teachers' professional opinions on the usefulness of innovative instructional approaches in raising achievement for their African American students.

Dr. Yolanda A. Johnson is an Associate Professor at Tarrant County College–South Campus, where she teaches developmental and core math classes, as well as math content for education majors. She also teaches graduate level math curriculum classes at Texas A&M University-Commerce. Her research interests include service learning and female students' mathematics experiences, achievement, and attitudes.

Dr. Jacqueline Leonard is an Associate Professor of Mathematics Education at Temple University. Her research interests focus on cultural pedagogy and social justice. She is the author of *Culturally Specific Pedagogy in the Mathematics Classroom* (Routledge, 2008). Her upcoming article, entitled *Using Multimedia to Engage African American Children in Classroom Discourse*, and co-authored with Marc L. Hill, will appear in the *Journal of Black Studies*.

Dr. Carol E. Malloy is an Associate Professor in mathematics education at the University of North Carolina at Chapel Hill. Her scholarly interests focus on equity in education and reform. She is responsive to concerns that many students have difficulty learning mathematics and, specifically, that African American, Latino, and Native American students often lack opportunities to learn quality mathematics and gain necessary skills to perform and understand rigorous mathematics. Recent publications include *Bringing Systemic Reform to Life: School District Reform and Comer Schools* (Hampton Press) and *The Education of African American Children in Charter Schools: Four Cases* (Handbook of African American Education).

Danny Bernard Martin is Chair of Curriculum and Instruction and Associate Professor of Mathematics at the University of Illinois at Chicago. He teaches content and methods courses in the undergraduate elementary education program as well as courses in the PhD. program in Curriculum and Instruction. Prior to coming to UIC, he was Professor in the Department of Mathematics at Contra Costa College for 15 years and was a National Academy of Education/ Spencer Foundation Postdoctoral Fellow from 1998–2000. His research focuses on mathematics education for African American learners and takes into account sociohistorical, community, school forces, and individual agency. His work draws from culture-practice theory, cultural-ecological theory, critical theories of race, and racial identity development theory. He is currently developing a perspective that frames mathematics learning and participation as racialized forms of experience. Dr. Martin is author of the book *Mathematics Success and Failure Among African Youth* (Erlbaum).

Dr. Lou Edward Matthews is an Assistant Professor of Mathematics Education in the Middle/Secondary and Instructional Technology in the College of Education. For the past 15 years, Dr. Matthews has addressed audiences of parents, teachers, and students throughout the nation regarding education reform and the schooling of African American children. A native of Bermuda, Dr. Matthews has also been actively involved in education reform efforts in Bermuda. He is the 2007–2009 President of the Benjamin Banneker Association, a national non-profit organization advocating excellence for African American children in mathematics.

Oren L. McClain is a graduate student in the Curry School of Education at the University of Virginia. His research interests are access and opportunities to learn in mathematics education.

Dr. Na'ilah Suad Nasir is an Associate Professor of Education and African American Studies at the University of California, Berkeley. She is interested in how issues of culture and race influence the mathematical learning, achievement, and educational trajectories of African American and other non-dominant students in urban schools. Recent publications include (with Paul Cobb) *Improving Access to Mathematics: Diversity and Equity in the Classroom* (Teachers College Press) and (with Victoria Hand) *Exploring Socio-cultural Perspectives on Race, Culture, and Learning* (Review of Educational Research).

Kathleen O'Connor is a graduate student in the School of Education at Stanford University.

Dr. Joi A. Spencer is Assistant Professor in the School of Leadership and Education Sciences at University of San Diego. Her research interests include mathematics equity, teaching mathematics for understanding, African American achievement and identity, effective schools for African American students, and improving the methodologies used to understand these issues. She is currently working on a 3-year longitudinal study at a conversion charter middle school in South East San Diego. This study investigates mathematics teacher practices and the mathematics learning opportunities of students across high and low-track math courses.

Dr. David W. Stinson is an Assistant Professor of Mathematics Education (and Affiliate Faculty in Women's Studies) at Georgia State University. His research interests include examining how mathematics teachers, educators, and researchers incorporate the philosophical and theoretical underpinnings of postmodern critical theory into their education philosophies, pedagogical practices, and/or research methods; and how students who are constructed outside the white, Christian, heterosexual male of bourgeois privilege successfully accommodate, reconfigure, or resist the hegemonic discourses of schooling, and of society generally. His recent publications include "African American Adolescent Males, Schooling (and Mathematics): Deficiency, Rejection, and Achievement" in *Review of Educational Research*; and "Negotiating Sociocultural Discourses: The Counter-Storytelling of Academically (and Mathematically) Successful African American Male Students" in *American Educational Research Journal.*

Dr. Marilyn E. Strutchens is a Professor of Mathematics Education at Auburn University, Auburn Alabama. Her research interests include African American students' mathematics achievement and teacher change in mathematics education. Dr. Strutchens is co-editor of NCTM's 2007 yearbook, entitled *The Learning of Mathematics: 69th NCTM Yearbook* and lead editor for the book *Changing the Faces of Mathematics: Perspectives on African Americans.*

Dr. Stephanie Timmons Brown, Ph.D., is a Research Associate in the College of Education, University of Maryland College Park. Her research interests focus on educational policy. Dr. Brown is the Executive Director of the Maryland Institute for Minority Achievement and Urban Education.

Jessica Tsang is a graduate student in the School of Education at Stanford University.

Dr. Erica N. Walker is an Associate Professor of Mathematics Education at Teachers College, Columbia University. Her research interests include the social and cultural factors related to success in mathematics for underserved students. In addition, she explores the relationship between teachers' perceptions of student potential and their classroom practice, and its impact on student mathematics outcomes. Her publications include "Urban High School Students' Academic Communities and their Effects on Mathematics Success" (*American Education Research Journal*, 2006). She has also published articles in *Educational Leadership*, *Teacher Education Quarterly*, and *The Urban Review.*

Dr. S. Kathy Westbrook taught mathematics at the high school level for 17 years before completing a Master's in Applied Mathematics and a PhD. in secondary mathematics curriculum and instruction in 2005. Dr. Westbrook is currently an Assistant Professor at the University of South Alabama with a joint appointment in the College of Education and Arts and Sciences. Her research interests include teacher change in mathematics education and African American students' mathematics achievement.

Sarah Wischnia is a graduate student in the School of Education at Stanford University.

Index

50–2; teacher instructional strategies and dispositions 96, 106–8, 108–11, 119–20
Student Support Services program 335
student-to-student activities 344
students: analyzing work on assessment tasks 161–8; direct-services school-university partnerships 333, 334–5, 335–6; framing 181, 182–3; giving students voice 103–4, 105; knowledge and behavior 217–18, 220; personal accountability and difficult circumstances 75–6
subject: discursive 268; marginalized 275
subversive repetition 275
success: forces shaping African American success in maths 200–30; key constructs in understanding 202–5
successful maths students 206–7, 212–15, 226; influence of sociocultural and sociohistorical discourses on agency 265–88
Sullivan, P. 153
summer jobs 319
Sunday schools 313
sustainability 348
Swafford, J. 93
synthesis 73
syphilis 310

Talent Quest 339
Talent Search program 335
talk, social 236–46
tasks: analyzing student work on 161–8; instructional strategies and conceptual understanding 94–5, 96, 106, 108, 109, 118, 119; teachers' instructional practice and student learning 153–61
Tate, W.F. 69, 126–7, 249–50, 250–1
Tatum, B. 202
Teach for America Program 304
teachers: Bermudian teachers and culturally relevant pedagogy 69–82; classroom practice 145–71; dispositions 88–122, 227; expectations 17, 75–6, 83, 272; extended roles of maths teachers 74–6, 82–4; forces affecting African American students' success 216–22; highly qualified maths teachers for African American children 26–7; knowledge 44–5, 141; researching African American maths teachers 39–62; resistance and school-university partnerships 336; shaping students' maths identity 297–8; students' perceptions of 208, 213
teaching strategies: classroom practice and

student achievement and understanding 145–71; and students' conceptual understanding 88–122; tenth-grade geometry 254–5, 261
teaching styles, contrasting 123–44
tenth-grade geometry 249–64
Texas Education Agency 322
Thernstrom, A. 7–8
Thernstrom, S. 7–8
Thornton, G. 314
three fifths rule 311–12
thug, discourse of the 274
Tillman, L. 22, 233, 311
tracks/tracking 200–1, 204, 219, 225
triarchic theory of intelligence 147
Trinity Church, Chicago 309–10
TRIO programs 335
Tuskegee experiment 310
Tyler, K. 336
Tyson, M. 221

underachievement 305; *see also* racial achievement gap
understanding: conceptual *see* conceptual understanding; procedural 184–5, 196
unemployment 304
United States Department of Education (USDE) 341
universities *see* higher education
university colloquia 345
university-school partnerships 333–50
unsuccessful maths students 207–12
Upward Bound program 335
Urban League 20
urban schools 51
Useem, E. 261
usefulness of maths 300–1; successful students' beliefs 213, 214; unsuccessful students' beliefs 209–10, 211, 212

Valadez, J.R. 345
Vietnam War 310
virtual manipulatives 137
Vithal, R. 92–3, 112
vocational education 317–18
voice, giving to students 103–4, 105
Vygotsky, L.S. 147

Waddle, J. 338
Walker, E.N. 233
Wallingford, Delaware County 314
Ward, C. 307
"warm demander" style 123–4, 132–4, 134–8, 141–2
Waters, M. 221